# ACTION THEORY

# SYNTHESE LIBRARY

STUDIES IN EPISTEMOLOGY,

LOGIC, METHODOLOGY, AND PHILOSOPHY OF SCIENCE

*Managing Editor:*

JAAKKO HINTIKKA, *Florida State University*

*Editors:*

ROBERT S. COHEN, *Boston University*

DONALD DAVIDSON, *University of Chicago*

GABRIËL NUCHELMANS, *University of Leyden*

WESLEY C. SALMON, *University of Arizona*

VOLUME 97

# ACTION THEORY

PROCEEDINGS OF THE WINNIPEG CONFERENCE
ON HUMAN ACTION, HELD AT WINNIPEG,
MANITOBA, CANADA, 9–11 MAY 1975

*Edited by*

MYLES BRAND

*University of Illinois at Chicago Circle, Chicago, Ill., U.S.A.*

*and*

DOUGLAS WALTON

*University of Winnipeg, Winnipeg, Manitoba, Canada*

D. REIDEL PUBLISHING COMPANY

DORDRECHT : HOLLAND / BOSTON : U.S.A.
LONDON : ENGLAND

Library of Congress Cataloging in Publication Data

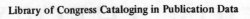

Winnipeg Conference on Human Action, Winnipeg, Man., 1975.
    Action theory.

    (Synthese library ; v. 97)
    Includes bibliographical references and indexes.
    1. Man  Congresses.  2.  Act
    (Philosophy)  Congresses.  3.  Agent
    (Philosophy)  Congresses.  4.  Decision-making
    (Ethics)  Congresses.
I.  Brand, Myles.  II.  Walton, Douglas.  III.  Title.
BD450.W54  1975    128    76–6882
ISBN 90-277-0671-9
ISBN 90-277-1188-7 (pbk.)

# TABLE OF CONTENTS

# PART 1

# INTRODUCTION

# INTRODUCTION BY THE EDITORS

## I

Gilbert Ryle, in his *Concept of Mind* (1949), attacked volitional theories of human actions; J. L. Austin, in his "If and Cans" (1956), emphasized the complexity and difficulty of analyzing the nature of human ability and opportunity. About the same time, Wittgenstein in the *Investigations* posed the question, without answering it, "What is left over when we subtract the arm rising from the raising of it?" These philosophers, among others, were pointing to the paucity of philosophically adequate knowledge and theoretical clarity concerning human action and related notions. They recognized, however, that clarity in such matters is essential if work on the freedom-determinism issue, moral responsibility, the social sciences and jurisprudence or any area where human action is a central concept, is to go forward.

During the decade following, a number of notable attempts were made to deal with the problems surrounding human action and ability. Some of the major efforts were A. I. Melden's *Free Action* (Humanities Press, 1961), Donald Davidson's "Action, Reasons, and Causes" (*Journal of Philosophy*, 1963), Charles Taylor's *The Explanation of Behavior* (Routledge & Kegan Paul, 1964), Arthur Danto's "Basic Actions" (*American Philosophical Quarterly*, 1965), Roderick Chisholm's "Freedom and Action" (in *Freedom and Determinism* (ed. by K. Lehrer), Random House, 1966), Richard Taylor's *Action and Purpose* (Prentice Hall, 1966) and Wilfrid Sellar's *Science and Metaphysics* (Routledge & Kegan Paul, 1967).[1] There were, needless to say, valuable contributions made by numerous other writers at this time, though these seem to have been the most influential. Several years later, Alvin Goldman in his *Theory of Human Action* (Prentice Hall, 1970) and Arthur Danto in his *Analytical Philosophy of Action* (Cambridge University Press, 1973) supplied syntheses and comprehensive theories.

How far, however, did this concerted effort take us? Had the analysis of human action progressed sufficiently to furnish results useful in dealing with related problems in philosophy of mind, metaphysics, moral theory and legal philosophy? If so, what were the cumulative findings of Action Theory? If not, what is the current state of the investigation into human action and where should future effort be directed? These, basically, were the questions that led to the Winnipeg Action Theory Conference. What the

*M. Brand and D. Walton (eds.), Action Theory, 3–7. All Rights Reserved*
*Copyright © 1976 by D. Reidel Publishing Company, Dordrecht-Holland*

conference seemed to show was that much groundwork analysis has been accomplished through the development of systematic and comprehensive views, but the evaluation of competing views remains. The centrality of the notion of human action in issues in philosophical psychology, metaphysics, moral and legal philosophy, and even the philosophy of science, was re-emphasized. It seems reasonable to say that the most fruitful work in this area is either in progress or will be undertaken in the next several years.

## II

In his *Analytical Philosophy of Action* as well as in a number of articles, Arthur Danto has attempted to clarify human action by concentrating on its simplest type, basic action, that is, action which requires no other action for its performance. In his contribution to the Conference 'Action, Knowledge, and Representation,' he discusses the internal structure of basic action, as it were; in particular, he is concerned with the relationship within basic action between representational or epistemic components and purely physical components, that is, bodily or physiological movement. His conclusion is negative: the structure of basic action does not involve the unification of the mental and the physical. Annette Baier in her 'Intention, Practical Knowledge, and Representation' takes up some of the same themes as Danto, using Descartes as a point of contact. But perhaps Baier's most interesting point concerns the presumption of Danto's entire program that human action is best clarified by concentrating on basic action. Baier claims that this presumption is myopic and has not led to an understanding of social or interpersonal action, an understanding that is necessary for dealing with issues in moral and political theory.

In 'Volitions Re-affirmed,' Wilfrid Sellars defends and elaborates his view that actions are caused by volitions. This view forms part of his larger project of clarifying the nature of practical reasoning, or said another way, mapping the logical geography of rational action. Although Sellars uses the term "volition," he is not subject to Ryle's charge of obscuranticism, since he carefully specifies the meaning of this technical term. Basically, a volition is a thought that has the force of saying to oneself "I shall do *a* here and now"; this thought, in turn, causes the performance of action *a*. Alvin Goldman, in his 'Volitional Theory Revisited,' agrees with Sellars that a volitional theory of action is not subject to the criticisms usually advanced against it. In particular, he is concerned with the issue of whether there is a one-one correspondence between volitions and movements that are voluntary.

Sellars holds that volitions cause actions. In contrast, Robert Binkley in his paper 'The Logic of Action' identifies an action with victorious decision, that is, a successful deciding that brings about the result in the appropriate way. Action *is* the mental event of deciding, not the causal consequence of that mental event. Binkley justifies his view, in part, by arguing that it is required by an adequate view of practical reasoning. In 'The Twofold Structure and Unity of Practical Thinking,' Hector-Neri Castañeda is also concerned with practical reasoning, especially judgments about duties and obligations. In this paper, Castañeda justifies and develops a formal system that incorporates the view that ought-statements are extensional and that they are two-sorted, in that they can contain components that behave like propositional functions and they can contain components that are non-propositional, components expressed by infinitive or subjunctive clauses.

The papers by Myles Brand, 'Particulars, Events, and Actions,' and Jaegwon Kim, 'Events as Property Exemplifications,' are concerned with the ontological status of actions. They approach this issue by dealing with the more general one concerning the status of events, since all actions are events. Brand argues that events are particulars, in much the same way that physical objects are particulars. The criterion for identity for events, however, is stricter than that for physical objects: physical object identity requires spatio-temporal coincidence but event identity requires necessary spatio-temporal coincidence. Kim, however, defends the view — which he has elaborated elsewhere — that events *are* physical objects exemplifying a property during a time. Even identity requires identity of the constitutive properties, physical objects and times.

There are, it might be said, two ways to clarify a key notion such as human action: one is to 'reduce' it to better understood or more fundamental notions, and the other is to explicate it within the context of related notions. In his 'The Agent As Cause,' Roderick Chisholm adopts the second strategy. He isolates an essential element in action, that of an agent undertaking to bring about a state of affairs, and outlines a general theory built on this notion.

Chisholm is especially interested in explicating those notions that are relevant to the free will issue. In brief, he argues that an action is free if the agent brings about the brain event that causes the appropriate bodily movement. Since the agent is not an event, but a substantial self, the relationship between the agent and the brain event is not efficient causation, but rather a type of causation Chisholm labels "immanent causation." (A similar analysis of free action has been advocated by Richard Taylor, for example, in his *Metaphysics* (Prentice Hall, 1963).) Irving Thalberg in his

'How Does Agent Causality Work?', however, raises several difficulties for this theory of free action. Basically, Thalberg asks first, whether the notion of immanent causation is circular, or if not circular, whether it is intelligible and, second, what can be the relationship between an agent's beliefs, intentions, emotions, and his action if it is not one of efficient causation.

In Keith Lehrer's ' "Can" in Theory and Practice' and Douglas Walton's 'Time and Modality in the "Can" of Opportunity,' the discussion of the modal auxiliary verb 'can' stemming from the early work of Austin and Nowell-Smith is continued. Lehrer recommends an analysis of the 'can' most directly involved in freedom of action, innovatively using the device of possible world semantics. His view is, basically, that an agent $S$ can at $t_j$ do action $A$ at time $t_n$ just in case there is a possible world that is minimally different from the actual one in which $S$ does $A$, where a world is minimally different from the actual one if it has the same natural laws and the least changes required to accommodate $S$'s doing $A$ at $t_n$. Walton is concerned with some syntactical problems in the 'can' of opportunity, rather than the all-in 'can' (to use Austin's term). He is especially concerned to examine some features of the double time-index in expressions of opportunity having the form '$S$ has the opportunity at $t_1$ to perform $A$ at $t_2$,' and related questions of whether and how actions may be said to be reversible. Walton concludes that the 'can' of opportunity exhibits the logical structure characteristic of the concept of possibility of normal modal logics, but needs to be further extended if we adopt the viewpoint of relative rather than absolute possibility.

In the remaining papers, the authors concentrate on applying the results of work in action theory, rather than attempting to amplify the analysis. Richard Taylor, in his 'Action and Responsibility,' argues that the notions of moral right and wrong are vacuous. Right and wrong, he says, are always relative to rules; for example, a wrong move in a chess game is one not permitted by the rules of the game. But there are no moral rules, since there being a rule presupposes a rule-maker and there is no moral rule-maker, the only possibility being God, who does not exist. Since moral responsibility presupposes moral wrongdoing (and moral rightdoing), moral responsibility is also vacuous. Faced with this challenge, P. H. Nowell-Smith argues that even if Taylor is correct, the notion of legal responsibility is an essential part of our ordinary conceptual framework and must be elucidated. Moreover, he argues that Taylor is not entitled to draw a hard and fast distinction between the deontological notions of right and wrong and the teleological ones of good and bad, as his argument requires.

Alex Michalos, in his 'Morality of Cognitive Decision-Making', critically examines arguments for and against an ethics of belief, that is, the view that cognitive states, such as believings, are subject to moral appraisal. His conclusion is positive; cognitive states can be assigned moral evaluations, in much the same way that actions can be morally evaluated. Richard Jeffrey presented a lecture during the conference in which he attempted to utilize the results of action theory to clarify some of the fundamental notions of game theory and decision theory, notions such as acting if certain conditions obtain and deliberate interpersonal action undertaken without complete knowledge of the circumstances. (Unfortunately, the manuscript for this lecture is not presently available.)

Several main directions for further research emerge from this Conference. These problem areas include notably the following: the relationship between thinking and doing, or put another way, the nature of practical reasoning; the structure of the action sequence, and in particular the role played by volitions (or intentions, wants, and beliefs); the ontological status of actions, and in general, of events; the nature of social and interpersonal action; and the analysis of human ability and opportunity. The papers in this volume also make obvious that action theory is the locus of a large number of issues, for example, those in moral and legal philosophy, especially concerning responsibility, those in the philosophy of science, including the foundations of psychology and decision theory, and those in the philosophy of language, in particular, the development and testing of formal semantical structures.

We would like to thank those agencies and institutions without whose generous support this conference would not have been possible. In particular, we should like to thank the Canada Council, the Program on Science, Technology and Society at Cornell University, sponsored by the National Endowment for the Humanities, and the University of Winnipeg. The University of Winnipeg has also been generous in providing facilities for the Conference.

MYLES BRAND<br>
DOUGLAS WALTON

NOTE

[1] See *The Nature of Human Action* ((ed. by M. Brand), Scott, Foresman, 1970) or *The Philosophy of Action* ((ed. by Alan R. White), Oxford 1968). These volumes concentrate on the work produced during the 1960's.

# PART 2

# BASIC ACTION

ARTHUR C. DANTO

# ACTION, KNOWLEDGE, AND REPRESENTATION

> And yet they ought to have made some
> mention of error at the same time, for error
> seems to be more natural to living creatures,
> and the soul spends more time in it.
>
> ARISTOTLE, *De Anima*

In this paper I seek to decompose the concept of basic actions in such a way that its philosophical components crystallize about one pole, and its scientific ones about the other. No doubt the scientific components will have a philosophical importance, but it will differ considerably from the philosophical importance basic actions themselves were originally believed to have. The latter derived from the pivotal role basic actions were cast to play in a massive restructuring of the mind-body relationship along lines which promised to re-unite bodies with minds and ourselves with both: to restore to an ontological unity what had been sundered by cartesian dialysis. That counter-cartesian program I now believe to have failed definitively, and its collapse, which I mean to demonstrate, entails the demolition of the concept of basic actions, at least so far as its hopeful philosophical significance is concerned. I hasten to mute this dour assessment, however: Descartes does not survive altogether the confounding of his rivals, only his distinctions do. But this does not compel us to follow him in housing the terms of the distinction in logically alien substances.

I

Philosophical theories of mind are philosophical theories of body by default. This is so whether, with Descartes, we radically distinguish properties of minds and by so doing isolate a class of predicates logically inapplicable to our bodies just because they are bodies, or whether, in the counter-cartesian orientation of contemporary philosophy, we psychologize the body and so isolate a class of predicates logically inapplicable to crass material objects

*M. Brand and D. Walton (eds.), Action Theory, 11–25. All Rights Reserved*
*Copyright © 1976 by D. Reidel Publishing Company, Dordrecht-Holland*

like sticks and stones, honoring the metaphysical line drawn by Descartes but locating it elsewhere, employing it to distinguish between orders of bodies rather than between bodies as an ontologically homogeneous order which contrasts in a global way with minds, spirits, *res cogitans,* or the like. By closing the gap between our minds and our bodies, we open a gap between *our* bodies, on the one side, and *mere* bodies on the other, even if this gap happens not to generate any of those deep perplexities, e.g., of causality, which motivated closure of the original gap: no special causal concept differentiates the way the hand moves the stick from the way the stick moves the stone. The only remaining problem, perhaps, concerns the way *we* move the hand. Suppose we speak of such movings as actions, perhaps as basic actions: then one consequence of treating our bodies as already having the properties cartesians relegated to minds, is that we are absolved from having to think that such movements of the hand are distinct effects of some special mental cause, acting mysteriously across what ought to be the metaphysically intraversable space between spirit and matter. The basic action, by filling this space, absorbs as its own the philosophical boundaries of the space and emerges as what the earlier philosophy of mind and body would have had to regard as a metaphysical monster, mental and crass at once, one thing, indissolubly compacted of thought and matter, and the world now seen as constituted of two sorts of bodies, unhaunted by asomatic ghosts. It is this dualism, enshrined, for example, in Strawson's distinction between entities exhaustively describable by sets of M-predicates alone, and entities only partially describable by these but fully describable if we augment our basic vocabulary to compass P-predicates (there being no entity exhaustively describable by P-predicates alone) which the new concept of action appears to have made feasible, and which explains in some measure the importance spontaneously felt to attach to the concept of action. It is not just that philosophers had hit upon an oddly neglected subject on which fresh work might be done, but that actions were suddenly felt to hold a metaphysical promise not appreciated from the limited contexts of law and morality in which they had traditionally been examined. The study of action must be considered as part of a general movement to rethink the philosophy of bodies, paralleling in Anglo-Saxon philosophy the deep reassessment of the body undertaken on the Continent by Sartre and others, and especially by Merleau-Ponty, a common, single philosophical enterprise, whatever may have been the differences in philosophical style and points of departure. It was Merleau's view, for example, that an exact understanding of the structures of the phenomenal field revealed features which only could be explained with reference to the body, which must itself have a structure radically distinct from that assigned it by Descartes — a thesis Merleau sought to confirm by showing the way in which bodily abnormalities induce structural distortions in the field of phenomenal experience.

The gap which Descartes opened up was not, of course, only in ontology: it was also, and more famously, an epistemological gap, bounded, under this perspective, on the one side by a mind and on the other by the so-called External World. The existence and nature of the gap made it difficult to be certain that the world underwrote our intended cognitions of it, as it made it difficult to see how any of the events which took place in it could be explained with ultimate reference to minds which necessarily stood outside it: it was a gap, in brief, which threatened us at once with radical ignorance and radical impotency, leaving us with knowledge only of ourselves, and with our repertoire of actions restricted merely to affirming or refusing to affirm our ideas. So the body, if it were, so to speak, to fill and hence obliterate the causal gap, might fill and obliterate the cognitive gap as well: just as there exists something already in the world and over which we have immediate control, which we are not required to control from without and across a hopeless distance, so might there be something and perhaps that identical thing, which is at once in the world and of which we have direct knowledge, which we are not required to address from without across a distance rendered hopeless by the logical unavoidability of skepticism. The body, and our special relationship to it as agents and knowers, locates *us* immediately in the world where our body had all along been supposed, on Cartesian assumptions, to have been located as a thing amongst things. The threats of ignorance and impotency are stunned with a single stroke, the remaining limitations on our powers of knowledge and action being practical only and, if insuperable in many cases are not *philosophically* insuperable, and hopeless from the outset. The triumphant double closure might have been expected if, as Sartre claimed, "knowledge and action are only two abstract aspects of an original, concrete relation."[1]

This relationship, as viewed by Sartre, is complicated by the overall structures of his philosophy, but in gist it is this, namely that "I *am* my hand"[2] when my hand is viewed as "the arresting of references and their ultimate end:" the body is the center of reference for the inter-referential system which is one's world: it is that through which the world is manipulated and known but which in *these senses* of manipulation and knowledge, is "at once the unknowable and non-utilizable term which the last term of the series indicates."[3] And Merleau-Ponty, whose views again cannot altogether be detached from the systematic structure in which they are embedded, insists that "the union of soul and body is not an amalgamation between two mutually external terms, subject and object, brought about by arbitrary decree. It is enacted at every instant in the movement of existence."[4] And again, "We have found underneath the objective and detached knowledge of the body that other knowledge which we have of it in virtue of its always being with us and of the fact that we are our body."[5] These thoughts are brilliantly anticipated in a neglected discussion of the concept of action by Gabriel Marcel, who wrote as early as 1927 that "I do not *use* my body, I am my body."[6]

Merleau speaks of 'that other knowledge' where Sartre speaks of the unknowability of the body and hence of ourselves, but this I take to be a lexical perversion not untypical of him: he means 'unknowable' relative to a model of knowledge which parallels if it is not identical with what he speaks of as 'objective consciousness,' the awareness we have of *objects* in contrast with that special sort of consciousness — *conscience (de) soi* — he alleges each of us has of himself: for if I *am* my hand, and if I do not know myself as an object, then I do not know my hand as an object either: or, to the degree that it is an object for me, as when I happen to see it, then I am *not* it. The central experience of moving a hand is supposed to be existential — or lived — and hence in figurative language internal rather than external, as any relation to an object by definition would be. And Merleau effectively concurs when he writes "My body is not an object."[7] So it is not so much not known as known differently, and in the case of either thinker the implicit claim is that, since I stand at no cognitive distance from my body, between my body and me there is no corridor for the skeptic to haunt, and we eliminate him by eliminating the place he needs to occupy in order to be effective. Predictably, then, Merleau rejects a representationalist theory of bodily knowledge, and he charges the classical psychologists precisely of having construed the knowledge we have of our bodies in terms appropriate to a scientific knowledge of our (or any) bodies (they did so, he explained, because they are scientists and charmed by the scientific model of knowledge), "separating what on the one hand belongs to the spectator or the observer and on the other the properties of the absolute object."[8] "Thenceforth," he concludes, "the experience of the body degenerated into a 'representation' of the body." And indeed this would have been the Cartesian picture, at least until Descartes complicated matters with his celebrated, cryptic claim that we are not in our bodies as pilots are in their ships — where we would otherwise have believed him committed to saying that we are in our bodies just that way. I am, Descartes appeared to hold, directly acquainted with my ideas (or representations, if you will), including some ideas of my body. But whether these representations are correct or not is altogether, here as with other ideas except perhaps the idea I have of God, a matter of external correspondences which nothing internal to the ideas themselves can assure me hold: and in fact, it is to suppose that I may have no body at all, or one utterly discorrespondent with my idea of it. For I can think of my body not existing but not of myself not existing, and so cannot be one with my body. The existentialist counter-claim may then be read as follows: if knowledge of my body is not representationalistic, then there is nothing between my body and which, in at least the central case, an external correspondence may or may not hold: where there is no gap, there is no need to *overcome* a gap: and so the skeptical frets cannot arise since the ground on which alone they could arise has vanished. "Experience of one's body runs counter to the reflective procedure which detaches subject and object from one another." Merleau summarizes, "and which gives us only thoughts about the body or the body as an idea, and not the experience of the body in reality."[9]

Exactly parallel considerations will apply in the domain of action. A basic action cannot be construed as a causal episode in which, perhaps, the representation of a bodily movement, say as a volition, causes the movement it represents (which was exactly Hume's theory of action): as I stand at no distance from my body, no distance has to be overcome by the dynamisms of causation. It may, of course, be argued that the Cartesian picture of knowledge and the Humean picture of action are philosophically incorrect descriptions of knowledge of, and action with *external* bodies, including those things physiologically credited as belonging to my body but which, since objects for me, are not part of what I am. But my concern will only be with what one might, in following these continental theorists, call representationalist theories of bodily knowledge and action. My question is whether these have in fact been discredited, and I suppose the issue will turn on the question of how we might handle in other terms just those things it seems to me representationalist theories were designed to handle philosophically, namely errors in the theory of our knowledge of objects, and misperformances in the theory of action. It is this to which my paper will address itself first.

II

The 'other sort of knowledge' to which Merleau-Ponty alludes may after all be what Miss Anscombe supposes "modern philosophy has blankly mis-understood: namely what ancient and medieval philosophers meant by 'practical knowledge.'"[10] For like her her continental counterparts, she sees 'modern philosophy' as committed to "an incorrigibly contemplative conception of knowledge," a conception according to which "knowledge must be something that is judged as such by being in accordance with the facts." So I suppose that if *practical* knowledge is knowledge of some quite different order, perhaps it is marked by the fact that *truth,* which presupposes at once a vehicle of knowledge — an idea or proposition or something at least to which truth-values may sensibly be attached — together with whatever it is ("the facts") that satisfies the truth-conditions of the vehicle, will not be a constituent in its analysis: for then the enjoined features of contemplativity will re-appear. So the knowledge, whatever may be its structure, is non-representational and in some way *immediate.* But if there is no place for truth, neither is their place for error, which on the contemplative model would be *disaccordance* with the facts. But surely there are misperformances or mistakes of action, which Miss Anscombe of all authors has especially taught us to appreciate. But how can this be if the knowledge of one's performance is practical and so lacks a truth-component? There are no misexecutions in the *world* — which is a spinozistic insight — and no misapprehensions in the understanding, save in relationship to one another: so some reference to a representation seems implied in the concept of errors of performance. So perhaps it is not so much that we can eliminate representations from our analysis of action as that we require a different relationship to a representation than that in which the facts are alleged to stand to representations in the contemplative model of knowledge: the satisfaction relationship, say. Still, practical knowledge is meant to refer to the sort of knowledge we have of our own actions, and possibly this is different from noticing, in an external manner, that one's arm is moving: or our knowledge that it is our arm which is moving is different somehow from our knowledge that someone else's arm is, or our knowledge that our own arm is moving when it happens to be moved by something external to ourselves and not, say, as a matter of basic action. So let us concentrate for a moment upon another feature Miss Anscombe appears to find in practical knowledge other than its acon-templativity: it is an instance of *knowledge without observation,* one of Anscombe's most interesting and puzzling notions.

An action *a* is not intentional under description *D* of *a* if the agent did not know that *D* was true of *a*: for not knowing that he was doing *D* renders inapplicable the question of why he did it, and the applicability of this question is analytical to the concept of intentional action as Miss Anscombe has reconstructed it. But not only must the agent know he is doing *a* under

$D$: he must know it in some special way, namely nonobservationally, for "the class of intentional actions is a subclass of things known without observation."[11] This move, I believe, is deeply controvertible. Nonobservational knowledge consists in knowing something $x$ where there is no sensation (for example), no "separately describable sensation" distinct from $x$ and on the basis of which knowledge of $x$ is had. So I suppose knowledge of our own sensations must be paradigmatically nonobservational on this construal. But then of how many of my *actions* is my knowledge nonobservational in this way? Do I know without observation, for instance, that I am cutting cheese? For surely if there is a sensation of moving my hand in some special cheese-cutting way, there must be a separately describable sensation of *cheese* being cut: the sort of sensation I have of cut cheese whether I am its cutter or not. Consider me cutting cheese without looking at what I am cutting. Nothing in the knowledge I may have of my own movements will differ from what I have while cutting cheese while looking at it: so what makes the difference is the separable presence of the perception of cheese in the one case and its absence from the other, the sensations of motility, supposing there are such, being invariant. So the sensation of cheese is separately describable. And suppose a stick of margarine has been substituted for the stick of *port salut,* and my movements remain the same though it is false that I am cutting cheese, even though the movements are the same as they would have been had I been doing so? How then can this be nonobservational knowledge I have when in fact I do have knowledge, viz, when I am cutting cheese and cheese indeed is being cut by me? And if nonobservationality is a criterion of intentional action, how can cutting cheese exemplify intentional action? Yet certainly a theory which makes it impossible for cutting cheese to be an intentional action is haywire *somehow.* What can have gone wrong?

Cartesian psychology would have allowed that I might have nonobservational knowledge of what my intentions are, e.g., to cut some cheese. There may be difficulties with this view, there may be unconscious intentions to which I refer in my own case as theoretical posits in order to make sense of my behavior, I may learn what my intentions are by observing what I do, and so forth. But Miss Anscombe does not wish to countenance intentions at all, as her strictures are not against Cartesian epistemology here but against the sorts of things the Cartesian supposes we can have direct and immediate knowledge of in at least the clearest cases, namely intentions: "Where is that to be found?" she asks rhetorically: "What is its vehicle?"[12] And her philosophical motives are transparent: to allow intentions to occur in separation from bodily movements which are then intentional in relation to them appears to her exactly to reopen the gap it was a deep Wittgensteinian project to hammer shut: their being intentional was supposed to be inseparable — 'not separably describable' — from the movements themselves. In a formulation she gives but claims others have found obscure, she writes: "I *do* what *happens*."[13] So if *I* cut cheese, the very sundering of cheese into slices — an event in the world — is what I do, no distinction being allowed between what takes place and what I do. "When the description of what happens is the very thing I should say I was doing, then there is no distinction between my doing and the thing's happening."[14] But what if there is a discrepancy? What happens if I should say I were cutting cheese and am doing something but not cutting cheese, margarine being there instead? A philosopher who wanted to say that I *believe* what is the *case* would have an easy time abolishing the distinction between world and representation — the world and representation are one — if there were in fact only true beliefs. But even in that fortunate case his would be a wrong theory, and it is exactly because we have to cope with false beliefs that we find our analysis of true ones has to be considerably more complex than we would have appreciated had error not been seen as a factor. Miss Anscombe's theory does not so much suffer from obscurity as from wrongness. And its wrongness shows the need for there being intentions, whatever may be the problem of their vehicle and location, and whatever the philosophical price of countenancing them.

III

Miss Anscombe's theory works best for mere bodily movements, for with these it may be argued that no separate sensation, say a visual one, tells me that my arm is moving when I move my arm: I know it to be moving, but not *through* anything apart from itself. In such cases, as she says, separate sensation "is merely an aid." And as much might be said regarding homeostatic sensations transmitted under alleged principles of feedback to the brain, which then sends out further signals bearing on the style of the movement. There is even scientific support for this: monkeys whose forelimbs were deafferented within hours of their birth nevertheless acquired the skills of ambulation, climbing and reaching; and deafferented monkeys whose eyelids were stiched shut so as to foreclose collateral visual aid were retarded in this acquisition by but a few weeks. So "topographic sensory feedback and autogenetic spinal reflexes are not necessary after birth for the development of most types of movement performed by forelimb musculature in monkeys."[15] So it very likely is with us. But it was our *bodies,* after all, of which we were to have had 'the other sort of knowledge' to begin with. If nonobservationality works here, enough of the anti-Cartesian program of her school may be salvaged to make the position respectable.

It is at this point that such phenomena as that of phantom limbs become vexing. Merleau appreciated this, and wrestled with it heroically, though more from the perspective of feelings referred to what in fact were sectioned limbs than from the perspective of moving them, but it is exactly here that the concepts of knowledge and action become so close as almost to justify by itself Sartre's view that there is only *one* 'concrete relation.' For Miss Anscombe, I think, the problem arises particularly in connection with the individuation of "separately describable sensations." For while there may indeed be a sensation or feeling of moving an arm as a basic action, the fact of phantom limbs allows the possibility to arise of this feeling being had without the arm moving since there *is* no arm to move. So something in addition to this feeling is required in the normal case, since the feeling is invariant: or one believes on the basis of a motor habit that it has gone up, in which case a secure glance at the rising arm confirms the belief, as an 'aid.' But this implies that the knowledge that ones arm has risen is after all not merely practical but contemplative, since the extra sensation is required, even if not normally sought for. And how are we to deal with this?

It may, to a degree correctly, be argued that the feeling of moving an arm is of a portion of a physiological process, where the latter is truncated in the case of the phantom limb and only the portion occurs, though in the normal case in which the arm is normally attached, the whole process and not merely the felt portion occurs: so the feeling stands proxy in the normal case for the whole process though strictly speaking it is only of the portion. Then of at least this fragment there is practical knowledge, upon which, as it happens, a body of beliefs and expectations has been formed about the behavior of the body, these being exactly confirmed when the body is normal or behaves in the normal way. It is then a matter of experience how far back in the process we may go before the feeling is obliterated — say by amputating more and more of the body until only that bit is left of which practical knowledge may be had.[16] Then all the *rest* is a matter not of practical but of contemplative knowledge.

There are some qualifications to be registered, however. The main one is that there may be basic performances unregistered by any feelings, known to be in our repertoire only through monitoring their outward somatic effects. Examples of this are available in the findings of Professor Miller, who has demonstrated the remarkable degree to which such functions as heart-rate and brainwave are subject to conditioning, enabling patients to modulate bodily states traditionally supposed immune to the intervention of the will, since nothing introspectively available ever led people to suppose they had such powers. And even with parts of our body whose movements we ordinarily would be supposed to know about directly, it has been shown, for example through Ralph Hefferline's experiments with thumb twitches, not only that subjects were unaware that their thumb-twitches were means by which certain noises were terminated — they did not even know they were twitching their thumbs. The other qualification is the traditional one, the possibility of illusions of motility, of dreams and the like: and as one knows, it is the argument from such illusions which generates the logical separation of representation from fact, and imposes upon us a Cartesian model of knowledge even of our bodies.

I shall not attempt to go further with these qualifications. I raise them only in order to suggest that "practical knowledge" is a seriously compromised concept which does not vanquish the *malin genie,* and that the philosophy of action, whatever we may have learned from its intense recent exploration, has not fulfilled the philosophical ambitions which generated it, namely to collapse forever the gap between our bodies and ourselves, and hence between the world and ourselves, by eliminating representationality altogether. To be sure, we may have something left we can call practical knowledge, as a sort of knowing-how which has application to our bodies, though I suppose we would wish to distinguish the knowledge of how to move our bodies gracefully, like dancers do, from mere bodily behavior. But this practical knowledge has a scientific name: it is operant behavior: it is that which is subject to conditioning. Operant behavior is the scientific component of the concept of basic actions, and it may indeed have a measure of philosophical importance. But it is something distributed throughout the animal domain, something we share with rats and paramecia, and it cannot, as I began by saying, have the philosophical importance which basic actions themselves were supposed to have. Moreover, our feelings of immediate contact with our schedules of operancy are of limited utility in determining the boundaries of conditionability. Briefly, there may be a great deal we in this sense know how to do, without our knowing that we have this knowledge. And we learn — or come to know — what are our powers through the despised avenues of con-templative knowledge.

But does this then mean that our bodies are to us nothing more than objects of knowledge, hardly different from the other things in the world of which we achieve successful representation? To this, I think, the answer is negative, for there is, I believe, another relationship in which we may stand to our representations, and it is to this that I now turn.

## IV

We may regard intentions as representations of how we should like the world to be in consequence of our actions, and it seems plausible that we regard the relationship between these representations and those actions as *causal*. Indeed, we may regard knowledge and action as having parallel if inverse structures, insofar as something is knowledge if it is, other factors bracketed, a representation caused by what makes it true, whilst something is an action if, other factors bracketed, it is caused by a certain sort of representation. There is a truth-component in the concept of actions so considered as well, but I want to introduce it in the course of making more precise the nature of the causal connection here. For the matter is not beneath controversy, since not everyone will admit that intentions, or more familiarly, reasons, could be causes of actions.

There is a class of very familiar arguments in the post-Wittgensteinian philosophy of action that since causes and effects are distinct events, and hence subject to separate and independent descriptions; and since reasons or intentions cannot be described save with reference to the actions in whose explanation they are enlisted, reasons or intentions cannot be causes of actions nor actions the effects of reasons or intentions. Donald Davidson has demonstrated[17] that, for any event counted a cause, a true description of it can be given which has the occurrence of the alleged effect as a truth-condition, so that such a description of the cause is not a separate and independent one. I suppose, for the matter, that we can give descriptions of anything which entails a reference to anything else we choose to formulate in the description, but this need not faze those who find the first argument compelling: it was not their claim that every description of a cause is separate and independent of reference to an effect, but that *some* such description can be found, whereas *no* individuating description of a reason can be given which does not make reference to the appropriate action. And Davidson's argument is powerless against this. Nevertheless, I feel that Davidson's essential point is correct, that reasons are causes of action, and I want to clarify the contrary intuition of the Wittgensteinians by showing *what* it is that their notion of non-independent description rests upon here. As we shall see, the thought behind their claim is quite similar indeed to that behind Miss Anscombe's flawed doctrine that what we do and what happens are one. And like her view, it is subject to an objection based upon misperformances or non-execution.

Reasons, like beliefs, are, I think, irreducibly intensional in their formulations. From considerations which parallel the phenomenologists' claim that consciousness always is *of* something, we may suppose that all reasons are reasons *that* something should happen or be the case: *that* I should marry, or be on the other side of the street, or become a father, or whatever. Such reasons will be cited in explanation of things I do when I believe the latter to be means to — causes of — that for the sake of which I do them. Suppose I am writing the King of Morocco that a certain prisoner should be freed. That he be freed is my reason for writing this letter, and explains my so doing. Since it is exceedingly unlikely that this prisoner be freed, or if he is that this will be in consequence of my letter, *that* for which I write the letter may not happen, or happen but not in consequence of my action. But my reason stands though no event occur of the sort without reference to which the reason allegedly cannot be formulated, and hence the formulation clearly cannot depend for its truth on the occurrence of such an event. So the truth of the description does not entail the occurrence of the event, or if it must, then it cannot be true that the given reason is my reason: and this seems flatly absurd. So what we must mean, I believe, is that reasons cannot be formulated without reference to what we might portentously speak of as intensional objects, or, less portentously, without reference to their *contents,* but this object or content cannot be identical with an event in real history of the sort which happens when my action is successful: if the prisoner is liberated and in consequence of my plea for amnesty. And now matters stand this way. Reasons cannot be formulated without reference to content, since their content is a logically inseparable part of reasons. But since reasons *cum* content are logically distinct from any events which may correspond to this content, reasons *cum* content can be causes of the latter. Perhaps they still are not causes, but not in consequence of the sort of argument alluded to above. For that sort of argument is now seen wrong. Briefly, a reason has the form '*a* in order that *p*' where '*a*' denotes an action, '*p*' is the content of the reason, and where, in the successful nonbasic action, *e* satisfies '*p*', *a* causes *e,* and the reason itself causes *a*. We then causally explain the performance of *a* by *m* with reference to that reason, presupposing, of course, that *m* believes *a* will bring about *e*. And this crude analysis preserves the insights of Davidson as well as of his opponents. Their views are not just consistent but complementary, each having a fragment of the truth. The relation between reason and content is logical, the relationship between reason *cum* content and action is causal.

But there is more to the matter than this. What more there is to say is that reasons are causal through their logical structure, and the theorists Davidson has attacked are right in believing that if causes at all, reasons are causes of a quite special sort: for ordinary causes are not such through their logical structure, having none. We may gain a measure of appreciation of what I mean by 'logical structure' here if we consider a parallel feature in the concept of knowledge. Take those cases of knowledge in which possession of a true belief is a necessary condition. Then the analysis might run as follows: the true belief that $p$ is knowledge that $p$, only if that state of affairs $o$ which makes $p$ true explains the fact that the person in question believes that $p$. Let this sort of explanation take 'causes' as a frequent instance. Then I know (for example) that the paper before me is yellow if the paper before me is indeed yellow, and if its being so causes me to believe that it is so. So the paper's being yellow enters into two relations with the belief: explaining its occurrence and making true the propositional content of the belief. Belief-that-$p$ has a logical structure, part of which is given by the logical structure of $p$ itself as part of the belief; and in the case of knowledge it is through this internal structure that belief is an *effect*. Seventeenth and eighteenth century philosophers were specifically interested in explaining the provenance of ideas as effects, when the ideas were construed intensionally, viz, as *of* red or *of* wax or *of* whatever. Indeed it would primarily have been through their content that ideas were of interest to them at all, though there plainly has to have been a polemical context for Berkeley's thesis that ideas just *are* their content to have been exciting. My concern, however, only is to utilize the parallels between the theories of knowledge and of action to propose that reasons or intentions are causes through their structure in just the way in which beliefs are effects through *their* structure. And perhaps it is this which is missing from Davidson's account.

In the simplest case, let 'in order that $a$' be $m$'s intention or reason for doing $a$, nothing ulterior intended: then not only must this reason cause $a$: $a$ must satisfy, confer truth upon, the description implicit in the reason. So as with belief in the context of knowledge, there is a causal as well as a semantical relationship between representation and the world to be accounted for. And it is the semantical relationship which requires the introduction of internal structure in our analyses of such causes. If I *shout* 'p' the echo comes back 'p'. I have caused the echo, but no truth-relationship holds here between cause and effect, and the internal structure of cause and effect are alike inscrutable or accidental, in contrast with what we require of causes and effects in the theories of knowledge and action. But this is very generally the case with causes and effects: effects do not routinely, and certainly not in the class of instances the collision of billiard balls is meant to exemplify, confer something like truth on their causes, nor causes on their effects. So I think that something more than just being causes of actions is required of reasons, supposing them to be causes to begin with, and the truth-connection may come to the somewhat more internal sort of connection the Wittgensteinians intuited has to be there: and this marks the difference between reasons and such other sorts of causes of action as there may be. But it is exactly this further component in the analysis that raises to prominence the representational factor in intentional action, whatever may be its vehicle.

V

I do not feel that reference to representation need, either in action or knowledge, drive us back to the pineal gland and then through some opening in it to a realm of spirit beyond. Elsewhere I have sought to argue for a materialistic account of representations, to which I merely can allude here. But representations, just because they admit of assessment in terms of truth and falsity, are logically external to the world in which they may in every other respect be located. As agents and knowers, indeed, we are within the world under the concept of causation, and external to it under the concept of truth. Within and without the world at once: that is the philosophical structure of man. In the respect in which representation has been misconstrued or underestimated, the modern theories of practical knowledge and of human action have failed. That we can change the world to fit our representations, as in action, or change our representations to fit the world, as in knowledge, are marvelous powers, but they require reference to representation, and this, I think, is finally what is going to distinguish the sciences of man — the *human* sciences — from the sciences of nature, where at least the subject matter of the latter is uncomplicated by representational elements.

Whatever the case, the basic action has been decomposed into a representation on the one side, and a piece of operant behavior on the other, with the former causing the latter and the latter satisfying the former. The two Cartesian substances have given way to two sorts of relationships instead, one causal and the other semantical, but the Cartesian distinction between representations and reality remains, and the powerful modern attempts to fuse them have failed.

*Columbia University*

## NOTES

[1] Jean-Paul Sartre, *Being and Nothingness* (transl. by Hazel E. Barnes), Philosophical Library, New York, 1956, p. 308.
[2] *op. cit.,* p. 323.
[3] *ibid.*
[4] Maurice Merleau-Ponty, *Phenomenology of Perception* (transl. by Colin Smith), Routledge and Kegan Paul, London, 1962, pp. 88–89.
[5] *op. cit.,* p. 206.
[6] Gabriel Marcel, *Journal Metaphysique* (Paris, 1927), p. 323.
[7] *op. cit.,* p. 198.
[8] *op. cit.,* p. 74.
[9] *op. cit.,* pp. 198–199.
[10] G. E. M. Anscombe, *Intention,* Blackwell, Oxford, 1957, p. 57.
[11] *op. cit.,* p. 14.
[12] *op. cit.,* p. 52.
[13] *Ibid.*
[14] *op. cit.* pp. 52–53.
[15] *Science* (7 September 1973), p. 959.
[16] This remaining bit may be thought of as a volition, something that causes the bodily movement which together with it forms the whole process designated as an action. See my *Analytical Philosophy of Action,* Cambridge University Press, Cambridge, 1973, Chapter III.
[17] Donald Davidson, "Actions, Reasons, and Causes", *Journal of Philosophy* **60** (1963), 685–700.

ANNETTE BAIER

# INTENTION, PRACTICAL KNOWLEDGE AND REPRESENTATION

Danto says "that we can change the world to fit our representations, as in action, or change our representations to fit the world, as in knowledge, are marvelous powers, but they require reference to representation." I shall make some fairly obvious points about representation, some more controversial claims about intentional action, taking my cue in both cases from things Descartes says on these topics. Since Descartes is said to have given us the problem of how a movement in the material world can be mind-imbued or mind-informed enough to count as an intentional act, it seems only proper to see what hints he gives of a solution. It is noteworthy that this problem is not a perennial one, it did have to be invented. Earlier philosophers, even those who believed the soul could be separated from the body, found nothing paradoxical in our intentional physical action. It is a special sort of achievement to become puzzled about the most familiar of things, and intentional action surely should be the most familiar of realities, even to a philosopher. Can it really be that the soul spends so much of its time in error, the discrepancy between intention and act so frequent in our 'community of spiritual animals' that we can, without special philosophical conditioning, find it problematic that act and intent should ever coincide, that we should find it puzzling when Anscombe says "I do what happens" (*Intention*, p. 52) and "the failure to execute intentions is necessarily the rare exception"? (*ibid.* p. 86). If our puzzlement is really due to our Cartesian upbringing, then possibly our cure will lie in a fuller realization of what that involved. The way into the flybottle is the way out.

Descartes' own philosophy of action is to be found in three places, first in a few references to the active life of the human person, secondly in his account of divine action, and thirdly in what he says about the actions and passions of the soul. If we want to find Descartes' views about intention and about representation, we must look in all these places.

On the active life of the human person he has a sensible and pragmatic philosophy to offer, one which involves a complete reversal of his official epistemology and metaphysics. When the goal is not truth but the well-

*M. Brand and D. Walton (eds.), Action Theory, 27–43. All Rights Reserved*
*Copyright © 1976 by D. Reidel Publishing Company, Dordrecht-Holland*

being of the whole person, the rule of withholding assent until rational
certainty is obtained gives place to this: "we must take sides, and embrace,
as regards ordinary affairs, the opinions that seem probable in order never
to be irresolute when it is a matter of action. For it is our irresolution which
causes us sorrow and remorse." (Letter no. 403, to Princess Elizabeth
(transl. by E. Anscombe and P. T. Geach), p. 285.) Whereas in the *Fourth
Meditation* sin lay in allowing the will to get ahead of the intellect, here the
diagnosis is reversed. Rogues are turned honest, cognitive vices become
practical virtues. Whereas for the purposes of the search for truth the ideas
of sensation are confused and in need of replacement or regimentation by
innate ideas, for practical purposes of harm-avoidance they are clear and in
"their own way more distinct than any I myself deliberately produced in my
meditations" (*Sixth Meditation*). The reversal is complete in ontology as
well as espistemology. That intellectually incomprehensible intimacy
between substances with distinct essences, the union of mind and body, is
said to be "understood very clearly by means of the senses" (Letter to
Princess Elizabeth) and even the dualism gives way to a considering of the
person as *one* thing. What is *its* essence? We are not told, but the rules for
finding essences seem to be altered, since we are told to feel free "to ascribe
matter and extension to the soul" (*op. cit.*) when our concerns are practical
not theoretical. The turn from theoretical to practical reason brings with it a
total reversal in ontology, epistemology, methodology. Yet Descartes
himself did not in the end see the search for truth as so sharply separable
from pursuit of the good. Kenny ends his book on Descartes with a
quotation from a letter to Chanut, in which the philosopher complains that
his medical studies are less successful than his ethical ones, and says
"instead of finding the means to preserve my life I have found another way,
far easier and far safer, which is not to be afraid of death" (quoted, Kenny,
*Descartes*, p. 226).

What I find instructive in Descartes' few scattered remarks about human
action is his clear recognition that his dualistic metaphysics could not there
be taken seriously. "The human mind is incapable of distinctly conceiving
both the distinction between body and soul, and their union," (Letter to
Princess Elizabeth) and, when our concern is action, it is their union not
their distinctness which is important. His attempt to save his official
dualistic metaphysics by a supporting dualism of theoretical and practical
reason presents an interesting foreshadowing of Kant's dualism, but its un-
satisfactoriness is obvious and his acceptance of it uneasy and halfhearted.

The other place in Descartes' thought where he gives any attention to
action by an agent with a foot in both worlds, thought and extension, is in

his claims about what God does. Here Descartes should perhaps be more embarrassed than he is, since his God escapes that intellectually incomprehensible combination of thought with extension which haunts the human person only by a trick, the trick of his 'eminent' possession of the attribute of extension. The Cartesian God, an infinite thinking thing, can be the cause and creator of an extended world although formally himself unextended. It is not very surprising that the materialists should turn the tables on Descartes and ask why the extended world should not, in the same mysterious way, contain the power to produce thinking things. For considering God as agent, however, it does not matter much just how he (or she) contains the attributes of thought and extension. What is interesting for our purposes is the fact that all the divine actions are intentional, and there are no failures of performance. To find out what a philosopher thinks successful intentional action consists in, look to his account of divine action.

The Cartesian God stipulates mathematical truths. It creates finite minds to which it gives the power to know and use those mathematical truths, and to share, innately, the divine self-knowledge, both in the finite mind's knowledge of itself, and in its knowledge of God. It creates a divisible and divided extended substance, sets it in motion, intimately conjoins body-sized and body-structured bits of it with finite minds, one per suitable body. All its knowledge is knowledge of what it has done, what it has made. Intention and knowledge go together, but intention or will calls the tune. This means that those disputed concepts, practical knowledge and knowledge without observation, apply to the Cartesian God, and indeed are the only sorts of knowledge that do apply. To act is to know what one is doing, to know what one has done. God needs no representation before his mind to have knowledge, since what he knows is his own work, itself present, needing no representative. Representation comes into the divine psychology not as the way God thinks but as the objective of action. Among the divine products are deliberate copies of other things. Man himself is made in the creator's image, and in him, as in the creator, intention or will dominates intellect. The universe in its variety, including in it man with his imperfections, is said in the *Fourth Meditation* to have a greatness suitable to that of its creator. Descartes, while claiming that it would be rash of him to investigate the aims of God, nevertheless portrays a God who is constantly expressing himself in his work.

Deliberate duplication or re-presentation is found also in man's innate ideas which copy their divine archetypes. But although Descartes' innate idea of triangularity is true because it represents the divine idea, the truth of God's idea of a triangle involves no correspondence between a representation and what is represented. God's idea of the triangle does not represent anything, it makes triangles what they are. God's thinking is constitutive. The divine archetypal triangle is not a blueprint for triangular shaped bits of matter to be cut out from the material world. "When I imagine a triangle," Descartes says in *The Fifth Meditation* "it may be that no such figure exists anywhere outside my consciousness or ever has existed, but there certainly exists its determinate nature which is unchangeable and external." Its nature has been determined. Triangles are no figment of Descartes' mind because they are authoritative 'figments' of the divine mind. To the extent that Descartes gives us a correspondence theory of truth, of truth as adequate representation in an idea of the formal reality that idea is of, this theory is supplemented by, and depends upon, a quite different theory of truth at the divine level. Even at the human level, Cartesian ideas 'represent' a very mixed ontological array. Geometrical ideas represent divine archetypes, clear and distinct ideas of material substance represent that substance, confused ideas of sense represent it badly but indicate clearly and well the features of it important for action; ideas of self and of thinking are reflexive or self-representational. (Does self-representation differ from self-presentation?) Ideas of God represent, distinctly but inadequately, the divine mind, none of whose ideas represent anything, since their role is to provide originals.

What I take from Descartes' off-guard philosophy of action, that is from his theology, are several truths about human action. The first is that action by the appropriate authority can create, by stipulation, universal rules within the constraints of which other agents will subsequently plan, think and act. Such institution-creating action has not been much considered by analytical philosophers of action, but has been left to the Hegelians and the Marxists. Secondly there is the Anscombe thesis that skilled successful intentional action carries with it knowledge without observation of what one is doing. If one has the know-how, one knows one has it and so knows that, in normal conditions, one's act succeeds. Practical knowledge is the human approximation to divine knowledge. Thirdly and negatively, I take the thesis that while representation may be the objective of some intentional action, it cannot be the very essence of intending.

This last thesis emerges more obviously from a consideration of Descartes' most direct treatment of action, namely his account of the actions and passions of the soul, or finite thinking thing. Here we do find unsuccessful attempts at action, happenings which are unintended, the full range of deviations from the norm of successful intentional action. One case to which Descartes devotes some attention is that of the failed attempt to imagine a geometrical figure. The mind can, with a special effort, call up the image of a pentagon, but it may fail to get an image of a ten-sided figure whose ten sides it can count, and it will not even attempt to imagine a chiliagon, since it knows its limitations. Descartes provides an explanation of the special effort needed to call up images, and of the limits of the mind's ability to construct images. The mind, he says, needs the cooperation of the body to call up an image. Whereas for pure thought it needs and has the cooperation of the divine mind which supplies those guiding constraints, innate ideas, for image construction it needs a finite cooperator as well. In the *Passions of the Soul* Descartes gives an elaborate account of the reciprocal actions and passions of mind and brain involved in the transaction. Mind is said to 'apply itself' to imagine something, say an enchanted palace. This 'applying' of itself is an action of the soul which has an effect in the body, namely a movement in the pineal gland which sends the animal spirits scurrying "towards the pores of the brain by the opening of which pores this particular thing can be represented" (Article XLII). This representation is relayed back to the mind, which then passively receives it and has an image to contemplate for as long as the gland sustains the brain motion needed to supply the image.

What is noteworthy about this account is that the calling up of an image is treated as an intentional activity. Not that having images is always intentional — in dreams images come to the mind unbidden, and these are passions of the soul precisely because the soul's desires are not what activates the image-construction activity. The intention to represent is what distinguishes the active from the passive imaginings. The soul's primary activity is willing. Representing, imagining, thinking about, withholding assent, are the things it can will to do. When what it intends to do is imagine, the soul must know, before it receives back the wanted image, what image it applied itself to get, and recognize what arrives as the correct one, or perhaps one too indistinct to be of any use. The representation is acceptable or not, depending on the intentions of the soul.

Could we treat the soul's willings or desirings as themselves representations, as Danto's account would seem to require? For the soul to want or will an image of an enchanted palace would then be for it to have a representation of an image of an enchanted palace, causally efficacious in bringing that image into being. But there would then seem little need for the intention to be causally efficacious, since the intention itself will contain its own fulfillment. By wanting to represent a palace, one will have represented one. And where intentions *are* representations, chiliagons can figure in representations, anything goes. Intentions become magical self fulfillers, and intending *followed* or *accompanied* by success becomes a pointless repetition or doubling of representations, as Danto himself half-realizes, in his discussion of imagining. (*Analytical Philosophy of Action,* pp. 142–3.)

At this point we need to recall Wittgenstein's simple mental exercise, "Consider the order 'Imagine a red patch.' You are not tempted to think that you must imagine a red patch to serve you as the pattern for the red patch you were ordered to imagine." (*Blue Book,* Harper, p. 3.) The moral here extends beyond images to anything which is given the role of a self-applying pattern. But, whatever the method of projection, a pattern is inert. A representation requires a representer whose intentions give it its status as representation.

The representations Danto speaks of are presumably not meant to be images, but they play a role suspiciously like that of Wittgenstein's mental samples. The mind Danto describes seems no more than a sequence of pictures or duplicates of states of affairs in the world. Causal relations to that world distinguish representations which are beliefs, caused by the world they picture, from representations which are intentions, exerting a causal force, self-realizing blue-prints for future states of the world. But mental states, even mental representations, do not come to us with their causal history or causal future stamped upon them, so it is unclear how I tell which of my representations are my intentions. Must my intentions, like my motives, declare themselves only retrospectively, when their causal role becomes clear? Must I wait to assess that causal role before recognizing my intentions? But who, in any case, am I, and what sort of thing is recognizing? If recognizing is itself representing the recognized, does the recognized occur twice before the mind on the occasion of recognition? Can it be its double occurrence which makes either representation of the twin-pair a case of something recognized? The busy purposeful life of the mind which Descartes described begins to degenerate into a series of self-repeating representations, a perpetual stuttering of images. Every effort to interpret a representation collapses into a duplication of the thing to be interpreted. With the meagre analytical tools of causal relation and correspondence or 'fit', the prospects are bleak for an account of the rich variety of the postures of the mind, for expectations, presentiments, forebodings, fears, admiration, hopes, wishes, aims, resolves, imitatings, envy, resentment, pride, shame, regret, remorse, wondering, revising, correcting, rejecting, ignoring, welcoming, repenting, forgiving, redeeming. With intentionality lost, absorbed into representation, the Cartesian active mind hollows out into Hume's empty theatre of the mind, devoid of actors, action, and of critical or appreciative audience.

I do not think it unreasonable to test a philosophy of action by applying its analysis to mental acts. There are intentional mental acts which must be accounted for, and whose relation to other intentional acts must be explained. Recent philosophy of action has been polarized into work, such as Geach's *Mental Acts,* which tackles mental activity, and work, such as that of Danto and Goldman, which analyzes physical action. The work of those who have recognized that physical action, in particular speech, is also mental, that is the work of Austin, Ryle, Sellars, Searle, Vendler, has not been of great influence on the treatment given to non-verbal physical action, nor to that accorded to mental acts. The exception is Vendler's interesting attempt, in *Res Cogitans,* to map the parallels between speech acts and thought acts. But, there too, we are given a parallel rather than a unified theory, and even the parallel does not extend from acts of mind through speech acts to other socially recognized and world-altering action. In Danto's book, *Analytical Philosophy of Action,* the special class of 'gestures' are recognized and thereafter ignored. They are even denied the label 'mediated actions', so little parallel does Danto find between gestures and other extensions of the power to act. For Danto, it is not enabling rules and habits of social recognition which mediate between the active subject and his substantial world, the mediators are intractable causal laws. Danto's agents' abilities to act are 'gifts', fixed by fate. Had more attention been given to those powers of action we possess in virtue of our necessarily shared ability to exchange and interpret 'gestures,' to teach, correct and extend our gesture-repertoire and with it our power to cooperatively understand and reshape our world and ourselves, a less blackly Schopenhauerian estimate of the prospects and freedom of the human agent might have emerged.

Danto does not discuss acts of mind as such, although he clearly wants to allow for such things, and instances imagining as an action. Unlike Descartes, Danto treats it as basic, indeed, not surprisingly he calls it the paradigmatic mental event (*Analytical Philosophy of Action,* p. 142). He suggests that imagining or mental picturing, like arm-raising, is to be treated as one among the normal person's repertoire of 'gifts', and even suggests that fate has denied this gift to Ryle (*op. cit.,* p. 131). He does not tell us if there are any mind-mediated mental acts, or any mental gestures. His discussion of feelings and forbearances concentrates on our power to inhibit expression of feeling, a power which is developed by socialization. No consideration is given to the possibility that socialization might not merely encourage our non-basic acts of inhibition, but might enlarge our repertoire of acts, responses, feelings and recognitions, including those acts and responses which are central to our cognitive life, subject to rational criticism and logical scrutiny. Our ability to think, the conclusions and beliefs which result, are treated as instances of grace or damnation, of that "fatality of gifts" (*op. cit.,* p. 133) which Danto thinks runs deep, deep into mental as well as bodily potencies and impotencies.

The importance of socialized or convention-generated action is more fully recognized by Goldman, who, in his *Theory of Human Action,* has basic actions raised to higher levels by conventional as well as causal generation. But the level-generation apparatus is not applied to mental acts, which, like Danto's 'gestures', are mentioned only to be put aside. Goldman treats cases where some overt action, like hiding or fishing, is given its distinctive feature by the wish, belief or aim of the agent, as cases of 'simple' generation, and he emphasizes that wanting and believing are not mental acts. Cases where two basic actions are co-temporal and together generate a higher-level compound act are cases of 'augmentation' generation, and this, like simple generation, is mysterious and anything but simple. The cases of compound augmentation-generation which Goldman discusses are ones where two co-temporal bodily movements are equally basic to one higher-level act, such as jumpshooting in basketball. What are we to say of cases where not just a mental state but a mental act gives a distinctive property to an overt action? Suppose I carry a precariously laden tray upstairs, thinking what I am doing and choosing each move carefully. Is my mental attention to my bodily movements basic to them, co-temporal with them, or generated by them? None of these answers seem satisfactory. There are not two independent co-temporal acts. I could not attend to my movements were I not moving, nor could I move with self-conscious care unless the requisite mental actions took place, the acts, that is, of in-tentionally thinking about the movements one is making. This may be a rare sort of thought, and most bodily movement, however intelligent or careful, need not be accompanied by such mental occurrences, but there surely are cases not just of careful but of self-conscious movement, where bodily action and mental acts cannot be kept segregated from one another. I do not know how a theory of basic actions could cope with such cases, nor give us a unified theory of basicness and of level generation which would cover mental acts and all the varieties of mind-imbued action. Analytical philosophy of action has neglected both the group action or co-operative action which is the prerequisite for 'gestures', and has neglected individual mental acts. If one concentrates exclusively on those middle-range actions which exercise neither the individual nor the collective mind, it will not be surprising if one ends wondering how mind can inform action.

I have argued that attention to intentional mental acts shows us that intention cannot be construed as representation of the intended. Whatever intentions are, they are not inner representations. I now want to look at the concept of representation itself, and at Danto's use of that concept. What is it that makes a mental state a representation of a state of the world, rather than the world-state a representation of a state of mind, especially when the mental state temporally precedes and causally affects the state of the world? How can the mind re-present what is not yet present? Representation is a non-symmetric relation but it is hard to see, on Danto's account, what determines which is representation, which the represented. Temporal or causal asymmetry cannot be what determines it, and the truth relation, seem as correspondence or 'fit', will not do the job since fitting too is a symmetrical relation. We need a way of determining what Austin called the onus of fit, but nothing about a state of affairs calls out for a belief to fit it, any more than a nightmare vision calls out for a fact to describe. Danto rightly says that beliefs are not merely inert furnishings of the soul, isolated introspectable interior decorations. "Beliefs spontaneously refer their holder beyond themselves to what makes them true" (*op. cit.,* p. 148). Beliefs may do this, although I would prefer to say that the believer does it, but the content of the belief, the 'representation', does not. We need an intender to determine onus of fit, to treat things, mental and physical, as representations, and to decide on the use of those representations. Without intention, without the will to represent, and without recognition of standards of correctness in representations, the world may be cluttered with matching states of affairs but not representations, with endlessly recurring events but, without a recognizing mind, no eternal return.

John Searle has recently[1] argued that within every speech act there is a representation. Completing every utterance which begins 'I warn you that', 'I assert that', 'I promise that' is a clause which represents some possible state of affairs in the world. The illocutionary force operator operates on representations. Searle also suggested that pictures, or even the represented thing itself, might stand in for the verbal representation. Instead of saying 'I warn you that the crankshaft is broken', I might, in a foreign country where my vocabulary did not extend to terms for crankshaft or other car parts, but included a few illocutionary expressions, say 'Achtung!' then indicate the crankshaft or draw a diagram of it in its broken state. The thesis that every illocutionary act has a representation as its content seems to me to run into trouble when we consider greetings, congratulations, christenings, where the only states of affairs referred to in the speech act seem to be those brought into being by the act itself. If I greet you, you are greeted, and the world changes to that extent. I represent nothing. I need not be glad to see you, nor do I purport to be so, when I acknowledge your arrival with a formal greeting. To construe a farewell as an utterance which really amounts to 'I wish that you fare well' is to force the facts to fit the theory, and to turn the distinctive speech act of farewelling into an instance of a different act, wishing. There are many wishes we can make, at the wishing well, or when we get the wishbone, but to wish that someone fares well is different from farewelling them, to wish that they end in hell is different from cursing them, to wish that they will enjoy one's company is different from welcoming them.

If, however, we grant that many illocutionary acts imbed representations of states of affairs independent of the illocutionary act itself, we could use this fact to get a way of distinguishing representations from what they represent. Where we have two matching or isomorphic states of affairs, one will represent the other only if it is imbedded within an illocutionary act. Vendler, in *Res Cogitans,* speak of the modes of thought, in the Cartesian sense, as *frames* for thought. The referents of verbs such as *doubt, intend, conclude, wonder,* will be thought frames. Adopting and adapting Vendler's felicitous term, we could say that a representation is what is inside a frame. The essence of a picture is to be framed.

If we take this line, then it will be true that most if not all thinking involves representing, but representing will now be dependent on framing, that is on the illocutionary acts which provide the frames, and so convert mere symmetric correspondence into asymmetric representation. This will drive us back to the mental and verbal actions and passions, and our account of representation will wait on our analysis of acts and their intentionality. The representations will be what follow the 'I think'.

The asymmetry of representing is not the only problem Danto's account appears to face. There is also the problem of reference. Wittgenstein asked, "What makes my image of him an image of *him*?" and gave us the beginnings of an answer, "not its looking like him". (*Philosophical Investigations,* II, iii.) What makes one of Danto's representations one of the future rather than of the past? Suppose I think about a painting I have seen and would like to see again. What makes my thought into a memory, or into an intention? A causal link with the past will be there whichever it is. Could one representation serve both as memory and as intention? Memory, as Hobbes said, supposeth the time past. Does the representation incorporate the *suppositio*? Are Danto's representations tensed, and have they mood as well as tense? Aquinas (*Summa Theologica,* §78, Article 4) discussed the view of Avicenna that the powers of the souls of men and animals include not merely Aristotle's common sense and imagination, to recognize, retain, and revive past perceptions, but phantasy to recombine them, and an estimative and memorative power to use and interpret them once revived, to assign them to the past or project them into the future as goals for action. Danto's representations will get that status only to a soul with estimative and memorative powers. As previously noted, Danto's differentiation of intentions from beliefs by their different causal relation to the world will not help explain how the believer or the intender knows that and what he believes or intends. Danto rejects Anscombe's knowledge without observation of what one is doing, but surely he would want to allow knowledge without observation of one's intentions. But if all our acts are inscrutable to us, our intentions will become equally alien.

Descartes attributes to the soul an immediate perception or knowledge of what it wills. "It is certain that we cannot desire anything without perceiving by the same means that we desire it; and although in regard to our soul it is an action to desire something, we may say that it is one of its passions to perceive that it desires. Yet, because this perception and this will are really one and the same thing, the more noble always supplies the denomination and thus we are not in the habit of calling it a passion, but only an action" (*Passions of the Soul,* Article XIX). Here we have, in its finite Cartesian version, knowledge without observation. This explains how the very concepts Danto criticizes and rejects can come from a translator of Descartes, Anscombe, and from Merleau-Ponty and Sartre, philosophers in the Cartesian tradition. Their Cartesian tradition, however, included its Hegelian development, which analytical philosophers of action have ignored to their loss. In Hegel's writings we find the most sustained pre-twentieth century explorations of intentional action, the varieties of conventional and institutional action, speech acts such as flattery, buying and selling. Had our attempt to discover what is basic to action taken its starting point in attention to actions of this sort, instead of remaining paralyzed in the hospital room where the amputee tries in vain to move his missing limb, we might by now have analyses of action of more use to the moral and political philosopher. We might have had a conference on transaction, interaction, cooperative action, instead of a retrospective conference on solitary action. Where the Hegelians demythologized Descartes' doctrine of the need for divine cooperation in human action, we imitated the surface individualism of his unhappy consciousness.

I want to conclude by a brief consideration of an action where recognizable intention in acting, practical knowledge, or knowing what one is doing, and knowledge without observation of what one has done, are clearly dependent on shared forms of activity, yet where the achievement is an individual one, no mere ritual act. It is the case of mimicking, an action which also exemplifies that derivative yet peculiarly fascinating family of intentional activities, re-presenting, and shows the difficulty, limits, and demands on cooperation such actions involves.

Suppose that someone entertains us by mimicking Kissinger. This action resists analysis into a basic action root from which sprout causal or conventional consequences. By doing what does the mimic mimic Kissinger? He speaks English with a German accent. Is his speaking basic, or does he do that by moving his mouth and larynx? This case is interesting precisely because the skilled mimic, unlike the normal skilled speaker, may need to make phonetic moves, not to speak English, but to speak like Kissinger. Descartes has interesting things to say about the skilled speaker's bypassing of the 'basic act', of his direct access to the language-mediated act: "When, in speaking, we think only of the sense of what we desire to say, that causes us to move the tongue and lips much more quickly and better than if we thought of moving them in all the ways requisite to utter the same words, in as much as the custom which we acquired in learning to speak caused us to join the action of the soul with the significance of the words which follow these movements, rather than with the movements themselves." (*Passions of the Soul,* Article XIV.) The normal speaker will make the movements themselves by speaking English, as well as speaking English by making those movements, if, that is, he has any powers of phonetic analysis he can call on when needed. The mimic probably will attend to some aspects of his phonetic act, not to speak English, but to get the right accent. Is speaking with a German accent simply or augmentatively generated by speaking? If it is either of these, then that speaking cannot have phonetic moves as basic to it, since the phonetic act is involved in the transformation of a case of speaking into one of speaking with an accent. Difficulties multiply when we try to move up the action tree, and ask what sort of level generation gets us from speaking with a German accent to speaking like Kissinger, and from that to mimicking him. A certain effect must be obtained, elicited from the audience, but it is a convention presupposing special effect. The audience must recognize that the mimic is not Kissinger, that he is not impersonating him or piously imitating him, but mimicking him. The prerequisites for the success of this act are a shared language, a shared knowledge that there are other languages, recognition of the distinctive phonemes of one of them, the German language, a shared knowledge of a particular individual and his speech habits, common knowledge of his public role, shared participation in or recognition of related forms of life such as pretending, quoting, playacting. The mimic's act is what Ryle calls a 'higher order' act (*Concept of Mind*, p. 193) which depends for its point and recognition on the recognition of a simpler act to which it makes reference. Its generation is complex, not simple. The audience must not only take it as some such higher order act, they must take it as one whose purpose is entertainment, realize that it is not a serious higher order act like legal representation, deputizing, forgery, fraud or false pretenses. The act of mimicking is one which can be performed and recognized in a community which has a large enough family of higher order relatives of mimicking, including such things as joking, commenting, alluding, practising, doodling, aping, clowning, re-enacting, trans-substantiating, performing masses both white and black, parading, advertising, self-advertising, confessing, lying, imposture, scandal-mongering, libel, biography, autobiography, parody, metaphor, sarcasm, irony, satire, coverup and exposure, scrawling graffiti, commemorating in plaques and monuments and statues, portraiture, forgery and defacing, making and faking graven images, and desecrating these images.

Mimicking is not gesturing, since no rule of interpretation licenses its description as mimicking, but, like rule-constituted conventional actions, it is necessarily intentional. One might unconsciously or unknowingly *imitate* someone's mannerisms, but one can no more *mimic* unintentionally than one can unintentionally bless, curse, greet, conceal, signal, telephone, pay, sell, buy, hire, dismiss, marry, or contract. (The list is Anscombe's.) There is of course room for failure, for mistakes and misfires. We may telephone or marry the wrong person. We may attempt to mimic Kissinger but succeed only in mimicking anyone with a German accent. Our conventions and shared forms of life make possible not only routine automatically successful intentional acts, acts where the agent must know what he is doing and that he is doing it, but they also give scope and opportunity for special individual talent, for innovative action, for new forms of social comment, new levels of self-reference and irony. The mimic's talents may be rare and distinctive, but he needs our cooperation to succeed in his act, and our cooperation is mediated by our common cognitions and recognitions.

There are, of course, many ways in which persons cooperate or do things together, and many ways in which individual actions and opportunities for action depend on cooperative or collective action. There are the cases which seem to involve the sharing and possibly the dividing and specializing of such action as might have been done singlehanded. If I am cleaning up the garden and you come and help, then I may do all the raking of leaves while you do all the carrying to the compost heap. This division of pre-existent labor, this joining of forces, will give scope for new forms of action and make room for coordinators, conductors, cheerleaders, coaches, coxswains, timestudy experts. When we have new games, religions, cults, we will introduce new forms of action in a different way, not ancillary to the division and specialization of old singlehanded acts. In such cases, doing things together will not be helping one another do more efficiently what some were already doing, but it will introduce genuinely new things to do. Such innovations, new forms of life, will usually involve a plurality of complementary roles, but these will multiply action possibilities without dividing what was already going on. For such roles, teaching and training will be not merely helpful but essential, since what we must learn is *what* we are doing, not just how to do it. The difference between learning how to walk and learning how to pray is that for the former we may use help, but for the latter we need initiation.

Once there are these roles into which new role players must be initiated, they will affect the roles resulting from division of labor. Once we have the roles of priest and penitent there will be room in armies for chaplains as well as for artillerymen, commanders, commissariat, and ship's captains will conduct prayers as well as chart the ship's course. The roles we find in any society will include all degrees of mixing of the natural and the conventional, the solitary and the social, the unavoidable and the arbitrary, of necessarily and of contingently shared actions, of divided tasks and multiplied action possibilities.

Pioneering work in exploring the complex web which results has been done by D. Shwayder in *The Stratification of Behavior,* and D. Lewis has analyzed in detail one form of self-consciously co-ordinated action in *Convention.* More recent work has been done by R. X. Ware, on 'The Mental Life of Groups'[2] and Gerald Massey has explored the logical behavior of sentences with conjunctive subjects.[3] Massey concentrates on sentences such as 'Tom, Dick and Harry are shipmates' and 'Tom, Dick and Harry moved the piano', which he thinks predicate logic ill-equipped to handle. Adapting the formal tools of Leonard and Goodman, he treats these conjunctive subjects as *sum individuals* and calls predicates *multigrade* at an argument place which admits of terms denoting sum individuals. A predicate such as 'presented the calculus of individuals' will be multigrade since it may be true of the sum individual Leonard and Goodman, but not of either singly. Massey suggests that most if not all predicates of natural languages are multigrade, and he notes the 'unigrade bias' of much analytical philosophy, including action theory. Now that the methodological individualists no longer have a monopoly of the formal tools, we can hope that this bias will be righted.

Are action predicates multigrade? The only plausible candidates for unigrade status are those mostly unmentionable actions, degenerate cases in that our control over them is limited and partial. Normal bodily functions may be unigrade but, following an operation, Jones' urinating may not be done singlehanded. Apart from such bodily quasi-actions, the other candidates for unigrade status are the controlled bodily movements which have been deemed basic actions. These, in a different way, suffer from unmentionability, since we have no criteria of individuation for hand movements, and a very poor vocabulary for specifying their variety.[4] I think that the search for basic actions has been to some extent motivated by the wish to find something which is unequivocally the doing of an atomic individual, all his own, some act of which he can say "I may depend on the world, and on my fellows, for what comes of this basic act, for the generation of my nonbasic actions, but my basic act is all my own, it is described by a predicate which is unigrade." Since no procedure separates agent from basic act, there is no room for helpers, no labor to divide, no room for shared responsibility or shared glory. The ironic thing is that to bodily movements as such no glory or responsibility attaches. It is for striking the right note, not for vibrating her vocal chords, that we give the soloist credit.

Most of the things we do singlehanded are done, at other times, multihanded, and some of the things we do together, like attending colloquia, are essentially multihanded. Yet others, such as electing a chairman, cannot be done even by sum individuals unless they have some accepted procedure for coordinated action. Whereas I can be said to attend a colloquium, provided others do as well, *I* do not elect a chairman even when I am a member of a committee which elects a chairman. The sum individual, Mary, Jane and Sally, elect a chairman if they act as members of a committee, but the atomic individual Mary, even as a member of the committee, does not do so. Actions such as electing are more than multihanded since they require, not merely coordination between the hands, but coordinating procedures. They could be called collective actions. The acceptance of the procedures which transforms multihanded action into collective action seems to be essentially multihanded. I cannot, by myself, accept majority rule, and even if I can, by myself, impose one-woman rule, only *we* can accept and legitimate it.

What makes some actions essentially multihanded?[5] I can't move the piano alone, but if I were stronger, I might. I can't play piano music for four hands alone, but if, like Siva, I had many arms, I might. To converse alone or to elect a leader alone, however, I would have to become several persons in one. (Descartes' claim to converse with himself alone is, significantly, preceded by his admission of confusion between his own existence and that of the triune deity.) Do all essentially multihanded actions involve conventions, or is it for collective action that convention is required? The difficulty of answering this question stems in part from that of sharply dividing the essence from the accidents of the human agent. Is it essentially or accidentally the case that human agents reproduce sexually? Were the actions taken in response to the command 'Go forth and multiply' essentially multihanded, was the successful action collective? Perhaps, to analyze what is basic to cooperative action, we will be driven back to bodily movements after all, perhaps we will find in the biological realm the basis not merely for solitary but for combined action. It would be pleasing if sex turned out to be the ur-convention.

Whatever we conclude are the proper answers to these questions, I am convinced that if we want to look for something basic to that action which reveals mind making a difference in the world, the direction to look is not towards some elusive basic action core, but towards all the complex inter-connections of common knowledge, convention, and recognition of individual originality and achievement which mediate between the individual agent and the world in which he acts. Danto began his presentation with a quotation from Aristotle, and I shall end by re-invoking him, with another passage from *De Anima*. Danto has described for us a mind which, in its representations, becomes all things, reduplicates them in a shadow world, and sometimes botches things, blots its copybook. I have tried to defend the thesis that its power to engage in this highly idiosyncratic act of re-presenting, and its recognitions of its success and failures in the great variety of its reflective activities, depends upon its cooperative, creative, constituting or presenting power, on that "other mind which is what it is in virtue of making all things". (*De Anima,* 430a, 14–16.)

*University of Pittsburgh*

## NOTES

[1] In a paper read at the Meeting of the Western Division of the American Philosophical Association at Chicago in April, 1975.

Since writing the above I have been able to see Searle's paper, whose theses I have somewhat oversimplified. Searle allows that a speech act like resigning brings about the state of affairs it represents, and he has states of affairs *expressed* rather than represented in acts like thanking. But for all speech acts, the form is $F(p)$, and different speech acts are regarded as different modes of representing or expressing reality.

[2] Unpublished.

[3] 'Tom, Dick and Harry and All The Kings Men', forthcoming in *American Philosophical Quarterly*.

[4] I discuss this in 'Ways and Means', *Canadian Journal of Philosophy,* **1** (1971), 275–294.
[5] In 'Mixing Memory and Desire', forthcoming in *American Philosophical Quarterly,* I argue that intending, like remembering, is dependent, for its first person singular instances, on its first person plural occurrences, so is essentially multihanded.

## BIBLIOGRAPHY

Anscombe, Elizabeth, *Intention,* Blackwell, Oxford, 1957.
Aquinas, St. Thomas, *Basic Writings* (ed. by Anton G. Pegis), Random House, New York, 1945.
Aristotle, *Basic Works* (ed. by Richard McKeon), Random House, New York, 1941.
Danto, Arthur, *Analytical Philosophy of Action,* University Press, Cambridge, 1973.
Descartes, *The Philosophical Works* (transl. by Elizabeth S. Haldane and G. R.T. Ross), University Press, Cambridge, 1911.
Descartes, *Philosophical Writings* (transl. by Elizabeth Anscombe and Peter Thomas Geach), Thomas Nelson and Sons, London, 1954.
Geach, Peter Thomas, *Mental Acts,* Humanities Press, New York, 1957.
Goldman, Alvin I, *A Theory of Human Action,* Prentice Hall, Englewood Cliffs, 1970.
Kenny, Anthony, *Descartes: A Study of His Philosophy,* Random House, New York, 1968.
Lewis, David, *Convention,* Harvard University Press, Cambridge, 1969.
Ryle, Gilbert, *Concept of Mind,* Hutchinson House, London, 1949.
Shwayder, David, *The Stratification of Behavior,* Humanities Press, New York, 1965.
Vendler, *Res Cogitans,* Cornell University Press, Ithaca, 1972.
Wittgenstein, Ludwig, *The Blue and Brown Books,* Blackwell, Oxford, 1958 and Harper, New York, 1965.

PART 3

THE VOLITIONAL THEORY REVISITED

# VOLITIONS RE-AFFIRMED

## I

1. What is a volition? It is a mental act, as conceptual a mental act as an occurrent believing.[1] Like the latter it is an event which finds overt expression — if one is in a thinking-out-loud frame of mind — in a sentential utterance, thus

> I will do A here and now.

In order that the trees not obscure the forest, it will be useful to regiment a little and adopt a philosophical idiolect in which it is 'shall' rather than 'will' which expresses intention. I will accordingly rewrite the above as

> I shall do A here and now

to bring it in line with

> The gardener shall mow the lawn.

2. As acts, volitions are episodes, as are occurrent believings. The basic grammar of 'volition' is

> Person wills to do A then and there.

3. The verb 'to will', so used, strikes many as not only contrived (which to a certain extent it is), but contrived to save a theory which urgently needs a verb to support the verbal noun 'volition'. But is it really a contraption? After all, it does occur in first person *expressions* of intention. As for second and third person *ascriptions* of occurrent here-now intentions to act, it must be confessed that the verb or its equivalent is more difficult to find. But how serious is this deficiency? In this respect the verb 'to will' and the verbal noun 'volition' are in the same boat. What we can say, and this is the heart of the matter, is that if the one is needed, so is the other. If the theory of volitions is a sound one, so is the theory that people will to do actions.

4. A parallel point can be made about occurrent beliefs. If the theory of occurrent belief is a sound one, there is a need for some such verb as 'to (occurrently) believe'. Now many philosophers believe (sometimes occurrently) in occurrent belief. Some of them seem to assume that ordinary

*M. Brand and D. Walton (eds.), Action Theory, 47–66. All Rights Reserved*
*Copyright © 1976 by D. Reidel Publishing Company, Dordrecht-Holland*

language contains an expression for this concept, among the candidates being 'to suddenly think that-$p$' and 'to be struck by the thought that-$p$'. But the latter imply, as the desired locution does not, that the thinking in question is not the conclusion of a process of reasoning.

5. The key to the situation, surely, is that our ordinary interest in mental events is highly specific and concerned to differentiate cases and contexts. This is particularly true of those *on the spot* intentions which result in action. What concerns us is whether the agent acted on impulse or did not act impulsively, considered alternatives or did not consider alternatives, deliberated or did not deliberate. From the standpoint of volition theory, in all these cases action is caused by volition. But the volitions themselves came about in importantly different ways.

6. Volitions, of course, though acts are not actions, pieces of conduct. They are mental *actualities* in Aristotle's sense of the term (*energeiai*). The same is obviously true of occurrent beliefs. Since what one wills is always an action, it doesn't even make sense to speak of willing to will, any more than it makes sense to speak of willing to (occurrently) believe something.[2] One can, of course, will to do something now which one thinks makes it likely that at a certain time in the future one will will to do a certain action. Similarly, one can will to do something now which one thinks makes it likely that at a certain time in the future one will occurrently believe a certain proposition.

7. Consequently, volitions are not tryings, for trying to do $A$ is acting in a way which one hopes will eventuate in a doing of $A$. (It should be noticed, however, that some philosophers who have flirted with volitions, while shying away from the term have given 'try' a technical use in which it comes close to standing for volition.)

8. Although volitions are acts, they should not be thought of as instantaneous. Here, again, we can draw on Aristotle, who distinguished between a continuing act and a change. One could sense-red for a minute (or contemplate an essence), without the sensing (or contemplation) being a process of change, even though it is accompanied, perhaps necessarily, by change. How long do volitions last? Long enough to do their job of getting actions going. It must be borne in mind that reference to volitions (and to mental acts generally) as well as to intentions, beliefs and propensities pertaining thereto, is part of our theory of persons, and they have the properties attributed to them by the theory — to the extent that, of course, the theory is a good one.[3]

9. Nor is it correct, I believe, to characterize volitions as parts of actions, the initial stages which bring the rest. Thus, when I move my finger and my finger moves because I will to move it, the initial stage of the moving is exactly that; the initial stage of the moving begins when the finger begins to move.

10. What makes it tempting to think that a volition is part of a willed action is that the *concept* of a volition is contained in — i.e. is a part of — the *concept* of an action. An action is essentially the sort of thing that is brought about by volition, though not necessarily the volition to do that action.

11. This implication is carried by action locutions (e.g. 'raising one's arm'), as contrasted with locutions which describe bodily occurrences which a person is (usually) able to bring about (e.g. 'one's arm going up'). Even if one takes the strong position that to ascribe an action to an agent is to imply the occurrence of a volition, it would be a mistake to conclude that the volition, though 'essential' to the occurrence of the action, is part of it. 'Part' is, indeed, said in many ways, and in many ways actions have 'parts'. However close the conceptual tie between volition and action, the decisive consideration remains that volitions are causes of actions, and it would, indeed, be a strange sense of 'part' in which a cause is part of its effect.

12. If volitions bring about actions, they do not always bring about the action which is willed. Indeed, no action at all may result. To explore these facts we must make use of the familiar concept of a minimal action, i.e. an action which one does not do by doing another action. Consider a volition which has the form,

> I shall do [minimal action] in order to bring about $X$ and thus do $A$

or,

> I shall do $A$ by doing $MA$

for example,

> I shall close my finger in order to cause the gun to go off and thus to fire it.

> I shall fire the gun by closing my finger.

Let us suppose that I am not paralyzed nor prevented from doing the minimal action. I do it, but instead of causing $X$, cause $Y$. As a result I do not do $A$, but rather $B$; thus, I dislodge the trigger — the gun being defective.

13. One does non-minimal actions by doing minimal actions which have certain results. Does this entail that one wills to do a non-minimal action by willing to do a minimal action *which one believes* will have a certain result? Here one must be careful, for this way of putting it implies that there occurs a separate volition to do the minimal action. The idea that this is in fact the case has proved tempting. I trace this temptation to a misuse of a (not unimportant) contrast between minimal and non-minimal action which is closely related to the conceptual distinction between them.

14. In addition to being actions which are not done *by* doing something else, minimal actions are as securely under our voluntary control as anything could be. Only abnormal states (e.g. paralysis) which deprive us of our very ability to do them remove them from our voluntary control. Even when physical restraint prevents us from doing one minimal action, we can resist by resorting to other minimal actions which we hope will have the same ultimate effect. In short there is a striking difference in the extent to which minimal and non-minimal actions involve the friendliness of circumstance.

15. It is this theme which makes possible the confusion. An analogy may be helpful. Suppose someone were to argue that perceptual 'takings' of physical objects are to be analyzed in terms of takings *proper* which are not of physical objects. One 'takes' there to be a red-topped table in front of one by virtue of *taking* there to be a red rectangular expanse, and 'accepting' the idea that the red rectangular expanse is a constituent of a near-by table top. And suppose that we were offered as a reason for this claim the fact that there is less epistemic risk in taking there to be a red rectangular expanse in front of one than there is in taking there to be a red-topped table in front of one. More can go wrong. Most of us, I believe, would reject the argument, even if embellished along familiar lines.

16. Unless circumstances are such as to make us wary, we simply take there to be a red-topped table over there. Similarly, unless the circumstances are such as to make us wary, we simply will *to open the window by pushing it,* where this does not mean that we will to push the window, believing that pushing it will cause it to become open.[4] In precisely this sense there is no separate volition to push. Volitions to do *A* by doing *MA* no more consist of volitions *proper* to do *MA* plus causal beliefs, than takings of tables consist of takings *proper* of expanses plus beliefs as to where these expanses make their home.

17. A related point is that if one wills to play a melody, there need be no

volition, with respect to each note, to sound that note. It is those who are learning to play the melody who are in this position, as was the fabled centipede who fell into confusion when he was asked how he walked.

18. There is, thus, an important place for the concept of an action being in one's voluntary control in the sense that if, just before doing it, one had willed not to do it, one would not have done it, a concept obviously akin to that of avoidable action as defined by Charles Stevenson.[5] Playing each note in a learned melody would be an action in one's voluntary control, even though playing the melody which is willed.

19. I shall conclude this initial stock-taking of volition theory with a bow and a wave of the hand to a question which raises central issues in metaphysics and the philosophy of mind, a serious treatment of which would take me far beyond the scope of this essay. How can a volition to raise one's finger have so close a conceptual tie with finger raising and yet be the cause of a finger raising? The crux of the answer must be that to specify the content of a mental act is analogous to saying what an expression means. In each case we classify by the use of a (usually) complex functional sortal built from expressions which have specifiable linguistic functions. The correct application of the sortal implies that the item is subject to pattern-governed uniformities which can be described without the use of intentional terms. Thus, to every explanation in mentalistic terms there corresponds *in principle* an explanation in non-mentalistic terms.[6] I say 'in principle' because, in even the simplest cases, the complexity of such an explanation would be unmanageable. Mentalistic explanations involve a cumulative wisdom which early researchers in artificial intelligence soon came to appreciate.[7]

II

20. I return to the task of locating volitions in the larger framework of mental activity. Once again it will be helpful, I believe, to take another joint look at volitions and perceptual takings. The latter, which can for our present purposes be construed as a variety of occurrent belief, are not, of course, actions. One acts, in perception, by opening ones eyes, looking, observing, focussing ones attention, etc. The point of all this action is to make possible a certain non-action, ones being caused to have a perceptual occurrent belief. If circumstances are favorable, the belief is true. Its content is available to serve as a *premise* in our thinking about how things stand in the world around us.

21. In perceptual taking the world impinges on our mind. In volition the mind impinges on the world — indeed, in many cases, on itself, for the mind is part of the world, and while the concept of a mental act must be carefully distinguished from that of a mental action, there obviously are mental actions. If circumstances are favorable, and we have the relevant abilities, a volition to do $A$ is the cause of ones doing $A$ and is *realized* (a concept closely akin to that of truth) by the doing of $A$.

22. Furthermore, just as it is an essential part of the function of perceptual takings to provide *premises* — though they may occur without the content they provide actually serving as a premise — so it is an essential part of the function of volitions that their content serve as *conclusions* of practical reasonings — though, as in the case of impulsive action, they may occur without their content actually having served as a conclusion.

23. This is not the occasion on which to elaborate a theory of practical reasoning. I cannot, however, dispense with some reflections on the topic. I have touched on it in print on a number of occasions, though not always, I am afraid, either clearly or distinctly.[8] I do, however, think that I was on the right track, and that in spite of serious blemishes and, on occasion, downright mistakes, the general picture was true. According to that picture, practical reasoning is genuinely, *reasoning,* reasoning in a full blooded sense.

24. The fundamental thesis is that one intention can imply another intention in that sense of 'imply' in which implication authorizes inference, just as one belief can imply another belief. Here, of course, we must be careful. In the latter case we distinguish between belief as someones state of believing, and belief as what is believed. We distinguish between what is implied by *what* Jones believes, thus p, and what is implied by the fact that he believes it. An ideally rational person would, of course, believe all the implications of what he believes. He would equally intend all the implications of what he intends. Neither, of course, is true of ordinary mortals.

25. I shall momentarily adopt a convention, which I shall not attempt to justify here,[9] according to which the content of a state of belief is represented by dot-quoting the sentence in our language which would be the appropriate expression of that belief. We can think of the dot-quoted expressions as standing for propositions. Thus ˙2 + 2 = 4˙ stands for the proposition that $2 + 2 = 4$. Suppose that Jones believes that he himself is

wise. Then the content of his state of belief is the proposition 'I am wise [Jones] where the bracketed 'Jones' serves as an index which informs us that the English sentence used to formulate this content is construed as one which would appropriately express Jones' belief state, if he belonged to the English speaking community. I put the bracketed 'Jones' outside the quotes, because, as Castañeda has pointed out, Jones may not believe that he himself is Jones, which "I (Jones) am wise" would imply.

26. It is a familiar story that other indices are necessary to represent other features of propositional contents, those features traditionally called 'ego-centric', but now appropriately called, following Pierce, 'indexical'. In what follows I shall abstract from these niceties. Indeed, I shall shortly fall back on the standard literary conventions by which authors represent what is going on in the minds of their characters.

27. But before taking a relaxed stance, I shall continue for a moment to regiment, for a parallel technical point needs to be made about intentions. Thus, if at $t_1$ Jones intends to do $A$ at $t_2$, the content of his intention is represented by "I shall do $A$ at $t_2$" (with appropriate indices). And if Jones at $t_1$ intends to do $A$ there and then, the content of his intention is represented by "I shall now do $A$" with appropriate indices. This content itself, as contrasted with the intending of which it is the content, can be said to be an intention, as the content of a believing can be said to be a belief (proposition).

28. Using '$I_i$' as a variable which ranges over intention-contents, as '$P$' '$Q$' ... range over propositions, we represent that one intention-content implies another intention-content by

$$I_i \text{ implies } I_j$$

as we represent that one belief-content implies another belief-content by

$$P \text{ implies } Q.$$

29. Volitions are, as I have emphasized, but one variety of occurrent intention (state), as perceptual takings are but one variety of occurrent belief (state). Volitions, accordingly, can be subsumed under the general thesis that one occurrent intention can have relevantly the same content as another occurrent intention, and as a disposition or propensity to be in a certain occurrent intention (state), just as one occurrent belief can have relevantly the same content as another occurrent belief and as a disposition or propensity to be in a certain occurrent belief (state).

## III

30. I now turn to a relatively informal treatment of some of the more important aspects of practical thinking to which the above distinctions are relevant.

31. I noted at the beginning that one kind of intention an agent can have is the intention that something come to be the case. In the kind of case we considered, the auxiliary 'shall' which expresses intention occurred within a grammatically simple sentence, directly modifying the main verb, thus

> The gardener shall mow the lawn

With an eye to constructing expressions for intentions that complex (e.g. conjunctive) states of affairs be the case, it will be useful to adopt the phrase 'it shall be the case that...' which has the desired flexibility.[10] As a notational convenience, let us rewrite

> It shall be the case that-$p$

as

> Shall be [$p$]

Using the same general style, intentions of the shall-do kind, thus

> I shall do $A$ at $t$

can be rewritten as

> Shall [I to do $A$ at $t$]

32. We clearly need a principle to relate 'shall be' to 'shall do'. In the absence of further distinctions which would be necessary to spell it out, I propose to rely on the intuitive (to me, at least) equivalence of

> It shall be the case that-$p$

with

> I shall do what I can to make it the case that-$p$[11]

which I shall rewrite as

> Shall make [$p$].

33. Another principle is to the effect that

> Shall make [I will $A$ at $t$]

implies

> Shall [I to do $A$ at $t$]

These principles connect intentions that something be the case with intentions to act.

34. Still another principle, the correct formulation of which would involve a return to the topic of indices, is to the effect that if at $t$ one intends

Shall be [$p$ is the case ten minutes from now]

then, if one minute later one intends

Shall be [$p$ is the case nine minutes from now],

in an important sense one has not changed ones mind. This connects the 'logic' of intentions with their 'chronologic'.

35. I now come to a key topic, my views on which have led Castañeda[12] to say that according to my theory practical reasoning is not reasoning 'in the full blooded sense'. I have steadfastly denied that expressions of intention belong in the scope of either truth functional connectives or quantifiers.

36. Thus, while I regard

Shall be [$p$ and $q$]

as well formed, I do not so regard

Shall be [$p$] and shall be [$q$]

Similarly, although I regard

Shall be [not-$p$]

as well formed, I do not so regard

Not (shall be [$p$]).

37. In my early writings on practical reasoning,[13] I claimed that it is governed by only one basic principle concerning implications pertaining to intentions. I formulated it thus

'Shall [$p$]' implies 'shall [$q$]' $\longleftrightarrow$ '$p$' implies '$q$'

I still think that this was not wrongheaded, but have come to see that it must be carefully embedded in a far more complicated framework than I then realized.[14]

38. To begin with, I made too crude an assimilation of

I shall do $A$

to

Shall be [I will do $A$]

for, although contrary indications were not lacking in my actual formulations, I tended to view the constituents of all intentions as future indicatives, thus overlooking, for example, the fact that my own future actions can enter into my reasonings *sometimes* as actions to be done and *sometimes* as actions which it is hypothesized that I will actually do.[15]

39. Before I end this breast beating and begin to accentuate the positive, one more confession is essential. In 'Thought and Action' I rejected the principle that

'Shall [p]' and 'shall [q]' imply 'shall [p and q]'

I am not clear why I did so, since it was clearly required by my basic principle together with Conjunction Introduction for propositions. I have long recognized and regretted this mistake — which, however, I tacitly circumvented in my treatment of what I called the "summative stage" of deliberation.[16]

40. Getting back to fundamentals, my strategy was to picture practical reasoning as presenting the agent with alternative scenarios between which a choice could be made. I regarded these alternative scenarios as having the form

Shall be $[p_i$ and $p_j \ldots$ and $\ldots$ I will do $A_i$ at $t_j \ldots]$

with appropriate sprinklings of negation to generate a family of intendible possible futures. Logical and causal implications between states of affairs served to enrich intendible futures with their implications, and to eliminate intendible futures with inconsistent constituents.

41. Thus I thought of a choice between scenarios as having the form of a set of questions,

Shall be [scenario$_1$]?
Shall be [scenario$_2$]?
$\vdots$
Shall be [scenario$_n$]?

42. If the chosen scenario included as a conjunct the agent's doing $A_i$ at $t_j$, then by simplification one would get

Shall be [I will do $A_i$ at $t_j$]

and, hence, in my idiolect,

I shall do $A_i$ at $t_j$.

43. How do states of affairs get into a scenario? The obvious, but un-illuminating, answer is that they are thought to be relevant. This points to a concept of preference. Here one must be careful to distinguish an *expression* of preference from an autobiographical *ascription* of a preference to oneself.

The former is the expression of a choice, and can be schematized in terms of the questions,

> Shall [$X$ and not-$Y$]? Shall [not-$X$ and $Y$]?

and an outcome,

> Shall [$X$ and not-$Y$]

the sequence representing a choice of $X$ as over and against $Y$. A person's preference of $X$ over $Y$ can be viewed as a disposition to make such a choice. Preference of an object of one kind to an object of another kind can be viewed as a preference concerning appropriate states of affairs involving such objects — thus, eating an apple as contrasted with eating an orange.

44. In general, preference is relative to an assumed context, $\alpha$. Thus,

> Shall [$\alpha$ and $X$ and not-$Y$]?
> Shall [$\alpha$ and not-$X$ and $Y$]?
> Shall [$\alpha$ and $X$ and not-$Y$]

Clearly, given a different context, $\beta$, one might choose $Y$ instead of $X$.

45. A concept of indifference is also needed, but I am concerned to sketch rather than map. It is essential to note, however, that the concept of preference I have been sketching has made no appeal to such concepts as desire, aversion, satisfaction, enjoyment, and disenjoyment.

46. Notice also that choice has been described in a way which involves no reference on the agent's part to his preferences. I do not, of course, deny that references to ones preferences — or, for that matter, intentions, desires and aversions — can occur in the scenarios between which one chooses. But such references are at a higher rung on the semantic ladder than first-level practical thoughts, and one should be clear about the latter before starting to climb.

47. It is as much a mistake to think of choice as essentially involving a reference to one's preferences, as it is to take as a paradigm of practical reasoning, an argument which has as its major premise

> I intend to bring about $X$.

If one is looking for a simple paradigm, neatly regimented into syllogistic form, one would do better to choose

> I shall bring about $X$
> [Bringing about $X$ implies doing $A$ at $t$]
> So, I shall do $A$ at $t$.

48. Notice that the account I have been giving implies that what is represented in the preceding paragraph by a syllogism can be expanded — for the purpose of getting insight into its depth structure — into a choice between two scenarios,

> Shall be [$\alpha$ and I will bring about $X$ and I will do $A$ at $t$]?
> Shall be [$\alpha$ and I will not bring about $X$ and I will not do $A$ at $t$]?
> Shall be [$\alpha$ and I will bring about $X$ and I will do $A$ at $t$]

(where '$\alpha$' represents that common part of the scenarios which is not in question at the time of the choice — i.e. has in some sense already been decided), an inferential move to

> Shall be [I will do $A$ at $t$]

and, from there to

> Shall [I to do $A$ at $t$]
> i.e. I shall $A$ at $t$.

49. The syllogism, however, implies, as the expanded version does not, that the *ground* of the preference for scenario₁ lies in the bringing about of $X$, rather than in the doing of $A$.


IV

50. Let us now take a closer look at constituents of scenarios other than actions by the agent. My concern is with the distinction between those which are up to the agent and those which are not. My linguistic intuitions tell me that we so use 'up to the agent' that a state of affairs, that $p$, is up to the agent if and only if

> Agent is able to bring it about that $p$ and also able to bring about that not-$p$

i.e. it is up to the agent whether or not $p$. It might be thought that the 'not-$p$' is redundant, but it seems clear that an agent might be able to bring it about that $p$, without being able to bring it about that not-$p$. I may be able to bring it about that Jones dies at $t$ by shooting him, but not able to bring it about that Jones lives at $t$ (since another gunman may shoot him just in case I don't).

51. Since most actions involve bringing about states of affairs by consisting in doing something which brings these states of affairs about, it is important

to see that the above does not conflict with the fundamental principle that if an agent is able to do *A* he is also able to do not-*A*. For

> Jones is able to bring it about that *p*, but not able to bring it about that not-*p*

is compatible with

> Jones is able to bring it about that *p*, and able not to bring it about that *p*.

52. In view of these considerations, the basic distinction we need is between those constituents of a scenario which the agent conceives to be in his power, including certain actions on his part, and those which he conceives not to be in his power.

53. All this, however, is rather crude, and needs to be refined and articulated. Unfortunately there is only time to sketch the essentials. I shall focus my attention on those constituents of a scenario which are common to a set of competing scenarios which practical reasoning has presented for a choice.

54. Suppose that an agent has decided that a certain state of affairs obtains. As I see it, we need a principle — which I have called the So-be-it principle,[17] but which might also be called the Reality principle, if the latter phrase had not already been pre-empted, to the effect that

> '*p*' and 'shall be [α]' imply 'shall be [*p* and α]'

The phrase 'so be it' is misleading; it implies a fatalistic attitude which has nothing to do with the principle. Indeed, there is an important class of cases where the agent's reason for deciding that *p* will be the case, is that *p* is in his power and he has decided to bring it about.

55. To swallow this principle, one must bear in mind that to intend

> Shall be [*p* and α]

a person need not *desire* that *p* be the case nor even *like* the idea of *p*'s being the case. The point of the principle is simply that the state of affairs gets into the logical framework of practical thinking.

56. By virtue of So-be-it, an agent who has the intention that α be the case,

> Shall be [α]

and has decided that *p* is (or will be) the case, is, if he is rational, confronted by the alternatives,

> Shall be [*p* and α]?
> Shall be [*p* and not-α]?

We can represent constituents which the agent has decided to be the case by
'$F$' (for 'Fact'). Thus,

> Shall be [$F$ and I bring about $X$ and I will do $A$]

It is by virtue of this principle that practical reasoning presents a family of
alternative scenarios which have '$F$' as a common constituent, thus

> Shall be [$F$ and ...]?
> Shall be [$F$ and ———]?
> ⋮

57. Needless to say there are many things which an agent has decided to be
the case which don't get into the scenarios he actually considers, because
they are taken to be irrelevant. But the same is true in the case of theoretical
reasoning. The role of Conjunction Introduction is always subject to considerations of relevance, otherwise premises would proliferate to absurdity.
I shall not pause to explore relevance, however, because the topic is in good
hands.

58. The 'reality' principle throws light on a topic about which I, at least,
have been confused. Thus consider

> If it rains, I shall study.

I have been torn in different directions. In the *first* place I have been
committed to the view that, when properly regimented, expressions of
intention do not occur in the scope of truth functional connectives. This
kept me from representing the above conditional intention by

> $p \rightarrow$ shall [I will study].

59. In the *second* place, my conception of practical reasoning as
culminating in a choice between intention scenarios which contain all the
states of affairs believed to be relevant, led me to think of the scope of 'shall'
in the above conditional intention as the entire hypothetical, thus

> Shall [If it rains, I will study]

60. In the *third* place I had convinced myself that the premise from which
an intention to act is derived is best construed — by an (I hope) rational
reconstruction — as a single, if complex, premise which has the form of an
intention.

61. In the *fourth* place, I was committed to the view that logical
connectives within the scope of 'shall' connect sentences in the indicative
mood. This pointed to

> Shall [It is raining at $t \rightarrow$ I will study at $t$].

62. As I now see it, none of these considerations was wrongheaded. They were, however, embedded in an inadequate framework of principles and distinctions, the result being paradox.

63. What led me up the garden path was a too simple minded equation of the 'if, then' involved in conditional intention with material implication, a mistake which at the time was not entirely idiosyncratic. I was so hypnotized by the idea that the 'if, then' does *not* represent even a weak entailment-like relation between 'It will rain' and 'Shall [I will study]' that I leaped from that frying pan into the fire of taking it to represent material implication, with the above results.

64. But, as Austin has made us emphatically aware, there are cases in which 'if, then', represents neither material implication nor entailment. I by no means agree with all the uses to which he put this insight. It did, however, open my eyes to possibilities I had ignored. Of direct concern to us are those cases in which

> If $p$, $q$

contextually implies that there is a valid argument which, perhaps with additional premises, would justify, given $p$, the conclusion that $q$; schematically,

$$p$$
$$[r, s, t]$$
$$\vdots$$
$$\overline{\phantom{xxxx}}$$
$$\text{So, } q.$$

Taking this as a cue, I found[18] it plausible to construe

> If $p$, I shall do $A$

as a commitment to the idea that there is a valid form of practical reasoning, all of the constituents of which, save $p$, have already been decided; i.e. are such that either I have decided on factual grounds that they are the case, or I have decided to make them the case. What I am waiting on is only my decision (if I should so decide) that $p$ is (or will be) the case.

65. The point I wish to make is that if I decide that $p$ is the case, and do not change my mind in other respects, the relevant reasoning does not have the form

$$\text{If } p, \text{ I shall do } A$$
$$\underline{p \phantom{xxxxxxxxxxxxx}}$$
$$\text{So, I shall do } A$$

but rather,

| | | |
|---|---|---|
| 1. | $p$ | premise |
| 2. | Shall $[\alpha$ and $(p \rightarrow$ I will do $A)]$ | premise |
| 3. | Shall $[p$ and $\alpha$ and $(p \rightarrow$ I will do $A)]$ | 1,2, So-be-it |
| 4. | So, shall be [I will do $A$] | MP (shall)[19] |
| | I shall do $A$ | |

Notice that the conditional intention implies not only that I believe that doing $A$ is up to me, but that I have not already decided that it is un-conditionally the case that I will do it.

66. Castañeda has argued that according to my original analysis, the following sentences

I.      If I don't press button $B$, I shall press button $A$

II.     If I don't press button $A$, I shall press button $B$

express logically equivalent intentions, although it is clear, after a moment's reflection, that they don't. He is right. In my original account they both transform into

Shall [either I will press $B$ or I will press $A$]

67. On the present account, the first expression, I, treats my not pressing $B$ as something which is to be decided to be the case, my pressing button $A$, on the other hand, as something to be decided to do — the reverse holding in the case of II.

68. Accordingly, the first conditional intention points to the validity of

| | | |
|---|---|---|
| 1. | I did not press $B$ | premise |
| 2. | Shall be $[\alpha$ and (I did not press $B \rightarrow$ I will press $A)]$ | premise |
| 3. | Shall be $[\alpha$ and I did not press $B$ and (I did not press $B \rightarrow$ I will press $A)]$ | 1,2, So-be-it. |
| 4. | So, shall be [I will press $A$] | 3, MP (shall)[20] |
| | I shall press $A$ | |

The second conditional intention points to the validity of a similar argument with an interchange of buttons $A$ and $B$.

IV

69. I have argued above (and elsewhere) that there are occurrent intentions, and that in the sense in which an occurrent belief can be said to be the

conclusion of a process of reasoning from certain premises, an occurrent intention can be said to be the conclusion of a process of practical reasoning.

70. I have argued elsewhere[21] that it is proper to think of the fact that a person has certain beliefs and/or intentions which serve as *premises* in his drawing of a *conclusion,* as the *cause* of his accepting the conclusion. Given his frame of mind, they are an essential part of the explanation of how he came to accept the conclusion.

71. It follows from these considerations that *reasons* can be *causes* of actions. For practical premises can be causes of practical conclusions, and practical conclusions, in the form of volitions, cause actions.

72. However, not every constituent in a premise of practical reasoning can be said to be part of the reason why the agent acted as he did. Thus, in the text book type of case which is regimented by the form

$$\text{I shall bring about } X$$
$$[\text{Bringing about } X \text{ implies doing } A]$$
$$\text{I shall now do } A$$

it is implied that the constituent of the alternative scenarios the agent has been considering which accounts for the preference

$$\text{Shall be } [\alpha \text{ and I will bring about } X \text{ and I will do } A]$$

is the bringing about of $X$. The agent is 'favorably disposed' toward the bringing about of $X$.

73. Shall we say that the agent *wants* or *desires* to bring about $X$? He clearly *intends* to bring about $X$. He clearly *prefers* bringing about $X$ and doing $A$ to not bringing about $X$ and not doing $A$.

74. According to the account of preference sketched in Paragraphs 43ff. above, to be favorably disposed towards $X$ is to be disposed to answer the questions

$$\text{Shall be } [X]?$$
$$\text{Shall be } [\text{not-}X]?$$

by

$$\text{Shall be } [X]$$

as contrasted with answering

$$\text{Shall be } [\text{not-}X]$$

or shrugging ones shoulders.

75. What is the relation between this, so to speak, purely conceptual sense of being favorably disposed, to the richer notion of desire? An intention is *realized* if the intended state of affairs comes to obtain. But desires can not only be *realized,* they can also be *satisfied.* How is this to be understood?[22] It seems to me that desiring that $X$ be the case implies something like being disposed to enjoy the thought of $X$ being the case. This, however, does not quite hit the mark. We must take seriously the fact that philosophers have traditionally connected desire with the will.

76. To connect desire with the will is, in our framework, to place it in the domain of intentions (and such cousins as hopes and wishes). This suggests that, in first approximation, to desire that $X$ be the case is to be disposed to enjoy thinking 'it *shall* be the case that $X$,' i.e. 'I shall do what I can to make it the case that $X$'. One must bear in mind, of course, that one can enjoy thinking 'It shall be the case that $X$' without enjoying thinking 'It shall be the case that $X$ and $Y$.'

77. It is a plausible psychological principle that if one is disposed to *enjoy* thinking 'It shall be the case that $X$' then one will have a propensity (other things being equal) to *think* 'It shall be the case that $X$.'[23]

78. Thus, in some cases at least, we can explain the fact that a person acts from a certain scenario in terms of his desires and aversions. I have been careful, however, not to imply that all dispositions to choose $X$ and not-$Y$ rather than not-$X$ and $Y$ are cases in which one desires $X$ more than $Y$ or has a greater aversion to $Y$ than to $X$.

*Pittsburgh*

## NOTES

[1] I use the phrase 'occurrent believing' in my dialectic, not because I think it is a particularly happy one, but because it implies the 'assertion' (not, of course, in the illocutionary sense) as contrasted with the 'entertaining' of a propositional content. I would be happier with 'occurrent thinking that'.

[2] The very centrality of the concept of volition in the theory of action has tempted philosophers to claim that in the last analysis what agents *really* do is will. 'Volitions are the true actions.' I certainly do not wish to deny either the essential connection between volition and agency or the fact that in a broad sense of 'do' willing is a doing. The fact remains, however, that in the specific sense of 'do' which is involved in the practical question 'What shall I do?' volitions are not doings.

[3] That a Scientific Realist can take seriously the Aristotelian conception of continuing mental acts which are not changes and yet envisage their 'identification' with neurophysiological processes which are essentially changes (in which, however, certain spatio-temporal patterns are preserved) is grounded in his view of the essentially functional and contentually gappy character of mental acts as conceived in the Manifest Image.

[4] This is not, of course, to deny that there is a sense in which if Jones willed to open the window by pushing it, he willed to push the window.

[5] *Ethics and Language,* New Haven, 1944, p. 298.

[6] This is the positive side of the argument for the identity theory which Davidson rests on the 'anomalousness' of the mental. (Donald Davidson, 'Mental Events', in L. Foster and J. W. Swanson (eds.), *Experience and Theory,* Amherst, 1970.)

[7] The metaphysics and philosophy of mind adumbrated in this paragraph are developed in *Science and Metaphysics,* London 1968. The essential points are made in 'Meaning as Functional Classification', in J. G. Troyer and S. C. Wheeler III (eds.), *Intentionality, Language and Translation* (*Synthese* **27** (1974), Dordrecht, Holland, and 'Language as Thought and as Communication', *Philosophy and Phenomenological Research* **30** (1969). (Reprinted in *Essays in Philosophy and its History,* Dordrecht, Holland, 1974.)

[8] See, for example, 'Imperatives, Intentions and the Logic of "Ought", in H. N. Castañeda (ed.), *Morality and the Language of Conduct,* Detroit 1965, and 'Thought and Action' in Keith Lehrer (ed.), *Freedom and Determinism,* New York 1966. For an attempt to single out the distinctive features of practical reasoning in the context of the moral point of view, see Chapter 7 of *Science and Metaphysics,* London 1968, also 'On Knowing the Better and Doing the Worse' and ". . . this I or he or it (the thing) which thinks" in *Essays in Philosophy and its History,* Dordrecht, Holland, 1974.

[9] But see Chapter 3 of *Science and Metaphysics;* for a brief presentation of meaning and intentionality which provides the metaphysical underpinning which the present essay obviously requires, see 'Meaning as Functional Classification', in *Intentionality, Language, and Translation* (*Synthese* **27** (1974), (ed. by J. G. Troyer and S. C. Wheeler III), Dordrecht, Holland.

[10] It has the drawback, from the standpoint of metaphysics, of involving the use of a that-clause, and, hence, of explicitly introducing propositions. The reader should reflect on the reading 'it is not the case that $p$ and $q$' for 'not ($p$ and $q$)'. This suggests that what is wanted is a 'shall' operator which has '. . .' as its scope without climbing the ontological (indeed, semantic) ladder.

[11] It should be borne in mind that intentions (as contrasted with hopes, wishes, etc.) carry with them the presupposition that what is intended is (in considerably more than the purely logical sense) possible. (From this point on I let the ontological chips fall where they may.)

[12] In an unpublished manuscript.

[13] E.g. The initial version of 'Imperatives, Intentions and the Logic of "Ought" ', *Methodos* **8** (1956).

[14] The many shortcomings in my published discussions of practical reasoning have been pointed out by patient and friendly critics — in particular Hector Castañeda and Bruce Aune, from both of whom I have learned a great deal.

[15] See paragraphs 66–7 below.

[16] *Op. cit.,* pp. 131ff.

[17] 'Notes for a Revision of "Thought and Action" ' (1971), an unpublished manuscript on which I have drawn heavily for this lecture.

[18] In the MS referred to in the previous note.

[19] I write 'MP (shall)' since, by virtue of the principle relating intention-implications to propositional implications, 3 implies 4.

[20] See previous note.

[21] 'Actions and Events', *Nous* **7** (1973), reprinted in *Essays in Philosophy and its History,* Dordrecht, Holland, 1974.

[22] My initial wrestling with this problem in Section III of 'Thought and Action' was not without its insights, but got bogged down in inessentials.

[23] I would hate to have to fill out the *ceteris paribus* clause. The topics of how one comes to have preferences between conceptually entertained states of affairs, and how one comes to enjoy (or disenjoy) contemplating the realization of certain states of affairs, as well as the

role of conceptual connections in building up complex preferences and in transmitting 'hedonic tone', take one to the heart of nascent psychological theory ('The Law of Effect and the Higher Processes'). It is to be hoped that philosophers will play a constructive part in this enterprise as they have in other areas of scientific theorizing. Keeping the theory which is embedded in our practice clear of conceptual confusions (e.g. psychological hedonism) is the least they can do.

ALVIN I. GOLDMAN

# THE VOLITIONAL THEORY REVISITED

The history of philosophy is replete with changes in fashion and taste. A piece of theoretical furniture which at one time adorns almost every philosophical household is relegated, at a later time, to the attic for unsightly monstrosities. Yet the same piece, the object of ridicule and derision in one generation, can sometimes be refurbished by the next generation, and re-introduced as a modish and handsome doctrine.

The theory of volitions has undergone at least the first change in philosophical fashion. Once regarded as virtually self-evident by practically everyone, it came to be regarded as a metaphysical curiosity, fabricated by careless philosophers without due concern for the facts. In the post-war period, especially, philosophers such as Ryle and Wittgenstein called for a spring-cleaning to rid the establishment of embarrassing mental entities, and one of the first items thrown on the rubbish-heap was the doctrine of volitions. A few friends of volitions, Wilfrid Sellars notable among them, have advocated their restoration.[1] But most members of the community, I suspect, still think of them as relics, which no really "contemporary" philosopher should allow on his premises.

I believe that the doctrine of volitions has been treated not only harshly, but unfairly. Much of the attack has been hastily conceived and executed. Some of the criticism, moreover, has been aimed at inessential flourishes or decorations that are not part of the dominant style or design. Setting these flourishes aside, and concentrating on the main lines of the doctrine, I think it is not altogether unattractive. A large part of the animus against volitions may be due to the term 'volition' itself, which has an outmoded and suspicious air about it. In the view of action that I have advocated, a doctrine quite close to the volitional theory was included,[2] but I avoided the term 'volition' partly because of the "odium theologicum" it has acquired. Since I still believe that something like a volitional theory is correct, I wish to review some of the considerations for and against it, and see whether a call for restoration is still in order.

Let me begin by trying to identify what is central to the doctrine of volitions. The primary aim of the theory is to distinguish voluntary from

*M. Brand and D. Walton (eds.), Action Theory, 67–84. All Rights Reserved*
*Copyright © 1976 by D. Reidel Publishing Company, Dordrecht-Holland*

non-voluntary events. (I say "events" rather than "action" or "behavior" because a theory of the voluntary cannot presuppose that the class of "actions" has antecedently been delineated. That is the job of the theory.) To this end, the theory begins by asserting that there is a class of conscious occurrences which are, or express, propositional attitudes, and the members of this class have the following property: each has a tendency to cause an event which satisfies or fulfills its propositional content. The members of this class are called "volitions". The theory goes on to say, at least roughly, that an event $E$ is voluntary if and only if there is another event $V$ such that (1) $V$ is a volition, (2) $V$ causes $E$, and (3) $E$ satisfies the propositional content of $V$.

Notice what is omitted from this characterization of the doctrine of volitions: we have not said what kind of conscious occurrence a volition is. In particular, we have not said whether it is a mental *action*, or a species of desire, intention, or other form of practical thought. I believe that the dominant, or at least *a* dominant, view of volitions is that they are a species of desire or intention. Hobbes, for example, defined an 'act of will' (a traditional synonym for 'volition') as "the last appetite or aversion immediately adhering to the action or to the omission thereof".[3] Locke had a similar inclination to regard willing or volition as desire, preference, or choice, and although he argued in the second edition of the *Essay* that will and desire are not precisely the same, the first edition contains a definition of 'volition' or 'willing' as (a form of) preferring.[4] Numerous other classical authors also viewed volition as a species of intention or desire (or wish). Bentham and John Stuart Mill used 'volition' or 'will' as synonyms of 'intention'.[5] John Austin defined 'volition' as a kind of wish or desire, and so did T. H. Green.[6] Among recent writers, Sellars has treated volitions as a species of intention, an intention to do something here and now.[7]

Not all volitional theorists, however, have taken this sort of position. In particular, some have regarded volitions as a species of *action* or *activity*. It might be thought that this ought to be the canonical view, since, as indicated, a traditional synonym for 'volition' is 'act of will'. But the phrase 'act of will' does not necessarily connote action or activity, in the sense of purposeful or intentional action. The term 'act' often denotes events or states that are clearly not voluntary or intentional. Peter Geach, for example, uses the phrase 'mental acts', in his book by that name, to include such events as hearing and remembering, obviously not *actions* in the full-bodied sense.[8] Some philosophers, nonetheless, *have* regarded volitions as actions or activities. Indeed, both Berkeley and Prichard held that volition is the *only* action or activity we perform.[9] Now this view of volitions naturally invites criticisms. The most famous is Gilbert Ryle's criticism in *The Concept of Mind*. Ryle begins by characterizing volitions as special executive acts:

> Volitions have been postulated as special acts, or operations, 'in the mind', by means of which a mind gets its ideas translated into facts. I think of some state of affairs which I wish to come into existence in the physical world, but, as my thinking and wishing are unexecutive, they require the mediation of a further executive mental process. So I perform a volition which somehow puts my muscles into action. (p. 63)

Objections to this view are familiar and obvious. First, there is the infinite regress argument, employed by Ryle (p. 67). If a volition is a voluntary action, and if something is a voluntary action only if it is caused by a volition, then there must be an infinite sequence of volitions, each being the "object" of its predecessor. Yet there is no such sequence of mental performances. Secondly, if volitions are actions, we ought to be prepared to describe them in at least some of the ways we describe purposeful actions, for example, as easy or difficult, as activities at which one can be efficient or inefficient, as tasks one can take lessons in doing, etc. Much of Ryle's criticism of volitions is that such descriptions are never made of any such thing as willing, and that therefore there must not *be* any such actions or activities.

The easy reply to these criticisms, as other writers have noted, is simply to reject the characterization of volitions as purposeful actions or activities. There are, we have seen, other plausible candidates for the kind of thing a volition is.

Let us turn to some other familiar objections against volitions, objections which also strike me as rather weak and ill-conceived. In this category is the alleged problem of counting volitions. Ryle formulates this as follows:

> ... when a champion of the doctrine [of volitions] is himself asked ... how many acts of will he executes in, say, reciting 'Little Miss Muffet' backwards, he is apt to confess to finding difficulties in giving the answer, though these difficulties should not, according to his own theory exist. (p. 65)

Why does Ryle believe that there should be no difficulty, according to the volitional theory, in saying how many acts of will one has executed? This assumption is unwarranted. Even if there were a definite answer to the question, 'How many acts of will?', a person may not have noticed how many there were unless he was attending to the question during the relevant interval. Furthermore, and more importantly, what reason is there for requiring a volitional theory to be committed to criteria for counting volitions? There do not seem to be criteria for counting other categories of mental events, so why should such criteria be demanded for volitions?

Consider the category of thoughts. Is there a definite number of thoughts one has during a two-minute interval? Thoughts can be chopped up into long units or short units, units of almost any length one pleases. The number of thoughts will be a function of the unit selected. Since there is no canonical unit, there is no straight-forward answer to the question, 'How many thoughts did you have during this period?'

It should be emphasized that counting criteria must not be confused with criteria of identity. There may be unambiguous criteria for saying when objects or events of a certain category are identical without there being criteria for saying how many such objects or events there are. Having specified an expanse *A* of sky and an expanse *B* of sky, there is no theoretical problem in saying whether or not they are the same. It doesn't follow that there are any criteria for numbering expanses of the sky.

The next argument against volitions is that they are "indefinable", "indescribable", or "characterless". This point is elaborated by Melden, both in his article 'Willing' and in his book *Free Action*.[10] Similar points are made by Taylor.[11]

Willing is *sui generis*, indefinable, a bit of mental self-exertion in which we engage, an activity not capable of further description but different from the wonderings, thinkings, supposings, expectings, picturings, and so forth, that comprise our mental episodes. Yet the appeal to indefinables is a desperate defence that purchases immunity from further attack only at the expense of unintelligibility.[12]

Now it is of course admitted that volitions can be characterized relationally, at least as events which cause bodily movements. The objection, presumably, is that there are no intrinsic, non-relational descriptions of volitions. Of course, if the psycho-physical identity theory is correct, that conclusion too is unwarranted. Whether or not we can *give* intrinsic descriptions of volitions, they will *have* neurophysiological descriptions, that is, descriptions "intrinsic" to them. But neurophysiological descriptions, it will be replied, are not descriptions we *know* to be true to them, and surely there must be some non-relational descriptions we know to be true of them. They must have some features we can recognize. After all, there is a difference between a volition for one movement and a volition for a different movement, and this must be a difference we can recognize or discern, hence a difference we can describe. Here I would object, however. Is is not quite common for us to be able to recognize a given mental state, and distinguish it from others, without being able tb *say* anything about their distinguishing characteristics? At the risk of belaboring the obvious, let me quote a lovely passage from William James.

Suppose we try to recall a forgotten name. The state of our consciousness is peculiar. There is a gap therein; but no mere gap. It is a gap that is intensely active. A sort of wraith of the name is in it, beckoning us in a given direction, making us at moments tingle with the sense of our closeness, and then letting us sink back without the longed-for term. If wrong names are proposed to us, this singularly definite gap acts immediately so as to negate them. They do not fit into its mold. And the gap of one word does not feel like the gap of another, all empty of content as both might seem necessarily to be when described as gaps. When I vainly try to recall the name of Spalding, my consciousness is far removed from what it is when I vainly try to recall the name of Bowles. Here some ingenious persons will say: 'How *can* the two consciousnesses be different when the terms which might make them different are not there? All that is there, so long as the effort to recall is vain, is the bare effort itself. How should that differ in the two cases? You are making it seem to differ by prematurely filling it out with the different names, although these, by hypothesis, have not yet come. Stick to the two efforts as they are, without naming them after facts not yet existent, and you'll be quite unable to designate any point in which they differ.' Designate, truly enough. We can only designate the difference by borrowing the names of objects not yet in the mind. Which is to say that our psychological vocabulary is wholly inadequate to name the differences that exist, even such strong differences as these. But namelessness is compatible with existence. There are innumerable consciousnesses of emptiness, no one of which taken in itself has a name, but all different from each other. The ordinary way is to assume that they are all emptinesses of consciousness, and so the same state. But the feeling of an absence is *toto caelo* other than the absence of a feeling. It is an intense feeling. The rhythm of a lost word may be there without a sound to clothe it; or the evanescent sense of something which is the initial vowel or consonant may mock us fitfully, without growing more distinct. Every one must know the tantalizing effect of the blank rhythm of some forgotten verse, restlessly dancing in one's mind, striving to be filled out with words.[13]

The point of the passage is that two mental states may be distinct from one another, and we may recognize this distinction, although we cannot "define" either state, or *say* what features distinguish them. This is true, I think, of many if not all mental states, not volitions alone.

I turn next to a more substantial difficulty for the volitional theory. This is the simple objection that there aren't enough of these conscious events to cover all the events or movements we classify as voluntary. A standard example in this connection pertains to complex skilled movements, such as playing a scale on the piano, or performing a complicated series of ballet steps. A skilled ballerina can execute the complicated series without attending to each separate component. There is, if you like, a volition that initiates the entire series. But it does not seem as if there is a volition for each separate element of the series.

Discussing the presentation of this point by Taylor, Wilfrid Sellars writes:

To this, the obvious answer is that learning to play a piece of music, and, in general, learning to play the piano, involves the building of behavioral elements into patterns which can be intended as wholes. It is only the beginner who has to think out each step as he goes along. The point is familiar to anyone who has learned to ride a bicycle or to swim.[14]

This reply is all right as far as it goes, but it is not clear that it fully resolves the problem; not, at any rate, if one accepts the rough formulation of the volitional theory I outlined earlier. According to that formulation, event *E* is voluntary if it is not only *caused* by a volition, but caused by one whose propositional content it satisfies. The latter requirement seems clearly necessary. Otherwise, efferent nerve impulses and muscle movements would count as voluntary, since they are all *caused* by volitions; also, extremely remote effects of volitions, e.g., bodily events that occur a week later, but are indirectly caused by the volition, would count as voluntary. Presumably none of these events should be classified as voluntary. Now once we note the requirement that an event must satisfy the content of the volition which causes it, it is not clear whether a given component of the ballerina's series of movements will count as voluntary according to the formula. But surely it should count as voluntary. The trouble is that no single element or component of the series satisfies the content of the initial, "holistic" volition; at least no component satisfies the *entire* content of that volition. It might be argued that we could allow an event to be voluntary if it satisfies only *part* of the content of the volition that causes it. Unfortunately, it isn't clear that a "holistic" volition has "parts" in the requisite sense. Of course, if we think of the volition as a conjunction, it will have some conjunct which a component movement satisfies. The very notion of a "holistic" volition, however, seems to imply that it is not "conjunctive" in the requisite sense. So the problem remains.

One solution to the problem is essentially a solution I proposed in my book, *A Theory of Human Action*.[15] It consists in revising our formulation of the volitional theory as follows. An event *E* is voluntary if and only if it either satisfies the original formula or is a *temporal part* of an event which satisfies the original formula. The ballerina's series of movements is voluntary according to the original formula; and each component of that series is a temporal part of it. Hence, according to the newly revised formula, each component qualifies as voluntary.

A second solution, at least a partial solution, to the problem is to deny the assumption we have been making, viz., that there is but one volition controlling the entire series. Admittedly, this assumption meshes with the view of some writers in the psychological literature, who regard the acquisition of a motor skill as the formation of a motor program, a pattern that is fired off by a single initiation of the program, in other words, that is fired off "open-loop", without the benefit of feedback. Other authors on the topic of motor performance, however, suggest that feedback still plays an important role, feedback that is used to monitor one's progress toward a goal and facilitate adjustments in one's execution.[16] The latter view seems to me more compelling. Although a single initiating volition may dominate the sphere of attention, there is continual control involving information and volition that guides a movement as it unfolds, though at a reduced level of attention. (Studies suggest that for visual feedback the interval of corrections of hand movements aimed at a target is between 190–260 milliseconds. For proprioceptive feedback corrections may be made at intervals as short as 112–129 milliseconds.[17]) Admittedly, this at best reduces the size of the unit subject to control, and the same principle embodied in our first solution may have to be invoked to handle the presumed voluntariness of smaller units. It is worth noting, however, that this principle may not be needed so early in the game.[18]

There is another kind of case that also suggests that there are too few volitions around to account for all voluntary events. It is a familiar fact that once a skill is acquired, a person does not concentrate on the bodily movements that execute the skill, but rather on more-or-less remote effects of these movements. A skilled typist concentrates on words to be typed, not finger movements. A skilled batter concentrates on where the bat is to go, not on his hands or feet. The agent's volition seems to be directed at *distal* rather than *proximal* events. When such a distal event occurs, we surely want to say that it is voluntary; at least the event of *his bringing it about* is voluntary. But don't we also wish to say that the proximal events, the movement of the fingers, hands, or feet, are voluntary? But has there been a volition whose propositional content these bodily events satisfy? The bodily events have been caused by a volition, viz., a volition to bring about the distal events, but the propositional content of that volition is not satisfied by these bodily events. Thus, by our original criterion of voluntariness, the bodily movements are not voluntary. Nor does our new addition to the formula help us, for the bodily events are not temporal parts of events which qualify as voluntary under the original formula.

To remedy the situation, one might try (as a first solution) to introduce another new principle. One might say that an event $E$ is voluntary if it either satisfies the earlier criteria or is an intermediate member of a causal chain the first member of which is a volition and the last member of which satisfies the propositional content of that volition. This will certainly allow bodily movements to qualify as voluntary; for even if they do not themselves satisfy the content of the volition, they are members of a suitable causal chain. Unfortunately, this principle is too liberal. It allows muscle movements and efferent neural events to qualify as voluntary; but presumably *these* events are not to be deemed voluntary.

This difficulty is not insuperable, however. An important distinction can be drawn between certain events in the causal chain — e.g., the finger movements — and other events in the chain — e.g., the efferent neural events. The former events are what I call *basic act-type* events, that is, instances of event-types which *can* be exemplified at will without the mediation of other volitions or beliefs.[19] The latter events, by contrast, are not instances of basic act-types. Willing these efferent events to occur would not, of itself, cause them to occur. With this distinction in mind, we could revise our principle by saying that, of the events in the actual causal chain, those (and only those) that are instances of basic act-types are voluntary (even though, on *this* occasion, they were not caused by a volition whose content they satisfy).

It might be objected, at this juncture, that although the newly revised principle avoids the difficulties at hand, it avoids them only at the cost of abandoning the spirit of the volitional doctrine. I am not sure whether or not this objection is correct. But in any case, I am not fully persuaded that we have to resort to the measures suggested above. Is it so clear in the examples discussed that there are no volitions whose propositional content is satisfied by movements of the limbs or digits? In the typing case, for example, is it perfectly clear that there are no volitions for fingers to move, as well as for a certain word to be typed? What is undeniable is that the *focus* of the agent's attention is on the word; this is what he concentrates on. But is his thought entirely exhausted by this content? Isn't he at least *dimly* thinking of the finger movements as well?

To lend support to this suggestion, consider another example. Suppose you are aiming to throw a baseball to a certain spot, say, home plate. You are concentrating not on your arm movement, but on the spot to which the ball is to be thrown. Are you not dimly thinking of your arm movement as well? Suppose you are perfectly ambidextrous, so that you *could* throw the ball with either arm. Would there not be a difference between the thought of throwing to home plate with your right arm, and the thought of throwing with your left? Even if the *focus* of your attention in both cases is on home plate, or the catcher's mitt, your intention or volition would be colored by the thought of throwing the ball with one kind of movement — e.g., a right-handed movement — or by the thought of throwing with another kind of movement — a left-handed movement. To draw an analogy between this practical thought and perceptual thought, we might say that the thought of home plate or the catcher's mitt is the *figure* of your thinking, the part that is "salient" or "prominent"; but the thought of the arm movement — indeed, the movement of the entire body — is a sort of *ground* against which home plate, or the thought of home plate, stands out. The thought of the arm-movement, or bodily movement, is peripheral or marginal, but it is not entirely absent.

The suggestion that there are non-focal processes is not foreign to cognitive psychology. In perception one frequently attends to certain signals rather than other, simultaneous signals. At a crowded, noisy party you may select one of several conversations within earshot to listen to: you "tune in" one and "tune out" the others. This does not mean that you don't *hear* the unattended conversations. In general, experiments show, one does extract some information from non-attended input. Subjects attending to material presented to one ear (e.g., through an earphone) still detect certain features of material presented through the other ear. At a minimum, they can tell whether or not a voice occurs in the non-attended material, and whether it changes from a man's to a woman's. Thus, non-attended material is perceived and analyzed, only not as vividly or fully as attended material. The "tuned out" signals are not really eliminated; they are merely attenuated.[20] Most of the time one hardly notices the piped-in music in a supermarket. But one does hear it, I think; it "colors" one's consciousness. Similarly, feelings of tension may "color" one's consciousness, though one does not explicitly attend to them or concentrate on them. It is characteristic of non-attended items that they tend not be registered in long-term memory. But that is not to say that they are not present to consciousness, and even short-term memory.[21]

Like the perceptual domain, I think, the domain of practical thought also contains peripheral or marginal elements. The "volitional field" may be occupied by non-focal as well as focal elements. When one learns a skill, one habituates to certain components of the activity, and no longer attends to these components in projecting the activity in question. Nonetheless, I suggest, they may remain as marginal ingredients in the phenomenal field. Similarly, when one has a mastery of typing or throwing a baseball, the precipitating volition may have the distal, or higher-level, factors as the focal point, but it will also include the proximal, or lower-level, factors (bodily movements) as peripheral elements. Thus, the "propositional content" of the volition may (partly) be satisfied by the bodily movements. (Talk of "*propositional* content" is not entirely felicitous; the ideas or thoughts in question are more spatial or sensory than verbal. This should not obscure the point being made, however.)

Until now I have been intentionally somewhat vague on the question of what kind of mental event a volition is (assuming that there are volitions). I have sided with the common suggestion that volitions are desires or intentions (I mean "occurrent" or "activated" desires), but I have been no more explicit than that.[22] However, more should be said, and I think can be said, on the subject.

Let me introduce the issue by citing the following facts. I am able to raise my left eyebrow (by itself) at will; but I am unable to raise my right eyebrow (by itself) at will. What is the difference between the two? Surely I can *desire* the rising (or raising) of the right eyebrow as much as I desire the rising (or raising) of the left. So why does a desire to raise the left eyebrow result in its rising, whereas a desire to raise the right eyebrow does not result in its rising?

Perhaps the only answer is that my desiring to raise my left eyebrow has somehow come to have a "neural hook-up" with that eyebrow's rising; whereas no such neural hook-up has been established in the case of the right eyebrow. That *might* indeed be all that can be said about the matter. But I think there is a more detailed story to be told.

The more detailed story is the *ideo-motor* theory, advanced in substantial detail by William James in 1890 and recently resurrected in the psychological literature.[23] Let us trace James' exposition of the theory. James begins by contending that a person can never perform an act voluntarily for the first time.

When a particular movement, having once occurred in a random, reflex, or involuntary way, has left an image of itself in the memory, then the movement can be desired again, proposed as an end, and deliberately willed. But it is impossible to see how it could be willed before.[24]

James goes on to say that the involuntary or random performance of movements leaves a supply of ideas in the memory, i.e., kinaesthetic sensations produced by the movements — in modern terminology, "feedback".

We may consequently set it down as certain that, whether or not there be anything else in the mind at the moment when we consciously will a certain act, a mental conception made up of memory-images of these sensations, defining which special act it is, must be there.[25]

In other passages James speaks of "images of peripheral sensations" and "an anticipatory image of sensorial consequences of a movement". The notion of an "image" of a response fell into great disfavor among psychologists during the early part of this century, especially under the pressure of behaviorism. Several recent psychologists, however, have returned to the Jamesian theory. The notion of a *"response image"* — the representation of sensory feedback from a movement or response — is employed by Mowrer, Anokhin, Adams, and Greenwald.[26] These psychologists have not simply re-affirmed James' theory, but have tried (especially Greenwald) to incorporate it into a learning-theoretical framework (which James himself attempted). The strength of agreement with James is indicated by the following passages from four authors.

... in his *Principles of Psychology*, published in 1890, in the chapter on 'Will', William James ... explicitly anticipated present-day developments ... perhaps the chapter's most remarkable feature is the extent to which the author makes sensory feedback from action essential to the continuation, and even initiation, thereof.[27]

James [clearly] saw the mechanism of voluntary movements, the mechanism at which he had arrived on the basis of astute introspection. It is most encouraging to know that we have come to exactly the same concept by quite different considerations — namely, through the physiological analysis of these movements.[28]

... in and through all this system of Jamesian suggestions [about the "will"] is ... the notion of ideo-motor action in which the central idea releases, triggers, gives life to, the waiting muscular system. How many times we hear today that our theories of learning do not tell us precisely how central functions, whether conceived in cerebral or in ideational terms, actually precipitate motor action! Yes, one reason is that we have forgotten James.[29]

Eighty years later, the basis for describing the ideo-motor linkage is hardly more satisfactory than James' introspective observation.[30]

Let us now return to the eyebrow raising case. My analysis of the situation is this. There is a sense in which I can desire the raising of the right eyebrow "on a par" with desiring the raising of the left eyebrow, namely, I can desire each event under a *visual* modality. Roughly speaking, I can "picture" my right eyebrow's rising and desire *that* to happen, or picture my left eyebrow's rising and desire *that* to happen. In neither case, however, is such a desire sufficient to produce the result. In order that my left eyebrow be raised, it is necessary that I desire its rising *under the guise of the response image*, which presumably includes, in large part, a relevant set of kinaesthetic or proprioceptive sensations. Now I *do* have such a response image, stored in memory, of the left eyebrow (alone) rising. But I do not have a corresponding image of the right eyebrow (alone) rising. In other words, I cannot imagine, at least not sufficiently distinctly, the muscular sensations attendant to raising the right eyebrow (by itself), and hence no such image functions as the object or content of a desire of mine. Thus, although there is a sense in which I can desire the right eyebrow's rising "on a par" with the left, I do not really have a relevant right-eyebrow desire to correspond with the relevant left-eyebrow desire.

What I wish now to propose is that a volition — or at least a *primary* volition — is not just any old desire or intention, even a desire or intention for a basic act-type. A primary volition is only a desire or intention whose "vehicle", or intentional object, is a *response image*. Only when I will *that* kind of thing to happen does the appropriate sequence of efferent impulses get started. (Not all volitions are primary volitions, however. A desire for the left eyebrow to rise, under a *visual* guise or description, might trigger a desire for the left eyebrow to rise, under the guise of the response image. The former desire would also be a volition, but a secondary one.)

Nothing I have said, of course, explains *why* a desire whose "vehicle" is a response image, rather than other kinds of desire, should trigger an appropriate set of efferent impulses. Central to Greenwald's defense of the ideo-motor theory, however, is to show why this is so; to show how, in terms of classical conditioning, a link can be established between an idea of feedback and efferent activity that results in a response productive of such feedback. The details of this defense are not a proper concern of this paper, however.

We are not yet finished with the ideo-motor theory, though. I have presented part of James' theory, but another, indeed, perhaps the most important, part has thus far been omitted. James' theory seems to be that it is not merely a *desire* embodying a response image that suffices to produce action, but that the mere *thought* or *occurrence* of a response image tends to trigger corresponding action. In other words, a response image tends automatically to evoke corresponding action, *whether or not it is "willed"*. James expresses this as follows:

> We may then lay it down for certain that every representation of a movement awakens in some degree the actual movement which is its object; and awakens it in a maximum degree whenever it is not kept from doing so by an antagonistic representation present simultaneously to the mind. ... We do not have a sensation or a thought and then have to *add* something dynamic to it to get a movement. ... Try to feel as if you were crooking your finger, whilst keeping it straight. In a minute, it will fairly tingle with the imaginary change of position; yet it will not sensibly move, because *its not really moving* is also a part of what you have in mind. Drop *this* idea, think of the movement purely and simply, with all breaks (sic) off; and presto! it takes place with no effort at all.[31]

As James notes, the reason why we feel disinclined to accept his suggestion is that we have so many ideas which *do not* result in action. His reply is that in every such case it is because other ideas rob them of their impulsive power. Even here, he goes on, when a movement is inhibited from *completely* taking place, it will *incipiently* take place. He quotes Lotze with the following anecdotal evidence (though he also cites clinical observations from various investigators):

> The spectator accompanies the throwing of a billiard-ball, or the thrust of the swordsman, with slight movements of his arm; the untaught narrator tells his story with many gesticulations; the reader while absorbed in the perusal of a battle-scene feels a slight tension run through his muscular system, keeping time as it were with the actions he is reading of.[32]

It is easy to cite other anecdotal evidence. Sitting in the front passenger seat of a car tends to be tiring, probably because traffic stimuli elicit incipient movements that are continually being inhibited. This is especially striking when one finds one's foot reaching for the brake in a dangerous situation.

These suggestions go along with current theories of perception that stress motor components. In these theories, implicit movements are assumed to be evoked by stimulus objects as part of the perceptual process. Motor theories of *speech* perception are particularly common. The hypothesis is that an auditory percept is formed with the aid of incipient movements of the articulatory muscles. Since this is a paper for philosophers, it is worth noting that a motor theory of speech perception was formulated by Henri Bergson:

I listen to two people speaking in a language which is unknown to me. Do I therefore hear them talk? The vibrations which reach my ears are the same as those which strike theirs. Yet I perceive only a confused noise, in which all sounds are alike. I distinguish nothing and could repeat nothing. In this same sonorous mass, however, the two interlocutors distinguish consonants, vowels, and syllables which are not at all alike, in short, separate words. Between them and me where is the difference? ... The difficulty would be insuperable if we really had only auditory impressions on the one hand, and auditory memories on the other. Not so, however, if auditory impressions organize nascent movements, capable of scanning the phrase which is heard and emphasizing its main articulations. These automatic movements of internal accomplishment, at first undecided or uncoordinated, might become more precise by repetition; they would end by sketching a simplified figure in which the listener would find, in their main lines and principal directions, the very movements of the speaker. Thus would unfold in consciousness, under the form of nascent muscular sensations, the motor diagram as it were, of the speech we hear.[33]

This theory obviously fits the ideo-motor theory rather well. For it may be assumed that auditory input links up with the mechanisms involved in the production of speech sounds. Thus, when there is an input from the speech of others, which is similar to one's own speech input, the motor images of speech production are activated, which, by the ideo-motor mechanism, results in at least nascent or incipient speech production. The following anecdotes, recently called to my attention, confirm this general picture. A singer, who gave up singing, found that merely listening to music was a strain on her throat; she was inaudibly mimicking what she heard. Doctors of patients recovering from throat operations instruct them not to read during the post-surgical period; just reading apparently elicits use of the throat musculature.

What I now wish to point out is that the development of the ideo-motor theory might seem to present difficulties for the volitional theory I have been advocating. If the mere thought or occurrence of a response image tends to trigger the corresponding behavior, then it appears that a volition — i.e., a willing of such a response image, or a willing whose "vehicle" is a response image — is not really necessary for voluntary behavior. But in fact there is no difficulty here at all. *When the behavior is initiated by the mere occurrence or thought of a response image, as opposed to a desire of which such an image is the vehicle (or content), then that behavior is not voluntary.* Consider the automobile passenger case. If the sight of the traffic elicits an actual foot movement, before it can be inhibited, we would *not* say that it was a *voluntary* movement. Similarly, we would not say that the incipient movements of the articulatory muscles are voluntary movements, when they are merely caused by auditory stimuli which evoke response images.

If the ideo-motor theory is correct, however, the matter of voluntariness is fairly subtle. Consider the driver of an automobile, for example. He notices danger, which elicits a foot movement response image, which in turn initiates impulses that would lead, unless inhibited, to movement of the foot. But these impulses are *monitored* by the volitional system; the impulses, in other words, are either *inhibited* by a volition or are *permitted* to continue along their natural path. When they are *permitted* to continue, the resultant movement is voluntary. This is to be contrasted with the case of the passenger whose foot moves *before* the volitional system has time to "approve" it. The difference here is admittedly subtle, for a volitional "permission to proceed" is not very prominent or salient in consciousness. Nonetheless, one can identify the kinds of processes I am describing introspectively. One has certainly had the experience of *catching* one's foot about to feel for the brake, but then inhibiting such movement, or the experience of not having caught it in time, that is, of one's monitoring activity having "arrived too late".

Since I have emphasized that volitional processes can be more or less in the forefront of consciousness, one may well ask under what conditions it comes to the forefront. A partial answer, I think, is that *conflict* among desires brings the matter into focal attention. When there are conflicting desires, indecision sets in, and indecision intrudes into a position of prominence in consciousness. The most vivid evocation of this fact is, once again, to be found in James, in his famous passage about getting out of bed.

We know what it is like to get out of bed on a freezing morning in a room without a fire, and how the very vital principle within us protests against the ordeal. Probably most persons have lain on certain mornings for an hour at a time unable to brace themselves to the resolve. We think how late we shall be, how the duties of the day will suffer; we say, "I *must* get up, this is ignominious," etc.; but still the warm couch feels too delicious, the cold outside too cruel, and resolution faints away and postpones itself again and again just as it seemed on the verge of bursting the resistance and passing over into the decisive act. Now how do we *ever* get up under such circumstances? If I may generalize from my own experience, we more often than not get up without any struggle or decision at all. We suddenly find that we *have* got up. A fortunate lapse of consciousness occurs; we forget both the warmth and the cold; we fall into some revery connected with the day's life, in the course of which the idea flashes across us, "Hollo! I must lie here no longer" — which at that lucky instant awakens no contradictory or paralyzing suggestions, and consequently produces immediately its appropriate motor effects. It was our acute consciousness of both the warmth and the cold during the period of struggle, which paralyzed our activity then and kept our idea of rising in the condition of *wish* and not of *will*. The moment these inhibitory ideas ceased, the original idea exerted its effects.[34]

When James says that he suddenly finds that he *has* got up, he does not (or should not) mean that his getting up is entirely automatic. On the contrary, as the passage goes on to indicate, his rising is the result of a desire to rise. But this does not attract much attention, because it is not *counteracted* by inhibitory tendencies. The earlier thoughts of rising, or not rising, were the focal points of consciousness, because they involved conflict or inhibition. When such conflict disappears, for one reason or another, a volition plays only a marginal role in consciousness. Nonetheless, I would contend, it *is* present in consciousness. What people ordinarily call an "act of will" is an event that terminates a relatively long period of conflict or indecision. It is therefore an event in the forefront of awareness. If we restrict the term 'volition' to such cases, it is obvious that no volitional theory can be correct, i.e., no theory claiming that *all* voluntary behavior results from such occurrences. But if we construe 'volition' to include desires or intentions — or, indeed, "permissions" or "approvals" — which may be only peripheral elements of consciousness, then there is a good bit more in favor of a volitional theory.

A further virtue of the picture I have been drawing is that it may enable us to explain why behavior that is not fully voluntary, like the automobile passenger's foot movements, still *feels* more-or-less voluntary, at least by contrast with events such as salivation or knee-jerks. One suggestion would be that the feeling of voluntariness is associated with the correspondence between the response image, i.e., the idea of feedback sensations that initiates a movement, and the occurrence of these very sensations that result from the movement.[35] This correspondence will obtain in fully voluntary cases, where the response image is the "vehicle" of a desire or volition, but also in cases where the response image has not been the "vehicle" of a desire or volition, like the passenger's foot movement case. There will be no such correspondence in salivation or knee-jerk cases, however, because there are presumably no response images involved in such cases.

Another possible explanation of the feeling of voluntariness would appeal to processes discussed in the literature which I have not yet mentioned. There are empirical reasons to believe that feedback from motor activity is not confined to exteroception and proprioception (i.e., feedback from muscles, joints, tendons, labyrinthine sensations, etc.). These are forms of *afferent* feedback. There is also evidence, however, of *efferent* feedback: signals returned to the cerebral cortex from the outgoing efferent impulses. If all goes well, efferent feedback will in some sense "match" the response image that initiates the efferent impulses. It is therefore sometimes called "efferent copy".[36] Such a concept seems required to explain Lashley's finding of reportably different perceptions of active movement of a patient's deafferented lower leg, and Taub and Berman's report of new response acquisition by a deafferented monkey.[37] A second hypothesis to explain the feeling of voluntariness, then, is that this feeling is associated with the receipt of "efferent copy". Such a feeling would be present in standard volitional cases and also in automobile passenger-type cases, but presumably not in cases of purely autonomic or reflex activity. Indeed, even if salivation or other autonomic behavior were (indirectly) caused by a desire (a type of case that has been discussed by some writers on action theory[38]), this would presumably not be accompanied by efferent copy that matches a response image; for although there is a desire, it does not embody a response image, at least not one with the appropriate causal properties. This would account for why we do not feel such events to be voluntary, even if they are (indirectly) caused by desires.

The story I have been sketching goes well beyond the rough formulation of a volitional theory given at the outset. I am not sure whether, or how, the elements of this story can be incorporated into an *analysis*, in the traditional sense, of the concept of voluntary action. In *A Theory of Human Action* I suggested that some reference to a "characteristic way" in which desires (and beliefs) cause behavior should be part of the analysis of intentional action.[39] I assumed that this "characteristic" causal process is linked with the feeling of voluntariness, as opposed to pure reflex or autonomic activity. I am no longer sanguine about including any such phrase in the analysis of the concept of voluntary (or intentional) action. But the task of explaining why we have a feeling of voluntariness is surely part of a general theory of action. Our remarks about the ideo-motor theory and the concept of efferent copy may be useful in this broader context. In any case, I hope that the ideas I have been sketching, if they are on the right empirical track, would help remodel the doctrine of volitions into a form that has at least some measure of plausibility.[40]

*The University of Michigan*

## NOTES

[1] Sellars, 'Thought and Action', in Keith Lehrer (ed.), *Freedom and Determinism*, Random House, New York, 1966. Also see Hugh McCann, 'Volition and Basic Action', *Philosophical Review*, **83** (1974), 451–473, and Lawrence H. Davis, 'Individuation of Actions', *Journal of Philosophy*, **67** (1970), 520–530.
[2] *A Theory of Human Action*, Prentice-Hall, Englewood Cliffs, N.J., 1970. See especially Chapter 4.
[3] *Leviathan* (1651), Chapter 6.

[4] *An Essay Concerning Human Understanding* (ed. by Alexander Campbell Fraser), Dover Publications, New York, 1959. See Volume One, pp. 313–315 and p. 331, including the editor's notes.

[5] Cf. Jeremy Bentham, *The Principles of Morals and Legislation* (1823), Chapter 8, section 2, and John Stuart Mill, *A System of Logic*, 8th edition, Longmans, Green and Co., Ltd., London, 1961, p. 35.

[6] In *Lectures on Jurisprudence*, 5th edition, John Murray, London, 1911, Austin writes: "These antecedent wishes and these consequent movements, are human *volitions* and *acts* (strictly and properly so called). ... Our desires of these bodily movements which immediately follow our desires of them, are therefore the only objects which can be styled *volitions*; or (if you like the expression better) which can be styled acts of the will" (pp. 412, 414). Green's discussion is in *Prolegomena to Ethics*, Clarendon Press, Oxford, 1883, sections 140–142.

[7] 'Thought and Action,' *op. cit.*

[8] *Mental Acts*, Routledge and Kegan Paul, London, 1957, pp. 1, 2.

[9] Berkeley, *Three Dialogues between Hylas and Philonous* (1713), Second Dialogue, and H. A. Prichard, 'Acting, Willing, Desiring', *Moral Obligation*, Clarendon Press, Oxford, 1949.

[10] A. I. Melden, 'Willing', *Philosophical Review*, **69** (1960), 475–84, reprinted in A. R. White (ed.), *The Philosophy of Action*, University Press, Oxford, 1968; Oxford University Press, London, 1968; *Free Action*, Routledge and Kegan Paul, London, 1961.

[11] Richard Taylor, *Action and Purpose*, Prentice-Hall, Englewood Cliffs, 1966; see pp. 68–69.

[12] Melden, 'Willing,' in White (ed.), *op. cit.*, pp. 72–73.

[13] *The Principles of Psychology*, Henry Holt, New York, 1890; Dover Publications, New York, 1950, Volume One, pp. 251–252.

[14] 'Metaphysics and the Concept of a Person', in Karel Lambert (ed.), *The Logical Way of Doing Things*, Yale University Press, New Haven, 1969, p. 244.

[15] The relevant principle concerning temporal parts occurs in the recursive definition of act-tokens, on page 45. Its pertinence to the present problem is discussed on pages 88–89.

[16] See Richard W. Pew, 'Human Perceptual-Motor Performance', in B. Kantowitz (ed.), *Human Information Processing: Tutorials in Performance and Cognition*, Lawrence Erlbaum Associates, Hillsdale, N.J., 1974.

[17] See Pew, *op. cit.*, who cites the work of several investigators.

[18] It may not be obvious that our revised principle is correct, since even the shortest temporal parts of voluntary events will be voluntary, according to the principle. It is important here to distinguish between an event or movement being voluntary and its being intentional. It would be a mistake, I think, to regard the briefest sub-parts of an intentional movement as themselves intentional movements. But it is correct, I think, to regard them as voluntary. Voluntariness and intentionality have considerable overlap, but they are not equivalent.

[19] For a precise definition of 'basic act-type', see *A Theory of Human Action*, Chapter Three, section 4.

[20] See Peter H. Lindsay and Donald A. Norman, *Human Information Processing*, Academic Press, New York, 1972, pp. 355–370.

[21] Many cognitive psychologists distinguish between three different types of memory, or memory storage systems: (1) sensory information storage, (2) short-term memory, and (3) long-term memory. (See Lindsay and Norman, *op. cit.*, pp. 287–290 and 329–355.) I am saying that non-attended material is present in (1) — which is tantamount to saying that it is perceived — and frequently retained in (2), but typically does not get retained in (3).

[22] As between desires and intentions, which is the better candidate for identification with volitions? One consideration favors desires rather than intentions (though these must be 'on-the-whole' desires). To say that $S$ intends to do $A$ implies that $S$ is fully confident that he will do $A$. But such confidence is not necessary, I think, for volition. If one's finger has recently

been paralyzed, and one is unsure whether the paralysis has worn off (as the doctor predicted it might), one might 'try' to move it without feeling confident that one will succeed. This trying involves a volition, but not an intention, at least not if intention necessarily involves the indicated sort of confidence or firmness of belief.

[23] The most explicit and sustained defense of the ideo-motor theory in the recent literature is Anthony G. Greenwald, 'Sensory Feedback Mechanisms in Performance Control: With Special Reference to the Ideo-Motor Mechanism', *Psychological Review* **77** (1970), 73–101. This is the main source on which I rely.

[24] *The Principles of Psychology*, Vol. 2, p. 487.

[25] *Ibid.*, p. 492.

[26] See Greenwald, *op. cit.*, for the other citations.

[27] O. W. Mowrer, *Learning Theory and Symbolic Processes*, Wiley, New York, 1960, p. 284. Quoted by Greenwald, *op. cit.*

[28] J. Konorski, *Integrative Activity of the Brain*, University of Chicago Press, Chicago, p. 194. Quoted by Greenwald, *op. cit.*

[29] G. Murphy, 'William James on the Will', Presidential address presented to Division 26, American Psychological Association (1968). Quoted by Greenwald, *op. cit.*

[30] Greenwald, *op. cit.*, p. 88.

[31] *Op. cit.*, pp. 526–527.

[32] *Ibid.*, p. 525.

[33] *Matter and Memory* (transl. by N. M. Paul and W. S. Palmer), MacMillan, New York, pp. 134, 136. Quoted by Ulric Neisser, *Cognitive Psychology*, Appleton-Century-Crofts, New York, 1967, pp. 190–191.

[34] *Op. cit.*, pp. 524–525.

[35] Cf. Greenwald's remark: "It is tempting to suggest, although it would be difficult to know how to document the assertion, that the subjective experience of volition corresponds to the operation of an ideo-motor mechanism in which an image of response feedback precedes overt performance of an action." *Op. cit.*, p. 98.

[36] See Pew, *op. cit.*, who cites von Holst and Anokhin.

[37] K. S. Lashley, "The Accuracy of Movement in the Absence of Excitation from the Moving Organ', *Americal Journal of Physiology* **43** (1917), 169–194, and E. Taub and A. J. Berman, 'Movement and Learning in the Absence of Sensory Feedback', in S. J. Freedman (ed.), *The Neuropsychology of Spatially Oriented Behavior*, Dorsey Press, Homewood, Ill., 1968.

[38] For example, Richard Taylor in *Action and Purpose*, pp. 248–250.

[39] See Chapter Three, section 3, esp. p. 62.

[40] I am grateful to Holly S. Goldman for comments on an initial version of this paper.

PART 4

# THE LOGIC OF ACTION

ROBERT W. BINKLEY

# THE LOGIC OF ACTION

## I

The title of this session, 'The Logic of Action', has an intriguing ambiguity which I propose to exploit. In one sense, it invites me to offer views on the formal properties of the concept of action; in the other it suggests that I discuss whatever it is about action that, sometimes, makes it logical. In my own thinking, I have found these two themes to be closely related. I have tended to begin with the question, what makes actions logical? and I have answered by saying that an action is logical if it is reasoned, and then I have tried to say what a reasoned action is. In doing so, I have found it necessary to make certain assumptions about what action is — the logic of action in the other sense — and so have felt under a growing obligation to work out an account of the concept of action compatible with these assumptions.

In this paper, I hope to make a move in that direction. I shall first give a quick sketch of my account of what it is for an action to be reasoned in order to elicit the constraints it places on the analysis of the concept of action. Then I will try to say something about the concept of action within those limits.

To anticipate, the main limit is that I am led to what might be termed a propositional analysis of action. To act is to cause a certain proposition to be true. Or, in the syntactical mode of speech, the sentence describing an action is to be formed by the application of a sentence-forming operator to another sentence. Schematically, I use

$$C_{a,o}(p)$$

to represent the logical form of action sentences, where this says that on occasion $o$, agent $a$ caused proposition $p$ to be true.

## II

I begin then with the account of reasoned action. What is it for an action to be reasoned? My approach has been to say that to represent an action as reasoned one must make it out to be as nearly like the conclusion of a

M. Brand and D. Walton (eds.), Action Theory, 87–104. All Rights Reserved
Copyright © 1976 by D. Reidel Publishing Company, Dordrecht-Holland

syllogism as possible, for that is my paradigm of reasoning. Now, it will be objected at once that actions do not *look* very much like the conclusions of syllogisms, so that a certain quantity of seductive discourse is required, and here begins.

What, after all, *is* the conclusion of a syllogism? Four answers suggest themselves: it is a sentence (or statement); it is a proposition; it is a judgment (or belief); it is knowledge. That is, the conclusion may be the sentence 'All Greeks are mortal', the proposition that all Greeks are mortal, somebody's judgment that all Greeks are mortal, or somebody's knowledge that all Greeks are mortal.

These four answers are closely related, and I find it useful to employ a notation that reveals these relationships. To begin with judgment, we note that the noun phrase, 'Jones's judgment that all Greeks are mortal', is derivative from the sentence, 'Jones judges that all Greeks are mortal'. I call such a sentence a *judgment description*; it describes a thinker as having a certain thought or being in a certain mental state. The sentence 'All Greeks are mortal' stands to this mental state as its *vehicle*; it is a sentence appropriate for expressing that thought or mental state in *our* language. Not necessarily the language of the thinker; there are many vehicles in many languages for this thought. What it takes to be such a vehicle is to stand for the proposition (or propositional sense) that all Greeks are mortal.

All this can be represented schematically as follows, where we are dealing with agent a on occasion o, and p abbreviates the sentence 'All Greeks are mortal':

| | |
|---|---|
| Judgment description | $J_{a,o}(p)$ |
| Judgment vehicle | $p$ |
| Judgment sense | $j(p)$ |

The judgment description and vehicle are both sentences, one about *a*, the other about Greeks. '$j(p)$', however, is a *name* of the judgment sense.

The fourth answer, that the conclusion of a syllogism might be knowledge, can also be provided for by introducing the

Knowledge description $K_{a,o}(p)$.

I turn now to the syllogism of which all these things are, in various respects, the conclusion. I suggest that the same principles apply, and that we should distinguish, with an admitted element of stipulation, (1) the agent's *reasoning,* or the syllogism in the mind, (2) the corresponding *argument* which is the vehicle of the reasoning and (3) the *inference,* which is the sense of the reasoning.

This enriches our schematism as follows, where $p$ and $q$ abbreviate premise vehicles, and $r$ a conclusion vehicle:

Reasoning description    $R_{a,o,}(p,q \to r)$

Reasoning vehicle        $p$
   (argument)            $\underline{q}$
                         $\therefore r$

Reasoning sense          $r[j(p), j(q) \to j(r)]$
   (inference)

While reasoning vehicles are easily expressed in ordinary language with 'since', 'therefore', and so on, we are not so well equipped for reasoning descriptions and names of reasoning senses. The description could perhaps be read 'On occasion $o$, agent $a$ concluded that $r$ on the grounds that $p$ and that $q$.' And we could name the sense of this with '(The inference) that $r$ on the grounds that $p$ and that $q$.'

There seems to be no concept related to reasoning as knowledge is related to judgment. This is curious. Reasoning the conclusion of which is knowledge, and especially reasoning the conclusion of which is made knowledge by that very reasoning, deserves, one should think, a special name. It would be easy enough to introduce one, but I will not on this occasion.

Of the three ways in which reasoning finds expression in language (description, argument and inference), we are most interested in the reasoning description, because that has to do directly with the reasoning in the mind of the agent. That must be regarded, I believe, as a single mental act or state with a complex content, and not as a series of mental acts or states. In this respect, reasoning is unlike calculation.

The premise-conclusion distinction, thus, must be drawn *within* the content of a mental act, and not *between* mental acts. Nevertheless, when a person reasons, judges that $q$ on the ground that $p$, he does also judge that $q$, and, for that matter judges that $p$. We want, I think, to avoid saying that there are three mental acts here, the reasoning and also the judging of premise and judging of conclusion. So we must say that there is only one mental act, which is characterizable by the three different descriptions. Or more accurately, that when a person reasons, *he* can be characterized by the three descriptions of being a reasoner, being a judger of premise and being a judger of conclusion. All the descriptions I have considered describe *persons on occasions,* not mental acts or states; I assume throughout a substance, not an event ontology. We must add that the description of the person as reasoning in a certain way entails the descriptions of him as judging premise and judging conclusion.

My purpose in the preceding remarks has been to elucidate the notion of the conclusion of a piece of reasoning as a step on the way to representing reasoned action as itself the conclusion of a piece of reasoning. However, I have so far considered only theoretical reasoning of which all components are judgments, and it is necessary now to extend the account to practical reasoning.

The first step in the extension is to introduce the notion which I call *decision*. This is a concept on the practical side parallel to the concept of judgment. Like judgment, it stands for a propositional attitude, but it involves commitment, roughly, to the making true of a proposition, not to the being true of it. It corresponds pretty well to what others have called intention, volition, etc.

To tend to the schematism first, we have, where $p$ abbreviates, say, 'The cat is on the mat':

Decision description     $D_{a,o}(p)$
[On $o$, $a$ decides that the cat is to be on the mat.]
Decision vehicle          $\$(p)$
[The cat shall be on the mat.]
Decision sense.           $d(p)$
[That the cat is to be on the mat.]

Thus decision, like judgment, is described by means of a sentence-forming operator on sentences. I shall say that the inside sentence of a decision description expresses the *result proposition* of the decision. I will be discussing later some problems about just what sorts of propositions can serve as result propositions. Here I will observe that typically the result proposition is not itself a proposition describing an action, though that is possible. In the present example, it is the proposition that the cat is on the mat, and not anything about *putting* the cat on the mat. This is, of course, a departure from our ordinary use of the word 'decide', for frequently we speak of deciding to *do* something rather than deciding that something is to be the case.

In addition, I believe, it is necessary to employ a concept of *withholding,* such that we may speak both of the withholding of judgment and the withholding of decision and, for that matter, the withholding of withholding.

In the schematism, this gives us:

Withheld judgment description $WJ_{a,o}(p)$
[On $o$, $a$ withholds judgment that the cat is on the mat.]

Withheld decision description $WD_{a,o}(p)$
[On $o$, $a$ withholds decision that the cat shall be on the mat.]
Withheld judgment vehicle $?(p)$
[Perhaps the cat is not on the mat.]
Withheld decision vehicle $?\$(p)$
[Perhaps the cat shall not be on the mat.]
Withheld judgment sense $wj(p)$
[That the cat may not be on the mat.]
Withheld decision sense $wd(p)$
[That the cat may not be to be on the mat.]

Next, the notion of reasoning may be extended to include these new ingredients. Thus we will countenance reasoning describable as

$$R_{a,o}(p, \$(q), ?(r) \to ?\$(s))$$

which describes $a$ as concluding on $o$ that $s$ may not be to be the case on the grounds that $p$, that $q$ is to be the case, and that $r$ may not be the case. The vehicles and sense names for these new reasonings can be easily constructed.

We now have a general concept of reasoning that covers the familiar judgmental reasoning together with reasonings involving decisions and withholdings. However, to justify all this as reasoning in anything more than name, it must be shown how a plausible distinction between valid and invalid reasoning can be made to apply to it. I have undertaken this task elsewhere,[1] and will here just sketch the grand strategy. It is first to define the concept of the Ideal Thinker. That is done by means of a logical calculus, a sort of modal logic made up out of the '$J$' and '$D$' of the judgment and decision descriptions treated as modal operators like necessity together with the '$W$' of the withholding description treated as a kind of negation. The second step is to define valid reasoning as reasoning such that an Ideal Thinker could not affirm its premises while withholding its conclusion.

One consequence of this definition is that the usual judgmental reasonings turn out to be valid. However, since the definition is not couched in terms of the transmission of truth from premises to conclusion, it applies also, and univocally, to reasonings involving decision and withholding.

It could be objected[2] that this definition places a logical obligation on the thinker to move ahead from the premises he accepts to such conclusions as he notices to follow from them whereas, it might be said, the validity of reasoning only *entitles* the thinker to move ahead, but does not oblige him to.

This difference in the conception of validity does not *make* a difference in the sphere of judgmental reasoning, since the same reasonings are viewed as valid. But differences emerge as soon as the notion of withholding is introduced. Consider, for example, a thinker of whom the following descriptions are true:

$$J_{a,o}(p \supset q)$$
$$J_{a,o}(p)$$
$$WJ_{a,o}(q)$$

On my view, logic must condemn such an assortment of thoughts, and so view as valid not only *modus ponens,* but also such forms as

$$\frac{p \supset q}{\therefore ?(p)}$$

This is the vehicle of the reasoning whereby one concludes that perhaps not *p* on the ground that if *p* then *q*, and perhaps not *q*, and is valid on my account. That my definition yields such intuitively desirable results seems to me to support my more stringent conception of the obligations of logic in preference to the objection's permissiveness.

A further manifestation of the difference between these conceptions, one more relevant to practical reasoning, has to do with the way in which we are to give expression to that generally recognized principle of practical wisdom which has to do with yielding to the inevitable. Not making use of the concept of withholding, some writers affirm as valid the following argument form:

$$\frac{p}{\therefore \$(p)}$$

This is Sellars' 'So be it' principle; one must positively support the inevitable. On my system, however, I can replace this with the weaker

$$\frac{p}{\therefore ?\$(\text{not-}p)}$$

which could be termed a 'So may it be' principle.

We have then concepts of reasoning and of valid reasoning that apply to decisions and withholdings as well as to judgments. This gives a concept of reasoned decision, which is simply decision that is the conclusion of the agent's reasoning. The next step is to move from the concept of reasoned decision to the concept of reasoned action.

## III

It is obvious, of course, in a general way that reasoned action will be action that derives from reasoned decision. But the sense in which the action derives from the decision requires analysis. At this point I appeal to the parallelism between the concept of action (as I analyse it) and the concept of knowledge. The crucial move is to say that action stands to the decision from which it 'derives' as knowledge stands to the judgment which it is. That is, that the relation between the action of causing it to be that p and the related deciding that p is to be is the same as the relation between the agent's knowing that p is the case and his judging that p is the case.

Consider the case of knowledge and judgment. There still is, I believe, wide support for the view that knowledge simply *is* judgment that is true in an appropriately non-accidental way. Knowing that p and judging that p are the same mental act or state; a knowing that p is simply a judging that p that meets certain further requirements. In the same sort of way, the winner of a race is simply a runner of the race who meets certain further requirements — those constituting victory; the runner and the winner are the same person.

Inspired by this comparison, I describe the further requirements that judgment must meet in order to be knowledge as *victory,* and so characterize knowledge as victorious judgment. And in parallel fashion, I view action as decision that is fulfilled in an appropriately non-accidental way. The action and the decision are the same mental act or state, and we may thus characterize action as victorious decision.

In what does victory consist? It consists in part in the truth of the proposition known or caused to be. But in addition to this, the truth of the proposition and the judging or deciding must be related in an *appropriately non-accidental* way. This means in part a causal relation, where this is to be analysed in terms of the idea of causal explanation. Roughly, in the case of knowledge, the being true of the proposition must enter in an appropriate way into the explanation of the judging, and in the case of action, the deciding must enter in an appropriate way into the explanation of the being true of the proposition.

It is necessary in each case to carry along that Pandora's box of a word "appropriately", and I shall not presume to open it here. But for an example, consider a man who, due perhaps to some bizarre brain injury, will believe that he has just been hit on the top of the head with a hammer by the Pope whenever he is hit on the top of the head at all. And suppose that the Pope, reaching out from behind a curtain, does hit him on the top of the head with a hammer, thus causing the characteristic judgment, which this time will be true. However, though its being true does enter into the explanation of the judging, it does not do so in an appropriate way, and so the judgment is not knowledge. Similarly, we can imagine a man so startled by his own decision to salute the enemy flag that a nervous spasm is produced which causes his arm to go through the motions of a salute. Here the deciding would enter into the explanation of the being true of the result proposition, but not in an appropriate way, and so it would not constitute action.

Victory, then, is what distinguishes knowledge from mere judgment and action from mere decision, and so is a very important notion. And I note in passing that it is important for another reason. For on my account of what it is for reasoning to be valid, it is victory, not truth, that is the desirable attribute that valid reasoning transmits from premise to conclusion. This is the feature that permits me to speak of a single sense of 'valid reasoning' applicable to reasoning in decision and withholding as well as judgment.

The definition of *reasoned action* in terms of reasoned decision is now straightforward. Action is victorious decision, and is reasoned just in case the decision is reasoned.

IV

I have now reached the pivot point of the paper. It is clear that this conception of what it is for an action to be reasoned depends crucially on the propositional analysis of action, since it is only in the terms of such an analysis that the requisite parallel between action and knowledge can be made plausible. I am now ready to take up the main task, which is to see if there is anything to be said in favour of this analysis over and above the fact that it supports my favourite theory of practical reasoning.

The discussion will be organized under three main heads. First, I will consider certain consequences that flow from the fact that on the analysis of action as victorious decision, action *is* decision, and so a mental act. Second, I will consider certain problems associated with the formulation of the result proposition, problems that arise on any propositional analysis of action. Finally, I will take up certain problems concerned with actions done by the same agent on the same occasion, problems which have led some writers to speak of a single action appearing under various descriptions, and have led Goldman[3] to introduce the notion of level-generation, and in this context I will be able to say a word about the concept of a basic action.

I first take up a very obvious restriction that must be placed upon the scope of this analysis. For it is clear that the view of action as victorious decision must be limited to action that is fully conscious and deliberate, even though our ordinary language of action has a much wider application. This limitation is not as damaging as it might seem, however, for I believe that fully deliberate action is the paradigm for all applications of the action concept, and that other uses can be understood by reference to it. But I will not pursue that theme here.

A second consequence of the interpretation of action as a form of decision is that the concept of action becomes a highly intensional one. An action on this view is, like judgment, a thought in the agent's mind having a certain proposition as content. We should expect, therefore, to find the same sort of intensionality in action descriptions as we do in descriptions of judgment and knowledge. Thus even though Jones strikes the shortest man in the group and the shortest man in the group is the general, it does not follow that Jones did the action, in my sense, of striking the general. We could of course define a sense in which he could be said to have done that action; the definition of that sense would amount in effect to the conjunction of the two premises of this suggested inference. That would be one of the many concepts of action derivative from the paradigm.

A third consequence is that the range of a man's action, like the range of his knowledge, cannot extend beyond the limits of his conceptual repertoire. He cannot think thoughts for which he does not have the conceptual equipment, though of course he may acquire new conceptual equipment. In describing action, therefore, we cannot employ concepts in expressing the result proposition that the agent does not possess. And more than that, we may employ only those concepts actually exercised by the agent in his decision. Thus it is possible for an agent to cause a board to be three feet long without causing it to be a yard long, either because he does not possess the concept of a yard or because he did not exercise it on this occasion. But again, a derivative sense of action could be defined in which the entailment would hold.

In describing action, we are thus limited to the agent's concepts. But of course, we are also limited to our own, since we cannot employ words in our description that we do not understand. It follows, then, that action in the paradigm sense can only be described within the overlap zone of the conceptual systems of agent and spectator. This is a point of some importance when it comes to the characterization of what we might term exotic actions, those, say, of savages or quantum physicists.

One final point on the conception of action as *being* decision. It was noted at the beginning that one of the possible objections to my view is that reasoned actions do not *look* very much like the conclusions of syllogisms. The analysis of action as victorious decision provides an answer to that of sorts. *Of course* actions do not *look* like the conclusions of syllogisms. Being mental acts, they cannot be observed, and so do not *look* like anything at all. This response, however, raises the question what it is that we do observe when we would ordinarily say that we are observing a man's actions, and the answer, which I will elaborate a bit below, is that we observe the bodily motions which make certain of the result propositions true.

V

So much, then for the points that arise from the fact that my analysis treats action as being a mental act or state. I turn now to problems associated with the formulation of the result proposition, and I take up first the question of time or occasion. It seems evident that human, if not divine, agents always act in time, and that therefore no decision could be victorious unless its result proposition carried some form of temporal determination. We cannot *produce* eternal verities. This is most conveniently dealt with by laying it down that the result proposition must always have the form of a predication of one or more occasions, and so will not simply have the form

$$p$$

but rather the form

$$P_o$$

or

$$P_{o,o'}$$

etc. For example, that the light is on on occasion $o$, or that it is on from $o$ to $o'$. I shall here limit the discussion to single occasion result propositions, and thus postpone consideration of such examples as causing it to be that one flies now while paying later.

Not only is our action limited to such temporal propositions; it is limited to only a subset of them, for those having to do with the past cannot be the objects of victorious decision. But this point requires a certain delicacy of formulation since in describing action we are concerned with the agent's conception of what he is doing, and so with the series of past, present and future occasions as he sees it.

Let us begin by noting that action may be concerned with futures of varying degrees of remoteness. When I pull the trigger of a gun, and so cause it to go off, my concern is with a very near future, whereas when I set my alarm clock, and so cause it to go off next morning, the relevant future is more distant. Let us start with the near end of this range, with action, that is, that involves the minimum of delay.

Can the delay be reduced to zero? That is, can we allow the form

$$C_{a,o}(P_o),$$

in which the two temporal references have the same sense? I believe that the answer is 'No' for a reason that is of fundamental importance for the concept of action; in acting, the agent must always conceive of himself as acting *in* the present and *on* the future.

This has two aspects. First, it means that when the agent considers the occasion of the result of his action, he must conceive it as related in some way to the present. This means that he must conceive it in terms of a *now*. That is, the vehicle of his thought of the result will involve an egocentric temporal reference. The gun is to go off now, the alarm clock is to go off on the morning after now, etc. The occasion references in the result proposition must therefore have an egocentric character, where the relevant ego is the agent. The occasion reference of the causing, on the other hand, may or may not be egocentric, but if it is, the ego will be that of the action describer.

A way of dealing with these egocentric references is provided by Castaneda's theory of quasi-indicators.[4] That theory is complex, and I will not review it here, but the central point can be put quite simply. Where the vehicle of a thought has an egocentric reference, the description of the thought has a quasi-indicator. When the agent thinks about himself in the first person, employing, say, the vehicle,

I am rich,

the describer of the thought employs a quasi-indicator (for which I use 'he*') and so says

Jones judges at 3:00 that he* is rich.

Similarly with 'now', and other egocentric temporal references. The thought for which an appropriate vehicle is

I am now rich

is described by

Jones judges at 3:00 that he* is then* rich,

'then\*' being a quasi-indicator for present tense reference, and the 'is' being timeless. It should be clear that this is not the same as

Jones judges at 3:00 that Jones is rich at 3:00,

for Jones might not realize that he is Jones and might not know the time of day.

Whenever an agent acts, then, he must be characterizable by an action description in which the temporal reference of the result proposition is given by a quasi-indicator, which is to say, with the form

$$C_{a,o}(P_{\text{then}*})$$

or the like.[5]

This excludes use of the form

$$C_{a,o}(P_o)$$

for the crucial egocentric case when describing the action of another because the form

$$C_{a,\,\text{then}*}(P_{\text{then}*})$$

is improper; the second 'then\*' occupies the place for the agent's temporal reference while the first fills that of the action describer's temporal reference. We would not get this form, even if the agent were to describe his own action as it occurred, since he would use

$$C_{I,\,\text{now}}(P_{\text{then}*}).$$

This still leaves us with the possibility of

$$C_{I,\,\text{now}}(P_{\text{now}})$$

for self-description, but that succumbs to a second argument.

The second objection to the idea of strictly contemporaneous action derives from the point that in acting the agent not only conceives himself as acting in the present, but conceives himself as acting on the future, and so as *initiating* the result. This means that his conception of the result must involve the idea of its *coming after* the causing of it. This point is best accommodated, I believe, if we conceive of the present as a division between a just ended past and a just starting future. We need then not only 'now', but also 'up to now' and 'starting now'. I suggest we use 'now—' and 'now+' for these ideas, reserving the unadorned 'now' for the moment in between. We can then put our point about action by saying that when the agent acts with minimum delay, the vehicle of his decision is

$$\$(P_{now+}),$$

and so the action must be described with the form

$$C_{a,o}(P_{then+*}).$$

Thus, even if the agent were to describe his own action at the time, he would use

$$C_{I,now}(P_{now+}),$$

not

$$C_{I,now}(P_{now}).$$

The logical structure of non-delayed action thus reveals an important feature of the way in which an agent must anchor himself in time. Another aspect of this would emerge if we considered the parallel case of knowledge by perception, for we would there be led to the form

$$K_{a,o}(P_{then-*})$$

since the perceiver perceives *in* his own present, and perceives his environment *up to then*.* The case of delayed action presents no special problem, in that we have such forms as

$$C_{a,o}(P_{then*+8})$$

as in the alarm clock case, but I will say a bit more about it later.

I turn now to the second feature of the result proposition that I wish to discuss, its actual content. At this point we must confront the fact that our ordinary way of talking about action is not built on the model of the propositional analysis. Rather, we have a whole vocabulary of verbs of action — 'walk', 'build', 'shoot', 'kill', 'raise the arm', 'flip the switch', etc. Indeed, the operation I employ in the propositional analysis, 'cause it to be that . . .' is just one among all the other verbs of action. The propositional analysis thus has the task of compressing all the verbs of action into a single canonical one, and then to find some other way of expressing the differences between the various ordinary verbs of action. And of course, we look to the result proposition to express these differences.

How, for example, are we to bring 'On occasion $o$, agent $a$ raised his arm' into approved form? What, exactly, is the result proposition here? It will not do simply to say that he caused it to be that his* arm was up, for there are other ways of producing this result than raising. (Lifting the paralysed arm with the other hand, etc., which would not be the ordinary sense of raising.) The solution in cases of this kind, I believe, though not in all cases, is to employ an artificial verb for what I shall call the *topological action*. I derive this verb from the verb of action proper, and speak of a person topologically raising his arm just in case everything goes on in space of the kind required for it to be the case that he raises his arm in the full action sense. The topological action, that is, consists in the right bodily motions and perhaps the motions of other objects. The action proper can then be viewed as the causing to occur of topological action. "Walk" is a verb of action; "sleepwalk" is not, but topological walking occurs whenever there is either walking or sleepwalking.

More precisely, let us suppose that we have a verb of action '$V$' so that in ordinary language we express the claim that agent $a$ did a certain action on occasion $o$ with a sentence of the form

$$V_{a,o}.$$

The proposal is to derive from this verb another verb for the related topological action, call it '$V^t$', *so that*

$$V^t_{a,o}$$

says that the topological action occurred. We then use this new verb to formulate the result proposition in the canonical action description,

$$C_{a,o}(V^t_{he*,now+*})$$

(Note, incidentally, the use of the quasi-indicators. It is of course essential that the agent conceive that the bodily motions will be motions of *his own* body.)

In these cases, then, the move is to begin with the ordinary verb of action, subtract the idea of agency to form the topological action verb, and finally restore the idea of agency with the 'cause it to be the case that . . .' operator.

It might be objected that this way of proceeding introduces a circularity into the account. I was supposed to be reducing verbs of action to the 'causing to be' form, and now it turns out that in order to do that I presuppose verbs of action as the sources of the topological action verbs. I have two responses to this.

First, it is only contingently the case that topological action verbs need to be derived from action verbs proper. Topological actions are simply matter in motion, and are in principle describable in purely physical terms. We have not evolved a purely physical vocabulary for them because our only, or main, interest in these particular motions of matter, unlike say the motions of planets, is that they constitute possible actions for us, and so our vocabulary has been linked to that. Further, we are free to introduce new topological active verbs unrelated to existing verbs of action. This is done, for example, when the dance instructor says "Do like *this*", and then gives a name to the motion.

My second response is that my account in fact *correctly* analyses the ordinary verb of action into the two components, agency and topological action, and that this correctly reflects the way in which an agent must think about his action. In his own deliberation, the agent must subtract agency from his conception of the possible actions among which he is choosing, if it is present, since he is then in the course of answering precisely the question whether or not to supply it, whether or not, that is, to *do* the action.

Very often, then, to act is to cause a topological action to occur, and this shows up in our ordinary language which frequently combines the topological action and the causing of it into the single verb of action. By no means all actions are of this type, but since all performable bodily motions are topological actions, and since it seems to be the case that it is only through bodily motions that we can produce any effects on the outside world at all, we may expect a topological action to be at least involved whenever anything is done to anything outside.

VI

I turn now to a discussion of some of the ways in which actions may be related to each other. This is required for the definition of the very important notion of a basic action, and will also help us to understand those cases in which some people have wanted to speak of the same action under different descriptions.

Let us begin by considering two actions of the same agent on the same occasion. We have, let us suppose,

$$C_{a,o}(p)$$

and

$$C_{a,o}(q).$$

How might they be related? There are two fundamentally different dimensions in which they may be related, and I shall refer to these as the internal linkage and the external linkage. The internal linkage is the relation between the causing of $p$ and the causing of $q$. It is called internal because these causings are decisions 'inside' the agent. The external relation is the relation between $p$'s being the case and $q$'s being the case. Typically, this will be 'outside' the agent.

For example, consider the case in which we say that the agent does one thing *by* doing something else. He causes the light to be on by flipping the switch. These two actions are described by

$$C_{a,o}(F^t_{\text{he*,then+*}})$$

and

$$C_{a,o}(L_{\text{then+*}}).$$

Here, the external linkage is causal; the topological switch flipping causes the light to be on. And the internal linkage is, in a sense, logical. Since action is victorious decision, these two actions must be in the agent's mind as decisions. And if the agent is to do the one action *by* doing the other, the decisions must be related. The required relation is that of serving as premise and conclusion of reasoning. The means decision to flip the switch, that is, must be the conclusion of reasoning having the end decision that the light be on as a premise. The vehicle of the agent's reasoning, that is, must be of the form

$$\$(L_{\text{now+}})$$
$$\cdots$$
$$\overline{\phantom{xxxxxx}}$$
$$\therefore \$(F^t_{\text{I,now+}}),$$

where the dots mark the place of the needed factual judgments. This constitutes my analysis of what might be termed the 'by' relation between actions. *a* causes it to be that *e* by causing it to be that *m* if and only if he decides that *m* is to be the case on the ground that *e* is to be the case, both these decisions are victorious and its being the case that *m* is cause or effect of its being the case that *e*. (Notice that I say 'cause *or* effect'. In most cases when I do *e* by doing *m*, *m* is the cause of *e*. But in special cases, as when in the course of my body-building program I cause a particular muscle to tense by lifting a weight, causality operates in the opposite direction — from end to means rather than from means to end.)

The 'by' relation between actions, then, consists in an internal linkage between the two decisions in that one must be premise, the other conclusion in the agent's reasoning plus an external linkage, which is a causal relation between the two result propositions. And this conception, I think, serves very well for defining the notion of a basic action. A basic action is simply an action that is not done by doing another.

Must all basic actions be contemporaneous? That is, must they all consist in causing the result proposition to be true, *starting now*? It is tempting to think that this is so because it is hard to see what reason there could be for attributing the coming true of a proposition at a remote time to the causality of an agent now unless the agent did something now to link him and the present occasion to that later event. It is easy enough to attribute the sounding of my alarm clock tomorrow morning to my causality tonight if I set the clock tonight. But then I cause it to sound tomorrow by setting it tonight. My two decisions have the vehicles

$(Clock is set now+)

and

$(Alarm sounds eight hours from now).

But this line of thought, I believe, may involve a mistake. It is true that something must occur now to link my present decision with the later event. And as a matter of contingent fact (our lack of psychokinetic powers), this must be something over and above the occurrence of the decision itself. But it is not clear that it has to be an action. That is, my present decision could cause a present effect, but one the causing of which did not constitute action, and then this effect might in turn cause the later event, the causing of which did constitute action. Thus, I might simply decide that the alarm is to sound in eight hours, and my hands would go through the necessary motions without my causing them to do that in the action sense, for I might not be aware of what those motions are. In that case, I might be said to have caused the alarm to sound tomorrow without causing in the action sense anything to happen now. This would be a non-contemporaneous basic action. However the issue cannot be settled without a more detailed analysis of what are the *appropriate* non-accidental ways for the truth of a result proposition to be related to a decision.

There are many more kinds of internal and external linkage, and consequently many more kinds of relations between actions. Another internal linkage, for example, occurs between premises of a single reasoning, and the external linkage may be logical rather than causal. One result proposition may entail another, either absolutely, or relative to some existing conditions and/or norms. Consider, for example, the action of running and the action of running at 8 mph. Here, topologically running at 8 mph logically entails topologically running absolutely. And the circumstances might be such that, relative to them, it entails topologically outrunning another runner. And relative also to certain norms it might entail topologically winning a race.

When an external linkage of this logical kind is combined with the ground-consequent internal linkage just discussed, we have actions that are related in a way often describable with the word 'in'. We can say "In running he ran 8 mph" and "In running he outran $X$", "In outrunning $X$ he won the race", etc., as well as the converses.

These are all examples of level-generation in Goldman's sense, and I hold out the hope that all such cases can be handled by appropriate manoeuvres with the internal and external linkages, and perhaps some moving down from the paradigm to derivative senses of 'action'. If that is right, the propositional analysis of action here defended will have passed a most important test.

*The University of Western Ontario*

## NOTES

[1] In 'A Theory of Practical Reason', *Philosophical Review* (1965), 423–448. An improved version was attempted in a paper, 'The Validity of Reasoning', which was presented to The Canadian Philosophical Association in June, 1973, and which may appear in *Noûs*. Behind these are some interesting but not much noticed papers by Reginald Jackson: 'Rationalism and Intellectualism in the Ethics of Aristotle', *Mind* **51** (1942), 343–360; 'Practical Reason', *Philosophy* **17** (1942), 351–367; and 'The Moral Problem — the Problem for Conduct', *Mind* **67** (1948), 420–458. Nor is my account uninfluenced by the work of Wilfrid Sellars.

[2] Bruce Aune has raised this point in correspondence.

[3] Alvin Goldman, *A Theory of Human Action,* Prentice-Hall, Englewood Cliffs, 1970.

[4] Hector Castañeda, '"He": A Study in the Logic of Self-Consciousness', *Ratio* **8** (1966), 130–157.

[5] The agent may *also* be characterizable by other action descriptions containing objective temporal references, for if he *knows* the time of day, and so forms judgments having such vehicles as 'It is now 3:00', then he will be able to relate his egocentric temporal references to objective ones, and equivalent decisions couched in terms of the latter will be as victorious as the primary decisions conceived egocentrically.

HECTOR-NERI CASTAÑEDA

# THE TWOFOLD STRUCTURE AND THE UNITY OF PRACTICAL THINKING

This is a contribution to the foundations of the theory of institutions. My immediate aim is to defend and formulate a comprehensive theory of the basic logical structure of judgments about duties or obligations. The theory is comprehensive in two respects: (i) it relates ought-judgments to the other contents of practical thinking, and (ii) it deals with the connections, seldom considered, between ought (or obligation) and identity (and quantification). The theory is systematized in rich formal system $D^{**}$ for propositions, imperatives, intentions, and deontic judgments with quantification and identity.

## I. A CENTRAL THESIS ABOUT PRACTICAL THINKING

We exercise our thinking powers in learning what things are and how they relate to one another; and we postulate hypotheses and invent theories about what things are and how they affect one another. These are all instances of thinking in which one contemplates the world, its contents, and its laws. They are pure or contemplative uses of reason. But we also exercise our thinking powers in finding out what to do ourselves and what others are to do. We propound hypotheses as to what we ought to do, or not to do. And we attempt to carry out our decisions and intentions. These are instances of practical thinking; they are practical uses of reason. Yet it is *one and the same reason* that one exercises in both cases; and it is one and the same world that is both the object of contemplation and the object of action.

That is in a nutshell the primordial, hence, trivial, datum of the philosophy of action and all its branches. That datum presents both the duality of contemplative-practical thinking and the unity of reason. Any truly elucidatory theory has to provide a unitary account of both.

Here I will develop the desired unitary account only with respect to the basic logical structure of ought-judgments. This account rests firmly on one of my oldest philosophical theses, which represents neatly both the duality

*M. Brand and D. Walton (eds.), Action Theory, 105–130. All Rights Reserved*
*Copyright © 1976 by D. Reidel Publishing Company, Dordrecht-Holland*

of practical thinking and the unity of reason. It is this: *Deontic concepts are modal operators that transform the purely practical, non-propositional contents of practical thinking into propositions.* By deontic operators I mean what is expressed by locutions like: 'it is obligatory (wrong, permissible, right) for $X$ to $A$' and 'it is obligatory (wrong, permitted, forbidden, required, unlawful) that $X A$'. By propositions I mean the thought contents that are true or false in the sense of corresponding to facts in the world, are characteristically expressed by indicative sentences, and are the *what*'s of believing (knowing, imagining, supposing) that something or other is the case. The non-propositional purely practical contents of practical thinking I call *practitions*. They are, on the one hand, the cores of commands, requests and acts of telling someone to do something; on the other hand, a practition is what one intends, plans, or decides to do. The former are second- or third-person thought contents, and I call them *prescriptions*. The latter I call *intentions*. I will explain this more fully below. My thesis is then that *deontic operators apply to practitions and yield propositions.* The basic duality of practical thinking is the duality proposition-practition; the unity of reason is in part the unity of deontic or normative thinking, whose primary concepts span the difference between purely contemplative thinking and purely practical thinking.[1]

The above thesis is one of the main prongs of my theory of both the structure of the contents of practical thinking and the nature and functions of practical thinking.[2] It is a theoretical thesis; it cannot, therefore, be proven deductively. But there is a lot of evidence in support of it as I have deployed before in several publications.[3] Here I want to discuss some evidence that I have not yet discussed in print before I proceed to the formulation of my favorite theory of the logic of the contents of practical thinking.

## II. PRACTICAL THINKING

The fundamental phenomenon of practical thinking is the phenomenon of coming to intend to do something. Its more glamorous manifestations appear in the occasions on which one decides to do something in the face of a very difficult choice. But glamor aside, when one intends to do some action $A$ one's attitude of intending toward $A$ *ipso facto* divides the world into several segments along three axes:

| Past | Future | |
|------|-----------|-----|
|      | A - Zone  | ~A  |
|      | Framework | |

(1) the world divides into the fixed Past and the pliable Future; (2) the Future divides into the *A*-Future Framework and the Future *A*-Zone of Indeterminacy; (3) the Future *A*-Zone of Indeterminacy divides into the endorsed *A*-Future and the rejected not-*A*-Future. This is all trivial, yet most of the work in deontic logic has not reached that minimal trivial complexity of practical thinking.

It is easy to see that the same threefold division of the world applies to the endorsement of an order or request or a piece of advice. I say "endorsement" rather than issuing because the primary phenomenon is the mental state involved not the speech acts which spring from, and presuppose, relevant mental state. If I am alone planning how to engage Josephine in my plans and am *not*, therefore, in a position to issue any orders or requests, I am in a position to *endorse* some orders and requests, and when I do so the world divides up along the lines (1)–(3).

The second-person case is derivative. It presupposes the requester's decisions, and the requested agent's own intentions.[4]

In all cases, then, practical attitudes divide up the world in three pairs of segments. I will not deal with the Past-Future division here. My main concern here is the division of the Future into a Framework and a Zone of Indeterminacy. It is often neglected.

The difference between the Future *A*-Framework and the *A*-Zone of Indeterminacy appears to the practical consciousness of the agent (as well as to that of a commander or requester) as fixed *with respect to action A*. The *A*-Framework appears as a network of facts or truths. It includes the circumstances and the laws of nature that are relevant to the contrast between the *A*-Future and the non-*A*-Future. The *A*-Framework is, then, thought of contemplatively, propositionally. On the other hand, the *A*-Zone of Indeterminacy is not thought of contemplatively: it is thought of in a way that appears to be under the control of thinking: it appears as a container that can be filled in with the *A*-Future as partially caused by, as a *consequence* of, the endorsing thinking of the *A*-Future itself.

This internal causal aspect of practical thinking is crucial: it connects the content of the thinking with the causality of thinking. Clearly, awareness of the causal powers of one's own thinking is not sufficient to make thinking practical. One can know that whenever one thinks of something a change happens in one's body which change may cause an alteration in one's environment. One may know this in detail so that on a given situation one contemplates the whole causal chain. Yet in such a case, the thinking of the something in question and the awareness of the causal chain leading to the alteration in the environment do *not* constitute an instance of practical thinking: one has no intention of bringing about the alteration, one is not carrying out any decision to produce the alteration.[5]

The ultimate analysis of the interval causality, i.e., the practicality, of practical thinking is a difficult problem. We will not deal with it here. We must note, however, that the content of practical thinking has a representation of the practicality of the thinking of that content. Consider, for example, my intending to go home soon. Suppose that I rehearse my state of intending and think (whether out loud or not is immaterial, since we are not primarily interested in speech acts):

(1)     I shall go home soon.

I think exactly the same agent as subject and the same action as predicate that I think when I consider the mere happening of my going home, namely, when I think the performance proposition corresponding to my intention (1) namely:

(2)     I will go home soon.

The central difference is that in the latter I think only of an event involving me as agent. This could very well be part of a fixed Future Framework with respect to some other actions I am interested in. Indeed, I can even consider that I will be going home soon, without any intention, driven without my consent by somebody else or by a hypnotically-induced impulse. Whatever the situation, (2) presents my going as a *circumstance* or as a *happening*. On the other hand, the expression of intention (1) presents my going home soon as an *open* component of the Future, and openness here is nothing but the availability of the causal space, so to speak, for the very thinking of (1) to enter and help bring about the truth of (2).

In short, then, the contents of practical thinking present agents and actions as related in a special causal way. First-person practical thinking is not only self referring in that it refers to the self that does the thinking: it is *self*-referring, or better, self-alluding in that it is the apprehension of a content that, without individuating (and thus truly referring to) the apprehension itself, includes an unindividuated signal of both the apprehension itself and the apprehension's causal power. That signaling role is part of the sense of the intentional use of the future tense and, derivatively, of the imperative mood. I speak of *signal*, because there is no conceptualization of that causal role. It is represented to consciousness as a way in which agent and action are *structured* in the thought content. I will say that primary practical thought contents have a special *copula* linking agent and action, namely, the structuring just described. Now, the contemplative or propositional copula is out there in world, so to speak, in that facts have a structuring of objects and properties. The practical copula is in the world only to the extent that *some* practical thought contents correspond to actual powers of internal causality of the practical thinking whose contents they are: Here we find the ontological primacy of pure contemplative reason over practical reason.

At any rate, the duality of copulae, which will be further analyzed in Section IV below, is one representation of the fundamental duality of *actions considered as circumstances*, i.e., as part of a Future Framework, and *actions considered practically*, i.e., as determining a Future Zone of indeterminacy. This duality is one that any study of practical thinking in general, or a segment thereof, like deontic or normative thinking, has to take into account. *Deontic logic, for instance, has to be two-sorted*: And on my view this is a sentential copulative two-sortedness, not a two-sortedness of predicates.

### III. SECOND-PERSON PRACTITIONS: PRESCRIPTIONS

Consider a transaction between Jones and Francis. The latter wants or would like the former to visit Mary, and depending on their relationships and circumstances she may order Jones:

(3)    Jones, visit Mary today. (This is an order.)

Or she may request him to do it:

(4)    Jones, please visit Mary today.

Or she may advise him:

(5)    Jones, you better visit Mary today.

Or she may entreat him, or beg him to visit Mary. I say that in all such cases Francis would articulate or express a *mandate*. In these cases the mandates Francis would express are different, and she would of course perform different speech acts; but in all of those speech acts she would be putting forward a common thought content at the core of all those mandates. We may call it a *demand*, or a *prescription*. It is, like a proposition, a subject-predicate type of content. Its subject and its predicate are precisely the same as those of the performance proposition,

(6)    You (=Jones) will visit Mary today.

But it is not the same as this proposition. While the proposition is true or false, neither the prescription nor the mandates containing it are true or false. I propose to use the infinitive construction as canonical notation for prescriptions. In our example, then, the prescription common to the above mandates is:

(7)      You (=Jones) to vist Mary today.

As I have argued elsewhere, the differences in grammatical person are ultimate and irreducible.[6] Thus, (7) is a second-person thought content, and I propose to recognize it as a distinct thought content from the third-person prescription

(8)      Jones to visit Mary today.

A mandate is a prescription embellished with a pragmatic character. The word 'please' in (2) is an operator expressing the request character of the mandate in question. But the word 'please' is not a logical operator in the sense that it affects the implications of the prescriptions expressed by the imperative sentences it applies to. Often the pragmatic character of mandates is expressed by performative operators, like 'This is an order (command, request, entreaty, petition, piece of advice, exhortation, suggestion)' and 'I am hereby ordering (commanding, requesting, etc.) you'. These might be called *Austin* operators, given that the late John L. Austin created the study of performative utterances in great scale. But care must be taken *not* to endorse Austin's strange view that the performative use of such operators precluded the sentences containing them from expressing propositions. Obviously there is no reason why sentence (9) below may not express both a statement and a command:

(9)      I am hereby commanding you to visit Mary today.

A very important fact to keep in mind is that, as part of the master unity of thinking, prescriptions and propositions combine into complex thought contents. But there is a psycho-biological primacy of the practical use of reason over the latter's purely contemplative uses. This is, of course, part and parcel of the survival value of reason. In consonance with this primacy, the mixed compounds of propositions and prescriptions are prescriptions. This is illustrated by examples like

(10)      Benson and Wilfrid, please do the following:
          (a) if Van comes, Benson *put him up in the mahogony room,*
              and if Ruth comes, Wilfrid *give her the blue room.*

In (10), clearly, the 'if'-clauses express propositions, while the italicized ones express prescriptions, and the whole of (a) expresses a prescription. In general,

(P.1)    The psycho-biological primacy of practical over pure reason is manifested in the logical dominance of prescriptionhood over propositionhood in the case of the so-called propositional connectives.

Examples like (10) show again that neither mandates nor prescriptions are propositions. Even if a prescription is the result of an operation on the corresponding performance proposition, a prescription is not a proposition. This raises the question as to what exactly is a prescription. It would be easy to take a prescription like *John to go home* to be the result of an operator $\pi$ on the proposition *John will go home* and then apply a fashionable possible-world formal semantics to $\pi$. But I do not believe that that is the philosophically illuminating approach. It is not clear to me that imperativity or prescriptivity is a modal operator involving more than one world. It is an operator that applies, as (10) shows, to primary propositions only, since compound prescriptions are prescriptions by virtue of their component prescriptions. The problem of elucidating prescriptivity is very serious. Yet the elucidation is not to come from a set-theoretical machinery, but from the way prescriptivity connects with action.

In order to build the basic logical structure of the contents of practical thinking we consider basic prescriptivity as a copula relating in an atomic prescription the agent subject to the action predicate in a way different from the one in which they are related in the corresponding performance proposition. That is, the operator $\pi$ reduces at last temporarily to a copula. For example,

(11)    Carl, read Carnap's *Meaning and Necessity*

contrasts with

(12)    Carl will read Carnap's *Meaning and Necessity*

in that (11) is

(11a)    Read [Carl, Carnap's *Meaning and Necessity*]

whereas (12) is

(12a)    Read (Carl, Carnap's *Meaning and Necessity*).

The truth-valued nature of proposition (12) is signaled by the copulative parentheses which express the propositional copula. The non-truth-valued nature of prescription (11) is similarly signaled by the square brackets, which signal the prescriptional, i.e., the practitional copula.

Alternatively, we can consider prescriptivity $\pi$ to be either an operator on the copula or an operator on predicates. On the former view the copula "[ ]" is the complex copula "$\pi(\ )$," thus indicating the ontological primacy of propositions, over practitions, i.e., of pure over practical reason. On the view that $\pi$ is an operator on predicates, we would analyze the prescription *John to go* as *John is $\pi$ (go)* or *John $\pi$ (goes)*. This view is convenient for developing set-theoretical models for imperatives. We can treat imperative logic as involving two sorts of predicates: the contemplative and the practical ones. The nonformal semantical problem of $\pi$ is, as we pointed out in Section II, the one of elucidating the way $\pi$ connects thinking and action.

## IV. FIRST-PERSON PRACTITIONS: INTENTIONS

We call the thought contents of intending and deciding *intentions*. As we pointed out in Section II above, *intentions are not propositions*. Yet this is a thesis that many philosophers find difficult.[7] I have argued in detail for this thesis elsewhere,[8] and I can be brief here. There is already evidence for that thesis in Section II above. The fact that intentions are the first-person counterpart of prescriptions makes the evidence for the duality proposition-prescription relevant to the contrast proposition-intention. Let us discuss some additional support for this thesis.

Consider the case of Nelson who has made two related decisions as follows, in his own words:

(13)    *I shall visit David next week,* if the Manager approves my leave;
(14)    *I shall visit David's brother next week,* if and only if I visit David next week.

In both (13) and (14) we find a duality of elements, which must be accounted for by any adequate theory of intentions. Clearly, the 'if'-clauses express circumstances that are conditions for the intentions expressed by the 'shall'-clauses. The conditions are true or false, and if true they create urgency of the consequent decisions. This is, of course, nothing but the duality discussed in Section II between what belongs to a Future Framework and what belongs to the corresponding Future Zone of Indeterminacy. For me that is sufficient to establish the need to differentiate intentions from propositions.

In (13) the primary intention or decision is *I (=Nelson) shall visit David next week*. In (14) the condition, both sufficient and necessary for Nelson's primary intention to visit David's brother is the proposition *I (=Nelson) (will) visit David next week*. It is obvious that intentions (13) and (14) do not imply Nelson's intention

(15)     I shall visit David's brother next week, if the Manager approves my leave.

Patently, (14) presents the visit to David's brother depending on Nelson's *actually* visiting David. It is true, by (13), that he intends to visit David, but there is always a causal gap between any person's states of intending and his actions. Such gaps have to do with the indeterminacy of the Future Zone of Indeterminacy. And such are precisely the gaps that prevent the flow of implication. We can see this formally. Precisely because of the gap between intending and doing, (13) and (14) are together compatible with the propositions

(16)     The Manager approves Nelson's leave

and

(17)     Nelson won't visit David next week.

Now, if intentions were the same as their corresponding performance propositions, both (i) the pair (13)–(14) would imply (15), and (ii) the quartet {(13), (14), (16), (17)} would be self-contradictory. For then the clause 'I visit David next week' in (14) and the clause 'I shall visit David next week' in (13) would express the same thought content, the same proposition. Then by trivial deductions we establish (i) and (ii).

To focus sharply on the present thesis, namely, that an intention is not identical with its corresponding future-tense performance proposition, I note that biconditional intentions of the following form are *not* all tautological:

(18)     I shall *A*, if and only if I *A*.

By positing the material equivalence (in a generalized sense) of the intention to its corresponding performance proposition, a compound intention of form (18) reveals something non-tautological, namely, that whatever the agent will do concerning action *A* will be intentional, *not* a mere happening. Consider, for instance, the case of a person subjected to certain electric tests that cause him to act, and at some juncture he declares his intention 'I shall jump, if and only if I jump.' (Of course, this sentence can be used by a person to make a tautological prediction.)

As in the case of prescriptions, compounds of intentions and propositions are intentions. This law is illustrated by (13) and (14) above.

Additional evidence for the difference between propositions and practitions appear in the different behavior of, on the one hand, infinitive and subjunctive clauses, and, on the other hand, indicative clauses in the scope of verbs of intention, like 'I intend', 'I have decided', 'I aim' and 'I want'. Consider, for instance,

(19)    I intend (have decided) to do the following this evening: *to discuss Myrna's problems with her* if she calls up or comes and is in the proper state of mind, and *to consult with Roger* if and only if I discuss Myrna's problems with her.

The italicized infinitive clauses express intentions; the other clauses express conditions, and the whole compound subordinated clause expresses an intention. I have elsewhere[9] pointed out how a counterpart of the deontic Good-Samaritan "paradox" can be developed for intending on parallel assumptions usually made in deontic logic, including the one-sortedness of the logic of deontic and intending operators.

In the non-first person subjunctive or infinitive constructions like

(20)    I intend that *Peter go,*
(21)    I want *Peter to go,*

the italicized subordinate clauses do not express intentions, but prescriptions — practitions in any case.


## V. DEONTIC JUDGMENTS

By *deontic or normative judgment* I mean the full thought content normally expressed when a person says something like

(J2)    It is *morally* **obligatory** that John keep his promise to Smith;
(J3)    Someone in the Philosophy Department **must,** *by the University rules on Commencements,* attend the May commencement.
(J4)    It is **required,** *by the Bank rules*, that employees enter by the North door.
(J5)    The Goodmans are **bound,** *by their agreement with the Pierces,* to deliver the latter's manuscript to the Museum.
(J6)    I **must** go!
(J7)    John **ought,** *everything relevant being considered*, to concentrate either on his political career or on his law office.

These examples and many more like them reveal a bewildering multiplicity and complexity of deontic judgments, which any adequate comprehensive deontic logic must take into account. To start with, there are many deontic expressions, like those in boldface in (J2)–(J7), each with different suggestions. For convenience we shall adopt the italicized word '*obligatory*' or '*ought*' as a technical term to represent the common deontic concept they express. Part of the different suggestions the different ordinary deontic expressions connote is that:

(N.1)    Deontic judgments belong in families: they have a systemic nature.

In the above examples the italicized *adverbial expressions* indicate the family. In all these cases the family appears to determine a network of reasons or *grounds* of obligation or requiredness. In some cases they point to some event of *endorsement* or acceptance of the family of deontic judgments. Clearly the University regulations or the Bank rules create requirements or obligations only for those persons who have accepted membership in the University or Bank personnel. The same is true of promises and agreements, as in (J5) and partially in (J2). There is a legend in certain philosophical circles that moral duties are binding on a person, regardless of whether he accepts them or not. We will not examine this legend or its basis on this occasion. In any case,

(N.2)    Each normative or deontic family determines a type of requiredness or obligatoriness, which depends for its actual applying to a domain of agents on some specific grounds or reasons and the endorsement by the agents in question.

(N.3)    In ordinary language a normative family is indicated by an adverbial phrase to be called a *qualifier*. Each family is determined, we shall say for convenience, by an *ought* and a *qualification*.

We must comment briefly on (J6) and (J7), however. Evidently, (J6) expresses a deontic judgment that is *assumed* as a matter of fact, so to speak, to override, or have overriden, all considerations against it as well as all contrary requirements. On the other hand, (J7) explicitly asserts that it is overriding all considerations opposed to it. I theorize that the 'must' of (J6) and the 'ought' of (J7) express the same type of requiredness, which I will call the *overriding oughtness*. The difference in the vocabulary of sentences (J6) and (J7) has to do with a difference in the context of utterance and thought. Normally, sentence (J6) expresses a judgment thought outside a conflict of requirements; even if it follows a deliberation, it is expressed after the deliberation has been finished and the conflict is over. On the other hand, the vocabulary of sentence (J7) indicates that judgment (J7) is involved in a conflict of duties; it may be asserted firmly in the midst of the conflict, or at the very end as an outcome of a deliberation and is still covered with the dust raised by the conflict of duties. In short,

(N.4)     Among the normative families is the special family of the *overriding ought* (or *must*). This connects directly with action and is expressed with the help of no qualifiers or with qualifiers like 'everything (relevant) being considered', 'overridingly' or 'above everything else'.

The above examples (J2)–(J7) are of the strong, demanding *ought*-type. There is also the *wrong*-type expressed with locutions like 'It is wrong (unlawful, forbidden, prohibited, etc.) that Jones go', the *may*- or *right*-type expressed with locutions like 'it is right to (that)' in the sense in which it is right to do what is obligatory, and the *optional*-type. But we shall concentrate on the *ought*-type on the grounds that:

(N.4)     It is *Qly wrong* for $X$ to $A =$ It is *Qly obligatory* for $X$ not to $A$.
(N.5)     It is *Qly right* for $X$ to $A =$ It is not *Qly obligatory* for $X$ to $A$.
(N.6)     It is *Qly optional* for $X$ to $A =$ It is neither *Qly obligatory* for $X$ to $A$ nor *Qly* obligatory not to $A$.

Here also the italicized words are our technical generalized deontic terms. The adverb schema '*Qly*' is a place holder for the qualifiers signaling deontic families.

General deontic logic is the logic of the deontic schema $X$ ought *Qly* to $A$ and the ones introduced by (N.4)–(N.6). For convenience, as I have done for over twenty years, I will write '*ought*$_i$' where the subscript 'i' is the qualifier slot.

The *Theory of Morality*, or moral philosophy proper, is primarily the theory of the adverb 'morally', which I have treated in detail in *The Structure of Morality*. The *Theory of law*, or philosophy of law, is primarily the theory of the adverb 'legally' in the slot 'i' in '*ought*$_i$' In general, the specific theory of any institution $N$ is the theory of an adverb family $N$ that determines a family of normative systems involving some types or types of *ought*-ness. I say family because an institution may be abstractly conceived as a system of normative systems. This is undoubtedly the case with the institution called the Law of a given country. It is the case also with morality, which is composed of several theories and three normative systems. Thus, as I have explained elsewhere,[10] the basic schema of a moral norm is '$X$ ought morally$_j$ to do $A$', where 'j' is a further adverb signaling a specific normativity.

The specific theory of an institution is the theory of a family of normative adverbs in that it is the theory of the truth-conditions of deontic judgments involving the qualifications expressed by the adverbs in question. Deontic logic deals with the general implication principles determined only by both the deontic concepts and the other logical concepts they interact with. Such implication principles demarcate the framework within which the special theories of institutions establish the truth conditions they study. Here we are dealing, then, with the logical foundations of *any* theory of any institution, especially, morality and the law.

Another of my main deontic theses is this:

(N*)      Deontic concepts are operators that apply to practitions and yield propositions.

Among the reasons for holding that deontic judgments are propositions are the following:

(A)      Deontic judgments are naturally said to be true or false, e.g., "It is true that one ought morally to avoid causing pain just for the enjoyment of the contemplation of pain behavior" and "It is false that one ought in accordance with the traffic regulations to turn left when facing a red light in normal circumstances."

(B)      Some deontic judgments have very clear and well delineated truth conditions. For instance, if the law makers enact a piece of legislation in compliance with the standard procedures prescribed in the books, then the citizens of the country in question *ought* legally$_L$ to do what $L$ says. Likewise, persons can and do easily make promises, which are mini-institutions with their own *ought*nesses.

(C)      Deontic judgments are characteristically said to be believed (or disbelieved), known (or unknown), conjectured, assumed, and in general, $X$-ed for all propositional attitudes of $X$ing — all of which are oriented toward truth.

(D)      Deontic judgments are said to be probably true or unlikely true.

(E)      Deontic judgments allow of modification by alethic modalities, e.g., "It is not logically necessary that one *ought* morally to keep one's promises" and "It is only contingently the case that one ought morally to pay income taxes."

(A)–(E) are powerful linguistic data that must be satisfied by a theory of deontic thinking. And I believe that the simplest theory is the subview, included in (N*), that deontic judgments are propositions. Naturally, this view must be complemented with an account of deontic truth-values, and I do not mean a set-theoretical account, which can only provide a formal model for their truth structure, whatever their truth may actually be. The modeling is, of course, alright. We can use it to illuminate the formal structure, but we must still have a *contentual* account of deontic truth. We cannot do this here, which we have in any case developed elsewhere.[11]

Among the data supporting the other half of (N*), namely, that the operands of deontic judgments are practitions, like the following:

(a)      In the scope of deontic operators producing complex judgments are two types of components. The components of one type behave like propositions or propositional functions. The other components are the focus of the deontic operators.

An example of (a) is this:

(23)     Roderick $ought_U$ [i.e., in accordance with the University rules U] to do the following: wear academic regalia if *he attends the May commencement*, and inform the Office of Ceremonies if *he intends to attend the May commencement*.

Very palpably, the italicized if-clauses express truth-valued, i.e., propositional components of what is in the scope of the qualified $ought_U$. The other components are clearly the focus of $ought_U$ness.

(b)      The focus of deontic operators are expressed with infinitive or subjunctive clauses, just as we have seen practitions are expressed.

Let us be clear on one point. The data in (a) and (b) definitely establish that there *is* a duality of components in some complex deontic judgments like (23). This is beyond dispute, and deontic logics that are not two-sorted either are very elementary, or are inadequate. That the duality in the scope of deontic judgments like (23) is *identical* with the proposition-practition duality studied in the preceding sections is a theoretical thesis. As such it is not a conclusion of a deductive argument, but must be supported dialectically by the relevant data. I claim that this identity theory is of great simplicity and explanatory power. But let us consider more data.

(c)      The internal duality of components of deontic judgments like (23) is further supported by the so-called Good-Samaritan paradox, the contrary-to-duty paradox, and the tense paradox, neither of which will be discussed here.[12]

The operands as wholes, or the focus in the operands, of deontic operators are not propositions. This is supported by data like the following, besides (b) and (c):

(d)    Deontic operators are not literally iterative. For instance, 'It is obligatory that John is obliged (ought) to do $A$' is a non-sensical sentence. In general, if $D^1(A)$ is a deontic judgment with operator $D^1$, then there is *no* deontic judgment of the form $D^2(D^1(A))$ for any deontic operator $D^2$.

There are non-literal or *apparent* iterations, like

(24)    It is morally obligatory that it *be* legally obligatory that nobody be sentenced to punishment without a fair trial

Here, as the italicized subjunctive 'be' signals, we are not dealing with the proposition

(25)    It is legally obligatory that nobody be sentenced to punishment without a fair trial.

Judgment (24) is addressed to legislators demanding of them the creation of the proper legislation. That is, (24) is the same as

(24a)    It *is* morally obligatory that in every society someone who has the authority make it that it be legally obligatory that nobody be sentenced to punishment without a fair trial.

The form of (24a) is $D^2(A^2)$, where $A^2$ is not of the form $D^1(A)$, but of the form $o(D^1(A))$, o being an operator forming the proper (subjunctive) operand for deontic operators out of the deontic judgment (25). On my view operator o is an operator that yields a practition out of (24) — being then an operator operating in the diametrically opposed direction in which deontic operators operate. In (24a) o is the operator '$x$ makes it that'.

(e)    The propositional components of complex deontic judgments like (23) can in many cases be taken out of the scope of the deontic operators constituting the judgment in question.

A little reflection shows that (23) is equivalent to:

(26)    If he attends the May Commencement, Roderick *ought$_U$* to wear academic regalia, and if he intends to attend the commencement he *ought$_U$* to inform the Office of Ceremonies.

Evidently *ought*$_U$ cannot let the non-propositions components *to wear* ... and *to attend* ... to escape its scope.

(f)      Propositional functions also behave in the scope of deontic operators propositionally.

An example of (f) is this:

(27)      It is *obligatory*$_i$ that someone who got a prize last year present the prizes to this year's winners.

Clearly, (27) implies

(28)      Someone got a prize last year,

but it implies neither

(29)      It is *obligatory*$_i$ that someone got a prize last year.

nor

(30)      Someone will present a prize to a winner this year.

(g)      Deontic operators are extensional with respect to propositional components.[13] That is the following implication schema holds:

(N.7)      'a *ought*$_i$ to do $A(B)$,

a = c, and

b = d'

implies 'c *ought*$_i$ to do $A$(b/d)', where $A$(b) has b occurring only in extensional positions and $A$(b/d) results from $A$(b) by replacing some occurrences of b with occurrences of d.

Since identity is a propositional relation, because it is an ontological one, it is never, by (e) and (f), essentially in the scope of a deontic operator. Thus, by (N.7) we have:

(N.8)      'It is *obligatory* that someone who alone is $F$ do $A$' is equivalent to 'Someone who alone is $F$ is *obliged* to do $A$.'

Examples of (N.8) are easy to come by. Here is one implication pair:

(31)      It is required$_U$ that someone who is the only professor of Classics attend the May Commencement.

(32)      There is just one professor of Classics and he is required$_U$ to attend the May Commencement.

There are more data. However, (a)–(g) suffice to establish the need of a two-sorted deontic logic. This I will do subsequently. But before I proceed to formulate my favorite system of deontic logic I want to discuss one celebrated example that has been adduced in support of a so-called dyadic or conditional deontic logic.

Here is Powers' famous Susy Mae example.

, (33)    John Doe has impregnated Susy Mae; so, he ought to marry her. But John kills Susy Mae and then it is not the case that he ought to marry her.[14]

Powers uses his example to refute, correctly in my opinion, a solution to the Good-Samaritan paradox offered by Aqvist,[15] and he embellishes it accordingly. Stripped to formulation (33) the example has been used by Van Fraassen to argue that a monadic deontic logic is inadequate, thus claiming support from it for a "conditional" deontic logic.[16] Van Fraassen argues that (33) shows that the schema (34) is false:

(34)    "If p, then it is obligatory that $A$" implies "If p and q, then it is obligatory that $A$."

I find the situation more complicated. First, it has been too quickly assumed that John Doe's killing Susy Mae automatically cancels his obligation to marry her — if he has one to start with. It is not out of order to suppose that some laws that demand marriage upon impregnation continue to require that the marriage be consummated with the dead Susy Mae, so that she goes away without the capital sin in question. The situation I am considering is in substance not different from the American practice of promoting George Washington posthumously to whatever may be the highest rank in the American Army, the latest one being to the rank of a five-star general when this rank was created during World War II. Note also that Susy Mae must be unmarried, unless we allow polyandria. It may be said that this quibbling is irrelevant, so that as long as *some* laws do not require John to marry a dead Susy, Van Fraassen's point holds. But what is Van Fraassen's point? That (34) fails. But this is not what the example establishes. The example with my commentary establishes that

(N.9)    Different normative systems may have different conditions for the "cancellation" of obligations.

Now the question is: How are we to represent (N.9) in general deontic logic? Undoubtedly, Van Fraassen's claim that (34) is false is one way. It has the prestige of having deontic logic converge with interesting systems for the logic of conditionals formulated by other philosophers.[17] Besides, so-called conditional logic solves the Good-Samaritan paradox. It also has certain parallelisms with the logic of causality.

Yet I remain unpersuaded. The denial of (34) is a negative solution that looks like overkill and also blurs some crucial distinctions. For one thing, it tampers with the extensionality of deontic operators. Secondly, the denial of (34) leaves unaccounted the fact that only in *very* few cases we *seem* to have the situation of an obligation cancelled by the addition of another circumstance. That is, the denial of (34) is a drastic reaction to the exceptional cases. Just consider that if John Doe ought to marry Susy Mae because he got her pregnant, then he ought to marry her if all sorts of things happen, or fail to happen, e.g., whether it rains, hails, etc., or not. So that for practically anything you can think of (34) holds obviously. *This too has to be explained.*

In any case, the evidence (a)–(g) just deployed together with the duality practition-proposition discussed in the preceding sections, establishes that we must distinguish between *circumstances*, which need not be obligations, that are necessary (or sufficient) conditions for obligations, and obligations that are conditions (necessary or sufficient) for other obligations. Thus, we cannot accept Van Fraassen's guiding principle below if we want a deontic logic that illuminates more than the simplest deontic implications:

> As a further criterion [Van Fraassen says], I propose that if something is a necessary *condition* of discharging an obligation then it is itself an obligation, given the same *conditions*.[18]
> [My italics.]

The notion of condition involved here perplexes me somewhat.

The so-called conditional deontic approach recognizes a duality of components in the scope of deontic judgment. A judgment like *If (given that) John Doe impregnated Susy Mae John Doe ought to marry Susy Mae* is taken by the "conditional" approach as having the connective 'if (given that) — ought' which treats the components *John Doe impregnated Susy Mae* and *John Doe marries Susy Mae* very differently. While I commend this duality of roles, I find it too limited to do justice to the duality of circumstances and focuses of obligations established above. The pervasiveness of the latter duality demands full recognition. Also it ignores (N.1) above.

The "conditional" approach recognizes also the relativity of duties or requirements to certain grounds or reasons. Again, this pleases me, but I am unhappy with the approach because it fuses several relativities and it fails to recognize a very crucial aspect of duties and requirements. Duties are relative to circumstances, and this relativity yields genuine conditional or disjunctive duties. Duties are also relative to acts or processes of endorsement, and, hence, to the reasons for such endorsements. *But this is an entirely different matter.* Here we do not have conditional duties, but the adverbial qualifications I have for over two decades been representing by means of the subscripts attached to deontic words. The standard "conditional" approach to the logic of deontic judgments (as contrasted with the study of uninterpreted mathematical formalisms called deontic calculi or deontic logics) does not distinguish this. In fact the examples often given, like "If John impregnated Susy, he ought to marry her", do not have a "condition" in the sense of the "conditional" approach. Note for instance that it is governed by transposition: "Only if John didn't impregnate Susy, is it not the case that he ought to marry her" is equivalent to it. It also implies "(Either) John didn't impregnate Susy Mae, or he ought to marry her." That 'if' looks very much like a material-implication 'if'. In general, since rules and norms are for the most part arbitrary stipulations, there is *no* relevant or logical connection between conditions of obligation and obligatory actions. More than that: the assumed freedom of practical thinking, which is presupposed in the creation of normative systems and in-stitutions, suggests very strongly, in one general stroke, that the con-ditionality of rules and norms is an arbitrary and stipulative conditionality, which can be fully grounded on the unrestricted conditionality of *material implication.* Normative "necessity" is to a large extent stipulative. And this is the profound rationale for the extensionality of the deontic operators. Thus, the "conditional" approach to deontic logic, which treats *ought*-ness as a form of alethic or intensional necessity seems *ab initio* to be proceeding in the wrong direction. The "conditional" approach ignores the crucial aspect of deontic judgments of belonging into systems. But, as noted, this belonging is not a connective linking two propositions. Each system is an arrangement from a certain point of view, as described briefly in Section II above, of *all* propositions and *all* practitions.[19]

In consonance with all the previous findings about practical thinking I submit, then, that.

(N.9)     Each deontic operator $D_i$ is paired with a set $C_i$ of necessary conditions for *ought*-ness.

Thus, *in* the normative system j that Powers and Van Fraassen are considering, where nobody marries dead people,

(33a)     At time t John Doe impregnated Susy Mae, and at time t (and later at $t_1$) John Doe *ought*$_j$ to marry Susy Mae *only if* Susy Mae is alive at t (or $t_1$).

I am accepting a truly conditional solution to Powers' problem, which allows (34) to explain the normal unproblematic cases. Hence,

(N.10)   Deontic operators are governed by (34).

The analogy between causality and obligation deserve a comment. It seems to me that the analogy actually goes the other way. Causality in science is a very obscure concept, and many conditions are left unspecified, so that the denial of (34) seems tempting. We tend to think of a general concept of causality. In the case of obligation, on the other hand, we deal with the different specific obligatorinesses of the varied specific normative systems. In such systems things need be specified and *are* specified arbitrarily. Especially in criminal law and in serious matters we want clearcut lines of responsibility. Thus, given our conception of ourselves and the world we fix conditions that are required for obligatoriness to hold. Since in many cases we depend on the causal participation of an agent, we have in fact impregnated the notion of cause with normative seeds. When we speak of causality in the abstract, independently of a set of normative considerations we are dealing with the schematic concept that is too anemic to provide a healthy model for deontic logic.

The preceding does not, of course, imply that the obligatoriness — 'cancellation' conditions $C_i$ of a normative system $N_i$ are always very simple and fully spelled out in some typescript publicly available and easy to read. In the very important case of a legal system there are wholly appropriate provisions that establish a fixed and clear procedure for determining the pervasive necessary conditions $C_L$ of a given obligatoriness$_L$, without the procedure specifying in advance what they are. For instance, judges or certain specified officers have as one of their primary roles to determine some of the conditions $C_L$ of obligatoriness$_L$. But the law, or the statutes of an institution, make the procedure final at a certain point. Obviously, there is no such finality in the abstract general conception of causality. And the law of the land and the by-laws of institutions are more efficient by having both an open-ended set $C_L$ of necessary conditions of obligatoriness$_L$ *and* a precise procedure for determining with finality certain elements of $C_L$. They can cope with changes in circumstances. Here is a very important phenomenon that the "conditional" approach leaves out.

## VI. A COMPREHENSIVE BASIC SYSTEM OF DEONTIC LOGIC

We proceed now to formulate a system of deontic logic that conforms to all the data and generalizations of data collected in the previous sections.

## A. Basic Deontic Languages

We start by constructing a large number of such syntactical structures, one for each qualified obligatoriness and one for the overriding ought. These languages will be called $D_i^*$, for $i = 1, 2, 3, \ldots$, where $D_1^*$ is the language of the pure overriding ought.

*Primitive signs:* Individual constants; individual variables; predicate constants; the connectives '$\sim$' and '&' expressing negation ('it is not the case') and logical conjunction ('and', 'but', 'although',), respectively; the square brackets '[' and ']' which paired constitute the sign of prescriptive copulation; the sign '$O_i$' of oughtness$_i$ or obligatoriness$_i$; the identity sign '=', and the parentheses '(' and ')', which are both signs of grouping as well as of propositional copulation.

*Rules of Formation:* We use Quine's corners implicitly throughout. Let the small letters 'p', 'q', 'r', range over *indicatives* (i.e., expressions of propositions or propositional functions); let the capital letters '$A$' and '$B$' range over *practitives* (i.e., expressions of practitions or practitional functions); let 'p*' and 'q*' range over both indicatives and practitives; let '$C$' range over predicates and 'x' and 'y' with subscripts or not range over individual variables, unless otherwise specified.

(a)    The Indicatives of $D_i^*$ are the sequences of signs of $D_i^*$ having one of the forms:

1. $C(x_1, \ldots, x_n)$, where $C$ is an n-adic predicate and each $x_i$ is an individual constant or variable;

2. $(\sim p)$;        3. $(p \,\&\, q)$;

4. $((x)p)$;        5. $(O_i A)$;

6. $(x_i = x_j)$, where each of $x_i$ and $x_j$ is an individual constant or an individual variable.

(b)    *Practitives* or *imperative-resolutives* of $D_i^*$ are the sequences of signs of $D_i^*$ having one of the following forms:

1. $C[x_1, \ldots, x_n]$, where $C$ is an n-adic predicate, each $x_i$ is an individual variable or constant;

2. $(\sim B)$;        3. $(p \,\&\, B)$;

4. $(B \,\&\, p)$;       5. $(B \,\&\, A)$;

6. $((x)B)$.

(c)    The Indicatives and the practitives of $D_i^*$ are all the wffs of $D_i^*$.

*Definitions.* We adopt the usual definitions of 'bound variable' and the definitions of the other connectives and the existential quantifier but we generalize them so as to cover practitives. The occurrence of an individual variable x in a wff p* is *bound* in p* if and only if it is an occurrence in a wff which is a part of p* and is of the form (x)q*. An occurrence of an individual variable x in a wff p* is *free* if and only if it is not bound in p*. The *bound* [free] *variables* of a wff p* are the variables which have bound [free] occurrences in p*.

Def. 1.    $(p* \lor q*) = (\sim((\sim p*) \mathbin{\&} (\sim q*)))$
Def. 2.    $(p* \supset q*) = (\sim(p* \mathbin{\&} (\sim q*)))$
Def. 3.    $(p* \equiv q*) = ((p* \mathbin{\&} q*) \lor ((\sim p*) \mathbin{\&} (\sim q*)))$
Def. 4.    $((\exists x)p*) = (\sim((x)(\sim p*)))$

We introduce the following deontic definitions:

Def. 11.   $(P_i A) = (\sim(O_i(\sim A)))$
           It is permitted$_i$ that $A$ if and only if it is not obligatory$_i$ that not-$A$.
Def. 12.   $(W_i A) = (O_i(\sim A))$
           It is wrong$_i$ that $A$ if and only if it is obligatory$_i$ that not-$A$.
Def. 13.   $(L_i A) = ((\sim(O_i(\sim A))) \mathbin{\&} (\sim(O_i A)))$
           It is optional$_i$ (or there is a liberty$_i$ that $A$) if and only if neither is it obligatory$_i$ that not-$A$ nor is it obligatory$_i$ that $A$.

We adopt the standard conventions on parentheses:

(1) we drop the pair of outermost parentheses of each wff; (2) we associate chains of conjunctions or disjunctions, to the left: e.g. $p* \lor q* \lor r*$ stands for $(p* \lor q*) \lor r*$; (3) we rank the connectives in the following order of increasing scope or bindingness: deontic operators and quantifiers; $\sim$; $\mathbin{\&}$; $\lor$; $\supset$; $\equiv$. Thus, for example, Def. 1, 3, and 13 can be simplified to:

Def. 1.    $p* \lor q* = \sim(\sim p* \mathbin{\&} \sim q*)$
Def. 3.    $p* \equiv q* = p* \mathbin{\&} q* \lor \sim p* \mathbin{\&} \sim q*$
Def. 12.   $L_i A = \sim O_i \sim A \mathbin{\&} \sim O_i A$

The desired interpretation for each language $D_i*$ is this: (1) indicatives should express propositions; (2) practitives should express practitions; (3) predicates should express properties or conditions. Patently, each language $D_i*$ satisfies some crucial data: (i) the difference between atomic propositions and corresponding atomic practitions is represented by the difference between the two expressions of copulation: '(. . .)' and '[. . .]'; (ii) deontic judgments are represented as propositions; (iii) mixed indicative-practitive compounds are practitive; (iv) the deontic operators expressed by

'$O_i$', '$P_i$', '$W_i$' and '$L_i$' apply to practitions, not to propositions; (v) there are no iterations of deontic operators.

The part of each language $D_i^*$ that includes neither quantifiers nor identity will be called $D_i^{c*}$. That is, $D_i^{c*}$ is $D_i^*$ without the wffs determined by rules (a)4, (a)6, or (b)6.

### B. The axiomatic systems $D_i^{**}$

We build on each deontic language $D_i^*$ an axiomatic system $D_i^{**}$, which is constituted by the axioms and rules of derivation enunciated below. We shall take advantage of the above definitions and conventions on parentheses. We shall also use the following convention. Let $X$ be a wff. Then an expression of the form '$X(a|b)$' stands for any wff resulting from $X$ by replacing some occurrences of a in $X$ with occurrences of b, where all occurrences in question of a or b (or both) are free if a or b (or both) are variables. $X(a||b)$ is the wff $X(a|b)$ that results when *all* occurrences of (free) a in $X$ are replaced with (free) occurrences of b.

*Axioms.* The axioms of $D_i^{**}$ are all and only the wffs of $D_i^*$ that have at least one of the following forms:

A0.  $O_i A \supset C_i$, where $C_i$ is the conjunction of the necessary or 'cancellation' conditions of *ought$_i$*-ness.

A1.  p*, if p* has the form of a truth-table tautology.

A11.  $O_i A \supset {\sim} O_i {\sim} A$

A11a.  $O_i A \supset A$     *Note*: A11a replaces A11 in the system $O_1(D_1^{**})$ for the overriding *ought$_1$*.

A111.  $(x)p^* \supset p^* (x||y)$

A1111.  $(\exists y)(x = y)$

We adopt the standard definitions of 'proof' and 'theorem':

1. A *proof* of $D_i^{**}$ is a sequence of wffs of $D_i^*$ such that each member of it is either (i) an axiom of $D_i^{**}$ or (ii) a wff derivable from previous members of the sequence by one application of the derivation rules R1, R11, or R111 of $D_i^{**}$, formulated below.

2. A theorem of $D_i^{**}$ is the last member of a proof of $D_i^{**}$. We write '$\vdash_i X$' to abbreviate '$X$ is a theorem of $D_i^{**}$'. We write '$\vdash_{i \text{-} a} X$' as short for '$X$ is a theorem of $D_i^{**}$ provable without axiom A11a'.

3. $p_1^*, p_2^*, \ldots, p_n^* \vdash_i q^*$, if and only if $\vdash_i p_1^* \& p_2^* \& \ldots \& p_n^* \supset q^*$.

*Rules of Derivation.* The rules of derivation of $D_i^{**}$ are:

R1.     *Modus ponens:* From p* and p* $\supset$ q*, derive q*.

R11.   OG: If $\vdash_{i-a} (p \& A, \& \ldots \& A_n \supset B)$, then $\vdash_i (x) (p \& O_i$
$A_1 \& \ldots \& O_i A_n) \supset O_i(x) B \& (x) O_i B$, where $n \geqslant 0$.

R111.  UG: If $\vdash_i p^* \supset q^*$, then $\vdash_i p^* \supset (x)q^*$, provided that $p^*$ has no
free occurrences of x.

R1111. ID: If $\vdash_i p^* \supset q^*$, then $\vdash_i x = y \supset (p^* \supset q^* (x|y))$

The axioms and the rules are labeled so that each pair $\{A_m, R_m\}$
characterizes one layer of implication:

1.      $\{A_1, R_1\}$ is the propositional calculus
        generalized to all practitions.

2.  $\{A_1, A_{11}, R_1, R'_{11}\}$, where R'11 is R11 without quantifiers, is the
basic propositional-practitional deontic calculus.

3.  $\{A_1, A_{111}, R_1, R_{111}\}$ is the calculus of quantification generalized to
practitions.

4.  R11 is restricted to theorems not depending on A11a in order to allow
the basic logic of conflicts of duties to be represented by the union of
deontic calculi $D_i^{**}$.

## VII. THE EXTENSIONALITY OF $D_i^{**}$

*It is an easy exercise that $D_i^{**}$* conforms to the criteria of adequacy
gathered in Sections I–V. We leave that exercise to the reader, except for
the proof that $D_i^{**}$ satisfies (N.8) of Section V.

THEOREM.   $O(\exists x)((y)(p(y) \supset x = y) \& p(y\|x) \& B(x)) \equiv (\exists x)((y)(p(y) \supset$
$x = y) \& p(y\|x) \& OB(x))$

*Proof.* I will use 'PC' to signal a set of applications of A1 and R1. The
sign '$\vdash$' is deleted before each formula for convenience. We take variables x
and z that do not occur free in $p(y)$, so that $p(y\|x\|z)$ is $p(y\|z)$.

1.   $(y)(p(y) \supset x = y) \supset (p(y\|z) \supset x = z)$                     A111

2.   $((y)(p(y) \supset x = y) \& p(y\|x) \& B(x)) \supset (p(y\|z) \supset$
     $x = z)$                                                              1;PC

3.   $((y)(p(y) \supset x = y) \& p(y\|x) \& B(x)) \supset ((y)(p(y) \supset$
     $x = y) \& p(y\|x) \& B(x))$                                           A1

4.   $x = z \supset ((y)(p(y) \supset x = y) \& p(y\|x) \& B(x) \supset (y)$
     $(p(y) \supset z = y) \& p(y\|z) \& B (x\|z))$                         3;R1111

5.   $(y)(p(y) \supset x = y) \& p(y\|x) \& B(x) \supset (p(y\|z) \supset$
     $((y)(p(y) \supset z = y) \& p(y\|z) \& B(x\|z)))$                      2,4;PC

6.   $\sim(p(y\|z) \supset ((y)(p(y) \supset z = y) \& p(y\|z) \& B(x\|z))) \supset$
     $(x) \sim ((y)(p(y) \supset x = y) \& p(y\|x) \& B(x))$                5;PC;R111

7.  $(\exists x)((y)(p(y) \supset x = y) \,\&\, p(y\|x) \,\&\, B(x)) \supset (p(y\|z) \supset$  
 $((y)(p(y) \supset z = y) \,\&\, p(y\|z) \,\&\, B(x\|z)))$    6;PC;Def. 4

8.  $p(y\|z) \,\&\, (\exists x)((y)(p(y) \supset x = y) \,\&\, p(y\|x) \,\&\, B(x)) \supset$  
 $((y)(p(y) \supset z = y) \,\&\, p(y\|z) \,\&\, B(x\|z))$    7;PC

9.  $p(y\|z) \,\&\, O(\exists x)((y)(p(y) \supset x = y) \,\&\, p(y\|x) \,\&\, B(x)) \supset$   8;R11.R111,  
 $O((y)(p(y) \supset z = y) \,\&\, p(y\|z) \,\&\, B(x\|z))$    PC

10. $(x)$ [9]                 9;PC,R111

11. $(\exists x)(p(y\|x) \,\&\, O(\exists x)((y)(p(y) \supset x = y) \,\&\, p(y\|x) \,\&\,$   10;PC,R111;  
 $Bx)) \supset (\exists x) \, O((y)(p(y) \supset x = y) \,\&\, p(y\|x) \,\&\, B(x))$    Def. 4

12. $(\exists x)(p(y\|x)) \,\&\, O(\exists x)((y)(p(y) \supset x = y) \,\&\, p(y\|x) \,\&\,$   11;PC,R11;  
 $B(x)) \supset (\exists x) \, O((y)(p(y) \supset x = y) \,\&\, p(y\|x) \,\&\, B(x))$    Def. 4

13. $\sim(\exists x)(p(y\|x)) \supset \sim(\exists x)((y)(p(y) \supset x = y) \,\&\, p(y\|x)$   PC,R111;  
 $\&\, B(x))$                  Def. 4

14. $\sim(\exists x)(p(y\|x)) \supset O \sim (\exists x)((y)(p(y) \supset x = y) \,\&\,$   13;R11,$(n=0)$,  
 $p(y\|x) \,\&\, B(x))$              PC, Def. 4

15. $O \sim (\exists x)((y)(p(y) \supset x = y) \,\&\, p(y\|x) \,\&\, B(x)) \supset$  
 $\sim O \sim \sim (\exists x)((y)(p(y) \supset x = y) \,\&\, p(y\|x) \,\&\, B(x))$    A11

16. $O(\exists x)((y)(p(y) \supset x = y) \,\&\, p(y\|x) \,\&\, B(x)) \supset (\exists x)$  
 $(p(y\|x)) \,\&\, O(\exists x)((y)(p(y) \supset x = y) \,\&\, p(y\|x) \,\&\, B(x))$   15,14;PC

17. $O(\exists x)((y)(p(y) \supset x = y) \,\&\, p(y\|x) \,\&\, B(x)) \supset$  
 $(\exists x) \, O((y)(p(y) \supset x = y) \,\&\, p(y\|x) \,\&\, B(x))$    12,16;PC

18. $O((y)(p(y) \supset x = y) \,\&\, p(y\|x) \,\&\, B(x)) \supset ((y)(p(y) \supset$  
 $x = y) \,\&\, p(y\|x)) \,\&\, OB(x)$         R11,R111,PC

19. $(\exists x) \, O((y)(p(y) \supset x = y) \,\&\, p(y\|x) \,\&\, B(x)) \supset (\exists x)$   18;R111,PC,  
 $((y)(p(y) \supset x = y) \,\&\, p(y\|x) \,\&\, OB(x))$     Def. 4

*20. $O(\exists x)((y)(p(y) \supset x = y) \,\&\, p(y\|x) \,\&\, B(x)) \supset (\exists x)$  
 $((y)(p(y) \supset x = y) \,\&\, p(y\|x) \,\&\, OB(x))$     17,19;PC

21. $(y)(p(y) \supset x = y) \,\&\, p(y\|x) \,\&\, B(x) \supset (\exists x)((y)(p(y) \supset$   3;A111,PC,  
 $x = y) \,\&\, p(y\|x) \,\&\, B(x))$          Def. 4

22. $((y)(p(y) \supset x = y) \,\&\, p(y\|x)) \,\&\, OB(x) \supset O(\exists x)((y)$   21;R11,R111,  
 $(p(y) \supset x = y) \,\&\, p(y\|x) \,\&\, B(x))$       PC; Def. 4

*23. $(\exists x)((y)(p(y) \supset x = y) \,\&\, p(y\|x) \,\&\, OB(x)) \supset O(\exists x)$   22;R111,PC,  
 $((y)(p(y) \supset x = y) \,\&\, p(y\|x) \,\&\, B(x))$      Def. 4

24. Theorem follows from 20 and 23 by PC.

For a set-theoretical modeling for $D_i^{**}$ see *Thinking and Doing*, Ch. 8.

*Indiana University*

## NOTES

[1] Castañeda, H-N., *Thinking and Doing: The Philosophical Foundations of Institutions*, Reidel Publishing Co., Dordrecht, 1975. An outline of the account appears in Castañeda,

H.-N., *The Structure of Morality,* Charles Thomas Publisher, Springfield, Illinois, 1974, Chapter 3.

[2] I first defended that thesis in 1952 in *An Essay on the Logic of Commands and Norms,* presented to the University of Minnesota as a Master's essay.

[3] For instance, in Castañeda, H.-N., (1) 'Actions, Imperatives, and Obligations', *Proceedings of the Aristotelian Society* **67** (1967–1968); (2) 'On the Semantics of the Ought-to-do', *Synthese* **21** (1970), 449–468, reprinted in D. Davidson and G. Harman, (eds.), *Semantics of Natural Language,* Reidel Publishing Co, Dordrecht, 1972; (3) 'Intentions, Practical Thinking, and Wants', in Norman Care and Robert Grimm (eds.), *Purpose and Action* (The *1974 Oberlin Philosophy Colloquium*), to be published by Yale University Press; (4) 'Intentions and Intending', *American Philosophical Quarterly* **9** (1972), 139–149. See also *Thinking and Doing,* Chapters 6 and 7, and 5.

[4] See Castañeda, H.-N., (1) 'On the Phenomeno-logic of the I', *Proceedings of the XIVth International Congress of Philosophy,* vol. 3, Herder, Vienna, 1969, pp. 260–266; (2) 'Indicators and Quasi-Indicators', *American Philosophical Quarterly* **4** (1967), 85–100, and (3) 'On the Logic of Attributions of Self-Knowledge to Others', *The Journal of Philosophy* **65** (1968), 439–456.

[5] For further discussion of this see item (3) mentioned in note 3, Part II, and *Thinking and Doing,* Chapter 10.

[6] See the papers mentioned in note 4.

[7] See, for instance, Goldman, Alvin, 'Comments on Castañeda's "Purpose and Action: An Integrated Theory"' in the book edited by Care and Grimm mentioned above in note 3.

[8] See the materials mentioned above in note 3, especially the very last ones.

[9] See item (4) mentioned in note 3, and *Thinking and Doing,* Chapter 6.

[10] See *The Structure of Morality,* Chapters 1, 6, 7, and 8.

[11] See *Thinking and Doing,* Chapter 8. A brief early discussion appeared in item (1) of note 3.

[12] See item (2) of note 3 and Castañeda, H.-N., 'Acts, the Logic of Obligation, and Deontic Calculi', *Philosophical Studies* **19** (1968), or *Thinking and Doing,* Chapter 7, §§ 10–12.

[13] This invalidates arguments, like Bas Van Fraassen's in his 'The Logic of Conditional Obligation', *Journal of Philosophical Logic* **1** (1972), 417–438, p. 424, if they are taken to apply to (genuine) deontic judgments. That the substitutivity of identicals does not hold in so-called systems of deontic logic that have deontic operators operate in propositions is an *inadequacy* of such systems. Note that attention is restricted to extensionality understood as substitutivity *salva veritate* of identical singular terms, and not to extensionality understood by means of different criteria.

[14] Powers, Laurence, 'Some Deontic Logicians', *Noûs* **1** (1967), 381–400.

[15] Aqvist, Lennart, 'Good Samaritans, Contrary-to-Duty Imperatives, and Epistemic Obligations'. *Noûs* **1** (1967): 361–379.

[16] See item mentioned in note 13, p. 418ff.

[17] See, for instance, Robert Stalnaker, 'A Theory of Conditionals', in N. Rescher (ed.), *Studies in Logical Theory,* Blackwell's, Oxford, England, 1968, who argues that conditionals do not obey antecedent conjunction, like (34), contraposition, and other standard laws.

[18] *Op. cit.,* p. 421.

[19] For other difficulties of the dyadic treatment of deontic logic, see Castañeda, H.-N., 'The Logic of Change, Action, and Norms', *The Journal of Philosophy,* **62** (1965), 333–344, which is a critical study of Von Wright, H. G., *Norm and Action,* The Humanities Press, New York, 1963, who is the founder of treatment, and does it in an impressive and large scale in this book. N. Rescher applied the 'conditional' approach to imperatives in his *The Logic of Commands,* Routledge & Kegan Paul, London, England, 1966. For difficulties with this work see H.-N. Castañeda's review of it in *The Philosophical Review* **79** (1970), 439–446. Some of these difficulties apply also to the conditional approach to deontic logic. A nice study of earlier 'conditional' systems of deontic logic by Von Wright and Rescher is Bengt Hansson, 'An Analysis of Some Deontic Logics', *Noûs* **3** (1969), 373–398.

# PART 5

# EVENTS AND ACTIONS

MYLES BRAND

# PARTICULARS, EVENTS, AND ACTIONS*

## I. INTRODUCTION

Philosophers of logic and language often make a distinction between three types of linguistic items:

   (i)    singular terms, including names;
   (ii)   predicates;
   (iii)  sentences.

There is a corresponding distinction between three types of objects:

   (i′ )  particulars;
   (ii′)  properties;
   (iii′) propositions.

Of course, this is a *prima facie* ontological division. Some persons have argued, for example, that there are no propositions, that propositions can be eliminated in favor of particulars having certain properties. Others have argued that there are no properties, that properties can be eliminated in favor of specifiable groupings of particulars. In any case, the tripartite division (i′)–(iii′) is a plausible working hypothesis, if not ultimately defensible.

The paradigm case of a particular is something in the world, say, an individual table, person, or pen. Examples of properties and propositions, assuming that there are such, are also specifiable. Events, however, are not paradigmatic members of any of these three ontological categories.

Three views about the ontological status and nature of events are generated by assimilating events to the categories (i′)–(iii′). On one view, events are particulars, in much the same way that my pen and my body are particulars. The Particularist Theory of Events, as I shall call it, has been vigorously defended by Donald Davidson.[1] On the second view, events are assimilated to properties. One version of this view takes events as properties of particulars: this thesis has been defended by Alvin Goldman.[2] Another

* I have received helpful comments on an earlier draft from Daniel Berger, F. Robert Bohl, Jr., Hector-Neri Castañeda, Alex Michalos, John Norman, Paul Teller, Irving Thalberg, and others. Work on this project has been partially supported by an NEH, 1974 Summer Stipend.

*M. Brand and D. Walton (eds.), Action Theory*, 133–157. *All Rights Reserved* version of the Property Theory of Events is that events are complexes of particulars, properties and times; this version has been defended by Jaegwon Kim and, at one time, Richard M. Martin, among others.[3] On all versions of the Property Theory, we must be able to express sentences about properties in our language; that is, we must be able to quantify over properties. Particularist Theories do not require quantification over properties; first order logic suffices to express sentences about events. This difference, however, will not be ultimately telling, if a Property Theory is coupled with a reductionistic view of properties or if a Particularist Theory makes a commitment to properties. On the third view, events are assimilated to propositions, or propositional-like objects, such as states of affairs or facts. Versions of this view have been supported by Neil Wilson and, most notable, Roderick Chisholm.[4] According to the Propositional Theory of Events, events are abstract, in the sense that they themselves are not spatio-temporally locatable; they are also repeatable, in the sense that they can occur or take place on more than one occasion. On the Particularist Theory, events are, at least in principle, spatio-temporally locatable and not, literally, repeatable. The Property Theory, at least Goldman's version of it, also construes events as abstract and repeatable, again unlike the Particularist Theory; and the Propositional Theory requires quantification over propositional-like objects, also unlike the Particularist Theory.

There are two, possibly three, *prima facie* advantages to Particularist theories. These theories, firstly, account for the obvious pre-analytic data that we talk about events in the same way that we talk about physical objects. We can speak about the button, as well as a button, about there being many buttons; and we can, standardly, count buttons. Similarly, we can speak about the button pressing, as well as a button pressing, about there being many button pressings, and we can, standardly, count them.[5] We assign proper names to physical objects, conventionally to all persons, but also to other physical objects, names such as 'The Empire State Building', 'The Brooklyn Bridge', and 'Mt. Everest'. Similarly, we assign proper names to events, names such as 'The Battle of Waterloo', 'The Civil War', 'Typhoon Shirley', and 'Superbowl VII'. It might be objected that we rarely assign proper names to events but frequently to physical objects. If we discount the assignments to persons and other animate objects and realize that proper names are also assigned to items other than physical objects and events, items such as places, then, I suspect, the frequency of assigning proper names to events approximates the frequency with which they are assigned to physical objects. In any case, the frequency of making assignments is otiose; it matters, rather, that our linguistic practice in dealing with events parallels our practices in dealing with physical objects.

The second advantage is a systematic one. Consider the event sentence

(1)      John is pressing the button.

Davidson has recommended that we parse it as

(2)      ($\exists x$) [Pressing (John, the button, $x$)]

which in quasi-English is

(3)      There is an event x such that x is a pressing by John of the button.[6]

Sentence (2) specifies that x is bound by a first-order quantifier, which is ordinarily interpreted to imply that the domain consists of particulars. This manner of parsing event-sentences has ramifications for the semantics for natural languages. Davidson and others have attempted to provide an extension of Tarski's truth definition from formal to natural languages. In order to accomplish this goal, it is necessary to recast natural language sentences into sentences using only the machinery available in first-order logic with identity, plus a list of singular terms and predicates. A recasting of this type allows for an extension of Tarski's convention T since it shows how the truth-conditions depend on sentential structure. Davidson has urged that we take the additional step of equating the meaning of the sentence with its truth-conditions.[7] I shall not comment here on the possibility or advisability of adding this component to Davidson's extensionalistic program (nor on its interesting historical predecessors). The main point is that there are *prima facie* broad systematic reasons for adopting a Particularist theory.

Another advantage of Particularist theories is their ontological simplicity, in that they require adding to the ontology the least kinds of existents. All agree that there are events that occur and all agree, I presume, that there are physical objects. Defenders of Property theories need, in addition to physical objects, properties, a relation of exemplification, and exemplifications in their ontology. Similarly, defenders of Propositional theories need propositions (or states of affairs), and the property of occurring or obtaining in their ontology. Particularists need only individuals, which come in two types, physical objects and objects that correspond to the exemplifications on the Property theory or occurrences on the Propositional theory.

However, there may be only the illusion of simplicity here. It can be forcefully argued that solutions to other philosophical problems require recognition of properties and propositions; for example, an adequate account of opaque contexts may well involve a commitment to propositions. Since we need properties or propositions in our ontology for other reasons, we are free to utilize them in event theory. Another plausible response to this alleged advantage is the Platonic one that considerations of ontological simplicity are of little, if any, importance.

In the remainder of this paper, I shall develop a version of the Particularist Theory of Events. I do so by addressing myself (in Sections III and IV) to the two most difficult problems facing Particularist theories, the problem of event identity and the problem of recurrence. To my knowledge, the only version of the Particularist Theory that addresses itself to these problems is Davidson's. In the next section (Section II) I argue that Davidson's views about event identity and recurrence are incorrect. There is, in general, a significant difference in emphasis and motivation between Davidson's account and the one developed here. Davidson is primarily interested in the semantics for natural language; his ontological commitments result from his semantical stance. I take less seriously this alleged systematic advantage of Particularist theories and concern myself primarily with the ontological status of events. An appropriate semantics is to be constructed only after the ontological issues are settled.

An investigation into the nature of events is fundamental in part because of its implications for semantics, but also because solutions to other philosophical problems depend on an adequate event theory. This dependency is clear in the cases of the theory of human action, the mind-body problem, causation, and explanation. In the final section, I develop some of the ramifications that my version of the Particularist theory has for action theory; in particular, I shall comment on the relation between events and actions, the reasons-causes debate, and the nature of nonbasic action.

## II. DAVIDSON ON EVENT IDENTITY AND RECURRENCE

Quine and others have pointed out that we must specify the domain before the machinery of quantificational logic can be utilized. That means, basically, that we need to specify identity conditions. The identity conditions for particulars given by Leibnitz's Law, $(x)(y)[x=y\equiv(Fx\equiv Fy)]$, suffice for the purposes of quantificational logic. These identity conditions, however, do not suffice for the purposes of specifying a Particularist event theory. Leibnitz's Law fails to be a useful or informative criterion. A useful identity criterion for, say, events is one that applies to events and is *minimal*, in the sense that it does not entail a weaker criterion that also applies to events. One of the reasons for stating identity conditions for events is to specify their ontological status; this is accomplished, in part, by requiring that the identity conditions be the weakest applicable conditions. Identity conditions for events must also be informative, in that they specify characteristics essential to events. Leibnitz's Law applies indiscriminately to all particulars, and hence, does not indicate any characteristic essential only to events. In general, when specifying the nature of a kind of object, we require minimal and informative identity conditions peculiar to that kind of object. The requirements for quantificational theory are less demanding; we need only specify identity conditions for the broadest ontological category to which that kind of object belongs.

Davidson has attempted to supply a useful and informative criterion by claiming that event-identity sentences are true just in case what is named have the same causes and effects. That is, letting e, f, . . . range over events and '. . . C ——' be the relation '. . . causes——',

(D1)     $e = f$ iff $(g)(gCe \equiv gCf)$ & $(h)(eCh \equiv fCh)$.

This criterion has a high degree of initial plausibility, and may well be the one that we employ for most practical purposes.[8]

However, there are serious difficulties for (D1). Let an ineffectual event be one that has no causes or effects. Then according to (D1), all ineffectual events are identical: for the definiens is trivially satisfied for these cases. Yet one should be able to distinguish among ineffectual events (if there are any). A defense might be that there are no ineffectual events. However, this defense assumes the truth of the substantive philosophical thesis of universal causal determinism. Aside from the point that the thesis is controversial, this defense fails to meet an adequacy condition for a criterion of event identity. An adequate criterion should be based on essential characteristics of events: it should not depend for its truth on any substantive claim; in this case, it should not depend on the truth of causal determinism.

Looking at this criterion in another way, counterinstances to (D1) can be generated. Suppose that there is a causal chain in which an object first undergoes fission and then is reunited by a process of fusion. Assume further that no other object causally interacts with it during this time. There are two events that are occurring from the time slightly prior to the fission to the time slightly later than the fusion, since each event involves distinct spatio-temporal objects. Nevertheless, these two events have exactly the same causes and effects. But according to (D1), these events are identical, since their causal histories and futures are identical. I understand that cases of this sort are common in particle physics. Such cases, anyhow, are logically possible. Philosophers concerned with personal identity have recognized situations of this sort.

Davidson says that "this criterion may seem to have an air of circularity about it, but if there is circularity it certainly is not formal."[9] It is true that (D1) is not formally circular. However, there are two kinds of informal circularity of consequence. The first is epistemological, and counts against using (D1) as a criterion for individuation, that is, a criterion for *judging* whether e and f are identical. As Davidson has rightly emphasized, the relata of the causal relation are events.[10] Now one event causes another only if they are distinct (that is, nonidentical), at least according to the ordinary notion of causation. By (D1), e and f are distinct only if there is some event causally related to e but not f, or conversely. Hence, it cannot be correctly judged whether the definiens is satisfied without first knowing whether the definiendium is satisfied *and conversely*. The second kind of circularity is logical, and counts against (D1) being an adequate statement of identity conditions. The definiens of (D1) requires quantification over events. But quantification over events in the definiens is permissible only if there is an identity criterion independent of (D1).[11]

The second major problem for Particularist theories is accounting for recurrence. "Any theory of events", Chisholm has said, "should be adequate to the fact of recurrence, to the fact that there are *some things* that recur, or happen more than once."[12] According to Chisholm, it is one single thing, a state of affairs, that occurs more than once. A state of affairs recurs if it occurs, and then it does not occur, and then *that same state of affairs* occurs again. Property theorists can also claim that some thing remains the same in recurrence by construing recurrence as multiple exemplifications of a single constitutive event property. Particularists cannot say that one and the same event happens again, since each event is a particular and, hence, nonrepeatable. It does not follow from this, however, that Particularists are unable to account for recurrence. They will have given such an account when they have explicated the notion of some things happening more than once.

Davidson's answer is that some things happen more than once when parts of a summational event occur at different times. "Events have parts that are events", he says, "and the parts may be discontinuous temporally or spatially (think of a chess tournament, an argument, a war). Thus the *sum* of all my droppings of saucers of mud is a particular event, one of whose parts (which was a dropping of a saucer of mud by me) occurred last night; another such part occurred tonight."[13] Summational events are comparable to summational physical objects, objects which retain their unity even if dismantled. If an automobile is dismantled and its parts scattered (though perhaps not grossly so), these parts nevertheless form a unity, a single automobile.

Davidson's solution, however, loses its plausibility when the events in question are spatio-temporally disparate. Consider the alleged summational events of electing a President every four years, men marrying women younger than themselves, persons losing bets. Each of these does not seem to be a single event with many parts. Or, in particular, consider

(4)     Socrates drank hemlock with his left hand at noon and so did my Uncle Frank.

Suppose that only two persons in history (and in the future) drink hemlock with their left hands at noon, Socrates and my Uncle Frank. This case is one of recurrence of drinking hemlock left-handedly at noon. However, it is implausible, if not absurd, to say that (4) specifies a single event with two constituents. It is difficult to specify conditions under which several events are constituents of a single, covering event. Some reference must be made to whether the events are spatially or temporally continuous, to whether a single physical object is involved in each, to whether they are brought about for a single goal if the events are actions, and so on. But in any case, it is not sufficient for events to be constituents of a single covering event that they share some properties in common, as Davidson's proposal requires.[14]

### III. RECURRENCE

Consider the sentence

(5)     Joshua performed the same action as Paul.

Suppose that the action is shouting. The problem of recurrence is to state truth-conditions for sentences like (5), when (5) is understood as being consistent with

(6)     Joshua performed it on Monday and Paul performed it on Tuesday.

That is, (5) is to be interpreted as being about two shoutings, not a joint shouting. There is a parallel problem for another kind of particular, physical objects. Consider the sentence

(7)     Joshua and Paul own the same thing.

Suppose that the object is a bicycle. The problem of repetition, as I shall call it, is to state truth-conditions for sentences like (7), when (7) is interpreted as being consistent with

(8)      That which Joshua owns is in the garage and that which Paul owns is on the street.

That is, (7) is to be interpreted as being about two bicycles, not a single one. Solutions to the problems of recurrence and repetition are parallel.[15]

Sentence (5), when interpreted as being consistent with (6), can be recast as

(5')      The action Joshua performed is the same type of action as the action Paul performed.

A similar recasting of (7) can be accomplished. The general problem is, then, supplying truth-conditions for sentences of the form

(9)      x is the same type of F as y,

where x and y range over particulars and F ranges over sorts or types. This sentence-schema is to be understood as entailing that there is a property that x has but that y lacks, that is, that x and y are distinct.

A sort, as I shall understand it, is such that it is possible that it have two or more members. On this view, "the sort consisting of all numbers identical with the third prime" does not name a sort, since it names something which must have exactly one member (if it names anything at all). However, "the sort consisting of all brontosauruses" and "the sort consisting of all unicorns" name sorts: the former because there were many brontosauruses, despite their extinction; and the latter because there could be more than two unicorns. Sorts are called "natural kinds" when they specify collections that are not artificially constructed, when, on one plausible view, they specify collections that could be referred to by the terms in natural laws.

Sorts, therefore, are to be distinguished from sets. Some sets are such that, necessarily, they have one member; and the null set has, necessarily, no members. There are no sorts such that, necessarily, they contain less than two members. Sorts, moreover, can gain or lose members while remaining the same sort; for example, the sort consisting of cats is constantly changing, as some are born and others die. Sets cannot gain or lose members while remaining the same set, since set-identity is defined in terms of actual membership. In general, sort F is identical with sort G *only if*, for every particular, during the time it is a member of F, it is also a member of G, and conversely. This condition is not sufficient since sorts need not contain actual members. The sort unicorn is distinct from the sort elf, though both sorts trivially satisfy the condition of having all their members in common at the same times.

Sorts and properties resemble each other, though not exactly. Like sets but unlike sorts, properties can have one or zero instances (members). It also seems reasonable to suppose that there are no universal sorts, that is, sorts such that everything belongs to them. But there are universal properties, properties such that everything has them (for example, the tautological property of being self-identical). An interesting conjecture and one that I shall take as a working hypothesis, is that sorts are properties satisfying certain conditions, that is, sorts are a subclass of properties.[16]

Information about the membership of sorts is obtained from two sources, the description (including the descriptive content of a name) and the background story, if there is any. Consider the description:

(10)     Jones' new car.

Suppose that we are also told the simple background story:

(11)     The car is a 1975 Ford and it was a gift.

The description (10) specifies that the object belongs to the sorts owned, owned-by-Jones, new-things, and cars. The background story (11) specifies that the object belongs to the sort cars, manufactured-in-1975, Fords, and gifts. (Information about which sorts particulars belong can be obtained from a source other than a written text or verbal report, namely, observation. For simplicity, I include as part of the background story, the information obtained from observation.)

The strategy, now, is to give an account of sameness of type in terms of particulars belonging to the same sort. Sortal sameness, in turn, is to be construed as relative to the available information.

Let F, G, . . ., range over sorts; let x, y, . . ., range over particulars; and let a, b, . . ., be constants standing for particulars. As a preliminary,[17]

(D2)     F is narrower than $G$ *iff*, for any x and time t, if x is of the sort F during t, then x is of the sort G during t, but not conversely.

Let $\mathscr{F}_x$ be the set of all sorts to which x belongs, as specified by the description and background story. Now,

(D3)     $\overleftarrow{\mathscr{F}_x}$ is the sortal set for $x$ *iff* for every F, F $\in \overleftarrow{\mathscr{F}_x}$ just in case F $\in \mathscr{F}_x$ and there is no G such that G $\in \mathscr{F}_x$ and G is narrower than F. (That is, $\overleftarrow{\mathscr{F}} = \{F : F \in \mathscr{F} \;\&\; (G)(G \in \mathscr{F} \supset G \geqslant F)\}$, where '$<$' is read 'is narrower than'.)

A sortal set is minimal, in that it is the set of all the narrowest sorts to which the particular is *known* to belong.

For example, the sortal set concerning Jones' new car in the previous case is

(12)    {The sort owned-by-Jones, the sort manufactured-in-1975, the sort Fords, the sort gifts-to-Jones}.

This set does not include the sort cars, since the background story specifies that the object belongs to the narrower sort Fords. The sort gifts-to-Jones is included in the minimal sortal set since it is independent of the other sorts specified in the description end background story.

Turning to the key locution,

(D4)    x is the same type of F as y *iff* there is a G such that G is narrower than F and $G \in \overleftarrow{\mathscr{F}_x}$ and $G \in \overleftarrow{\mathscr{F}_y}$.

That is, $x$ is the same type or sort as $y$ just in case there is a narrower sort to which they both belong that is specified by either the descriptions or the background story.

Recall the example

(5)    Joshua and Paul performed the same action.

As background information we were told that the action was one of shouting, and Joshua did it on Monday and Paul on Tuesday. Hence, we can formulate the following sortal sets:

(13)    {The sort performed-by-Joshua, the sort shouting, the sort taking-place-on-Monday}.

(14)    {The sort performed-by-Paul, the sort shouting, the sort taking-place-on-Tuesday}.

Is the action performed by Joshua *the same type of action as* the action performed by Paul? According to (D4), the answer is affirmative. The sort shouting is narrower than the sort action and (13) and (14) each contain this sort.

If it had been asked whether Joshua and Paul performed the same type of shouting, whether for example, they shouted angrily, the output from (D4) would be negative. For the minimal-descriptive sortal sets fail to specify a sort narrower than shouting to which both these events belong. These sortal sets contain sufficient information to indicate that the events are the same types of actions, but contain insufficient information to indicate that they are the same types of shoutings.

It might be objented that Joshua and Paul did not perform the same type of action since, despite both being shoutings, one might have been done in a loud squeaking voice and the other in a deep throaty voice. This objection is based on the view that sentences of the form 'x is the same type of F as y' are to be judged true or false on context-independent grounds.

One might try to accommodate this objection by producing a context-independent notion of sortal set and using that notion in (D4). A context-independent sortal set should not be confused with a set containing a complete listing of the sorts to which the particular belongs. A context-independent sortal set, on the other hand, is one that would indicate the significant features of an event; presumably, it would include the narrowest sorts specifying the physical object (if any) involved in the event, the causal ancestry and future of the event, the purpose (if any) for which it took place, the circumstances under which it took place, and the manner in which it occurred. A similar listing of significant features would obtain for physical objects.[18]

The information required to formulate context-independent sortal sets is enormous and rarely if ever obtainable in practice. More important than the practical difficulty in obtaining this information is that substituting a notion of context-independent sortal set into (D4) would make it counter-intuitive. Suppose that x and y are machines as different as imaginable; suppose also that, unknown to everyone, they share the property of being slightly rusted. Since being a slightly rusted machine is a narrower sort than being a machine, and since context-independent sortal sets of these machines would include that they are slightly rusted, the reconstructed (D4) would yield the untoward result that these machines were of the same type. Rather, judgments of sameness of type are made in the context of persons' knowledge and interests, not simply on the basis of the particulars sharing some property or other. This kind of context-dependency is reflected by defining sortal set relative to the available information, as in (D3), and in using *that* notion in explicating sameness of type.

In summary, a Propositionalist, like Chisholm, interprets recurrence as a single event happening more than once. A Particularist can make sense of recurrence despite not being able to say that one and the same event occurs more than once. For the Particularist, locutions concerning event recurrence are best understood as locutions about events of the same type occurring. In doing this, the claim that events are particulars in much the way that physical objects are particular is taken seriously; for talk about sameness of physical objects is to be understood in terms of physical objects being of the same type. Further, sameness of type is a context-dependent notion. It seems possible to construct a context-independent notion of sameness of type, but that notion would not reflect our ordinary way of judging these matters.

## IV. EVENT IDENTITY

Let me emphasize a distinction that is sometimes made, that between *individuation* and *identity conditions*. Individuation is an epistemic matter; it is concerned with telling or judging whether or not there are distinct events on the basis of available information. Identity conditions for events are logically necessary and sufficient conditions for the truth of sentences of the form '$e = f$'. Practical affairs often require decisions of individuation; for example, in cases of assigning or excusing responsibility and in cases of praising or blaming. Suppose that, as result of falling asleep, Casey trips the airbrake switch, which causes the train to stop and prevents a collision. It would be inappropriate to praise Casey for his deed, since his preventing the accident is a distinct event from his alertly pressing the airbrake switch. Identity conditions are required to determine membership for a kind of object in the domain. Identity conditions for some types of objects might also serve as an individuating criterion; but that need be the case in general.

In the literature on event theory we are often given partial descriptions of events, usually without any background story, and asked to make a judgment as to whether these partial descriptions are descriptions of a single event. In a well-known example,[19] we are given, and only given, the following partial descriptions:

(15a)    Jones' flipping the switch

(15b)    Jones' turning on the light

(15c)    Jones' illuminating the room

(15d)    Jones' alerting the prowler.

From (15a), (15b), (15c) and (15d) alone, it is not possible to judge whether these are partial descriptions of one, two, three or four events. We simply lack the information to make this decision. I shall be concerned with identity conditions in the remainder of this paper, and leave the epistemic issue of individuation for another time.

Identity conditions for physical objects can be given in terms of spatio-temporal regions — though there are some problems concerned with assigning spatio-temporal regions to physical objects, especially if we countenance high-velocity small particles as physical objects. It might be suggested, then, that the identity conditions for events be in terms of spatio-temporal regions, since events too are particulars.[20] That is, let s range over spatio-temporal regions and let R be the relation '... occurs within ...'; then,

(D5)      $e=f$ iff $(s)(eRs \equiv fRs)$

Note that (D5) does not require that events occur within continuous spatio-temporal regions. For example, the event of the playing of the 1967 World Series consists in a series of spatio-temporally separated constituent events, the playing of the first game, which took place in Fenway Park, Boston, on October 4, and the playing of the second game, which also took place on October 5, and so on.

However, (D5) is inadequate. Two or more events can occur in exactly the same spatio-temporal regions. For example, given an appropriate background story,

(16)      My swimming the Channel (now)

(17)      My catching a cold (now)

are distinct, despite these occurring at the same time and place.[21] Similarly, 'it's raining in Chicago between 8–9 P.M. on August 21, 1974' and 'it's growing dark in Chicago between 8–9 P.M. on August 21, 1974' describe two events occurring at the same time and place. One more such case is:

(18)      This metal sphere's rotating (now)

(19)      This metal sphere's becoming warm (now).

Though not himself advocating (D5), Davidson suggests a defense by claiming that (18) and (19) are not distinct, since each is identical with motions of molecules.[22] But this defense will not work. Descriptions (18) and (19) might each specify something identical with molecular motion, but it does not follow that they are each identical with the *same* molecular motion. The molecular motion that appears macroscopically as rotation is different from the molecular motion that appears macroscopically as growing warmer.

Moreover, we should not expect (D5) to be adequate. If variables ranging over physical objects are substituted for '$e$' and '$f$' in (D5), then we obtain adequate identity conditions for physical objects. Although events are particulars, the identity conditions for these particulars have to be different from the identity conditions for physical objects; otherwise there would be no difference at all between physical objects and events, which is clearly counter-intuitive. Since events are particulars, we should expect something like (D5) to be adequate, though not precisely (D5).

The alteration of (D5) required to differentiate events from physical objects and to account for multiple occurrences in the same spatio-temporal regions is (with a qualification to be added):

(D6)    $e = f$ iff $\Box(s)(eRs \equiv fRs)$.

According to (D6), (16) $\neq$ (17) since I could have caught the cold someplace else and could have swam the Channel while remaining healthy. Similarly, (18) $\neq$ (19) since the sphere could have rotated in the same spatio-temporal region without growing warmer. The identity conditions stated by (D6) entail those stated by (D5), but not conversely.

The identity conditions for events are stricter than those for physical objects, while exemplifying the same underlying rationale. It is important to realize that (D6) does not supply adequate identity conditions for physical objects. As indicated earlier, identity conditions must be minimal, if they are to be conditions giving the ontological nature of a kind of object. If the variables e and f were taken to range over physical objects, then the resulting alteration of (D6) would not be minimal, since there would be another statement of conditions (namely, (D5)) which is entailed by the altered (D6) and which apply to physical objects.

Definition (D6), however, is not wholly unproblematical. It might be objected that there is difficulty in assigning spatio-temporal regions to events. Strictly speaking, this is not a difficulty for (D6), since (D6) states identity conditions, and does not purport to be an individuating criterion, that is, a criterion for judging or telling in every case whether e and f name a single event. To use (D6) as an individuating criterion requires supplying an additional theory for locating events.

All events take time — at least in the ordinary sense of 'event'. If an event involves physical objects, then it occupies at least all the space occupied by the physical objects during the time of the event. If the event does not involve a physical object, such as a magnetic field increasing in strength or a flashing of lightning, the event occupies at least all the space in which the change takes place. However, difficulty arises for spatially or temporally discontinuous events, for example, my phoning my mother long-distance.[23] Where does this event take place? At the places at which my mother and I are located? Are the locations of the telephone wires, the switching devices, the operator, and so on, to be included? In general, problems of locating events are weakened by taking '. . . $R$ ———' to be '. . .

occurs within ———', rather than some relation requiring precise location, such as '. . . exactly occupies ———'. Cases involving events having evential parts, such as the telephone call to my mother, are similar to cases involving complex physical objects. Where, for example, is my house to be located? Does it include the empty space within the house? The detached garage? The space between the house and the garage? It would seem that a solution to the problems of locating complex events parallels that of locating complex physical objects. Another kind of difficult case involves so-called Cambridge events, that is, changes in objects resulting from their entering into relations with other objects (for example, my becoming an uncle when my sister has a child).[24] One way to proceed in these cases is to distinguish between relational and nonrelational changes, and restrict events to non-relational changes.[25] Answers to these difficulties must be supplied if (D6) is to form the basis of an individuating criterion. Undertaking such an extension, it seems, is a worthy project, though not one I shall attempt here.

Compare the following pair of event descriptions

(20)     Nixon's resigning

(21)     The 37th President's resigning

with this pair:

(22)     Hesperus' rising today

(23)     Phosphorus' rising today.

Now (22)=(23), since, to use the common idiom, in every possible world, each occurs in the same spatio-temporal region. In possible worlds in which Hesperus does not exist, Phosphorus does not exist, and hence, they trivially occupy the same spatio-temporal regions in those worlds. Kripke labels proper names like 'Hesperus' and 'Phosphorus' (and some other designators) *rigid*, meaning that they name the same object in every possible world in which that object exists and name no objects in other possible worlds.[26] The pair (20)–(21) name the same event; however, there is a possible world in which (21) did not occur but in which (20) did. For 'the 37th President' is not a rigid designator and hence picks out individuals other than Nixon in some worlds. That is, counter-intuitively, (D6) yields (20)≠(21).

Kripke credits David Kaplan with suggesting an operator, *Dthat*, that transforms descriptions into terms rigidly designating the object picked out in the actual world.[27] In brief, *Dthat* transforms descriptions into proper names. More carefully, let $\alpha$ be a singular term containing one or more descriptions or names occurring transparently, and let $\alpha^+$ be the result of applying the *Dthat* operator to $\alpha$. Then, if all the descriptions and names in $\alpha$ are rigid, $\alpha$ is $\alpha^+$; if some or all the descriptions and names contained in $\alpha$ are not rigid, then $\alpha^+$ is exactly like $\alpha$ except where $\alpha$ contains nonrigid designators, $\alpha^+$ contains rigid designators picking out the objects designated in the actual world by the names or descriptions in $\alpha$. We can then revise (D6) as follows:

(D6)$^+$ $\quad e = f \text{ iff } e^+ = f^+$
$\qquad\qquad e^+ = f^+ \text{ iff } \Box(s)(e^+ Rs \equiv f^+ Rs)$

Thus, for example, (D6)$^+$ yields the correct result that (20)=(21). For (20)=(20$^+$) and

(21)=(the 37th President's resigning)$^+$

and, by (D6)$^+$

(20$^+$)=(the 37th President's resigning)$^+$.

The question might be raised whether these identity conditions can be accommodated by Davidson's semantical program of giving truth conditions for natural language sentences by extending Tarski's convention T. The problem arises because we require truth-conditions for sentences of the form $\Box A$ without appealing to intensional objects such as propositions. At the outset, it should be noted that if Davidson's program is to be plausible, it must deal with modal sentences, both alethic and nonalethic ones. It is not open to Davidson to deny the intelligibility of modal sentences, as Quine is purported to have done, since his semantical program is not prescriptive but rather descriptive in that it must provide truth-conditions for all ordinary natural language sentences.[28]

I know of no treatment of modal sentences in Davidson's published corpus; one might, however, suggest such a treatment taking a cue from his comments on indirect discourse.[29] Consider the sentence "Aristotle said that Plato practiced nepotism." Davidson proposes that we treat 'said' as a two place predicate, taking as arguments expressions referring to speakers and a demonstrative, 'that', referring to an utterance. "Aristotle said that Plato practiced nepotism", that is, is really two sentences "Aristotle said that" and "Plato practiced nepotism", where the "that" of the former refers to the utterance by Aristotle. There is no logical or semantical connection between these two sentences. Of course, Aristotle said it in Greek and I have repeated it in English. We must add, then, that Aristotle and I are *samesayers*, that is, there was an uttering of his that has the same import as my uttering does here and now. Utterings are actions, hence events, and we can quantify over them. A similar treatment of "It is necessary that A" proceeds by construing "It is necessary" as a one-place predicate, taking a demonstrative referring to an utterance. If the utterance was originally made by someone other than myself, it must be added that we are samesayers.

This account is problematic; there is, for example, the question of explicating 'samesaying'. Do we require quotation to explicate it, in which case Davidson's account of indirect discourse suffers from the same problems as the metalinguistic account? Or is samesaying to be understood as a type of synonymy, in which case the metalanguage will not be purely extensional as Davidson's program requires? The cost of a non-Fregean semantics seems to be rising; and we may wonder about the extent to which it is an advantage of a Particularist theory that it suggests an extensional semantics. However, we should realize that a Particularist theory of events does not *require* an extensional semantics. Indeed, given the criterion of identity (D6)$^+$, we might do well to seek a nonextensional semantics.

## V. ACTIONS AND EVENTS

The version of the Particularist event theory sketched has ramifications for action theory. I shall consider three, the relationship between a bodily movement and an action, reasons and causes, and the nature of nonbasic action. The focus of these issues is the proposed event identity conditions.

1. Wittgenstein asked what remains when we subtract the bodily motion of our arm's rising from our action of raising it.[30] Actually, there are two questions being asked. Suppose that the following descriptions obtain:

(24)   Jones' left arm's rising (now)

(25)   Jones' raising his left arm (now).

First, do they describe a single event, that is, does (24)=(25)? And second, if not, what is the difference? Event theory yields an answer to the first question; action theory yields one to the second question.

The answer to whether (24)=(25) depends on how the event (or events) are located. There are four reasonable options, obtained by permutating the first two claims with the second two:

(a1)   the arm rising occurs within, and only within, the spatio-temporal region occupied by the arm during the period of its movement;

(a2)      the arm rising occurs within a spatio-temporal region larger than that occupied by the arm during the period of its movement;

(b1)      the arm raising occurs within, and only within, the spatio-temporal region occupied by the arm during the period of its movement;

(b2)      the arm raising occurs within a spatio-temporal region larger than that occupied by the arm during the period of its movement.

Of (a1) and (a2), the former is more acceptable. (Aristotle's interesting point, that something is not an arm if removed from the person, however, lends some support to (a2).) Of (b1) and (b2), the latter is, at least *prima facie*, more acceptable. We associate an overt action with muscle movements, nerve impulses, brain events, and perhaps other parts of a person's body, and not simply the bodily limb that moves, as Irving Thalberg has rightly emphasized.[31] Using (a1) and (b2), yields the result that $(24) \neq (25)$, since event identity statements are true just in case what is named by each description necessarily occupies the same spatio-temporal regions.

2. The result that $(24) \neq (25)$, or in general that actions are distinct events from the bodily movements involved, has consequences for the reasons-causes debate. This debate has been confused, it seems to me, because of a failure to keep clear several alternative theses. These theses should not be formulated in terms of the having of a reason, since it is implausible, at best, to construe the having of a reason as the primary causal factor in action.[32] It makes better sense to construe the causal factor either as a mental action, say, a willing, or as a (mere) mental event, say, the having of an appropriate want and belief. Four alternative theses can be distinguished, where S ranges over persons, a over bodily (or mental) actions, and where the statements are universally closed.

(T1)      If S performed a, then there was an appropriate wanting and believing of S such that this wanting and believing caused S's performing a. (Mere event causes action)

(T2)      If S performed a, then there was an appropriate wanting and believing of S and there was a bit of bodily (or mental) behavior associated with S's performing a such that this wanting and believing caused the bit of behavior. (Mere event causes mere event)

(T3)     If S performed a, then there was a willing of S's such that this willing caused S's performing a. (Action causes action)

(T4)     If S performed a, then there was a willing of S's and there was a bit of bodily (or mental) behavior associated with S's performing a such that this willing caused the bit of behavior. (Action causes mere event)

The first thesis is central to the causal theory of action advocated by Davidson and others.[33] According to it, actions are distinguished from other events in virtue of the causal sequences into which they enter. To explain an action's occurrence on this view, it is necessary to cite the causal antecedents, namely, the agent's wants and beliefs.

Thesis (T1) is false, however. A consequence of event theory is that a person's performing an action is not identical with the associated behavior. An action, rather, is a complex event involving at least bodily motions (if any), neurological events and brain events. If the Mind-Brain Identity Theory is correct, some of the brain events are the wanting and believing; if it is incorrect, then, in addition to the brain events, there are mental events of wanting and believing: but in either case, the wanting and believing are parts of the action. Now A causes B only if A and B are distinct. It follows from this that if A and B are complex causally related events, then there is an event that is part of A but not part of B and conversely. Since the complex event of wanting and believing is wholly a part of the action, it follows that the wanting and believing does not cause the action.

Theses (T2)–(T4) are volitional-type theories. The latter two take the cause to be an action; (T3) also takes the effect to be an action; (T4) takes the effect to be a bodily event. Thesis (T4) has been held by Prichard, among others[34]; I do not know of anyone who has held (T3). Theses (T3) and (T4) are subject to well-known problems, perhaps the telling one being that they fail to make clear the nature of human action. Since willing is itself construed as an action, they do not specify an essential feature of actions. The essential feature cannot be that of being caused by a willing, for that would yield a vicious regress.

Thesis (T2) is central to what I shall label *the old-time volitional theory*. It was a theory advocated by, for example, John Stuart Mill and John Austin, the nineteenth century jurist.[35] According to this theory, an action *is* a bodily movement caused by a mental event. It is a reductive theory: actions are nothing over and above bits of behavior having mere mental events as causal antecedents. Of the alternatives, only the old-time volitional theory is reductive.

This theory is not subject to the above objection against (T1); for the bodily (or mental) behavior associated with the action is a distinct event from the wanting and believing. It remains intact, moreover, against the usual objections brought against volitional theories; for example, unlike (T3) and (T4), the mental event involved is not an action, and hence, no vicious regress threatens. However, the old-time volitional theory is not without its problems. A serious one is that of explicating the notion of a bit of behavior being associated with an action. A first attempt might be to say that a bit of behavior is associated with an action just in case it is logically impossible that the complex event that is the action occur without the bit of behavior also occurring. In any case, the theory of events proposed leads to the rejection of (T1), the causal theory of action. Together with the seeming difficulties with (T3) and (T4), this result focuses attention on (T2), the old-time volitional theory, which I believe is the most interesting of the four alternatives.

3. Following the lead of Arthur Danto, many philosophers divide actions into basic and nonbasic ones.[36] At the intuitive level, the mark of a nonbasic action is that it is appropriate to use a *by-sentence* in describing what happens. For example, in 'Jones lifted the staff by raising his arm', 'Jones' having lifted the staff' describes the nonbasic action. A basic action is one the agent performs without doing anything in order to perform it. Here 'Jones' raising his arm', describes a basic action. Basic actions are named, if at all, by the description following 'by'. Of course, a by-sentence can contain two nonbasic action descriptions, for example, 'Jones moved the stone by lifting the staff' and a basic action can be described without using a by-sentence, as in 'Jones (simply) raised his arm'.

Being more careful, consider the following descriptions:

(26)    Stravinski's lowering his arm (now)

(27)    Stravinski's lowering the baton (now)

(28)    Stravinski's signaling to the cellos (now).

The first describes a basic action — though there is controversy on this matter.[37] The issue I want to focus on is the nature of nonbasic action, or in terms of this example, the relationship of (27) and (28) to (26).

One view, urged by Davidson, is that there are no nonbasic actions.[38] He would say that (26) is the only action performed and it causes

(27e)    the lowering of the baton (now)

and

(28e)    the signaling to the cellos (now).

We indicate that Stravinski brought about events (27e) and (28e) by using descriptions (27) and (28). Hence, Davidson collapses the basic-nonbasic action distinction (since there are only basic actions), but allows for nonbasic action-descriptions.

It seems correct, however, to credit Stravinski with lowering the baton and signaling to the cellos. Descriptions (27) and (28) are not the result of inaccurate ordinary talk. Our actions reach out into the world; we are not merely a causal island, as it were, but a part of the world that is larger than our bodies. This objection to Davidson loses some of its force, however, if he can provide an acceptable method for attributing agency and responsibility. In any case, let us take (27) and (28) to be genuinely nonbasic actions.

The next question concerns counting nonbasic actions. Here (27) and (28) are the same in that they both include the basic action of Stravinski's lowering his arm, which causes the event of the baton being lowered. There is some temptation to add that (27)=(28) since there is nothing over and above lowering his baton that Stravinski has to do in order to signal to the cellos. However, (27)≠(28). There is a possible world, different from the actual one, in which the spatio-temporal region occupied by Stravinski, the baton, and so on, is not also occupied by his signaling to the cellos. Conventions, clearly, will be different in alternative worlds. Since (27) and (28) do not occur in all possible worlds, they are distinct according to the proposed criterion of event identity.

If (27) is distinct from (28), then the problem of their relationship arises. Following Danto's recent view of taking nonbasic action to be comprised of a basic action plus one or more event components, the problem focuses on the relationship between (27e) and (28e). They are, we can say, *conventionally related*.

The events (27e) and (28e) occupy the same spatio-temporal region in the actual world. Not all conventionally related events are alike in this way: they can be either spatially or temporally distinct. A conventionally related spatially distinct pair, suggested by Kim, is 'Socrates' dying' and 'Xanthippe's becoming a widow'.[39] This pair also illustrates a case of noncausally conventionally related events. Since these events are simultaneous, they could be causally connected only if we accepted the untoward principle of causation at a distance. Suppose, now, that it is a convention that a bill becomes law ten days after being signed by the President. Nothing other than the President's signing it has to take place in order for it to become law. Then the pair 'the President's signing the bill' and 'the bill's becoming law' are conventionally related though temporally distinct. Those who are straight-jacketed by Laplacian thinking will attempt to reduce these cases to causal ones. The correct course seems to be, however, to recognize that there are noncausal conventional connections between events and to provide a detailed account of these connections.

Counting events using the criterion of necessary spatio-temporal coincidence yields more actions than Davidson's countenances. It does not, however, yield as many actions as others have found. Goldman, for example, argues that (27) and

(29)     Stravinski's lowering the baton quickly

name distinct actions: he would say that (27) *augmentatively generates* (29). In cases of this sort "the generating act is entailed by the performance of the generated act".[40] But acts do not entail each other, rather sentences formed from the description of acts do. The event-sentence formed from (29) entails the event-sentence formed from (27), but not conversely. However, non-equivalence of event sentences is not sufficient for the correlated descriptions naming distinct events. In cases in which the descriptions are dissimilar insofar as one involves predicate modification absent in the other (as in the case of (27) and (29)), they can (usually) be taken as partial descriptions of a single event. But in order to substantiate this claim and to deal with the exceptions to it, it would be necessary to develop a theory about basic event descriptions and predicate modifications of them — a difficult but worthwhile task.[41]

*University of Illinois at Chicago Circle*

NOTES

[1] See especially: 'The Logical Form of Action Sentences' in Nicholas Rescher (ed.), *The Logic of Decision and Action*, Pittsburgh University Press, Pittsburgh, 1967, pp. 81–95; 'On Events and Event Descriptions' in Joseph Margolis (ed.), *Fact and Existence*, Blackwell, Oxford, 1969, pp. 74–84; 'The Individuation of Events' in Nicholas Rescher *et al.* (eds.), *Essays in Honor of Carl G. Hempel*, D. Reidel, Dordrecht, 1970, pp. 216–234; 'Events as Particulars', *Nous* **4** (1970), 25–32; 'Eternal vs. Ephemeral Events', *Nous* **5** (1971), 335–349.
[2] See especially, *A Theory of Human Action*, Prentice Hall, Englewood Cliffs, 1970, Chapter 1, pp. 1–19. Cf. my review in *The Journal of Philosophy* **69** (1972), esp. pp. 250–254.
[3] See Kim, 'Events and Their Descriptions', in Nicholas Rescher *et al.* (eds.), *Essays in Honor of Carl G. Hempel*, pp. 198–215; 'Causes and Events; Mackie on Causation', *The Journal of Philosophy* **68** (1971), 426–441; 'Causation, Nomic Subsumption, and the Concept of Event', *The Journal of Philosophy* **70** (1973), 217–36; 'Noncausal Connection', *Nous* **8** (1974), 41–52. See Martin: 'On Events and Event Descriptions' in Margolis (ed.), *Fact and Existence*, pp. 63–73; *Language, Logic and Metaphysics*, New York University Press, New York, 1971, Chapter IV.

[4] See Chisholm: 'Events and Propositions', *Nous* **4** (1970), 15–24; 'States of Affairs Again', *Nous* **5** (1971), 179–180; 'Problems of Identity', in Milton Munitz (ed.), *Identity and Individuation*, New York University Press, New York, 1971, pp. 3–80. Neil L. Wilson, 'Facts, Events and Their Identity Conditions', *Philosophical Studies* **25** (1974), 303–321.

[5] Cf. Davidson, 'Eternal vs. Ephemeral Events', pp. 336ff.

[6] See Davidson, 'The Logical Form of Action Sentences', esp. p. 92.

[7] See Davidson: 'On Saying That', *Synthese* **19** (1968–69), 130–146; 'Theories of Meaning and Learnable Languages', in Y. Bar-Hillel (ed.), *Proceedings of the 1964 International Congress for Logic, Methodology and Philosophy of Science*, North-Holland Publishing Co., Amsterdam, 1965, pp. 383–394; 'True to the Facts', *The Journal of Philosophy* **66** (1969), 748–764; 'Truth and Meaning', *Synthese* **17** (1967), 304–323. For an interesting summary of Davidson's project see Robert Bohl, Jr., 'Davidson and Chisholm on Events', unpublished dissertation, Brown University, 1973.

[8] 'The Individuation of Events', p. 231. (Also see *Synthese* **22** (1970), 502.)

[9] *Ibid.*

[10] See his 'Causal Relations', *Journal of Philosophy* **64** (1967), 691–703.

[11] Cf. Wilson. 'Fact, Events and Their Identity Condition', pp. 303–304.

[12] 'Events and Propositions', p. 15. Italics added.

[13] 'Events as Particulars', p. 28.

[14] Notice that the claim that a single covering event cannot be formed from any two or more events, that the constituent events must somehow be 'relevant' to each other, has serious ramifications for the logic of event sentences. The following principle for example, is untenable:

(i)        $(Oe \& Of) \supset O(e \wedge f)$,

where '$O \ldots$' is a monadic predicate read '$\ldots$ occurs' and '$\wedge$' symbolizes singular term 'conjunction'. (Statement (i) is isomorphic to Axiom 2 of Patrick Suppes' logic of event sentences: see Suppes, Patrick, *A Probabilistic Theory of Causality*, North-Holland, Amsterdam, 1970, pp. 37–41.)

[15] After suggesting his summational account in 'Events as Particulars', Davidson hints at the following way of looking at recurrence. He says "recurrence may be no more than similar, but distinct, events following one after another", p. 28.

[16] See Nicholas Wolterstorff, *On Universals*, University of Chicago Press, Chicago, 1970, Chapter II. Given this conjecture, there is a close relationship between the Particularist theory developed here and some Property theories: cf. Kim's 'Events as Property Exemplifications: Considerations and Reconsiderations' in this volume.

[17] For this and other definitions, assume universal closure.

[18] The only attempt known to me to clarify a notion resembling context-independent sortal sets is a treatment of adequate action descriptions in Nicholas Rescher's, 'On the Characterization of Action', in Myles Brand (ed.), *The Nature of Human Action*, Scott, Foresman, Glenview, Ill., 1970, pp. 247–266.

[19] Davidson, 'Actions, Reasons, and Causes', *The Journal of Philosophy* **60** (1963), 685–700. Reprinted in Brand; see pp. 68–69, including note 2.

[20] A suggestion of this sort has been made by E. J. Lemmon. See his 'Comments on D. Davidson's "The Logical Form of Action Sentences",' in Nicholas Rescher (ed.), *The Logic of Decision and Action*, pp. 98–100.

[21] This case is similar to Davidson's in his 'Reply to Comments' in Nicholas Rescher (ed.), *The Logic of Decision and Action*, p. 117.

[22] 'The Individuation of Events', pp. 230–231.

[23] These cases were brought to my attention by Alvin Goldman.

[24] Cf. Kim, 'Noncausal Connections'.

[25] Cf. Lombard, L. B., 'Events, Changes, and the Nonextensionality of "Become",' forthcoming *Philosophical Studies*.

[26] Kripke, Saul, 'Naming and Necessity', in Donald Davidson and Gilbert Harmon (eds.), *Semantics for Natural Languages*, Reidel, Dordrecht, 1972. Those who find (informal) possible world semantics unilluminating, or who have some other favorite semantics, should feel free to make the appropriate translations. The substantive point, that identity conditions for events must be modal, is independent of the semantical interpretation given to the modal notions.

[27] *Ibid.*, p. 346, note 22. I may well be deviating from Kaplan's own view, though it follows Kripke's brief comments. (Cf. Kaplan's unpublished mimeo 'Dthat'.)

[28] In 'Truth and Meaning', Davidson says "... the task of a theory of meaning as I conceive it is not to change, improve or reform a language, but to describe and understand it" (p. 314).

[29] See 'On Saying That', esp. pp. 140–145.

[30] *Philosophical Investigations* (transl. by G. E. M. Anscombe), MacMillan, New York, 1953, paragraph 621, p. 161.

[31] See his 'Constituents and Causes of Emotion and Action', *Philosophical Quarterly* 23 (1973), 2–14 and Vivian Weil and Thalberg, 'The Elements of Basic Action', *Philosophia* 4 (1974), 111–138.

[32] See my 'Causes of Actions', *Journal of Philosophy* 67 (1970), 932–47, where I argue this claim in detail.

[33] See Davidson's 'Actions, Reasons, and Causes'. Sellars appears to hold a similar view, except that the causal antecedent is taken to be an intention to perform the action, construed as a saying to oneself 'I shall do *a* now'; see his 'Actions and Events', *Nous* 7 (1973), 179–202.

[34] Prichard, H. A., *Moral Obligation*, The Clarendon Press, Oxford, 1949, pp. 187–198. Reprinted in Brand (ed.), *The Nature of Human Action*, pp. 41–49. This view has recently been defended by Hugh McCann, 'Volition and Basic Action', *The Philosophical Review* 83 (1974), 451–73.

[35] Cf. Brand, Myles, 'Action and Behavior', in Brand (ed.), *The Nature of Human Action*, pp. 3–21, esp. pp. 8–13.

[36] See Arthur Danto, *Analytical Philosophy of Action*, Cambridge University Press, Cambridge, 1973, Chapters 1–5. Cf. my review, forthcoming in *Metaphilosophy*.

[37] Cf. Annette Baier, 'The Search for Basic Actions', *American Philosophical Quarterly* 8 (1971), 161–170, and her 'Intention, Practical Knowledge, and Representation' in this volume. Also see McCann, *op. cit.*

[38] 'Agency' in Binkley, Robert, Bronaugh, Richard and Marras, Ausonio (eds.), *Agent, Action, and Reason*, Basic Blackwell, Oxford, 1971, pp. 3–25, esp. pp. 20ff.

[39] See his 'Noncausal Connections'.

[40] *A Theory of Human Action*, p. 30. See also pp. 28–30. Cf. Kim's 'official line' in his 'Events as Property Exemplifications: Considerations and Reconsiderations'.

[41] See Table I for a way in which the major literature on the nature of nonbasic action can be indicated.

TABLE I

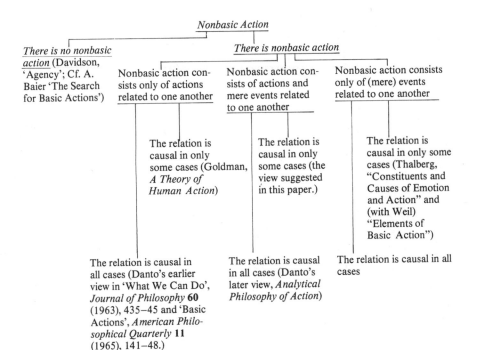

*Nonbasic Action*

*There is no nonbasic action* (Davidson, 'Agency'; Cf. A. Baier 'The Search for Basic Actions')

*There is nonbasic action*

Nonbasic action consists only of actions related to one another

Nonbasic action consists of actions and mere events related to one another

Nonbasic action consists only of (mere) events related to one another

The relation is causal in only some cases (Goldman, *A Theory of Human Action*)

The relation is causal in only some cases (the view suggested in this paper.)

The relation is causal in only some cases (Thalberg, "Constituents and Causes of Emotion and Action" and (with Weil) "Elements of Basic Action")

The relation is causal in all cases (Danto's earlier view in 'What We Can Do', *Journal of Philosophy* **60** (1963), 435–45 and 'Basic Actions', *American Philosophical Quarterly* **11** (1965), 141–48.)

The relation is causal in all cases (Danto's later view, *Analytical Philosophy of Action*)

The relation is causal in all cases

JAEGWON KIM

# EVENTS AS PROPERTY EXEMPLIFICATIONS*

## I

The term 'event' ordinarily implies a change, and most changes are changes in a substance. Whether coming into being and passing away can be construed as changes in substances is a question we shall not consider here. A change in a substance occurs when that substance acquires a property it did not previously have, or loses a property it previously had. Whether fissions and fusions of substances can be considered as cases of losing or acquiring properties is, again, a question we shall not discuss in this paper. By 'substance' I mean things like tables, chairs, atoms, living creatures, bits of stuff like water and bronze, and the like; there is no need here to associate this notion with a particular philosophical doctrine about substance.

Besides events, we also speak of "states". If "events" signal changes, "states" seem to be static things, "unchanges", to use a term of C. J. Ducasse's;[1] some examples of states would be my body's weighing 140 pounds, the earth's being nearly spherical in shape, and the presence of oxygen in this room. There are, however, good reasons for not taking this dichotomy of changes and unchanges, or of events and states, too seriously at the initial stage of developing a theory of events. For one thing, there are cases that are hard to classify; e.g., the whirring of my typewriter, having a throbbing pain in the right elbow. Then there are "conditions", which, it seems, can be either events or states depending on essentially pragmatic contextual factors. And what of "processes"? A deeper analysis may reveal subtle and important differences among these entities, but I think that can wait until we have a good enough grasp of them as a distinct ontological category. Of course, this may turn out to be a wrong move; there may not be a single, unitary ontological category of interest comprising all, or even most, of them. But if we are wrong here, it would be philosophically profitable to find out that we are.

Moreover, it is a philosophical commonplace to use the term 'event' in a broad sense, not only to refer to changes but also to refer to states,

* I have benefited from discussions with, or unpublished materials furnished by, the following persons: David Benfield, Richard Cartwright, Roderick Chisholm, Donald Davidson, Fred Feldman, Michael A. Slote, Ernest Sosa, and Ed Wierenga.

*M. Brand and D. Walton (eds.), Action Theory*, 159–177. *All Rights Reserved*
Copyright © 1976 *by D. Reidel Publishing Company, Dordrecht-Holland*

conditions, and the like. When universal determinism is formulated as "Every event has a cause" or "the aim of science" is said to be the explanation and prediction of events in nature, it surely is not intended that states, narrowly so-called, escape the net of causal relations or that it is not the business of science to explain why certain states obtain, e.g., why the sky looks blue or why the earth is pear-shaped. To give one more reason for playing down the differences between events and states: some properties already imply changes in the substance that has them; for example, fading in color, falling, and freezing. This means that a change need not necessarily be characterized as a losing or acquiring of some property; it may simply be the *having* of some property at a time.

Just as changes are changes of properties in substances — again leaving aside such difficult cases as coming into being, passing away, fusion and fission — states and conditions are states and conditions *of* or *in* substances or systems of substances. Add this to our earlier reasons for underplaying the differences between changes and unchanges, and we naturally arrive at a conception of events and states as *exemplifications by substances of properties at a time.* This account can be called 'the property-exemplification account' of events; it has also been called a theory of events as "structured complexes", since it attributes to an event a complex structure: an event (or state) is a structure consisting of a substance (an *n*-tuple of substances), a property (an *n*-adic relational attribute), and a time. This in essence is the view of events I have advocated in several earlier papers.[2]

This view of events has been criticized from many quarters, notably by Donald Davidson. The present paper aims at providing further clarifications of the theory, in part in light of some of these criticisms, and also raise some further issues concerning events and actions. In order to do this we need to state a few more details of the property-exemplification account. According to this account, each individual event has three unique constituents: a substance (the "constitutive object" of the event), a property it exemplifies (the "constitutive property" or "generic event"), and a time. An event is a complex of these three, and I have used the notation $[x, P, t]$, or variants thereof, as a canonical notation for events in general. There are two basic principles in the theory, one stating the conditions under which an event exists (occurs, if you like) and the other stating the conditions under which events are identical.

*Existence condition:* Event $[x, P, t]$ exists just in case the substance $x$ has the property $P$ at time $t$.

*Identity condition:*   $[x, P, t,] = [y, Q, t']$ just in case $x=y$, $P=Q$, and
$t=t'$.

(For simplicity's sake we won't bother with dyadic and higher-place events, although these will show up later as examples. For details see my 'Causation, Nomic Subsumption, and the Concept of Events' cited in note 2.) We shall sometimes use the expression 'event structure'[3] when we want to refer specifically to entities satisfying these conditions, i.e., events under the property-exemplification account.

As far as monadic events are concerned, i.e., events involving non-relational, one-place attributes as constitutive properties, the theory can easily be developed along a different line: dispense with the existence condition and define the *predicate* 'is an event' over ordered triples of substances, properties, and times. An ordered triple $\langle x, P, t \rangle$ would be an event just in case the substance $x$ has the property $P$ at time $t$. The existence of the triple would be guaranteed by the principles of set theory, provided $x$, $P$, and $t$ exist, whether or not $x$ has $P$ at $t$. And the identity condition for events would merely be a special case of the identity condition governing $n$-tuples. For dyadic and higher-place events, this approach of defining the event predicate within set theory introduces some complexities in regard to the identity condition, complexities which are by no means insuperable. In any case this approach has the advantage of using the familiar set-theoretic apparatus and of doing away with a special operator '[ , , ]', which some people seem to find mysterious (but given the identity condition, '[ , , ]', may be taken as a special case of the familiar definite description operator, and in this regard it is not different from the set-abstraction operator '{v|...v...}'). It would also allow us to speak of "possible events", i.e., the ordered triples $\langle x, P, t \rangle$, whether or not $x$ has $P$ at $t$, which might be useful for certain philosophical purposes.[4]

What is essential is that we are assuming as primitives the three functors on events: 'is the constitutive property of', 'is the constitutive object of', and 'is the time of the occurrence of'. The theory states that just in case a substance $x$ has property $P$ at $t$, there is an event whose constitutive object is $x$, whose constitutive property is $P$, and whose time of occurrence is $t$ (the existence condition), and that events are identical just in case they have the same constitutive property, object, and time (the identity condition). This is the core of the account of events under discussion. The introduction of the notation '[ , , ]' is merely abbreviatory; the use of the set-theoretic machinery *may* have certain metaphysical consequences, depending on one's metaphysical views of sets, as regards, say, the "essential properties" of events. But I regard these as peripheral issues pertaining largely to the mode of presentation of the theory; the basic elements of the account are not essentially altered thereby.

The account so far presented is not an "eliminative" or "reductive" theory of events; that is, it does not attempt to show that events are in some eliminative sense "reducible" to substances, properties, and times. (It may be remarked, though, that a better case for the elimination or reduction of events might be made if we take the ordered triple approach sketched above.) I do not know exactly when a metaphysical theory is "reductive"; the account, however, attempts to tell us something about the metaphysical nature of events by relating them to such other ontological categories as substances, properties, and times. And I have tried to show, in several earlier papers, how this view of events can provide a useful framework within which to develop and discuss theories of causation and explanation, and the mind-body problem; I believe it also provides a framework in which an account of the relation between micro-events and macro-events can be developed.[5]

I have said little about what properties are allowable as constitutive properties of events; namely, what "generic events" are. It clearly will not do to count as an event the exemplification of any arbitrary property by an object. This becomes obvious if one thinks, as many do, that there is a property expressed by any open sentence, or if one thinks of properties in the way modal logicians do nowadays, namely as functions from possible worlds to sets of individuals. There is also the problem, a difficult and important one, of properties ordinarily considered generic events, e.g., becoming a widow, which give rise to "Cambridge events".[6] It will only beg the issue to try to explain 'generic event' in terms of such notions as 'change' and 'alteration'. And it may be tempting, but no less question begging, to try to define it in terms of overtly causal concepts, for "real changes" or "real events" seem to be just those that make a causal difference, and generic events seem to be just those properties whose possession by an object bestows upon it a causal power or potency, or whose possession by an object indicates its being subjected to such powers.

This causal approach, I think, may turn out to be the correct one — but in a roundabout way: the basic generic events may be best picked out relative to a scientific theory, whether the theory is a common-sense theory of the behavior of middle-sized objects or a highly sophisticated physical theory. They are among the important properties, relative to the theory, in terms of which lawful regularities can be discovered, described, and explained. The basic parameters in terms of which the laws of the theory are formulated would, on this view, give us our basic generic events, and the usual logical, mathematical, and perhaps other operations on them would yield complex, defined generic events. We commonly recognize such properties as motion, colors, temperatures, weights, pushing, and breaking, as generic events and states, but we must view this against the background of our common-sense explanatory and predictive scheme of the world around us. I think it highly likely that we cannot pick out generic events completely a priori. If generic events are understood along these lines, not all of the Boolean combinations of generic events can be relied on to yield generic events; for example, if two generic events are from different theories or rival theories about the same subject matter. It isn't even clear that if F is a generic event, non-F is also a generic event in every case.

There is also the following problem: generic events are often picked out by verbs and predicates. Now there is a group of words that modify them — adverbs and, generally, predicate modifiers. The question arises: if 'F' is a predicate or verb designating a generic event and $a$ is a predicate modifier, under what conditions does '$a(F)$' designate a generic event? The answer will of course depend on the particular properties of '$a$' and of '$F$'. If walking is a generic event, walking slowly seems to be one also. What about walking while chewing gum, walking toward the Eiffel Tower, and walking exactly two thousand years after the death of Socrates? Are they *kinds of events*? Or should we treat the modifiers as indicating properties *of* the individual events arising from the generic event of walking — e.g., treat '(being done) while chewing gum' as designating a property of the event of my walking at a particular time $t$? We shall briefly recur to this problem below.

## II

A metaphysical theory of events of the sort just sketched must be distinguished from a theory of the "logical form" of event and action sentences — a theory that attempts to exhibit the relevant logical and semantical structures of sentences about events — of the sort initiated essentially by Donald Davidson in an influential series of papers.[7] To call attention to this distinction is not to say there are no important connections between the two. Davidson has made ontological claims based on his work on the logical form of event and action sentences; most notably, he has claimed that his investigations have shown that events and actions must be admitted into our ontology as values of bound variables, and that they are "particulars" that can be described and referred to in various nonequivalent ways. However, Davidson has also emphasized a distinction between a logical and semantical theory of event discourse and a metaphysical theory of events:[8]

> On the score of ontology, too, the study of logical form can carry us only a certain distance. ... Given this much, a study of event sentences will show a great deal about what we assume to be true concerning events. But deep metaphysical problems will remain as to the nature of these entities, their mode of individuation, their relation to other categories.

Davidson did go beyond a theory of event sentences: in his paper 'The Individuation of Events'[9] he has given us a principle of individuation for events. It is this: events are the same just in case they have the same causes and the same effects. This criterion has been criticized as covertly circular, since causes and effects themselves are events.[10] If the criticisms are correct, it may be unsound as a "criterion" of individuation; nonetheless, it may be true that events having the same causes and same effects are in fact one and the same, although one wonders how the criterion would fare in an indeterministic, causally irregular world (this world could be such a world). Further, it may in fact turn out that my criterion of event identity is coextensive with Davidson's; that is, for events $x$ and $y$, $x=y$ under the identity condition of the property-exemplification account of events if and only if $x=y$ under Davidson's criterion.[11]

Let us now look into the question whether the property-exemplification account of events is incompatible with Davidson's theory of event sentences and his metaphysical claims based on that theory. The two are often considered as competing theories,[12] and it is a matter of some interest to see what differences, if any, exist between them.[13]

Central to Davidson's theory of event sentences is the point that a sentence like:

(1)     Flora dried herself with a towel on the beach at noon,

which is just the sort of sentence often said to "describe" or "represent" an event, contains a covert existential quantification over concrete events, and its logical form should be brought out thus:

(2)     There is an event $e$ such that $e$ is a drying of Flora by Flora, $e$ was done with a towel, $e$ occurred on the beach, and $e$ occurred at noon.

Now there seems to be no reason why the variable '$e$' cannot take as its values the event structures of the property-exemplification account: in fact, no reason why the particular event structure [(Flora, Flora), ① dries ②, noon] isn't just the value of '$e$' that makes (2) true. As (2) affirms, this event

— an action, as it happens — has the property of being done with a towel, the property of occurring on the beach, and so on. Notice, by the way, that the first clause in the matrix of (2) says '*e is a drying* of ....'; this 'is a (verb)-ing' construction and other verb nominalizations are good clues for identifying the generic events involved in Davidsonian paraphrases of event sentences. To cite two of his own examples:[14]

(3a)    The boiler exploded in the cellar

(3b)    There exists an $x$ such that $x$ was an explosion and $x$ was in the cellar and $x$ was of the boiler

(4a)    Jack fell down ...

(4b)    There is an event $e$ such that $e$ is a falling down of Jack ...

On my account exploding, falling, and the like are generic events in the intended sense; the boiler and Jack, in the above examples, are the constitutive substances of the two events respectively.

Obviously, my events can be quantified over; and there is no problem about quantifying *into* the event structures unless of course there happen to be other barriers to quantification such as psychological modalities. My events are "particulars" and "dated". That they are dated is obvious. I am not clear what "particulars" are; but events in my sense have locations in space, namely the locations of their constitutive substances (if mental substances have no spatial location, then mental events would have no spatial location either, which presumably is what some dualists want to claim). And my events are not "eternal" objects; they do not exist in all possible worlds; they exist only if the existence condition is met, which is a contingent matter of fact. If this doesn't show that something is "concrete" or "particular", what does?[15]

Davidson has considered it an important mistake to regard a sentence like

(5)    Doris capsized the canoe yesterday

as picking out a unique event, for she may have capsized the canoe more than once yesterday. Generally speaking, it is a mistake, according to him, to think of such sentences as playing the role of singular terms for events. Now my account does not compel us to render (5) into:

(6)    The event [Doris, capsized the canoe, yesterday] occurs.

(Here we disregard the fact that a dyadic event may be involved; we also disregard the tense.) For we may put (5) thus:

(7)        (∃t) ([Doris, capsizes the canoe, *t*] exists and *t* belongs to
           yesterday).

But we are not quite through with Davidson on this point. According to the
existence condition, as I intended it, if an object *x* exemplifies *P* at *t* in the
sense of *throughout t*, then the existence of a *unique* [*x*, *P*, *t*] is guaranteed
by the identity condition. Davidson writes:[16]

> Some actions are difficult or unusual to perform more than once in a short stretch of time,
> and this may provide a specious reason in some cases for holding that action sentences refer
> uniquely to actions. Thus with 'Jones got married last Saturday', 'Doris wrote a check at
> noon', 'Mary kissed an admirer at the stroke of midnight'. It is merely illegal to get married
> twice on the same day, merely unusual to write checks simultaneously, and merely good
> fortune to get to kiss two admirers at once.

Let us assume that kissing some admirer or other is a generic event. My two
conditions, then, imply that there is the unique event of Mary's kissing an
admirer at the specified time. From the existence of this event, however,
nothing follows as to how many persons she kissed at the time, although
ordinarily, it would be safe enough to assume she kissed one person.
Suppose she in fact kissed two admirers. Steve and Larry. If we take the
dyadic kissing, *x*'s kissing admirer *y*, as the generic event involved, the two
conditions entail the existence of two unique dyadic kissings, Mary's kissing
Steve and her kissing Larry. Thus, there are three kissings here, which some
might find a bit disconcerting; but once it is realized that they are one
monadic kissing and two dyadic kissings, the situation need no longer strike
us as implausible or incoherent. In fact, it seems to me that that is what we
should say to describe Mary's kissings.[17]

Another point of some importance, though obvious, is this: there is
nothing in my account that implies that from any sentence about an event
we can read off what the event's constitutive components are. From the
sentence 'A momentous event occurred yesterday' we can only approx-
imately locate the time of the event; we can tell nothing about its
constitutive property or substance. From the sentence 'The momentous
event that occurred yesterday caused the event now under discussion by the
regents of the university' we can say nothing about the constituents of these
events, except, again, the time of the first event. This is as it should be. The
situation is quite similar with sentences about physical objects. In a sense
knowing what the constitutive object, property, and time of an event are *is*
to *know what that event is*. Although we are here treading on uncertain
grounds, my canonical description of an event, I believe, gives an "intrinsic
description" of an event (assuming that the three components are given
"intrinsic descriptions"), in the sense in which such descriptions as 'the

momentous event yesterday' and 'the event now under discussion' are "extrinsic". I am not here prepared to explain, much less define, what is to be meant by 'intrinsic' and 'extrinsic'; perhaps they are explainable in terms of a combination of modal and epistemic concepts.

There are other points of apparent disagreement between Davidson's views and mine, some of which will be taken up in succeeding sections. But overall it seems to me that there are no irreconcilable *doctrinal* differences between Davidson's theory of event discourse as a semantical theory and the property-exemplification account of events as a metaphysical theory. True enough, Davidson and I disagree about particular cases of individuation of events; for example, whether Brutus's stabbing Caesar is the same event as Brutus's killing Caesar. But most of these differences about particular cases seem traceable to possible differences in our views about causation, explanation, and intensionality. Where Davidson says, with regard to a sentence like

(8)    The collapse was caused, not by the bolt's giving away, but the bolt's giving away so suddenly

that here 'was caused' should be understood in the sense of 'is causally explained', and that explanations "typically relate statements, not events".[18] I would take (8) more literally and be inclined to take it as evidence for saying that in virtue of their different causal properties, the bolt's giving away and the bolt's giving away suddenly are different events, though one is "included" in the other. But here we are coming dangerously close to difficult problems about the relationship between causation and explanation, and the intensionality of causal and explanatory relations, problems well beyond the scope of the present paper.

III

One of the most frequently voiced objections to the theory of events as property exemplifications is the point that this theory multiplies events beyond necessity. Not only is Brutus's stabbing Caesar distinct from his killing Caesar and also from his assassinating Caesar; but in fact no stabbings are killings, and no killings are assassinations.[19] What seems worse, Brutus's stabbing Caesar is also a different event from Brutus's stabbing Caesar with a sword, since stabbing and stabbing with a sword presumably are different properties; and neither of these events is the same as Brutus's stabbing Caesar in the heart; and so on. These considerations seem to have led some philosophers to think that the property-exemplification account does not permit redescriptions of events,[20] since any addition or deletion from a given description would alter the constitutive property of the event in question.

Let us first examine the problem of redescribing an event. It is true that if an event description is altered so that a different generic event is picked out, then the resulting description, on my view, would pick out a different event. That much is clear enough. And the same applies to the names and descriptions of the constitutive objects and times of events. On the other hand, it is not part of the account in question that the use of different predicates — nonsynonymous, logically nonequivalent predicates — invariably leads to a multiplicity of properties. 'Is blue' and 'has the color of the sky' pick out the same property, namely the color blue.[21] Moreover, as noted earlier, events themselves *have* (exemplify) properties; Brutus's stabbing Caesar has the property of occurring in Rome, it was intentional, it led to the death of Caesar and caused grief in Calpurnia, and so on. Needless to say, the properties an event exemplifies must be sharply distinguished from its constitutive property (which is exemplified, not by an event, but by the constitutive substance of the event). It is also a property of Brutus's stabbing Caesar that its constitutive property is stabbing. Thus, events can be redescribed by the use of different predicates expressing the properties *of* (exemplified by) them; what cannot be done is to redescribe them by tampering with their constitutive properties. The point I am making should be obvious if we consider such "extrinsic" descriptions of events as 'the event we are talking about' and 'the most unforgettable event in David's life'. What the theory implies is that if 'the most unforgettable event in David's life' refers, then the event thus referred to must have a structure of the sort the theory attributes to events; for example, the event could have been David's falling off a horse at age five.

But the foregoing isn't likely to satisfy the critics as allowing us a full range of describing and redescribing events. 'Brutus stabbing Caesar' and 'Brutus killing Caesar', they insist, *are* redescriptions of the same event; and what seems even more obvious, 'Brutus's stabbing Caesar' and 'Brutus's stabbing Caesar with a sword' are two descriptions of the same event, one being somewhat more detailed and more informative than the other. Similarly, for such examples as 'Sebastian's stroll', 'Sebastian's leisurely stroll', and 'Sebastian's limping stroll'. Here we return to the initial objections mentioned at the outset of this section.

I do not want to discuss here the question of whether Brutus's stabbing Caesar is the same event at Brutus's killing Caesar; for I have little to add to the existing arguments in favor of their distinctness.[22] Also, intuitively, it is more plausible to deny identity in cases like it than in cases like Sebastian's stroll and Sebastian's leisurely stroll (where, we suppose, Sebastian did stroll leisurely).

So what of Sebastian's stroll and Sebastian's leisurely stroll? First of all, there is the question whether being leisurely is to be taken as a property exemplified by the event of Sebastian's stroll, or as modifying the generic event of strolling, thereby issuing in another generic event, namely strolling leisurely. If the former line is taken, there is no special problem — no more problem here than there is in the case of 'this red rose on the table' and 'this withered red rose on the table' where there is ône unique red rose on the designated table which is withered. So on this approach Sebastian's stroll, after all, turns out to be the very same event as Sebastian's leisurely stroll, i.e., Sebastian's stroll, which, as it happens, was leisurely.

Thus, the general strategy is this: we deny that strolling leisurely or stabbing with a knife are generic events, although strolling and stabbing are. The modifiers 'leisurely' and 'with a sword' are taken, not as modifying 'strolling' and 'stabbing', but rather as indicating properties of the individual events which arise from the exemplifications of the generic events designated by 'strolling' and 'stabbing'. We could say, somewhat more generally, that predicate modifiers indicating means-manners-methods, may be construed in this way.[23] Taking this way out, however, is not entirely appealing, for at least two reasons: first, it would place a very severe and urgent burden on us to produce an account of generic events and of the modifiers of expressions designating them, although this is a problem that one has ultimately to face in any case. Second, this approach neutralizes one of the initial motivations for developing the structured complex view of events. Whatever else events might be, they were intended to be entities that enter into causal relations with one another, and that can be objects of explanations. But it is clear that we may want to explain not only why Sebastian strolled, i.e., Sebastian's stroll, but also why he strolled leisurely, i.e., his leisurely stroll. Under the approach being considered, the second explanation would be of why Sebastian's stroll was leisurely; we would be explaining why a certain event had a certain property, not why a certain event occurred. But perhaps it was a mistake to bring very broad and general considerations about explanations into a theory of events, to begin with. The desire to have events as the relata of causal relations could, I believe, be accommodated within this approach, although some of the specific things I have said in earlier articles about causation would have to be retracted (especially, the claim that for Humean causation there must be a lawlike connection between the generic events of any two causally connected individual events).

The other strategy for dealing with Sebastian's stroll and his leisurely stroll, which one might call "the official line" of the property-exemplification account, is to affirm that these are different, if not entirely distinct, events. Not entirely distinct since the latter *includes* the former.[24] I will not try to give a characterization of 'inclusion' for events here; a completely general characterization gets, as far as I know, to be very complicated without being philosophically interesting; also, various different kinds of "inclusion" have to be distinguished (obviously, the sense in which as assassination *includes* a killing or strolling leisurely *includes* strolling is very different from the sense in which, say, my walking to the door *includes* my moving the left foot to take the first step, or the burning of the barn *includes* the burning of the roof of the barn). But I assume that it's intuitively plausible to say there is some relation here that can be called "inclusion". Difference need not be total distinctness or absence of any significant relation whatever. Once this is granted, there being two events (actions) here, and not one, impresses us as not such an extravagant claim after all. Take this table: the top of the table is not the same thing as the table. So there are two things, but of course one table — in fact, there are lots of things here if you include the legs, the molecules, the atoms, etc. making up the table.

Unfortunately, we are not through with the proliferating events. The new difficulty I have in mind is this: Granted there are two events here, of which one is included in the other. Now, Sebastian's strolling is a strolling — a stroll event, if you like — and Sebastians strolling leisurely is also a stroll event. You say they are two events, not one; so it follows that there are two stroll events, both strolled by Sebastian on that memorable night through the streets of Bologna, In fact, given such generic events as strolling with a cane in hand, strolling with a limp, and so on, there were indefinitely many strolls strolled by Sebastian that night! And of course indefinitely many stabbings administered by Brutus on Caesar!

The analogy with tables and other sundry physical objects may still help us here. We normally count this as *one* table; and there are just so many (a fixed number of) tables in this room. However, if you believe in the calculus of individuals,[25] you will see that included in this table is another table — in fact, there are indefinitely many tables each of which is a proper part of this table. For consider the table with one micrometer of its top removed; that is a table different from this table; and so on.

It would be absurd to say that for this reason we must say there are in fact indefinitely many tables in this room. What I am suggesting is merely that the sense in which, under the structured complex view of events, there are indefinitely many strolls strolled by Sebastian may be just as harmless as the sense in which there are indefinitely many tables in this room. The proliferation of events with which my account of events is often charged is not in itself serious; for "the number of *events*" is very much like "the number of *things*" or "the number of *facts*"; 'event' isn't an ordinary run-of-the-mill count noun. What is bothersome is the seeming fact that the number of stabbings or strollings seems to go beyond any bound. 'Stabbing' and 'stroll' seem to be as good count nouns as 'table' and 'apple'. In any case I hope that I have succeeded in mitigating this difficulty. If I have not, the earlier strategy of handling the proliferation problem would merit more serious consideration.

IV

The question has been raised whether my account of events has implausible consequences concerning the essential properties of events.[26] Take Sebastian's leisurely stroll at midnight. According to the structured complex account, it is thought, there are three essential properties of that event: one, that the stroll was strolled by Sebastian; two, that it was a leisurely stroll; and three, that it occurred at midnight. More generally, it is alleged that the account is committed to the thesis that the three constituents of an event constitute the essential properties of the event. It is then argued that, at least, the time of the occurrence of an event is not an essential property of it. Sebastian's stroll could have taken place five minutes before or after midnight. And perhaps its being a leisurely stroll isn't an essential property of the stroll either; if Sebastian had been pressed for time, the stroll would have been a brisk one. Similarly, the stroll could have been taken by someone else. Suppose that the midnight stroll was done as some sort of ritual by a member of a secret society chosen by lottery, and that it so happened that Sebastian was so chosen. If Mario, Sebastian's friend, had been chosen, then Mario would have strolled that stroll.[27]

It isn't clear to me what, if anything, an analysis or metaphysical theory of something implies about the essential properties of that thing. There is a metaphysical theory of physical objects, which is of respectable vintage and tradition, that asserts that a physical object is a "congerie of properties" or something like that. So this table is a "congerie" of such properties as brown color, the mass it has, and so on. But presumably it is not a consequence of the theory that the table has essentially the properties it actually has, that the brown color of the table is an essential property of it.

Why should it be thought, then, that the structured complex view of events is saddled with the essentialist consequences mentioned above?

But perhaps it is my identity condition for event structures that is the chief focus of the objections. Here, too, analogy with other cases makes it difficult to see how any essentialist consequences necessarily follow from identity criteria. It is at least a respectable identity criterion for physical objects that they are the same just in case they are completely co-incident in space and time. From this it does not follow that a physical object is essentially where and when it in fact is. To give another, possibly controversial, example, the extensionality criterion of set identity does not entail that a given set has its members essentially. It seems at least arguable that the set of the planets could have comprised eight planets rather than nine; even if this is wrong, it's not easy to see how the extensionality criterion (or any part of the usual mathematical theories of sets) shows it; we would need an independent metaphysical argument.

On the other hand, I don't want to claim that the essentialist consequences attributed to my account are in themselves false. At least, I find it plausible to think of the constitutive substance of an event as essential to the identity of that event. The fact that someone other than Sebastian could have taken a stroll in his place does not make it the case that the very stroll that Sebastian took could have been taken by someone else. If Mario had been chosen to stroll that night, then there would have been another stroll, namely Mario's. It has been remarked by some philosophers that, although you could have a pain that is qualitatively identical with the pain I am now having, you could not, logically or metaphysically, have the very same, numerically identical pain that I have.[28] The event of my strolling could not, logically or metaphysically, occur to anyone else any more than the event of my being in pain could. Only Socrates could have died *his* death. It seems not implausible to think that events and states are essentially individuated with respect to their constitutive substances.

The essentiality of the constitutive property to the identity of an event is less certain. For one thing, the question seems to depend on some of the issues earlier raised concerning generic events. If strolling leisurely is a generic event, there seems to be a case for saying that the generic event is not essential to the identity of an event which exemplifies it. But it is highly dubious that Sebastian's leisurely stroll could have been a run or a crawl, and it certainly could not have been a coughing or dozing, although Sebastian could have stayed home that night with a cold, coughing and dozing. The case seems still weaker for the essentiality of the time of occurrence: it seems correct to say that the stroll could have occurred a little earlier or later than it actually did. The stroll, we suppose, could have taken place five minutes later than it actually did, but could it — the very same stroll — have occurred five months later? Five years? In any case, caution is required: we should not infer, from the mere fact that Sebastian could have strolled at a different time, the conclusion that this very stroll Sebastian took could have occurred at that different time.

Some of these issues may have important bearings on other philosophical problems, such as the identity theory of mind; also, what we want to say about the bearing of generic events on the essential properties of events may in turn constrain what we want to pick as generic events. And what I said earlier about "knowing what a given event is" and "intrinsic description of an event" is likely to have a bearing on these issues. There is at present only a mass of intuitions, some conflicting with others, which need to be sorted out by a theory. We don't have such a theory, and in any case, events don't seem to be much worse off than anything else with respect to these problems about essences.

There is an essentialist consequence I am willing to accept: events are, essentially, structured complexes of the sort the theory says they are. Thus, events could not be substances, properties, and so on. But this should not be confused with the assertion that *each* event structure has *its* constituents essentially. This assertion is at least partially true, as I argued; but the general problem is still open.

V

Actions are usually taken as a subclass of events. How to characterize this subclass is a problem considered very important, but we shall not be concerned with it here. Killings are actions — at least, those that involve agents (I assume falling rocks and lightnings can also kill) — and thus events as well. But what is a killing? As has frequently been observed of late, 'kill' is a near synonym of 'cause to die'. Since killing presumably isn't a basic action, not for humans at any rate, it must involve two events, one an action performed by the killer and the other the death caused by the action. Thus, Brutus's killing Caesar seems to be nothing other than some action of Brutus causing the death of Caesar. The action event of Brutus's killing Caesar thus threatens to turn into a *relation*, a *causal* relation, between two events. And Brutus's stabbing Caesar, the cause event in this causal relation, itself may turn into a causal relation between two events, in the same way. Thus, killings so analyzed don't seem to fit the model of events under the property-exemplification account; they do not seem to have the complex event structure it attributes to events; instead, they seem to be relations between events.

This feature isn't limited to action events. As noted some time ago by C. J. Ducasse, many transitive verbs are implicitly causal; e.g., 'pull', 'push', 'break', 'shatter'. When the wind blows the door open, a causal assertion is made: the pressure of the wind on the door causing the opening of the door. So the event of the wind's blowing open the door appears to turn into a causal relation between two events, the wind's pressure on the door and the door's opening. The question arises: Are we to accept these causal relations themselves, i.e., one event's causing another, as events?[29] Or should we fit them into some other ontological category, say, facts?

One argument for treating, say, killings as events may be this: they are just the sort of thing that can have causes and effects, and just the sort of thing that can be given causal explanations. Brutus's killing Caesar may have been caused by Brutus's political ambitions and personal jealousies; it in turn caused Calpurnia's grief and caused Caesar to be absent from the Roman Senate the next day. It is of the essence of events that they can enter into causal relations. So why not treat killings and other actions as events?

This argument isn't decisive, however. As earlier noted, there are two events involved in Brutus's killing Caesar: Brutus's action, which was his stabbing Caesar, and Caesar's death. When we cite Brutus's motives and beliefs as causes of the killing, we do not seem to be saying that they are the causes of the stabbing's causing the death; rather, we seem to be saying that they are causes — or among the causes — of Brutus's undertaking the action, namely the stabbing of Caesar, which he believed would result in Caesar's death. I would venture the hypothesis that what we normally take to be a cause of the killing will ultimately turn out to be a cause — or among the causal conditions — of the basic action which was undertaken by Brutus in the endeavor that Caesar be dead and which in fact did cause the death.

What of the effects of the killing? Calpurnia's grief may very well have been caused by her *belief* that Caesar was dead, or that Caesar was so brutally murdered, or that it was Brutus who killed him. As for Caesar's absence from the Senate the following day, we can attribute it to his death as one of its effects. I think that what we normally take as an effect of a killing is often attributable to the death of the person killed or someone's cognitive attitude, such as belief, toward some aspects of the killing.

I believe similar things can be said of events that do not involve agents. The rock shatters the window. This we normally call an event. But it involves a causal relation: the rock's impact on the window caused it to shatter. What is the cause of the rock's shattering the window? Well, Johnny threw the rock. But we can take Johnny's throwing the rock as the cause of the rock's impact on the window, namely the first of the two events in the causal relation. The rock's shattering the window caused a cut on my hand. Again, the cut can be construed as an effect of the shattering of the window, namely the second of the two events in the causal relation, and not as the effect of the rock's shattering the window. One might object: But what of the fragility of the window glass? Why isn't that a cause of the rock's impact's causing the shattering? We do say: If the glass in the window had not been so fragile, the rock's impact would not have caused the window to shatter. Furthermore, the fragility of the window glass is not a cause of the rock's impact on the window. My reply is this: we still need not say that the fragility is a cause of one event's causing another; it is a cause, along with the rock's impact and perhaps other things, making up the complete cause of the window's shattering.

So the thesis I am suggesting is this: the causes and effects of actions and events exhibiting the causal features under discussion are attributable to the events in the causal relation that constitute such an action or event. (I leave aside here effects like Calpurnia's grief that may be caused by beliefs about such actions and events.) The thesis has two interpretations, one stronger than the other: (1) all causes of, say, a killing are among the causes of the action that caused the death, and all effects of the killing are among the effects of the death; and (2) all causes of the killing are among the causes of the action that caused the death or of the death, and all effects of the killing, too, are among the effects of the action or of the death. (1) The stronger thesis, appears to be false; suppose that as a result of the wielding of the heavy sword, Brutus dislocated his right shoulder. It would be correct to say that Brutus's dislocating his right shoulder was caused by his killing Caesar, but clearly it is not caused by Caesar's death. The weaker interpretation (2) of course accommodates this sort of example. In any case, if the thesis is correct in either interpretation, we can block the argument that killings must be treated as events since they enter into causal relations.

If we decide not to regard killings and such as events, then it would be open to us to regard them as *facts* (which should not preclude us from taking events simpliciter as a special subclass of facts): Brutus's killing Caesar is the fact that some action of Brutus caused Caesar to die, and the rock's shattering the window is the fact that the rock's impact caused the window to shatter. Such events and actions turn out to be causal facts. Treating them in this way may affect the ontology of action theory, theory of explanation, and the analysis of causation. And it may lead us to the talk of "basic events", namely those events not involving causal and other relations among other events.

But the above is not the only course open to us. If we are prepared to accept causal properties as generic events, that is, if we are prepared to allow causal relations between events to appear in generic events, then we could accommodate killings and its ilk within our scheme. For we can render

(9)      Brutus's doing some action which caused Caesar's death

into

(10)     [(Brutus, Caesar), for some generic action event $P$ and time $t^*$ [(①, ②), $P_{①②}$, $t^*$] caused [②, dies, $t'$], $t$].[30]

Which way is better? I think that the second way leads to a messy situation with regard to the problem of characterizing generic events, and creates complications in the theory of causation, explanation, and so forth. The first way is largely unexplored at this stage, but I would look upon it more favorably; I think it presents us with interesting possibilities to explore.[31]

*The University of Michigan*

## NOTES

[1] In Ducasse, C. J., *Causation and the Type of Necessity*, Univ. of Washington Press, Seattle, 1924

[2] "On the Psycho-Physical Identity Theory", *American Philosophical Quarterly* 3 (1966), 231–32; 'Events and Their Descriptions: Some Considerations', N. Rescher *et al.* (eds.), *Essays in Honor of Carl G. Hempel*, Reidel, Dordrecht-Holland, 1969; 'Causation, Nomic Subsumption, and the Concept of Event', *Journal of Philosophy* 70 (1973), 217–36. A similar account of action was given by Alvin Goldman in *A Theory of Human Action*, Prentice-Hall, Englewood Cliffs, N.J., 1970; an account of events very much like mine is found in R. M. Martin's 'On Events and Event-Descriptions', J. Margolis (ed.), *Fact and Existence*. See also N. L. Wilson, 'Facts, Events and Their Identity Conditions', *Philosophical Studies* 25 (1974), 303–21.

[3] This expression was suggested by Richard Cartwright.

[4] For a treatment of 'possible facts' somewhat along these lines see Bas van Fraassen, 'Facts and Tautological Entailments', *Journal of Philosophy* 66 (1969), 477–87.

[5] Interesting results have been obtained along these lines by Terence Horgan in his doctoral dissertation, *Microreduction and the Mind-Body Problem* at The University of Michigan, 1974.

[6] See my 'Noncausal Connections', *Noûs* 8 (1974), 41–52. The term 'Cambridge change' comes from Peter Geach, *God and the Soul*, Routledge & Kegan Paul, London, 1969, p. 71.

[7] To cite a few: 'The Logical Form of Action Sentences', N. Rescher (ed.), *The Logic of Decision and Action*, Univ. of Pittsburgh Press, Pittsburgh, 1967; 'Causal Relations', *Journal of Philosophy* 64 (1967), 691–703; 'Truth and Meaning', *Synthese* 17 (1967), 304–23.

[8] 'Action and Reaction', *Inquiry* **13** (1970), 140–48, 146–47.

[9] In N. Rescher (ed.), *Essays in Honor of Carl G. Hempel.*

[10] E.g. by N. L. Wilson in 'Facts, Events and Their Identity Conditions'; and by George Sher in 'On Event-Identity', *Australasian Journal of Philosophy* **52** (1974), 39–47.

[11] In 'On Kim's Account of Events and Event-Identity', *Journal of Philosophy* **71** (1974), 327–36, Alexander Rosenberg claims that, with a slight revision in my account of events, Davidson's criterion and my criterion are equivalent under the Humean, constant-conjunction view of causation.

[12] Davidson himself refers to my account as a 'rival' account, in his 'Events as Particulars', *Noûs* **4** (1970), 25–32, p. 26, footnote 4.

[13] I shall not discuss here Roderick M. Chisholm's very different theory of events as 'states of affairs' in his sense of abstract intensional entities, developed in his 'States of Affairs' (forthcoming). See also his 'Events and Propositions', *Noûs* **4** (1970), 15–24.

[14] The first pair comes from his 'Eternal vs. Ephemeral Events', *Noûs* **5** (1971), 335–49, p. 337; the second from 'Causal Relations', p. 696.

[15] Chisholm refers to both Davidson's and my account as variants of 'the concrete event theory' in 'States of Affairs'.

[16] 'The Individuation of Events', p. 220.

[17] Especially if we keep in mind that fact that there being three different kissings does not entail that there can be no intimate and significant relations between them.

[18] 'Causal Relations', p. 703. (8) is a slightly altered version of Davidson's own example.

[19] Davidson in his 'Comments' on Martin's 'On Events and Event-Descriptions', Margolis (ed.), *Fact and Existence*, p. 81. Also Rosenberg in 'On Kim's Account of Events and Event-Identity'.

[20] E.g. Carl G. Hedman claims this in his 'On When There Must Be a Time-Difference Between Cause and Effect', *Philosophy of Science* **39** (1972), 507–11.

[21] On property identity, see Peter Achinstein, 'The Identity of Properties', *American Philosophical Quarterly* **11**, 1974, 257–75.

[22] I have in mind: Lawrence H. Davis, 'Individuation of Actions', *Journal of Philosophy* **67** (1970), 520–30; Judith Jarvis Thomson, 'The Time of a Killing', *Journal of Philosophy* **68** (1971), 115–32; Alvin I. Goldman, 'The Individuation of Action', *Journal of Philosophy* **68** (1971), 761–74.

[23] Such a view is suggested by Judith Jarvis Thomson in her 'Individuating Actions', *Journal of Philosophy* **68** (1971), 774–81.

[24] Goldman would say that the former 'level-generates' the latter; see *A Theory of Human Action*, Chapter 2.

[25] In the sense of Nelson Goodman, *The Structure of Appearance*, Harvard University Press, Cambridge, 1951.

[26] Ed Wierenga has raised this question in his doctoral dissertation, *Three Theories of Events*, University of Massachusetts at Amherst, 1974.

[27] This is substantially what Davidson says in 'Eternal vs. Ephemeral Events' to answer a question raised by Chisholm.

[28] Jerome Shaffer in 'Persons and Their Bodies', *Philosophical Review* **75** (1966), 59–77.

[29] From similar considerations N. L. Wilson concludes "... 'alerting', 'killing' and all the other causative verbs do not refer to events" in 'Facts, Events and Their Identity Conditions', p. 318.

[30] The question of the relationship between $t^*$, $t'$, and $t$ is discussed by Judith Jarvis Thomson in 'The Time of a Killing'.

[31] The problem of generic events that contain causal relations is related to Bernard Berofsky's problem of characterizing 'R-sentences' in his *Determinism*, Princeton Univ. Press, Princeton, 1971, Chapter V, Esp. pp. 157ff.

# EVENTS AND ACTIONS: SOME COMMENTS
## ON BRAND AND KIM

After noting that "the paradigm case of something particular is something in the world, say, an individual table, person, or pen", Myles Brand says, in his interesting paper, that "examples of properties and propositions are also specifiable".[1] He tells us nothing more concerning this latter. Just how are properties and relations specifiable? Brand thinks it is a "plausible working hypothesis" that properties are legitimate objects, as good as "specifiable groupings of particulars" — which presumably sets or classes are. But sets, remember, are specifiable wholly in terms of their membership. A set $\alpha$ is ordinarily regarded as identical with a set $\beta$ if and only if every member of $\alpha$ is a member of $\beta$ and conversely. Properties, however, are not specifiable in terms of the particulars that have them. In fact, it is to be feared that no one has ever quite told us adequately just how properties are to be specified, and consequently what the condition for identity between them actually is. It thus seems to me doubtful that the assumption of properties is on a par with that of sets or classes as a plausible working hypothesis. Similar comments apply to the assumption of propositions. If properties are available propositions are also, and conversely. The most sophisticated recent attempt to construct a logic accommodating both is perhaps that contained in Alonzo Church's Presidential Address to the Pacific Division a year ago entitled 'Russellian Simple Type Theory'.[2] (That theory seems to many so appallingly artificial and complicated, however, as to throw no light upon mathematics, natural science, or the structure or ordinary language. And yet it is just this sort of theory that Brand opts for by way of a background logic.) In any case, it would be of interest to be shown specifically how his theory would fit in with some such well-developed logic as that of Church.

Brand's espousal of a particularist theory of events is surely welcome. It is not easy to say *exactly* what particulars are, however, as has often been observed, but at least they are entities at the lowest type level. The problem arises as to whether we may base the theory upon only a first-order logic or rather whether we should presuppose one of higher order or even a full axiomatic set theory. Brand admits a higher-order (even intensional) logic,

*M. Brand and D. Walton (eds.), Action Theory, 179–192. All Rights Reserved*
*Copyright © 1976 by D. Reidel Publishing Company, Dordrecht-Holland*

whereas only a first-order extensionalist one is acceptable to some. More on this in a moment.

Brand thinks there are "two, possibly three, *prima facie* advantages to particularist theories". The first is that we can name and even count events just as we can name and count physical particulars. But would not the same hold of non-particularist handlings of events? Especially if properties and propositions are "specifiable," as Brand thinks they are? If specifiable, properties may presumably be named and counted just as particulars are. For this first advantage to have point, Brand should not have allowed property- and proposition-talk at all.

The second advantage is that in order to "provide an extension of Tarski's truth definition from formal to natural languages . . . it is necessary to recast natural language sentences into sentences using only the machinery available in first-order logic with identity plus a list of singular terms and predicates." Brand suggests that "Davidson and others" have attempted to do this. Nowhere it seems, however, has Davidson attempted any such thing. He in no way parts from Tarski in this regard. There is no such thing as a "Davidsonian truth-definition" not due to Tarski. The object-language for Tarski may be of first order, it will be recalled, but it need not be. In either case, however, the metalanguage *must* be of order at least one higher than that to which it is applied. Brand's second advantage thus seems no more to favor particularism than his first.

A third possible advantage of particularist theories is "their ontological simplicity, in that they require the least kinds of existents." Brand thinks that this advantage may be illusory, however, and that the response to "this alleged advantage is the Platonic one that considerations of ontological simplicity are of little if any importance." To many, however, this third advantage will seem a genuine one, and in fact the only real one thus far. We will return to this point again in a moment.

Brand follows Davidson in using 'C' to stand for a relation for efficient causation between events. Thus '$e_1 C e_2$' expresses that event $e_1$ causes event $e_2$. But axioms are never given and no attempt is made to analyze the notion of cause thus symbolized. It has been argued elsewhere that the form '$e_1 C e_2$' is too simple and that causation must be handled intensionally in terms of the Fregean *Arten des Gegebenseins* or modes of linguistic description.[3] Causation, in the sense Davidson needs it, seems to be a quadratic relation, where '$e, a C e', a'$' expresses that event $e_1$ as taken under the linguistic description a causes event $e'$ as taken under the linguistic description $a'$.

Let us turn now to Brand's comments on event identity in terms of spatio-temporal location. Recall that a modal operator for necessity is required in the definiens ([D6] and [D6]+). Event $e_1$ is identical with $e_2$ if and only if necessarily $e_1$ occurs within spatio-temporal region s if and only if $e_2$ does also for all s. (The additional proviso of [D6]+ is of no concern for the moment.) Just what kind of necessity is involved here we are not told. Logical necessity? — if so, just what kind, i.e., on the basis of just what logical principles? And with or without meaning postulates? If with, what are they? Physical necessity? If so, in accord with what physics? Technological necessity? If the latter two, does necessity become time-bound, in accord with say the present state of physics or technology? These are not rhetorical questions — they are Reichenbachian ones and should be answered satisfactorily, it seems to me, by those who use the modal operators without analysis. And not much help is gained by talk of possible worlds, that talk itself being at least equally obscure if not more so. To try to explicate the *obscurus per obscurius* seems of little help in making any genuine — in Hempel's splendid phrase — "progress in clarification."

At two or three places Brand speaks of the disadvantages of a "metalinguistic account" of indirect discourse. Perhaps he would include here a metalinguistic account of the modalities also. It is not clear just what these disadvantages are supposed to be, however. (On some specious disadvantages, see my *Belief, Existence, and Meaning*, New York University Press, 1969, pp. 57ff.) And in any event, Brand seems to accept the usual kind of metalinguistic account of the modal operators in terms of possible worlds. Thus not only does he accept a higher-order object language with modalities, he must accept also a still higher-order metalanguage in terms of which possible-world talk may be carried out. He is thus driven to accept a metalinguistic account, whatever "disadvantages" he thinks it involves. Curiously, however, he never seems to worry about the *axiomatics* of these frameworks. The metalanguage contains of course a modal theory, which in turn presupposes a set or type-theory of great power. Some of the axioms needed are highly dubious, especially the axioms of existence.

The point of mentioning the axiomatic framework is that it goes hand in hand with matters of ontological commitment, which, Brand suggests, "are of little if any importance." The real situation is quite the opposite: Nothing under the sun is more important in our theorizing about anything at all, it would seem, than being clear about our assumptions. So close is the relationship between ontic commitment and axiomatics that the latter may be said to determine what our theory actually is. Equally significant of course is what objects our assumptions determine the theory to be about — this is precisely what our assumptions do, in addition to interrelating these objects in suitable ways. Economy of ontic commitment thus goes part and parcel with economy of axiomatic assumption, this latter being of the highest import in metalogic, metamathematics, and in their various applications to methodology and the empirical sciences.

Let us skip on now to the example concerning Stravinsky. Let '$\langle s, L, $ (his arm)$\rangle e_1$,' express that $e_1$ is some specific action of Stravinsky's lowering his arm, '$\langle s, L, $ (his baton)$\rangle e_2$', that $e_2$ is an action of Stravinsky's lowering his baton, and '$\langle s, S, $ (the cellos)$\rangle e_3$', that $e_3$ is an action of Stravinsky's signalling to the cellos. Note here that '(his arm)' is a deictic description where 'his' is taken as cross-referential to 'Stravinsky's'. Also '(the cellos)' is an anaphoric Russellian description of the fusion of the cellos in such and such a given class of cello players. The question is now as to whether $e_1$, $e_2$, and $e_3$ should be regarded as distinct events or not. Concerning identity we should wish the usual Hilbert-Bernays laws to obtain:

*Id1.*     $\vdash e = e$,

*Id2.*     $\vdash e = e' \supset (Fe \supset Fe')$, where in place of '$F$' any event-descriptive or other suitable predicate is placed.

The condition for diversity is then the usual one of exhibiting explicitly some $F$ applicable to one but not to the other. On this basis, it would seem that $e_1 \neq e_2$, $e_2 \neq e_3$, and $e_1 \neq e_3$. Surely we can find some $F$ applicable to $e_1$ and not to $e_2$, e.g., $e_2$ bears the By$_{\text{Means}}$-relation to $e_1$ but not to itself — the lowering of the baton is accomplished by means of the lowering of his arm. Similarly $e_2 \neq e_3$, for $e_3$ By$_{\text{Means}}$ $e_2$ but not $e_3$ By$_{\text{Means}}$ $e_3$. And likewise $e_1 \neq e_3$ for $e_3$ By$_{\text{Means}}$ $e_1$ but not $e_3$ By$_{\text{Means}}$ $e_3$. Perhaps all three of these events are simultaneous in which case it is interesting to consider the sum event $(e_1 \cup e_2 \cup e_3)$. Clearly this sum event is not itself a $\langle s, L, $ (his arm)$\rangle$ nor a $\langle s, L, $ (his baton)$\rangle$. It is more than this, being a $\langle s, S, $ (the cellos)$\rangle$. Could we than say that $e_1$ is a *part* of $e_2$ and that $e_1$ and $e_2$ are both *parts* of $e_3$? (Of course they are trivially parts of $(e_1 \cup e_2 \cup e_3)$.) Perhaps we can, in the sense that every spatio-temporal part of $e_1$ is also a part of $e_2$ and every spatio-temporal part of $e_2$ is a part of $e_3$. The relevant spatio-temporal parts of the baton are not spatio-temporal parts of the lowering, so that $\sim e_2$ P $e_1$. Also the whole signalling to the cellos presumably consists of something more than just the lowering of the arm or baton, so that $\sim e_3$ P $e_1$ and $\sim e_3$ P $e_2$. What more is involved? A nod in the direction of the cellos, perhaps, or some other gesture with the baton, eyes, arm, or body. (And also there are the cellos and their players. If there are no cellos or players of them, Stravinsky can hardly be said to signal to them. Of course he can signal even if there are none, but not *to them*. It is a logical consequence of

'$\langle s, S, (\text{the cellos})\rangle e_1$,' that there are cellos and players of them being signalled to. The whole event $e_1$ concerns thus both the location of Stravinsky as well as the cellos.)

Whenever we speak of events and actions it is of interest to consider various adverbial constructions upon them.[4] Suppose we were to say that Stravinsky lowered his arm skillfully. This would mean — in accord with one analysis of adverbs — that the action $e_1$ was skillful in the sense appropriate for lowering of arms. To say that Stravinsky lowered his baton skillfully means rather that $e_1$ was skillful in the sense appropriate to lowerings of batons. And, more strikingly, to say that Stravinsky signalled the cellos skillfully is to say that $e_3$ was skillful in still a third sense, that appropriate to skill in signalling to cellos in the art of conducting. We have then three quite separate senses of 'skillfully', each applicable to one of $e_1$, $e_2$, and $e_3$ but not to the two others. In such a way as this, discernible adverbial differences among $e_1$, $e_2$, and $e_3$ are brought to light, to assure their diversity.

Note that as a result of our identity laws, Brand's (D6) may be transformed into a one-way implication. In other words, occurring within the same spatio-temporal regions becomes a necessary condition for identity but not a sufficient one. My swimming the channel (now) and my catching a cold (now) are very different even though occurring at the same place and time. The event of its raining in (the whole of) Chicago between 8–9 p.m. on August 21, 1974 is not the same as the event of its growing darker in (the whole of) Chicago between 8–9 p.m. on August 21, 1974. And similarly for other examples.

In addition to events we should recognize, it would seem, event-*concepts* as well, not as anything mysterious in the sense of Carnap's intensions or the Frege-Church *Sinne* or meanings, but as something quite definite and "specifiable," namely events taken under a given *Art des Gegebenseins*.[5] Let the ordered couple $\langle e, a\rangle$ be such that the one-place predicate $a$ denotes $e$. Such a couple is merely $e$ taken under the linguistic description $a$. We see than that the notation for causation suggested above is essentially one involving event-concepts. The event $e$ of Nixon's resigning is the same event as the 37th President's resigning. But the *concept* of $e$ under the description '$\{e' \ni \langle n, R\rangle e'\}$' is very different from the *concept* of $e$ under '$\{e' \ni \langle (\text{the 37th Pres.})R\rangle e'\}$'. And even the concept of Hesperus's rising today is a different concept from Phosporus's rising today, unless 'Hesperus' and 'Phosporus' are taken as logically equivalent or synonymous in some suitable sense. Intentional contexts may be handled by bringing in event-concepts, and indeed virtual-class and relation concepts as well.

"A basic action," Brand notes, "is one that the agent performs without doing anything in order to perform it." Presumably we should insert 'else' here after 'anything', so that a basic action is an action the agent performs without doing anything else to perform it. Thus, perhaps we may define

'$BA$ e' as '($Ep$) (Per p · p Do e · $\sim$($Ee'$) (p Do e' · $\sim e' = e \cdot e$ By$_{\text{Means}}$ e'))'.

For this definition to be very helpful, a good deal must be spelled out concerning the By$_{\text{Means}}$-relation. In fact a whole logical theory of means and ends is needed, which seems not to have been supplied. In the absence of such a theory, it is difficult to say whether there are any basic actions at all. Much depends on the analysis of the lexical verb 'do' as well as on the meaning postulates concerning 'By$_{\text{Means}}$'. Brand would not disagree with this perhaps, at least in principle. In accord with the definition of '$BA$', our $e_2$ and $e_3$ above come out as nonbasic, as Brand thinks they should. However, it should be noted that the By$_{\text{Means}}$ relation is not the same as the C-relation for causation. It seems that this latter is always somehow related to a law of causal form. Where $\langle e, a \rangle$ C $\langle e', a' \rangle$ there is always lurking in the background a causal law to the effect that events to which the predicate a applies cause events to which a' does — that all a's cause a''s, or something of the sort. No such condition need be placed upon the By$_{\text{Means}}$-relation. The sentence 'I drove here by car' presupposes no one general causal law. It seems that Danto and others have sometimes confused these two relations and inadvertently have slipped into causal talk, where they had been speaking wholly in terms of 'By$_{\text{Means}}$'.

When we speak of the By$_{\text{Means}}$-relation, it is essential to specify the subscript 'means'. Strictly there is no "By" relation at all; there is a whole family of them, with some family resemblances perhaps. Thus 'He was standing by the car' involves By$_{\text{Relative Position}}$, the By-relation of *relative position*. 'He jumped by me' involves that of *relative passage*. 'By noon I will have arrived' involves one of *time*. 'The window was broken by a stone' involves the *instrumental* By. 'We were observed by a stranger' involves By in the *agentive* sense. It is this last that is needed to handle agency and responsibility. Thus 'John stole the car' may be given a logical form

'($Ee$)(e Before$_{\text{Time}}$ *now*$_{sp}$ · $\langle S \rangle$ e · e By$_{\text{Agent}}$ $j$ · e Of$_{\text{Object}}$ (the car))',

and

'John is responsible for stealing the car'

a form such as

'$(Ee)j$ Responsible e,' $\{e' \ni (Ee'')(Ep)$ (e'' Before$_{Time}$ $now_{sp}$ · $\langle S \rangle e''$
· e'' By$_{Agent}$ p · e'' Of$_{Object}$ (the car))$\}$''.[6]

The form 'j Responsible e, '$F$'' here expresses that John is responsible for performing e under the (speaker's) description of its having been a stealing of the car by someone. The intentionality of the context is handled by bringing in the predicate '$F$' as the speaker's *Art des Gegebenseins* of the action. Note that John is said to be responsible for e under this description, but not necessarily under some equivalent description. Note that the given sentence is ambiguous as between

'John is responsible for John's stealing the car'

and

'John is responsible for someone's stealing the car'.

The form given is for the second only.

Brand makes a number of interesting comments concerning recurrence, "the second major problem for Particularist theories." It will be instructive to consider logical forms for some of the sentences he suggests, thereby throwing light on some of the problems involved. Consider first

(1)     'Socrates drank hemlock with his left hand at noon and so did my Uncle Frank'.

Brand rightly wants two separate actions here, both being broadly of the same sort. The two actions involved are both drinkings of hemlock. (The addition of the phrases 'with (his) left hand' and 'at noon' (of the same day?) may be handled by additional clauses.) To specify this much seems sufficient. Grammatically, an interesting feature of this sentence is the presence of the pro-verb 'so'. Pro-verbs may be handled as other deictic words such as pronouns used referentially. In other words, the deep structure for this sentence should indicate that the speaker is using 'so' to refer to just the action type drinkings of hemlock, no other. Let a be an inscription of the form (1) as uttered (or written or whatever) by the speaker *sp* (me). Let b be the inscription of the form 'so' occurring in a. Further, let the speaker use b to refer in a to the virtual class of drinkings of hemlock. Thus we have that

(2)     (1) a · 'so' b · b Occ a · *sp* Ref b, $\{e \ni (Ee')$ $(Ex)$ $(\langle Drink \rangle$ e · e Of$_{Object}$ x · x P hemlock)$\}$, a.

Here 'hemlock' is for the totality of the world's hemlock (drink), and 'x P hemlock' expresses that x is a suitable *part* or *bit* of it. Where (2) obtains then, we have as a deep structure of (1) something like

'$(Ee)(Ee')((Ex)(\langle Drink\rangle$ e $\cdot$ e Before$_{Time}$ $now_{sp}$ $\cdot$ e Of$_{Object}$ x $\cdot$ x P hemlock). e By$_{Agent}$ Socrates $\cdot$ e With$_{Instrument}$ (Socrates' left hand) $\cdot$ e At$_{Time}$ noon $\cdot$ $sp$ So e', b, a $\cdot$ e' Before$_{Time}$ $now_{sp}$ $\cdot$ e' By$_{Agent}$ (my Uncle Frank) $\cdot$ e' With$_{Instrument}$ (my Uncle Frank's left hand) $\cdot$ e' At$_{Time}$ noon)',

Here '$sp$ So e', b, a' is merely an abbreviation for

'(2) $\cdot$ {e $\ni (Ex)(\langle Drink\rangle$ e $\cdot$ e Of$_{Object}$ x $\cdot$ x P hemlock)} e'',

to the effect that the speaker takes b to be a 'so' occurring in a and uses it to refer to such and such a virtual class one of whose members is e'. Sentences containing pro-verbs, like those containing directly referential (as over and against cross-referential) pronouns and other deictic words are thus seen to be occasion sentences and not eternal ones. (The use of 'his' and 'my' here are left unanalyzed.)[7]

Note that e and e' here are clearly distinct events, there being discernible differences between them. The e has Socrates as its agent, the e' my Uncle Frank. Likewise e is done with one instrument (Socrates' left hand), the e' by another (my Uncle Frank's left hand). Still both are of a common sort or kind, namely, drinkings of hemlock. Also there is a compound action (e $\cup$ e') with its own special properties. It is doubtful that we would wish to call this compound action 'a drinking of hemlock', nor is it done by Socrates, nor by my Uncle Frank. On the other hand, it takes place at noon, where 'noon' is taken to refer to noon of the same day. (A deeper analysis of the use of 'noon' here should of course be given.) Given any two events, if both occur *at* a given time, then their sum occurs at that time also. And conversely. Concerning 'during', however, the situation is different. If e and e' both occur during some time, their sum does also. And conversely. But e might occur during some part of a time, and e' during some other part, but (e $\cup$ e') would not occur during either, but only during the sum of those two times.

Consider next

'Joshua performed the same action as Paul'.

If interpreted co-agentially, this becomes

'$(Ee)(\langle Do\rangle$ e $\cdot$ e Before$_{Time}$ $now_{sp}$ $\cdot$ e By$_{Agent}$ $(j \cup p))$'.

Here there is a single doing, a joint shouting, as it were, done by Joshua and

Paul together, collectively, as co-agents, but not necessarily separately. Brand construes this sentence in such a way that there are two shoutings, not a joint shouting. Here the two doings are similar or match each other, somewhat as Russell's *sensibilia* and Goodman's *qualia* are allowed to do. The same action-kind or -sort is involved, but different action-events. (It is very important to distinguish, as Brand in effect does, action-types from action-events. The failure to do so, or even to recognize the distinction, seems to have led to a good deal of confusion.) Let 'e Sim e'' express that e and e' are similar. Then

$$\text{'}(Ee)(Ee')(\langle Do \rangle e \cdot \langle Do \rangle e' \cdot e \text{ Sim } e' \cdot e \text{ Before}_{\text{Time}} \, now_{sp} \cdot e'$$
$$\text{Before}_{\text{Time}} \, now_{sp} \cdot e \text{ By}_{\text{Agent}} j \cdot e' \text{ By}_{\text{Agent}} p)\text{'}$$

comes pretty close to expressing what is wished here.

Note that

'Joshua did the same shouting as Paul'

is at best a dubious sentence semantically. It might be construed as

'Joshua and Paul separately shouted the same thing'

or

'Joshua and Paul together shouted the same thing',

but less likely as

'Joshua and Paul both shouted'.

All of these renditions may be easily handled using the methods above. ('The same thing' here refers to similar inscriptions, the relation of syntactic similarity being well spelled out in inscriptional syntax.)

In sum, however, it does seem to me that Brand is on the right track in contending that "locutions concerning event recurrence are best understood as locutions about events of the same type" and that sameness of type is a "context-dependent notion," depending, that is, upon just what kind of sameness is required in the given sentential context — sameness of shouting, sameness of drinking hemlock, of drinking hemlock with the left hand, of drinking hemlock with the left hand at noon, and so on. It is doubtful that a context-independent notion of sameness of type is definable or even intelligible.

In his "Events as Property Exemplifications"[8] Jaegwon Kim writes that a "change in a substance occurs when that substance acquires a property it did not previously have, or loses a property it previously had." It is

interesting to compare this contention with a famous passage from Russell's
*The Principles of Mathematics* (p. 468).

> Change is the difference, in respect of truth or falsehood, between a proposition concerning
> an entity and a time T and a proposition concerning the same entity and another time T',
> provided that the two propositions differ only by the fact that T occurs in the one where T'
> occurs in the other. Change is continuous when the propositions of the above kind form a
> continuous series correlated with a continuous series of moments.

Change for Kim has to do with acquiring and losing a property; for Russell
it has to do with the difference in truth or falsity of two closely allied
"propositions." But, as noted above, propositions and properties go hand in
hand, and the two characterizations seem substantially the same. Russell
goes on to describe a continuous change in terms of a continuous series of
propositions. To handle this latter, of course, a considerable bit of set theory
or higher-order logic is required. Kim thinks he can "dispense with the set-
theoretic framework," but this is doubtful. If his theory is to be developed at
all extensively, it would seem that fundamental use will have to be made of
essentially the resources Russell needs.

The question arises as to just what kind of entities events are, for Kim,
and as to whether he has variables ranging over them. According to him,
"each individual event has three unique constituents: a substance (the
'constitutive object' of the event), a property it exemplifies (the 'constitutive
property' or 'generic event'), and a time. An event is a complex of these
three." Thus $[x, P, t]$ is an event with $x$ as its constitutive object, $P$ as its
constitutive property, and $t$ as its time. But just what is this "complex" $[x,
P, t]$? Clearly it is not itself a substance, a property, or a time. Is it some
new kind of entity to be taken as a value for a new kind of variable, or is it
rather a construct in some fashion? If the former, it could probably be
identified as an ordered triple within set theory or higher-order logic.[9] If the
latter, and this seems to be Kim's view, principles must be given concerning
*all the permissible linguistic contexts* in which these complexes are allowed
to occur. Kim gives only two, the context in which a complex is said to exist
and the context in which two complexes are said to be the same. Many
more contexts must be provided for, however, if this reductive account of
events is to be made workable. Also, quantifiers over events must
presumably be available, as well as quantifiers over classes of and over
relations between or among events. It is difficult to see how these could be
provided for, on Kim's views, without a very strong underlying logic — in
which case the complexes might as well be identified with ordered triples *ab
initio*. Kim contends, however, that "whether we use a new notation . . . or
use the set-theoretic machinery is really beside the philosophical point. The

metaphysical account of events is not essentially altered by such differences in the mode of presentation." It is doubtful that the difference is merely one of presentation, however. There is a vast logico-metaphysical difference between using the set-theoretic machinery or not, the set theory itself carrying its own assumptions and ontic commitment.

Kim thinks that a "metaphysical theory of events of the sort . . . sketched must be distinguised from a theory concerning the language and logic of events, or a theory of the 'logical form' of event and action sentences." It is difficult to see precisely just what this difference is, however, a well-developed theory of one carrying with it a well-developed theory of the other. A metaphysical theory is couched in a language with its own assumptions and ontic commitment, and its sentences thus have certain logical forms. If events and actions are to be considered metaphysically, sentences containing expressions for them are needed. And conversely, any well-developed theory of logical form is itself tantamount to the statement of a metaphysical view.

Let us turn again now to the matter of event identity, the problem of the individuation of events. Brand, Kim, and Davidson all seem to agree that this is the *Hauptproblem* in formulating a satisfactory theory. It is surely an important one, but perhaps not quite so fundamental as they would have us believe. There are conflicting intuitions here, just as there are conflicting intuitions among set theorists concerning the existence assumptions to be made. Set theorists go about their work in an admirable way, explicitly enunciating their assumptions and exploring the logical consequences of them. Brand, Kim, and Davidson seem content to defend their conflicting intuitions rather than to show us why their particular intuitions are of any special interest and how a workable theory can be developed on the basis of them. When intuitions conflict, alternative theories are needed accommodating them. We can then judge the success or failure of the theories as a whole. Seen in this light, the question of event identity may not be quite so important as is commonly supposed. The problem becomes one rather of formulating a theory to accommodate our intuitions concerning event identity as best we may. And if something has to be given up along the way for the sake of systematic coherency, *tant pis*. The principles of logic are rather basic to the whole enterprise and should be tampered with only as a last resort — and not at first blush, as is so common.

When one reflects upon identity, it is always good to start with Leibniz's definition, or with *Id1* and *Id2* above if the underlying logical framework is of first order. Entities are discrete then, as noted, if there is some discernible *F* applicable to one but not to the other. Why should these principles not hold of events? There seem to be no good reasons at all, merely that some intuitions will be violated if they do. Here it is a question of weighing the intuitions, which are usually rather feeble at best, against fundamental laws that hold throughout mathematics and natural science. It would remain a rather profound mystery why these should hold in such generality everywhere except in the theory of events. (Intensional and intentional contexts may be handled in terms of the *Arten des Gegebenseins*.) The use of a wise methodology would suggest rather that we adjust our intuitions to logic, rather than abrogate fundamental laws in favor of some *a priori* intuitions.

One simple way of handling event identity is to assume *Id1* and *Id2*, and then append an additional principle. Let $Prep_1$, $Prep_2$, ..., $Prep_n$ be the basic prepositional relations — it is assumed for the present that these are all dyadic — in terms of which others are definable. And let 'e $Under_{sp}$ a' express that the speaker takes e under the *Art des Gegebenseins* of the one-place predicate a, and 'a $Prphs_{sp}$ b' that the speaker takes a as a *paraphrase* of b.[10] '$\langle R \rangle$' and '$\langle S \rangle$' are any event-descriptive predicates standing for ⸱eneric events. Our rule is then that

$Id3.$ ⊢ $(\langle R \rangle e_1 \cdot \langle S \rangle e_2) \supset (e_1 = e_2 \equiv (\langle R \rangle = \langle S \rangle \cdot (e')(e_1 \ Prep_1 \ e' \equiv e_2 \ Prep_1$
$e') \cdot (e')(e_1 Prep_2 \ e' \equiv e_2 \ Prep_2 \ e') \cdot \ldots \cdot (e')(e_1 \ Prep_n \ e' \equiv e_2 \ Prep_n$
$e') \cdot (a)(b) (a \ Prphs \ b \supset (e_1 \ Under_{sp} \ a \equiv e_2 \ Under_{sp} \ b))))$.

'$\langle R \rangle = \langle S \rangle$' here expresses merely that every $\langle R \rangle$-event is an $\langle S \rangle$-event and conversely, and is equivalent to '$R = S$'.

Perhaps the generic events can be listed. There is presumably only a finite number of them. The "basic generic events may be best picked out relative to a scientific theory" — this contention of Kim recalls Hempel on meaningfulness — "whether the theory is a common-sense theory of the behavior of middle-sized objects or a highly sophisticated physical theory." Or, for that matter, of a protolinguistic source system for a natural language such as English. Even in the latter the vocabulary is specifiably finite, and thus in principle any suitable subset of it can be listed. Thus we may let $G_1, \ldots, G_k$ be the required generic events. We may then let

'$e_1 = e_2$' be defined as '$((G_1 e_1 \equiv G_1 e_2) \cdot \ldots \cdot (G_k e_1 \equiv G_k e_2) \cdot (e')$
$(e_1 \ Prep_1 \ e' \equiv e_2 \ Prep_1 \ e') \cdot \ldots \cdot (e') (e_1 \ Prep_n \ e' \equiv e_1 \ Prep_n \ e')$
$\cdot (a)(b) (a \ Prphs_{sp} \ b \supset (e_1 \ Under_{sp} \ a \equiv e_2 \ Under_{sp} \ b)))$'.

*Id1*, *Id2*, and *Id3* are then forthcoming as theorems. (This definition is merely an adaptation of one suggested by Hilbert and Bernays.)

Events are distinguished, on the basis of either of these two methods, by finding some suitable $F$ applicable to one rather than to the other. These are in accord with the *separatist* tendency to allow a plurality of simultaneous co-placial events. All such events may be summed, however, in accord with the calculus of individuals, and especial interest attaches to such sum-events. The whole totality of what is going on here now, say, or there then, might be thought of as the fundamental kind of event to admit. Such a view would be in accord with the *summationlist* tendency. Event-identity could then be handled essentially as in Brand's (D6). Even so, all manner of differences may be handled by bringing in events-concepts as discussed above. The *concept* of its growing dark in Chicago at such and such a place-time is a very different concept from its raining at that place-time. Still only one event is taking place, the whole complex of what is happening. This alternative way of handling the matter — in accord with alternative intuitions — could no doubt be made to work. Synonymy and paraphrase, as well as hyponymy, would be needed metalinguistically to handle matters that, in the other methods, are handled by identity and the part-whole relation.

Incidentally, note that Kim's *Existence condition*, that $[x, P, t]$ exists just in case the substance $x$ has the property $P$ at time $t$, is very close to that of Reichenbach.[11] Kim's *Identity condition*, that $[x, P, t] = [y, Q, t']$ just in case $x = y$, $P = Q$, and $t = t'$, purports to account for intensional contexts, $P$ and $Q$ being properties, not classes. Kim is no better off than Brand here, however, he also needing an obscure intensionalist logic of some kind to account for identity of properties, an account that seems never adequately to have been given. Also, as noted earlier, Kim provides only these two contexts for expressions for his complexes to occur in. But such complexes must themselves be allowed properties, stand in relations, be characterized by adverbs, and so on. A good deal more is needed here than Kim seems to realize. He seems to suggest that this can be done in terms of "three primitive functors on events: 'is the constitutive property of', 'is the constitutive object of', and 'is the time of occurrence of'." For these primitive functors to behave properly, however, contexts containing complexes must already be available primitively. Thus a whole syntax and semantics concerning expressions of the form '$[x, P, t]$' is needed, the square brackets and commas being additional primitives.

Also a good deal of spelling out of the theory of time is needed for Kim's program to get under way.[12] It is surely legitimate to take times as part of the primitive ontology with a special kind of variable upon them — both Peirce and Frege favored such a method. It harks back to older conceptions of time, however, and the most sophisticated contemporary views regard time as a construct in terms of events. Kim regards events rather as constructs in terms of times. Perhaps this latter view can be made to work, but a good deal of detail must be supplied before we can be sure that it can be made adequate for relativity physics, quantum mechanics, and the like.

*Northwestern University*

## NOTES

[1] 'Particulars, Events, and Actions', presented at the Winnipeg Conference on Action Theory, Map 9–11, 1975.

[2] In *Proceedings and Addresses of the American Philosophical Association* **47** (1973–4), 21–33.

[3] See especially the author's *Events, Reference, and Logical Form*, The Catholic University of America Press, Washington: to appear, pp. 29ff.

[4] See especially 'On How Some Adverbs Work', in *Events, Reference, and Logical Form*.

[5] Cf. *Events, Reference, and Logical Form*, pp. 15ff.

[6] Cf. the author's 'On Some Prepositional Relations', in *The Logical Enterprise*, the Fitch *Festschrift*, New Haven, Yale University Press, 1975, pp. 51–59, and 'On Prepositional Protolinguistics', to appear in the *Festschrift* for Paul Lorenzen (ed. by K. Lorenz).

[7] Cf. also some remarks in the author's 'Why I Am Not a Montague Grammarian', *Theoretical Linguistics*, **2** (1975), 147–157.

[8] Also presented at the Winnipeg Conference.

[9] As in the author's 'On Events and Event-Descriptions', in *Fact and Existence* (ed. by J. Margolis), Blackwell's, Oxford, 1969, pp. 63–73 (and also pp. 97–109). Cf. in addition the author's *Logic, Language, and Metaphysics*, New York University Press, New York, 1971, pp. 101ff.

[10] On paraphrase, see especially H. Hiż, 'The Role of Paraphrase in Grammar', in *Monograph Series on Language and Linguistics* (April, 1964).

[11] See his *Elements of Symbolic Logic*, The Macmillan Co., New York, 1947, p. 271.

[12] See Salmon, W., 'Events and Time', in *Fact and Existence*, pp. 95–97.

MYLES BRAND

# REPLY TO MARTIN

Professor R. M. Martin has made helpful comments on my paper 'Particulars, Events and Actions', some of which are amplificatory and some of which are critical. I should like to reply to several of these comments.

## I. CLASSIFYING EVENT THEORIES

At the beginning of my paper, I classified event theories into three types, on the basis of whether an ontological commitment is made only to particulars, to properties as well as particulars, or to propositions as well as particulars. If there is an adequate theory that 'reduces' properties to particulars, or one that 'reduces' propositions to properties and particulars, then this tripartite division is not ultimately tenable. Martin believes that such reductive theories are not available, and hence the tripartite division does not collapse.

The interesting case is the distinction between Property and Particularist theories. Martin argues that these types of theories are indeed distinct, since they involve different underlying logics which carry with them different ontological commitments (pp. 188f). Professor Kim in his paper 'Events as Property Exemplifications' claims, on the contrary, that his theory and Particularist theories are not ontologically distinct; his theory, he says, gives the internal structure of those particulars that are events.

It is not clear to me that Kim is correct here. For one reason, Martin seems to be correct in saying that additional logical machinery is needed in Kim's case, and that this machinery, namely, second-order logic, involves commitments not made by first-order logic (or some extension of it, modal or otherwise), where first-order logic is all that is required by a Particularist theory. For another reason, on Kim's view, events depend for existence on there being physical objects, since events *are* physical objects having a property during a time. On my view, events do not depend on there being physical objects; physical objects and events are ontologically independent (though they are both particulars). As a consequence, if events and physical objects are construed as having ontological parity, we can expect to learn

*M. Brand and D. Walton (eds.), Action Theory, 193–196. All Rights Reserved*
*Copyright © 1976 by D. Reidel Publishing Company, Dordrecht-Holland*

something about events by studying physical objects. I attempted to capitalize on this parity in my discussion of recurrence. This method of clarifying the nature of events, however, is not fully at Kim's disposal, since physical objects and events lack ontological parity on his view.

## II. CAUSATION

Martin criticizes the lack of axiomization for the relation "... efficiently causes –––". But surely, there is a great deal of philosophical groundwork to be done before undertaking an axiomization. One of the reasons for clarifying the nature of events is to become clear about causation. As Davidson has persuasively argued in his 'Causal Relations' (*Journal of Philosophy* **64** (1967, 691–703), and with which Martin apparently agrees, the arguments of the relation "... causes –––" include variables or names ranging over events. I would not inveigh against the view that axiomizations produce clarity; rather, I urge that such projects be undertaken only after the locutions in question have been carefully examined. In the case of causation, much foundational analysis remains to be done.

Martin also suggests that causation should be represented by a quadratic relation, namely, an ordering of events under linguistic description. On this view, there are causal relations only if there are linguistic descriptions. But, presumably, there are linguistic descriptions only if there are agents, human or otherwise, who can use language. However, it is highly counter-intuitive, to me at least, that there being causal relations depends on there being language-using agents. In a world differing from ours only in there being no such agents, there would be, it seems, causal connections. Suppose that there is a nuclear holocast completely killing all such agents, or suppose that we consider the universe at an early stage of its development. In these cases, it is correct to claim that the rain's falling causes the ground to become wet, the eruption of a volcano causes lava to flow, or so on. The connection between the eruption of a volcano and the flowing of lava does not depend on any agent being able to describe what happens.

## III. NECESSITY

Martin is correct in saying that I have not produced a full account of necessity; it would be helpful to have done so, though one cannot solve all problems at once. The situation in regard to necessity is better than that for causation. In recent years, a great deal of work, both in axiomatics and semantics, has been done; I intended to capitalize on some of this work, especially that of Kripke.

Martin's positive suggestion, that an account of necessity should proceed metalinguistically, is however problematical. There are at least two *prima facie* objections that must be defeated before such an account can be accepted.

By a metalinguistic account of necessity, I mean one that entails that

(1)       It is necessary that p

and

(2)       'p' is necessary

are logically equivalent. First, there are problems of the type pointed out by Alonzo Church. When a sentence is substituted for the variable in (1), the German translation of that instance of (1) will be different from that of (2), since the sentence-variable in (2) is contained in quotation marks which resists translation. Hence, the instance of (1) has a property, namely, having a certain German translation, that (2) lacks; thus, in general, (1) and (2) are not logically equivalent.

Second, a metalinguistic account seems to obscure the difference between *de dicto* and *de re* modalities. Consider the sentence

(3)       Necessarily, the number of planets is greater than 7.

This sentence has two readings:

(3a)       $\Box(\exists x) (x = \text{the number of planets} \ \& \ x > 7)$;

(3b)       $(\exists x) [x = \text{the number of planets} \ \& \ \Box(x > 7)]$.

It is difficult to see how to represent these alternative readings on a metalinguistic account.

## IV. EVENT IDENTITY

Martin argues against the sufficiency of my criterion of event-identity. He says "occurring within the same spatio-temporal regions becomes a necessary condition for identity but not a sufficient one. My swimming the Channel (now) and my catching a cold (now) are very different even though occurring at the same place and time" (p. 183). There is a mis-understanding here. I did not claim that spatio-temporal coincidence is necessary and sufficient for event-identity; rather, I claimed that *necessary* spatio-temporal coincidence is required. Indeed, it was the Channel example, among others, that led me to reject mere spatio-temporal coincidence and to propose the stricter criterion of necessary spatio-temporal coincidence.

Martin also questions the view, taken by Kim, Davidson, and myself (though actually having its genesis with Quine), that an identity criterion is vital for developing a theory of events. Conditions of event-identity are needed in order to use the machinery of quantificational logic. But, as I see it, they serve an even more important role: they specify the nature of events, their ontological status. A useful criterion of event-identity would indicate that which distinguishes events from all other types of phenomena. A criterion of event-identity states essential properties for events (though I do not want to deal with the complex issue of essential properties here). In this respect, the problem of specifying conditions of event-identity is the *Hauptproblem*. Incidentally, contrary to Martin's claim (on pp. 189f), it is not being denied that the Hilbert-Bernays laws (Id1 and Id2, on p. 182) obtain. Rather, it is being claimed that conditions must be added to these laws in order to make the identity criterion serve the function of specifying the nature of events.

*University of Illinois at*
*Chicago Circle*

# PART 6

# THE AGENCY THEORY

RODERICK M. CHISHOLM

# THE AGENT AS CAUSE

## I. INTRODUCTION

I assume that a theory of agency should be adequate to the following: (1) such statements as 'Jones killed his uncle' and 'Jones raised his arm' are sometimes true; (2) they imply that there is a certain event or state of affairs that an agent caused or brought about ('Jones killed his uncle' implies that the death of Jones' uncle was caused or brought about by Jones, and 'Smith raised his arm' implies that the raising of Smith's arm was something that was caused or brought about by Smith); and (3) such statements may, on occasion be supplemented, by the true statement "But at the time there was something else he could have done instead."

In making the first of these assumptions, I am presupposing that as philosophers we cannot escape our problems by taking refuge in a merely expressive or emotive theory of action. ("We say such things as 'Jones killed his uncle' when we want to express praise or blame or get something done, but strictly speaking such statements are neither true nor false.")

In making the second assumption, I am, or so it seems to me, saying something trivial and obvious. The same point has been put by Alvin Goldman this way: "When S's act A causes event E, we say that S is exemplified by the property of causing E. In other words, we say that the event E was caused, or brought about, by the agent S."[1] We take it to be unproblematic, then, that there is such a thing as 'agent causation'. I would say, therefore, that some of the philosophical issues about agent causation have been misplaced (by myself in earlier writings and by others). The question is not whether there *is* such a thing as agent causation. But one may ask whether agent causation can be reduced to 'event causation'. Can we, for example, express 'Jones killed his uncle' without loss of meaning into a set of statements in which only events are said to be causes and no one of which presupposes that there is anything of which Jones may be said to be the cause? (In what follows I will try to explicate agency by reference, in part, to the concept of an agent *undertaking* something, as expressed in '*S* undertakes to bring it about that *p*.' But I know of no way of expressing '*S*

*M. Brand and D. Walton (eds.), Action Theory, 199–211. All Rights Reserved*
*Copyright © 1976 by D. Reidel Publishing Company, Dordrecht-Holland*

undertakes to bring it about that $p$' as affirming merely a relation between events.)

I assume, thirdly, that people do things when they could have done something else instead. This, I would say, is one of those things that we have a right to believe about ourselves — at least until we have a positive reason for believing them to be false. Like the proposition that I am now awake and in a room with other people whom I can see and hear, it is a proposition I may regard as being innocent, epistemically, until I have positive reason to think it guilty. In the case of a conflict between such a proposition and a philosophical theory, the burden of proof should be upon the philosophical theory.

Some of the views I will express here, I have also expressed, often less clearly, in previous writings. Most of the points are discussed in considerably more detail in my Carus Lectures, *Person and Object: A Metaphysical Study* (Allen & Unwin, and Open Court, 1976).

## II. 'HE COULD HAVE DONE OTHERWISE'

Since the theory of agency, if I am right, presupposes that 'He could have done otherwise' is sometimes true, it is essential that we try to explicate this important concept. I will begin by summarizing what I believe to be the correct analysis.[2]

I suggest that any adequate analysis of what is intended by 'He could have done otherwise' must make use of the following three concepts: (a) that of *physical necessity*, expressible in the locutions, 'p is physically necessary' or 'p is a law of nature', where the expression replacing '$p$' designates a state of affairs; (b) that of *causal contribution*, expressible in the locutions, '$p$ contributes causally to $q$' or 'the occurrence of $p$ contributes causally to the occurrence of $q$'; and (c) that of *undertaking* or *endeavor*, expressible in the locution, '$S$ acts with the intention of contributing causally to the occurrence of $p$' or '$S$ undertakes, or endeavors, to contribute causally to the occurrence of $p$.' I will comment briefly on each of these concepts.

(a) It is generally agreed, I think, that the concept of physical necessity, or a law of nature, is fundamental to the theory of causation and, more generally, to the concept of nature. Some universal generalizations, expressible in the form, 'For every $x$, if $x$ is $F$, then $x$ is $G$' are physically necessary, or lawlike, and some are not. (A mark of a physically necessary, or lawlike, generalization is the fact that the corresponding, singular counterfactual, 'If $a$ were $F$, then $a$ would be $G$' is also true.[3]) The lawlike generalizations may be said to express laws of nature — the physical necessity of certain states of affairs.

(b) The concept of *causal contribution* is to be distinguished from that of a *sufficient causal condition*. If *c* is a sufficient causal condition of *e*, then it is physically necessary that if *c* occurs then *e* occurs. But *c* may contribute causally to *e* without it being physically necessary that if *c* occurs then *e* occurs. If we say, for example, that the presence of oxygen in the room contributed to the fire, we do not imply that it is physically necessary, or a law of nature, that if there is oxygen in the room then there is a fire. A sufficient causal condition may be thought of as a conjunction of events. If it occurs, then some of its conjuncts may be said to contribute causally to its effect.[4] And so when we speak of one event *contributing causally* to another, we presuppose that the first event is a part of a sufficient causal condition of the second and that this sufficient causal condition in fact occurs.

(c) I will discuss *undertaking*, or *endeavoring*, in detail below. The concept in question is sometimes expressed by means of the word 'trying', as in the following quotation from G. E. Moore:

That the bird's *body* moves away, owing to its wings moving in a certain way, is not *all* we mean by saying it *flies* away: as Wittgenstein says, if *I raise* my arm, something else happens *beside* that *my* arm is raised: that *I raise* it is a *Handlung*, and this is what we mean by saying that the raising is due to my *will*, though I neither *choose* nor *decide*. When I *choose* or *decide*, all that happens may be that I *try* to raise it.[5]

But our expression 'to undertake' should not be taken to connote the effort or that doubt that is sometimes associated with 'to try'.

Let us now turn to the analysis of 'He could have done otherwise.'

The 'could' that I will attempt to explicate is *indeterministic* in this respect: our definitions will imply, in effect, that if our agent had it within his power at 10 o'clock this morning to arrange things so that he would be in Boston now, then there were certain things such that at 10 o'clock this morning there had occurred no sufficient causal condition for his not then *undertaking* those things. (But presumably in the case of the underdetermined subatomic particle, the absence of the equipment necessary for undertaking or endeavoring constitutes a sufficient causal condition for *its* not undertaking anything, and our definitions, therefore, will not apply to it.)

In addition to being thus indeterministic, our 'could' will also be constitutionally iffy. For the definitions will imply that *if* our agent had undertaken some of the things just referred to, and *if* further conditions, which I shall try to specify, had obtained, then he *would* be in Boston now. (We will not, however, make use of any contrary-to-fact conditional in the formulation of our definitions.)

I shall formulate three definitions: first, a definition of what it is for our agent to be *free to undertake* a certain activity; secondly, a definition of what it is for a state of affairs to be *directly within his power*; and thirdly, a definition of the more general concept of what it is for a state of affairs to be *within his power*. By making use of the third of these definitions, we will be able to explicate 'He could have done otherwise' as 'Doing otherwise was within his power.'

Our first definition, then, will be this:

(D1)     *S* is *free at t to undertake p* = $D_f$. There is a period of time which includes but begins before *t* and during which there occurs no sufficient causal condition either for *S* undertaking *p* or for *S* not undertaking *p*.

Our second definition concerns the things that are *directly* within an agent's power. These are his free undertakings and anything that *they* would cause. If a state of affairs is directly within an agent's power, then something he is free to undertake is such that his undertaking it would bring about that state of affairs. In other words:

(D2)     *p* is directly within *S*'s power at *t* = $D_f$. There is a *q* such that: *S* is free at *t* to undertake *q*; and either (a) *p* is *S* undertaking *q* or (b) there occurs an *r* such that it is physically necessary that, if *r* and *S*-undertaking-*q* occurs, then *S*-undertaking-*q* contributes causally to *p*.[6]

Perhaps we should remind ourselves that, when we say 'there *is* a *q* such that he is free to undertake *q*', we do not mean that *q occurs*, or *obtains*. For many of the states of affairs that our agent is free to undertake are events or states of affairs that do *not* occur or obtain.

Our third definition concerns the broader concept of being *either directly or indirectly in one's power* — or, as we may put it more simply, the concept of *being within one's power*. Roughly, we may say that a state of affairs is within our agent's power if it is one of a series of states of affairs such that the first is directly within his power and each of the others is such that it would be made possible by its predecessor. More exactly:

(D3)     *p* is within *S*'s power at *t* = $D_f$ *p* is a member of a series such that (i) the first is directly within *S*'s power at *t* and (ii) each of the others is such that its predecessor in the series is a sufficient causal condition of its being directly within his power.

Since a series of states of affairs may have just one member, our definition allows us to say, as obviously we should be able to say, that the things that are thus within an agent's power include the things that are directly within his power.

Applicability of the second and third definitions presupposes what we might call the principle of the diffusiveness of power:

If (i) $q$ is within $S$'s power at $t$, (ii) $p$ occurs, and (iii) not-$p$ is not within the power of anyone other than $S$, then $p$ & $q$ is within $S$'s power at $t$.

### III. FREEDOM AND INDETERMINISM

I have said that, if there is anything that is within an agent's power, then there is something that he is 'free to undertake' — there is something such that there occurs no sufficient causal condition for his undertaking it and there occurs no sufficient causal condition for his not undertaking it.

One familiar objection to any such indeterministic account may be put this way:

(i) According to your account, if anything is ever within anyone's power, then certain events occur which are not preceded or accompanied by any sufficient causal conditions. But (ii) if an act which is within an agent's power is thus indeterministic, it is not possible for another person to exert any influence upon such an act. Yet (iii) we do exert influence upon the actions of other people, including those actions they could have refrained from performing. We do this, for example, by giving them motives or reasons. And so (iv) your theory is false.

The error in the argument lies in the second premise: 'if human action is thus indeterministic, it is not possible for us to exert any influence upon the actions of other people.'

One way, of affecting another person's behavior is to restrict his options. We prevent him from making choices he otherwise could have made. We may indeed thus cause him to act in a certain general way and leave the further particulars up to him.

But *restricting* his options is not the only way we can affect another person's free behavior. We can also affect him by *enabling* him to do what *he* otherwise could not have done. For if he then does what we have enabled him to do, we have brought about some *necessary* causal condition of his act.

I have said that one event is a *sufficient* causal condition of another provided it is a law of nature that, if the first event occurs, then the second occurs, either at the same time or later. We may also say, analogously, that one event is a necessary causal condition of another provided it is a law of nature that, if the second has occurred, then the first has also occurred, either at the same time or before. Now even if a man's undertaking has no sufficient causal condition, it has indefinitely many necessary causal conditions, indefinitely many conditions each of which is a *sine a qua non* of his undertaking what he does.

Our abilities are thus necessary causal conditions of what we do. Thus if you provide me with the necessary *means* for getting to Boston, means without which I wouldn't have been able to get there, then, if I do go there, you can be said to have contributed causally to what I do even though my undertaking the trip had no sufficient causal conditions. Or perhaps I would not have undertaken the trip unless I had thought it would involve something pleasurable or worthwhile. If now you had persuaded me that the trip *would* be pleasurable or worthwhile, then you gave a *motive* or *reason* for going, a motive or reason without which I would not have been able to undertake the trip. And so, once again, if I did go, then you contributed causally to my act even though there occurred no sufficient causal condition for my doing what I did. This last example makes clear one way in which our reasons and motives can be said to contribute causally to what we do.

And, of course, I can also affect *my own* subsequent free behavior in these ways. Thus, with every act I perform, I restrict my subsequent activity. Moreover, in planning ahead and taking preliminary steps, I *enable* myself to do things I otherwise could not have done. I may even supply myself with reasons and motives by trying to insure that the subsequent act, if it is performed, will be pleasurable or worthwhile.

## IV. AGENCY

What is it for an *agent* to bring about a state of affairs?

Sometimes a distinction is made between 'event causation' and 'agent causation' and it has been suggested that there is an unbridgeable gap between the two. But if we take the standard concept of 'event causation' — the concept of one event contributing causally to another — along with the concept of undertaking, or endeavoring, then we can say what it is for an agent to contribute causally to the occurrence of an event or state of affairs.

The concept of event causation, as we have said, may be expressed in the locution '$p$ contributes causally to $q$' — or, if one prefers, 'the occurrence of $p$ contributes causally to the occurrence of $q$.' (The latter locution has the advantage of enabling us to say 'the occurrence of $p$ at $t'$ contributes causally to the occurrence of $q$ at $t''$'; but for simplicity we will ignore such temporal references in much of what follows.)

In terms of event causation, so considered, and our undefined concept of undertaking, we may now define agent causation.

We will say first that, if a man's undertaking contributes causally to something, then the man *does* something which contributes causally to that something:

(D4)    $S$ does something at $t$ which contributes causally to $p = D_f$
There is a $q$ such that $S$'s undertaking $q$ at $t$ contributes causally to $p$.

Given the concept just defined, let us now attempt to characterize a broader concept of agent causation that we may express by saying '$S$ contributes causally to $p$.' We wish to construe this broader concept in such a way that we say each of these things:

(a) If a person does something that contributes causally to $p$, then *he* contributes causally to $p$;

(b) If a person undertakes something, then he contributes causally to his undertaking that something; and

(c) If a person does something that contributes causally to $p$, then he contributes causally to his thus doing something that contributes causally to $p$.

I would propose, then, the following definition of this broader concept of agent causation:

(D5)    $S$ contributes causally at $t$ to $p = D_f$. Either (a) $S$ does something at $t$ that contributes causally to $p$, or (b) there is a $q$ such that $S$ undertakes $q$ at $t$ and $S$-undertaking-$q$ is $p$, or (c) there is an $r$ such that $S$ does something at $t$ that contributes causally to $r$, and $p$ is that state of affairs which is $S$ doing something that contributes causally to $r$.

(Shouldn't we also be able to say that the agent contributes causally to some of his own *omissions*? We will provide for this possibility in the following section.)

We assume that, if a state of affairs $p$ occurs and if an agent $S$ contributes causally to a *necessary* causal condition of $p$, then $S$ contributes causally to $p$. This fact, as we have noted, enables us to say that an agent may contribute causally to subsequent free actions of other agents and of himself.

We may now formulate and reply to still another familiar objection to the type of theory here defended. The objection is:

Your account presupposes that there are certain events which men, or agents, cause to happen. Suppose, then, that on a certain occasion a man does cause an event $p$ to happen. What, now of *that* event — that event which is his thus causing $p$ to happen? Your account implies that there occurs no sufficient causal condition for his causing $p$ to happen. Will you say, then, that it's not caused by anything at all? But if you say that, then how can you ever hold *him* responsible for his causing an event to happen?

The answer to this objection will be clear if we consider certain schematic theorems about agency. The theorems are consequences of: the ontology of events and states of affairs we have presupposed; the interpretation we have given to the undefined concept of undertaking; and what we have said about event causation.

(T1)    If $S$ contributes causally to $p$, then $p$

(T2)    If $S$ does something that contributes causally to $p$, then $S$ contributes causally to his doing something that contributes causally to $p$

(T3)    If $S$ contributes causally to $p$, then there exists a $q$ such that $S$ undertakes $q$

(T4)    If $S$ undertakes $p$, then $S$ contributes causally to $S$ undertaking $p$.

But the following principles, it should be noted, are *not* consequences of what we have said:

If $S$ undertakes $p$, then $p$

If $S$ contributes causally to $p$, then $S$ undertakes $p$

If $S$ undertakes $p$, then $S$ undertakes $S$'s undertaking $p$.

And so we may reply to the above objection by saying this:

If a man does something that causes a certain event $p$ to happen, then, *ipso facto*, he contributes causally to his doing something that causes that event $p$ to happen. It is a mistake, therefore, to say that nothing causes his causing that event to happen.

The schematic letters in our formulae, then, may be replaced by expressions designating actions; e.g., 'His raising his arm' 'His stealing the money', and 'His breaking his promise.'[7] And we may say that, whenever an agent performs such an act, he contributes causally to the fact that he performs that act.

One normally does not have to do things for the purpose of bringing about the actions that one performs. But to say that the agent contributes causally to the fact that he performs the act is not to say, as some critics have assumed, that the agent thereby does or undertakes something for the purpose of bringing it about that he performs the act. The concept suggested by 'He does a certain thing for the purpose of bringing it about that he do a certain other thing' is discussed in detail in Sections VI and VII below.

We next introduce an expression fundamental to the theory of agency:

(D6)     By contributing causally at $t$ to $p$, $S$ contributes causally at $t$ to $q = D_f$. $S$ contributes causally at $t$ to $p$, and everything he then does that contributes causally to $p$ also contributes causally to $q$.

Thus we may say that, by contributing causally to the replenishment of the water-supply, the worker contributed causally to the household being poisoned. The second clause of the definiens ('everything he then does that contributes causally to $p$ contributes causally to $q$') assures us that things needn't be the other way around. We needn't say that, by contributing causally to the household being poisoned, the worker contributed causally to the replenishment of the water-supply. We may also say that, by contributing causally (by making it happen) that his hand was extended out the car window, the driver contributed causally to his signaling. And to say this is *not* to say that his extending his hand out the window caused him to signal. Other replacements for '$p$' and '$q$', respectively, might be: 'His jumping 6 feet 3 inches' and 'His outjumping George'; 'His moving his queen to King-knight 7' and 'His check-mating his opponent'; and 'His trying to save Jones' life' and 'His doing his duty.'[8] (It should be noted, in connection with the final example, that one of the consequences of what we have said is that an agent contributes causally to his own undertakings.)

We next comment briefly on those acts that are deliberate omissions.

### V. A NOTE ON DELIBERATE OMISSION

Doesn't a person also contribute causally to some of his own *omissions* — those omissions he may be said deliberately to commit? Suppose one man greets another and the second man does not respond. If the second man was unaware of the fact that he was addressed by the first person, then his failure to respond may have been a mere omission. But if the second man intended to snub the first man, to insult him by failing to respond to his greeting, then the second man could be said to have *committed the omission*; he omitted the act *deliberately*.[9]

We may characterize deliberate omission in this way:

(D7)     $S$ deliberately omits undertaking $p$ at $t = D_f$. $S$ considers at $t$ undertaking $p$ and $S$ does not undertake $p$ at $t$.

(Here we appeal to the concept of *considering*, or *entertaining*, a state of affairs — an intentional concept that is essential to any adequate theory of thought.)

Now our definition (D4), above, of '$S$ does something that contributes causally to $p$', does not cover those cases in which a person $S$ may be said to do something by committing an omission. But if we choose, we may remedy this defect by replacing (D4) by the following:

(D4.1)　$S$ does something at $t$ which contributes causally to $p = D_f$. There is a $q$ which is such that either (a) $S$-undertaking-$q$ at $t$ contributes causally to $p$, or (b) $S$ deliberately omits $q$ at $t$ *and* $p$ is that state of affairs which is $S$ deliberately omitting $q$.

If we make use of this revised definition, then we may say, in accordance with (D5), that $S$ contributes causally to his own deliberate omissions and to their results. (He may be *morally* responsible for the results of some of his non-deliberate, or uncommitted omissions — those omissions he should not have made. But, I assume, it would not be accurate to say that he is *causally* responsible for such results.)

## VI. PURPOSIVE ACTIVITY

We are now in a position to look somewhat more deeply into the structure of purposive activity and into some of the philosophical questions to which this concept gives rise.

Let us begin with the distinction between means and ends:

(D8)　　$S$ undertakes $p$ and does so for the purpose of bringing about $q = D_f$. $S$ undertakes to bring about (i) $p$ and (ii) his-undertaking-$p$ contributing causally to $q$.

We may also say that $S$ undertakes $p$ as a *means* to bringing about $q$. We will assume that, if he thus undertakes one thing as a means to a second thing, then he also undertakes the second thing.[10]

The expression we have just been considering — '$S$ undertakes $p$ and does so for the purpose of bringing about $q$' — is intentional with respect to both variables; it does not imply that either of the states of affairs, $p$ or $q$, obtains. But the following expression is intentional only with respect to the second variable: '$S$ contributes causally to $p$ for the purpose of bringing about $q$.' This concept is, of course, readily reducible to the terms we have been using.

### VII. SOME FURTHER PHILOSOPHICAL QUESTIONS

We undertake certain things $p$ by undertaking certain *other* things $q$; in such cases, we undertake $q$ for the purpose of bringing about $p$. And so it must also be the case that we undertake certain things $p$ without undertaking certain other things $q$ for the purpose of bringing about $p$. The things $p$ that we thus undertake could be said to be things we *undertake directly*.

When we are successful with respect to the things we undertake directly, we may be said to perform certain *basic actions*. These are the things we succeed in doing without undertaking still other things to get them done. For most of us, raising our arms and blinking our eyes are thus basic. But people have different 'repertoires' of basic acts and what one person can perform as a basic act another may be able to bring about only by undertaking a lengthy chain of causes.[11]

We may characterize the present sense of basic act as follows:

(D9)     $S$ brings about $p$ as a *basic act* at $t = D_f$. (i) $S$ undertaking $p$ contributes causally at $t$ to $p$ and (ii) there is no $q$ such that $S$ undertakes $q$ at $t$ for the purpose of bringing about $p$.

In other words, our agent performed as a basic act provided he brought about something he *undertook* to bring about and provided further there was nothing he undertook for the *purpose* of bringing that thing about.

Given this definition of basic action, we need no say, as some have said, that a man's basic actions are actions 'which he cannot be said to have caused to happen."[12] And we may say, if we choose, that a man may undertake a basic act on a certain occasion and fail. (Presumably this would happen, if unknown to himself, the man had lost some member of his 'repertoire' of basic actions and then discovers the loss.)

Let us now contrast the things we thus *undertake directly* with the things we *bring about directly*.

We bring about some things by bringing about other things that cause them. Or, in other words, we bring about certain things $p$ by bringing about certain other things $q$ such that $q$ brings about $p$. Therefore, it would seem, we also bring about certain things $p$ *without* bringing about certain other things $q$ such that $q$ brings about $p$. Let us say:

(D10)   $S$ brings about $p$ *directly* at $t = D_f$. (i) *$S$ contributes causally at $t$ to $p$ and (ii) there is no $q$ such that (a) $S$ contributes causally at $t$ to $q$ and (b) $q$ contributes causally to $p$.*

If a man brings about anything at all, then, presumably, he brings about some things as *basic acts* and he also brings about some things *directly*. But we must distinguish the things he brings about as basic acts, and the things he brings about directly.

If what I have been saying is true, then a man's undertakings are things he brings about directly. But, given our definitions, we cannot say that undertakings are basic acts; for basic acts are undertaken and undertakings are not. The mark of a basic act is that, although it is undertaken, nothing is undertaken as a *means* to bringing it about. And the mark of what one brings about directly is that, although it is brought about, it is not brought about by some *other* thing the agent brings about.

I think we can say that anything a man brings about directly is an internal change, a change within himself. Using a scholastic term, we could say that the things a man causes directly are *immanently* caused; as states of the agent himself, they may be said to "remain within the agent".[13]

This way of looking at direct causation should be contrasted with that suggested by H. A. Prichard: "Where we have willed some movement of our body and think we have caused it, we cannot have directly caused it. For what we have directly caused, if anything, must have been some change in our brain." Prichard's view would be compatible with that suggested here if our undertakings could be said to *be* "changes in our brain".[14] But whether or not our undertakings are themselves changes in our brains, it would seem that they contribute causally to certain changes in our brains that we know next to nothing about.[15]

*Brown University*

## NOTES

[1] Goldman, Alvin I., *A Theory of Human Action*, Prentice-Hall, Inc., Englewood Cliffs, N.J., 1970, p. 25.

[2] I will not here criticize alternative theories. I have discussed a number of other possibilities in 'He Could Have Done Otherwise', in Myles Brand (ed.), *The Nature of Human Action*, Scott, Foresman and Company, Glenview, Ill., 1971, pp. 293–301.

[3] Compare Rescher, Nicholas, *Hypothetical Reasoning*, North-Holland Publishing Company, Amsterdam, 1964; Walters, R. S., 'Contrary-to-Fact Conditional', in Paul Edwards (ed.), *The Encyclopedia of Philosophy*, Crowell Collier and Macmillan, New York, 1967, Vol. II, pp. 212–216; Kneale, William, 'Natural Laws and Contrary-to-Fact Conditionals', *Analysis* **10** (1950), 121–125; Chisholm, Roderick M., 'Law Statements and Counterfactual Inference', *Analysis* **15** (1955), 97–105.

[4] It might be supposed that causal contribution could readily be defined in terms of sufficient causal condition; e.g., that '$c$ contributes causally to $e$' might be defined as saying 'there occurs an event $s$ such that $s$ is a sufficient causal condition of $e$, and $c$ is a part of $s$.' But this definition is not satisfactory, since sufficient causal conditions may have parts that are

superfluous. For if $s$ is a sufficient causal condition of $e$, and if $c$ occurs before $e$, then $c$ & $s$, no matter what $c$ may be, will also be a sufficient causal condition of $e$; and so $c$ may be a part of a sufficient causal condition of $e$ without $c$ itself contributing causally to $e$. The problem thus becomes that of finding a suitable definition of 'a causally superfluous part of a sufficient causal condition of $e$.' The problem is discussed by Mackie, J. L., in 'Causes and Conditions', *American Philosophical Quarterly* **2** (1965), 245–264. As a result of lengthy discussions and correspondence with Robert S. Keim and Ernest Sosa, I am convinced that no solution to this problem is at hand. See Sosa, Ernest, *Causation and Conditionals*, Oxford University Press, 1975.

[5] Moore, G. E., *Commonplace Book 1919–1953* (ed. by C. Lewy), George Allen & Unwin, London, 1962, p. 410.

[6] Why not put the second clause more simply and say: 'There occurs an $r$ at $t$ such that it is physically necessary that, if $r$ and $S$-undertaking-$q$ occurs, then $p$ occurs'? The simpler formulation would guarantee that, if $S$ undertaking $q$ occurs, then there would occur a sufficient causal condition of $p$. But it would not guarantee us that $S$-undertaking-$q$ contributes causally to $p$. For this simpler formulation is consistent with supposing that $S$ undertaking $q$ is a superfluous part of the sufficient causal condition of $p$.

[7] I would assume, however, that what is intended by most such action expressions could be paraphrased (doubtless sometimes cumbersomely) into our 'undertaking' and 'making happen' vocabulary without using terms that themselves designate actions. But an adequate explication of *some* action expressions ('His signaling for a turn', 'His checkmating his opponent') would also involve reference to what is *required* by certain laws, customs, rules, or conventions. This point is stressed by Hart, H. L. A., in 'Ascription of Responsibility and Rights', *Proceedings of the Aristotelian Society* **49** (1949), 171–194, and by Melden, A. I., in *Free Action*, Routledge & Kegan Paul, Ltd., London, 1961. I would disagree, however, with the suggestion that such reference to laws, rules, customs, or conventions constitutes the mark of action.

[8] All but the first of these examples are taken from Goldman, Alvin I., *A Theory of Human Action*, Prentice-Hall Inc., Englewood Cliffs, N.J., 1970, pp. 23–27. They all illustrate what he calls 'act generation', one act, so to speak, arising out of another. The first example is from Anscombe, G. E. M., *Intention*, Basil Blackwell, Oxford, 1968, p. 40ff.

[9] See Brand, Myles, 'The Language of Not Doing', *American Philosophical Quarterly* **8** (1971), 45–53.

[10] I have discussed the concept of undertaking in further detail in 'The Structure of Intention', *Journal of Philosophy* **62** (1970), 633–647. Compare Hector-Neri Castañeda, 'Intentions and the Structure of Intending', *Journal of Philosophy* **68** (1971), 453–466. I am indebted to Richard Taylor's, *Action and Purpose*, Prentice-Hall, Inc., Englewood Cliffs, N.J., 1966.

[11] The term 'basic act' and the expression 'repertoire of basic acts' are due to Arthur Danto; see his 'What We Can Do', *Journal of Philosophy* **60** (1963), 435–445, reprinted in White, Alan R., *The Philosophy of Action*, Oxford University Press, London, 1968.

[12] Compare Arthur Danto, *op. cit.*

[13] Compare Rickaby, Joseph, *Free Will and Four English Philosophers*, Burns and Oates, London, 1906, p. 177. St. Thomas is speaking of *immanent action* in the following passage: "For action and production differ, because action is an operation that remains in the agent itself, as choosing, understanding and the like (and for this reason the practical sciences are called moral sciences), whereas production is an operation that passes over into some matter in order to change it, as cutting, burning and the like (and for this reason the productive sciences are called mechanical arts)." *Commentary on the Metaphysics of Aristotle*, Henry Regnery Company, Chicago, 1961, paragraph 1152.

[14] I suggest that such an identification would be correct only if we ourselves are identical with our brain or with some proper part of our brain.

[15] I am indebted to Jaegwon Kim and Ernest Sosa.

IRVING THALBERG

# HOW DOES AGENT CAUSALITY WORK?*

My purpose is to understand, sympathetically but critically, the novel concept of agent causality, which Professors Roderick Chisholm and Richard Taylor have championed in recent philosophy of action. I want to appreciate, and determine the viability of, this notion which they alone have bothered to exposit in detail. I have encountered just one clear anticipation of it:[1] C. D. Broad's tentative hypothesis that perhaps we engage in "non-occurrent causation of events" when we act (1952/reprinted 1962, p. 131; see pp. 119–122, 124, 129f). Chisholm's and Taylor's own views of the unique causal tie of deed to doer hardly coincide in all particulars. For that matter, Chisholm's present "concept of an agent *undertaking* something, as expressed in 'S undertakes to bring it about that p'" (p. 199),[2] does not seem to me to fit Chisholm's earlier notions of agent-causing — as I show in Section I. Yet Chisholm's previous work does share with Taylor's and Broad's accounts one challenging fundamental idea: that a person may bring about movements of his own body, but without doing anything else, then or antecedently, in order to accomplish this. The causal relationship here is supposed to be radically unlike what we find when one or more events propagate another. It is not only unnecessary for the agent-causer to do anything overt as a means of making his limbs move. He also need not perform 'acts of will'. Nor does movement result from his conative, affective and cognitive attitudes, from happenings in his nervous system — and especially not from 'external' influences.

In Sections I through IV, I add to this sketch. Beginning in Section V, I attend to significant doctrinal differences between Taylor and Chisholm.

* I thank Professors Daniel Berger, Myles Brand, Alan Donagan, Patricia Greenspan, Arnold Levison and Norman Malcolm for their critical reactions to various drafts of this paper. I read an early, and much shorter, version of it to the Illinois Philosophical Conference, devoted to the Philosophy of Roderick Chisholm, at Illinois State University, November 2, 1974. I am grateful to many participants there, notably Professor Chisholm, for comments. Over the years, Professor Chisholm has been most generous with his time, helping me with my work in action theory and in several other fields of philosophy — to which he has made so many lasting contributions.

When I read my penultimate draft at Winnipeg, it goes without saying that I received very useful suggestions from a large number of conferees.

*M. Brand and D. Walton (eds.), Action Theory, 213–238. All Rights Reserved*
*Copyright © 1976 by D. Reidel Publishing Company, Dordrecht-Holland*

During my expository discussion I register several small grumbles; but from Section VI onward I set forth a couple of major dilemmas which I think these writers, and all would-be agent causationists, ought to deal with. The first is whether or not agent-causing is supposed to be an active relationship. If it is, then don't we risk circularity when we define action as agent-causing our limbs to move? But if we deny that agent-causing resembles any ordinary performance, then on what model are we to understand it? My second dilemma occupies Sections IX through XI, and it concerns the beliefs, emotions, intentions and impulses on which we sometimes act. Do agent causationists envisage any rapport between the phenomenon which interests them — viz., our propagating movement of our limbs — and the event or state which consists in our having reasons of these types? Either a 'Yes' or a 'No' answer may entail awkward consequences, and these might dissuade some potential converts to agent causality. Naturally I would not want to drive any hard-core believers from their comfortably fortified positions.

In order to set these dilemmas in context, I want to gaze first at some pitfalls which I think agent causationists may have been trying to avoid. This should enhance our comprehension and our respect for their approach.

## I. THREE POSSIBLE SOURCES OF AGENT CAUSALITY DOCTRINES

To begin with, I imagine that philosophers who developed notions of agent causality were dissatisfied — and rightly so — with quasi-official 'volition' theories of what it is to act. Here I am alluding mainly to orthodox Bentham-Austin-Mill analyses of action as comprising a movement of one's body, or perhaps a contraction of one's muscles, together with a mental act of willing by means of which one produced the movement or contraction. Prototypes of this view appear in the work of Hobbes, Descartes, Locke, Berkeley, Hume, Reid and Kant. Full-fledged volition analyses won virtually unanimous assent in jurisprudence, and went unchallenged in philosophy until the era of Wittgenstein and Ryle. A cognate theory I mean to include is Prichard's narrower and somewhat less intuitively appealing doctrine. Prichard deletes the corporeal movement, and argues that, in a strict sense, an action consists in willing alone (1945, pp. 89–98, esp. p. 94; see Aune, 1974).

Richard Taylor, like Wittgenstein and Ryle, devises what I consider decisive arguments against the whole idea of volitional capers (1960/1962, pp. 85–88; 1966, pp. 49, 64–68, 75–79, 88ff, 113). They should not need repeating here. In Chisholm's earlier work we find few analogues to acts of will (but see 1971b, p. 53). His new stress on "undertaking" — as contrasted with what one undertakes, namely "to bring it about that $p$", "to contribute causally to the occurrence of $p$" (this volume, pp. 199, 200) — sounds rather volitional. Especially when we read that "a man's undertakings are things he brings about directly", and that "anything a man brings about directly is an internal change", which may in turn "contribute causally to certain changes in [his brain] that we know next to nothing about" (this volume, p. 210). Chisholm's notion of "undertaking" also sounds volitional when he admits that what you undertake may not happen (this volume, pp. 208f). This is like willing a movement which fails to occur. But whenever you cause $E$, $E$ takes place.

Whether or not we decide that Chisholm has now countenanced something like an act of will, we can see how easy it is for agent causationists to dispense with such regressive antics. They need not imagine that I activate my conative faculty, or that I engage in "undertakings", to get my limbs going — much less that all I ever do is execute volitional stunts. Instead, agent causationists can declare that I simply and "directly" make portions of my body budge, without prefatory inner jabs.

## II. A DIFFICULTY ABOUT ACTION AND BODILY HAPPENINGS

So far so good. I turn now to a more contemporary knot which may have provoked theories of agent causation. What is left when we exorcise volitions? Apparently just corporeal movement. For brevity I follow current philosophical practice and interpret our key verb 'move' quite broadly, so that even if a person is holding still, and his limbs are motionless, it will nevertheless be true that his body moves (see Davidson, 1971, p. 11; Honderich, 1972, p. 187). In this elastic sense, it would seem that corporeal movement always does coincide with action. Might our deeds then be nothing but these physical goings-on? Isn't action something more? Here, to distinguish act from bodily happening, and to articulate the link between doer and deed, one may be tempted to introduce agent causality. Thus Taylor reasons:

Such things as the beating of my heart and the growth of my hair ... are motions and changes of my body, but in a familiar though somewhat baffling sense they are not things with which I have anything to do ...

My arms and fingers sometimes move, on the other hand [sic], or my body moves from place to place, carried hither and thither by my legs, and these motions seem clearly to be events of a wholly different kind ... Indeed, if they happen at all it is *because* I make them happen. And this seems manifestly different from my body, or my brain and nervous system, making them happen.

... we can say that ... I cause the motions of my fingers but not those of my heart (1966, p. 57f; see Chisholm, 1971b, p. 68f; 1971b, p. 40).

Who doesn't feel an urge to deploy causal terminology in order to mark off action from bodily movement? Even if we withhold the overworked verb 'cause' itself, then we at least want to introduce one of the kindred expressions which Taylor considers: "make happen", "initiate", "bring about", "originate" (1966, pp. 111, 113, 262; 1974, p. 56). In desperation, we may enlist verbs like 'engender' and 'call forth', or Chisholm's "endeavor" (1971b, p. 53) and "undertake". In his Winnipeg paper, Taylor spoke of "absolute creation".

The apparent snag to all this, which we will run across throughout our inquiry, is that the phenomena we are attempting to analyse diverge radically from established causal models — from those familiar situations where causal verbs have a relatively straightforward meaning. Remember that our concern is with circumstances in which a person is supposed to bring about movements of his own limbs. But typically, when there is some event that a person is said, in any down-to-earth sense, to have caused, you can always distinguish between the occurrence which he brought about, and whatever he did to make it happen (see my 1967/1972, pp. 39–45). We bring about $E$ (a riot, a reconciliation) by doing something else $A$ (by shouting, by meeting with husband and wife). That is, our causing of $E$ consists in a separable performance $A$, which produced the event $E$. But when we move our limbs in the normal way, there is no other performance to sunder from their agitation or stillness, which might qualify as something we did to bring about the latter. And what else could we have in view when we speak of 'causing' here? Thus, while we comprehend how events, including our purposive and our accidental behavior, work to produce their effects, we have great trouble understanding the mechanism of agent causation — as well as Chisholm's new "undertaking to bring about".

Broad's early discussion touches on this snag (1952/1962, p. 131). For his part, Taylor begins one book maintaining that the notion of agent causality is more "archaic", "primary", "original" and "natural" than the notion of one event resulting from another (1966, pp. 10, 14f, 18, 21, 111). Yet elsewhere he admits that his "conception of the causation of events by beings or substances that are not events is ... so different from the usual philosophical conception ... that it should not even bear the same name" (1974, p. 56). Examining statements like "A brick caused that window to break" Taylor remarks:

objects or substances seem to be referred to as causes ... But this is simply a common manner of speaking ... It is not, for example, just the brick as such that causes the window to break. It is, rather, the impact of the brick against the window; and this impact is not itself a substance, but a change ... [I]n all typical cause-and-effect situations, the causal connections are between changes or states of substances, and only indirectly between the substances themselves (1974, p. 93f).

I am also troubled by the fact that our usual notion of causality involves predicting and explaining. If event $A$ causes $B$, then as a rule you can confidently expect a $B$-like occurrence whenever you observe an $A$-like one. And if both $B$ and $A$ events have taken place, in suitable spatio-temporal proximity, you can explain why $B$ happened, by citing the occurrence of $A$. But in the cases of someone moving his body, which preoccupy adherents of agent causality, we find no analogue for the $A$ event which would justify us in forecasting $B$. Obviously the mere existence of some agent at any given time neither allows us to predict how his body will move at that time, nor to explain why it moved that way at that time (see Taylor, 1966, p. 218ff).

Whatever causal verb we select — 'make happen', 'originate', 'initiate', 'endeavor', 'undertake', 'create' — similar questions about what we could possibly mean will plague us. Should we then abandon causal verbs, as Taylor suggests at one juncture, and say instead that an agent merely "does" or "performs" the movement of his body? (Taylor, 1974, p. 56; see Danto, 1970, pp. 110–113, and 1973, pp. 7, 38f, 50–60, 119). I am suspicious. The verbs "do" and "perform" are, syntax aside, virtual synonyms for "act" — and no better understood. So how can it advance our analysis of the relationship of an agent to his bodily movement when he acts, if we say that he "performs" or "does" the movement? Incidentally, if you specify my corporeal movement in certain perfectly standard ways, for example as 'the rising of my hand', it will be ungrammatical to say that I do or perform it. And I think it is a fairly reliable sign that a metaphysician is in deep trouble if he thereupon declares our ordinary grammar inadequate to express the real nature of agency or anything else.

Before we go on to a third possible source of agent causality doctrines, however, I want to reiterate my sympathy — both for the metaphysician's impatience with the limits of what is grammatical, and for his obsessive use of causal terminology to mark off those movements of our bodies with which, as Taylor recognizes, we have something to do. I also share Taylor's reluctance to identify our actions with bodily happenings that result from certain events in our "brain and nervous system". This brings us to what I regard as the fountainhead of agent causality doctrines: the determinism, indetermism, free will and responsibility conundrum.

### III. BETWEEN THE HORNS OF DETERMINISM
### AND INDETERMINISM?

Chisholm and Taylor both believe, as I do, that sometimes a human being has power over his own behavior, and is free to act in alternative ways.

Chisholm believes, and I agree, that such free agents are sometimes justly held accountable for harm they have wrought. But how can these assumptions be true, if it is also true that every event — including our physical movement when we act, and any volition or other mental caper which is supposed to engender our movement — has resulted from antecedent or contemporaneous events? It does not matter to Taylor and Chisholm whether a determinist says that electrical activity within our cerebrum makes our limbs move, or that in favored circumstances our own decisions, impulses, ambitions, and more or less reasoned beliefs are what do the trick. Chisholm and Taylor would point out that by the determinist's account, ultimately we have no control over these 'inner' causes of our behavior. I am unsure what Taylor and Chisholm think it would be like for us to possess such mastery (see Taylor, 1966, p. 74). But they certainly think these mental antecedents make it impossible for any other motion of our limbs to occur. In that case, how can we act freely, have it within our power to behave differently, and be reponsible? A characteristic passage from Taylor goes:

Whether a desire which causes my body to behave in a certain way is inflicted upon me by another person, ... or derived from hereditary factors, or ... from anything at all, matters not ... [I]f it is in fact the cause of my bodily behavior, I cannot but act in accord with it (1974, p. 51).

Like Taylor, Chisholm worries that an agent may lack "power either to bring about or not to bring about" those attitudes which are said to cause his movements. Chisholm argues:

... if these beliefs and desires ... caused him to do just what he did do, then, since *they* caused it, *he* was unable to do anything other than just what he did do. It makes no difference whether the cause of the deed was internal or external; if the cause was some state or event for which the man himself was not responsible, then he was not responsible for what we have been mistakenly calling his act (1966, p. 13; see pp. 23–28; 1964b, p. 24f; and cp. Campbell, 1951/1968, p. 161).

Would it comfort Taylor and Chisholm if determinism proved altogether false — if, for example, scientists discovered some totally uncaused bodily motions, or even movements resulting from uncaused decisions and thoughts? That would vindicate "simple indeterminism", of which Taylor jibes: "We ... avoid picturing a puppet ... but ... the conception that emerges is ... that of ... an erratic and jerking phantom, without any rhyme or reason" (1974, p. 51; see 1958, p. 225).

What if Libertarian theorists add a noumenal Self, which barges into the causal order and overpowers our "character as so far formed"? (see Campbell, 1951/1968, p. 170). In these situations we would experience random breaches of "causal continuity", which may somehow coincide with our "effort of will" to " 'rise to duty' in the face of opposing desires" (Campbell, 1951/1968, pp. 166, 169f; cp. Chisholm, 1966, p. 25). Taylor plausibly interprets such talk of the Self as an obscurantist way of emphasizing that it is the person himself who performs his action. Otherwise, Taylor feels, the Libertarian form of indeterminism seems to imply that we are in constant danger of losing command over our behavior to an unpredictable though dutiful Self which we somehow "possess" (1966, pp. 134f, 263).

Chisholm incisively sums up the apparent failure of both indeterministic and deterministic outlooks to explain how an individual can exercise control over what he does, and to justify our practice of holding such an individual accountable. Chisholm sees the puzzling situation as follows:

'Human beings are responsible agents; but this fact appears to conflict with a deterministic view of human action (the view that every event that is involved in an act is caused by some other event); and it *also* appears to conflict with an indeterministic view ... (the view that the act, or some event that is essential to the act, is not caused at all).' To solve the problem ... we must make somewhat far-reaching assumptions about ... the agent ... (1966, p. 11; see 1969, p. 199).

## IV. DISCONTENTS THAT I SHARE WITH CHISHOLM AND TAYLOR

Before we probe those "assumptions", I want to endorse some of Chisholm's and Taylor's complaints. How could one be said to exercise command over undetermined, chance movements of his limbs — or perhaps movements engendered by random resolutions and beliefs? Absence of events which cause my behavior is no guarantee that I act freely. I would certainly not be in charge of movements inflicted upon me by a will-of-the-wisp Self.

So much for indeterministic views. I have also recently come to believe that the stock deterministic picture, of action generally as well as free action in particular, is hardly more adequate. But my reasoning is rather different from Chisholm's and Taylor's. I still dissent from their 'incompatibilistic' supposition that a person's own motivational states take away his freedom whenever they cause his bodily movement. I would block Chisholm's inference: "since *they* caused it, *he* was unable to do anything other than just what he did do". I do not automatically conclude that the person here must have been powerless to act otherwise. Taylor's reasoning on this topic is less obviously open to challenge. From the premise, "existing conditions are causally sufficient for my not moving my finger", Taylor says "it follows that it is causally impossible for me to move my finger" (1960, p. 86). What does Taylor mean? Imagine that among "existing conditions" there figured prominently my wish to test the breeze for velocity and direction, and my conviction that I could do so by holding my moistened index finger rigid in the wind. My finger is motionless as a result of these undramatic "existing conditions". Suppose we deduce, *ohne Weiteres*, that it is "impossible for me to move my finger". Then aren't we assuming, without evidence of paralysis, disability or impediments, that digital motion is beyond my power? Does Taylor's modifier, "causally", attenuate the impossibility here? If so, can Taylor mean by "causally impossible for me" anything more worrisome than that my finger is *caused not* to bend? And this is a far cry from saying that my own motives, along with other "conditions", hinder me — leave me unable to crook my finger.

Obviously I do not share Taylor's and Chisholm's fear that determinism must undermine our belief that we are sometimes free to act otherwise than we do. But I join them in rejecting the determinist's overall picture of what it is to act upon one's beliefs, guesses and other attitudes. As I reconstruct it, the deterministic model of motivated behavior, both free and unfree, presents the agent as a field of causes. More precisely, he is like an arena where 'his' calculations, his perceptual judgments, his noble and base inclinations, perhaps his repressed fantasies, his conscious terrors, rages, lusts and devotions, either contend or blend with each other. Even if these proceedings do generate agitation of his limbs, why should we say that this is "his act"? I would echo Chisholm's phrase: "*they* caused it"; that is, movement has resulted from the protagonist's "beliefs and desires", but he seems to have had very little to do with it.

Determinists may respond by emphasizing that, after all, it is the person who calculates, desires and so on; consequently we do not merely have cause-effect sequences running through him. And since these antecedent mental states are his own conative, affective and cognitive feats, the resulting bodily goings-on — at least the ones he wanted or expected — rank as his deeds.

I admit that this re-drawing of the deterministic tableau connects up the agent with various mental states inside himself, thereby giving him a more active role. But his activity now seems limited to engaging in mental high jinks which somehow affect his limbs. And this revised deterministic scenario sounds, I think, suspiciously Prichardian. In fact, how can determinists now say that we really do anything more than form beliefs, wallow in or resist emotions, and carry out acts of willing?

The only way out for determinists would be to clarify the analytical goals they may have in presenting a cause-and-effect story of human behavior. They could say that they are only recording what transpires when a person acts: there are mental episodes, either identical or mysteriously paired with neural goings-on, and one or both these sets of events in turn bring about agitation or stillness of our limbs. The whole sequence amounts to an action. Since "every event that is involved" results from some distinguishable earlier or concurrent happenings, the principle of universal causation holds. But this deterministic story should be read as only a catalogue of what happens when someone acts; it is not intended to tell us what makes him an agent, or what makes the sequence "his act". The determinist's *compte rendu* reveals no essences; it does not lay bare the hidden 'nature' of action. In particular, it no longer implies that any of the sub-events which are listed as composing one's action are themselves mini-deeds. For example, determinists need not imagine that the agent 'does' or 'acts upon' his brain processes, his motivational states or even (*pace* Danto, 1970, pp. 108ff; 1973, pp. 7, 39, 57, 75ff) his large-scale bodily movements. All these can be sub-events constituting what he does, without being further things he does.

This dispute is for us a side issue, which determinists may thrash out at their leisure. For present purposes I shall go along with Taylor and Chisholm in opposing both indeterminism and determinism as *analyses* of what it is to act, either freely or unfreely; and with them I shall look to doctrines of agent causality for a better account.

### V. COMPARING TAYLOR AND CHISHOLM: WHAT WE AGENT-CAUSE

Before we decide whether agent causality is what we need, we must peruse both Chisholm's and Taylor's systems, inasmuch as they differ on a few crucial points — for instance, on what it is that agents bring about. Taylor nominates concrete, individual, ephemeral events — specifically those events which are motions of our bodies. Chisholm would also say that it is events we agent-cause; but for him events are a species of non-concrete, quasi-propositional, sempiternal "states of affairs". What Chisholm says we agent-cause sound propositional because often, when registering a case of agent causation, Chisholm deploys a full sentential clause in the direct-object position — for example: "He makes it happen that his arm goes up" (1969, p. 206). Chisholm's official view is that states of affairs are to be delineated in gerundive rather than sentential form — e.g., "that state of affairs which is John sitting" (1970, p. 20; see 1971b, p. 39). At any rate, states of affairs resemble propositions in their identity conditions. To update an example of Chisholm's: the proposition that Gerald Ford is in

Washington at time t is not identical with — not numerically the same proposition as — the proposition that Nixon's successor is there at t; similarly, Chisholm admits that the corresponding states of affairs, and also the matching events, must be numerically distinct (1970, p. 21; 1971b, p. 41). States of affairs further resemble propositions in having negations — Ford not being in Washington at t.

When I call Chisholmian states of affairs sempiternal, I allude to their ontological status. *There is* the state of affairs of my arm going up, and of Ford being in Washington, even while my arm is held down, and while Ford is away from Washington. This is analogous to the way that propositions 'exist' even when they are false. And parallel to the 'true'-'false' distinction among propositions, we hear that "there *are* states of affairs, some of which obtain and some of which do not obtain" (Chisholm, 1971b, p. 38; 1971c, p. 33). Perhaps the terms "obtain" and "do not obtain" have an uniformatively technical or 'stipulative' ring. Then Chisholm will permit us to say instead " 'takes place' or 'occurs' or 'is actual', or even 'exists' " (1971b, p. 40). I confess that I remain unenlightened; but I shall save my requests for clarification until Section VII.

For now I want to elucidate Chisholm's contrast, now de-emphasized (this volume, pp. 109, 204), between agent causation and ordinary "transeunt" or "event causation". We meet the everyday species whenever one state of affairs, in occurring, makes another occur (1966, pp. 17–20; 1971b, p. 42). With transeunt causation, effects always result from other, spatio-temporally separable occurrences. Agency is a different matter. Chisholm sees it only when "there is some event, or set of events, that is caused, *not* by other events or states of affairs, but by the man himself, by the agent" (1966, p. 17; see pp. 23–28). There is immanency when "we cause certain events to happen and no other events — or agents — determine us to cause those events to happen" (1971c, p. 34; cp. this volume, pp. 201ff, 203ff).

Chisholm's earlier writings give me the impression sometimes that he would prohibit any state of affairs from having both immanent and transeunt ancestry at a given time. Chisholm definitely appears to take this line with regard to actions from which the agent could have abstained. His reasoning goes:

A responsible act is an act such that, at the time at which the agent undertook to perform it, he had it within his power . . . not to perform the act. But what it is that he thus accomplishes is caused by certain physiological events. (The man raises his arm; yet certain cerebral events cause his arm to go up.) Hence, it [would appear to be] false that it is within his power not to perform the act, and therefore he [would appear to be] not responsible . . .

. . . The things he makes happen directly may well be certain cerebral events, and therefore they will be things he is likely to know nothing about . . . [T]hese events in turn made his arm go up (1964a, pp. 19f; see 1969, p. 216; 1971c, p. 38).

As I understand his dialectics here, Chisholm seems to be retreating from the view that our arm-raiser immanently made his arm rise. Why? Because the movement was transeuntly caused by "cerebral events". So it sounds as if the two forms of causation may not co-exist. But Chisholm keeps agency in the picture by having his arm-raiser bring about the cerebral processes. And since these are what he "makes happen directly" when he performs actions which he is able to refrain from, we might as well say that he does likewise whenever he acts. At any rate, Chisholm generalizes: "whenever a man does something $A$, then (by 'immanent causation') he makes a certain cerebral event happen, and this cerebral event (by 'transeunt causation') makes $A$ happen" (1966, p. 20).

If I am right in suspecting that Chisholm's earlier works do not allow a single event to have both immanent and transeunt origins, then Chisholm might be forced to deny that there can be earlier or simultaneous brain processes which transeuntly cause the "cerebral events" we immanently bring about.

To gain perspective on this issue, we should consider Taylor's position. Taylor definitely permits a single event to be both immanently and transeuntly caused. For this reason, perhaps, Taylor does not entertain the idea that we agent-cause those cerebral happenings which may transeuntly bring about our bodily movements. His most detailed illustration of immanent-transeunt co-existence has to do with motivational rather than neural factors. Taylor asks us to suppose:

> that I am the cause of ... a motion of my finger. Suppose further, however, that there are [transeunt] conditions causally sufficient for my doing just that — such as, among other things, my conviction that only by doing so can I save my life ...
> ... what is entailed by this concept of agency, according to which men are the initiators of their own acts, is that for anything to count as an act there must be an essential reference to the agent as the [immanent] cause of that act, whether he is, in the usual [transeunt] sense, caused to perform it or not (1966, p. 114f).

Taylor's view, that agent-caused movements may have transeunt causes, will enable him to distinguish between actions in general and free actions. Taylor modestly concedes that "[t]here are doubtless other and indeed more adequate meanings [sic] for the expression 'a free act' "; nevertheless he suggests that

> ... we ... define ... "a free act", not as an uncaused bodily motion ... but as an uncaused act ... not as something that just happens from no cause, but rather, as something that is in fact [immanently] caused to happen by some agent, but under circumstances which are such that nothing [transeuntly] causes him to do it ... (1966, p. 127f; see p. 34f).

It is unclear to me whether Chisholm can use this or any other definition to single out free acts. Professor N. L. Ranken states the problem neatly:

immanent causation is understood [by Chisholm] in such a way as to preclude any change happening to the *agent* in his causation of the act ... there is no foreign causal influence ... A man is free with respect to an act, and therefore, responsible, says Chisholm, if he has the power both to perform and not to perform that act. *Immanent causation accounts for the presence of that power.* Now, if all our actions are immanently caused by us — and this is analytically true —⁀ then all our actions are free, and we are, all of us, equally responsible for all our actions (1967, p. 405).

I shall not attempt to resolve any of the issues I have raised about what we are supposed to agent-cause. The principal questions are: Do we agent-cause concrete individual events, or instead proposition-like states of affairs? Do we agent-cause movements of our limbs (bodily-movement states of affairs), or only "cerebral events" (cerebral states of affairs)? Finally, is overdetermination possible? That is, can whatever we agent-cause also have transeunt causes? My purpose has been mainly 'retrospective' here and in foregoing sections. I wanted primarily to see what standard doctrines agent causationists like Taylor and Chisholm might have been trying to avoid, and secondarily to gain a clearer view of agent causation by investigating its 'objects' or results.

Now we can shift to a more critical perspective. Besides inquiring what a person agent-causes, we should wonder what the agent-causing is like. We saw in Section II that we cannot model agent-causing on ordinary causing, where you make $E$ happen by doing something else, $A$. Nevertheless I think we are naturally inclined to picture agent-causing as some kind of active relationship between a doer and the movement of his limbs. But I feel sure that this 'active' conception of immanency will create a major dilemma. To test my hunch, I shall ask:

## VI. IS AGENT-CAUSING ACT-LIKE?

I must consider this problem in two stages, beginning with Chisholm's theory that we agent-cause states of affairs to obtain. I shall investigate whether he might mean that we act on them. Next I shall focus on Taylor's doctrine that we immanently bring about motion of our body.

I believe this rather crude line of questioning is legitimate, given our conceptual dead-end. For example, suppose we learn that "there is" some state of affairs $B$. Why should we not inquire how a person can make contact with $B$, and operate on it in such a way that he "makes $B$ happen"? (Chisholm, 1964a, p. 615). Why can't we ask if the state of affairs suddenly or slowly begins to look different as the agent succeeds, and it "obtains"? I must admit that I have trouble visualizing the hapless state of affairs when he fails, and it "does not obtain".

Now we do speak quite literally and seriously of acting upon familiar objects — for instance, of doing repair work on a phonograph, and thus making it run more smoothly, or causing it to break down altogether, or perhaps failing to bring about either of these results. Do causal verbs have a different meaning in Chisholm's theory than they do in an ordinary situation like this? If so, we should not be afraid to ask what that meaning is. Then we can compare ordinary with Chisholmian situations, and decide whether there are enough similarities to justify using the same causal verbs in both. I feel insufficiently enlightened by the negative assertion that, unlike a hi-fi repairman who acts on the turntable to make it rotate more evenly, the agent-causer does *not* do anything to his brain, limbs or cerebro-bodily state of affairs when he acts. I still want to know what does transpire, and whether the goings-on resemble any paradigmatic form of causal behavior.

It is doubly difficult to pursue this investigation into Chisholm's theory, because he seems to interpose a state of affairs between agent-causers and their brain and body. Is this additional move justified?

## VII. THE NEED FOR A "SOMETHING"

Chisholm urges us to consider

such true statements as these: 'There is something he knows that we do not know'; 'There are things he believes that no other rational person would believe'; 'What Jones desires is the very thing that Smith fears'; 'I've been thinking about what it is that obsesses him' and 'There is something we have all wished for at one time or another that only he had the courage to try to bring about'. So far as I know, there is no adequate analysis of such statements which does not presuppose that there *are* certain things — other than attributes and individuals — which the attitudes in question may take as their objects. The following seems to me to be a sound procedure methodologically: if (1) there are certain true sentences which can be taken to imply that there *are* certain things other than attributes and concrete individual substances, and if (2) we are unable to paraphrase these sentences into other sentences which can be seen *not* to imply that there are those things, then (3) it is not unreasonable to suppose that there are in fact those things (1971d, p. 24; see 1967b/1970, p. 135).

Only Chisholm's last example concerns action — namely an attempt to "bring about" a "something we have all wished for". I see no metaphysical significance in the case where a speaker is being coy, and refuses to specify *what* "we have all wished for", and consequently *what* the person referred to as "he" tried to bring about. If the speaker will not provide these details, perhaps we must continue talking vaguely of a "something". But this seems to have no significance for the analysis of action — or of agent-causing. After all, you cannot do merely an unnamed "something" of this sort. I doubt that even an agent-causer is able to immanently bring about a characterless "something". I am sure that we cannot all merely wish for "something". I for one cannot visualize the state of affairs which is only "something".

Perhaps then we should turn our attention to "true statements" which apparently "imply that there are" certain more definite state-of-affairish items. For simplicity, I'll take a case which does not involve wishing along with trying. My goal will be to decide whether or not agent-causing could be like acting upon a state of affairs — whatever that might be like.

Here is the situation: "there is something" I have done each morning before breakfast during the past week — namely a deep knee-bend. But last night, in a drunken stupor, I fell and sprained my knees. This morning I wake up late, and "there is something" I have done each previous day which I now attempt but fail to do (see Chisholm, 1970, pp. 15–19; 1971c, p. 33; 1971d, pp. 18–24). In sum, this is a story of how I have moved, and now try to move, my limbs. Can we paraphrase it so that we presuppose only "concrete individual substances": me; my knees, their individual flexings last Monday, Tuesday, etc; and my unsuccessful effort to bend them today? My proposal would be to say: "I bent my knees fully on Monday, January 27, 1975; I bent them fully on Tuesday, . . .; but today, Sunday, . . . I huffed and puffed, and only managed to move them a few degrees." In Taylor's vocabulary: "I agent-caused my knees to bend fully on Monday . . .; but today I only agent-caused myself to huff and puff, and my knees to move a short distance."

What advantage would accrue if we introduced a superterrestrial deep knee-bending state of affairs, and declared that I immanently caused it to obtain, or to occur, Monday through Saturday, but that on Sunday I tried and failed to make it recur? Nor is it more helpful to say that I made an unidentified cerebral state of affairs occur today, in a vain endeavor to make the deep knee-bending state of affairs occur as well. Both neural and behavioral states of affairs are paraphrasable, hence supernumerary. But that may not be all. If we insist on keeping them anyway, they are sure to complicate the already puzzling 'immanent' analysis of action. As I remarked in Sections V and VI, we are altogether unsure what it means to talk of states of affairs 'obtaining' and 'not obtaining'. Suppose a novice metaphysician has just heard about states of affairs. He comes to you seeking advice on how to get in contact with one, and how to make it obtain. What instructions would you give him?

At this juncture some state-of-affairists might urge us to stop wondering what their key terms mean, and instead to look upon the language of states of affairs as a purely technical axiomatization, neither corresponding with any sector of everyday language, nor intended to introduce ontological novelties. But against this line we ought to object that a purely technical system of notation can provide no insight into metaphysical riddles about action and bodily movement, determinism and the like. Thus we can put aside states of affairs, and confront again our dilemma about whether agent-causing is like acting — to see how it bears upon theories which only presuppose individual bodies and their particular movements.

## VIII. HAVE WE OTHER MODELS FOR IMMANENT CAUSATION BESIDES ACTING?

Could agent-causing resemble a mere event, which involves no activity? Chisholm actually says that agent-causings *are* events. He takes this position while struggling with the puzzle we discussed in Section III, that both deterministic and indeterministic outlooks seem to invalidate our belief in responsibility. Chisholm imagines "that on a certain occasion a man does [immanently] cause a certain event e to happen". Then Chisholm asks:

> What now of *that* event — the event which is his thus causing e to happen? . . . Shall we say that it was not caused by anything? . . . [T]hen we cannot hold *him* responsible for his [immanently] causing e to happen. What we should say, I believe, is that . . . if a man contributes causally to the occurrence of . . . e, then he contributes causally to his contributing causally to the occurrence . . .
> . . . [The agent] will . . . be a causal contributor to that event which is his being a causal contributor . . . (1971c, pp. 40ff; see 1969, p. 214; also pp. 205–207 this volume).

I shall not worry about the prospect of an infinite series of simultaneous agent-causings of agent-causings, nor about the distinctions Chisholm might draw between agent-causing and being a causal contributor (1971c, pp. 44f; this volume, pp. 200f). Other questions interest me. The first is quite general: When one or more events cause another, would we ever speak of "*that* event — the event which is [their] thus [transeuntly] causing" the latter? If we did reify transeunt causing into a separate occurrence, we would have to explain how it is related to the original events, and to the final effect. No doubt we would soon have an infinite series of transeunt causings of transeunt causings. But that is beside the point. My first question is simply why immanent causing merits this preferential treatment. Why should it be a separate occurrence?

My next question is whether it may not be self-defeating to reify episodes of agent-causing. My guess is that this undermines the innovative, fundamental contrast between immanency and transeuncy. For suppose we register an "event" of agent-causing, followed by "cerebral event" or a bodily motion, e. Why should we not assert that the former "event" transeuntly brought about e? We could bank upon e-like events whenever we learn of other incidents of immanency resembling this "event which is [someone's] causing e to happen". We could investigate whether or not such agent-causings of e-like events have any regular antecedents themselves. But the point is that once we classify agent-causing as an event, we may have to stop explaining e as "caused, *not* [transeuntly] by other events ... but by the man himself, by the agent". Thus e would begin to look like the ordinary, transeunt upshot of a simultaneous, or an already progressing, display of immanent causality. The only contrast left in our metaphysical analysis of agency would be relatively unexciting. Previously we could distinguish the way agents are related to their actions, and the way events are related to their effects. Now we only have a minor disparity between the peculiar internal structure of episodes of agent-causing, and the banal transeunt relationship of such episodes to their e-ish consequences.

Here we should ask what kind of event agent-causing could be. Unfortunately Chisholm gives no details — for example, as to how long an agent-causing event might take to unfold; whether it might be instantaneous, uniform, or possibly intermittent; and how the event of agent-causing is spatially related to the cerebral process or the bodily movement e. Taylor, for that matter, does not even consider the possibility that agent-causing is itself an event. But maybe Taylor was short-sighted. Perhaps any display of our immanency really must be somewhat event-like. After all, we can say generally where and when any agent-causing occurred. Moreover, the time interval we specify must not be later than the time e began, nor may it be 'over' a long time before e started occurring.

The most expeditious procedure might be to see if any events which are not human actions can serve as models for agent-causing. This leaves it open whether it is literally an event. For simplicity I take examples which only involve inanimate objects. First we might look at events in which an object is merely on hand, neither actively participating in, nor affected by, what is going on. For instance, a layer of mud remains on the hillside while a tornado sweeps over. A second kind of event is that in which the object is acted upon — as when a rainstorm washes the layer of mud downhill. Could an agent-causer be related to his brain process or bodily movement in these ways? I do not think so. It sounds incongruous to liken his relationship to his cerebral processes or limb motions with either kind of occurrence. It is hardly enough that he merely be present; and we cannot suppose that either neural or bodily motion episodes are things which overcome him — which happen to him.

One type of event remains: that in which an item figures actively. For instance, the layer of mud breaks loose, and careens downward — perhaps thereby demolishing a cabin in its path. If we were now to return from the domain of inanimate objects like the mud, and incidents like its slide, what would our understanding of agent causation amount to? It seems to me that we would be elucidating the hookup between agent-causers and their cerebral or bodily motions by analogy with ordinary agents and either what they do 'directly', or what they transeuntly cause. Our analytic procedure would appear to be circular, in a clear sense: the agent causationist first informed us that acting really is immanently bringing about certain processes in your brain, or else motions of your limbs; and he went on to tell us how different this form of causation was from the familiar 'transeunt' kind. But when we got up enough nerve to request a more positive characterization of agent-causing, we only learned in the end how similar it is to the ordinary forms of action we began with.

A defender of immanent causation may quash this charge of circularity, but not without sacrifice. He can maintain that acting is agent-causing, and then announce that the latter is primitive — totally uncharacterizable. Or, to vary this strategy, he could offer his theory as a purely formal calculus of definitions and axioms. As I objected at the end of Section VII, when discussing the introduction of states of affairs, it seems unlikely that these countermoves will generate much metaphysical illumination. What do we learn about action when it is reduced to an unanalysable relationship between doer and brain process or bodily movement — or when we are given an uninterpreted, technical system of notation? How can either view furnish us an alternative to volition theories, clarify the distinction between act and bodily happening, or unravel the determinism-indeterminism-freedom knot?

I should boil down the dialectical *ragout* which I have been brewing. We noticed as early as Section II that we are unsure what agent-causing is. We wanted to know more than that it differs radically from its transeunt sibling. Therefore in Section VI I asked if we have any other model for agent-causing besides human actions or the 'activity' of inanimate objects. Apparently not. And our alternative to circularity is the rather unenlightening position that the immanent relationship may not be analysed.

Perhaps champions of immanency are undaunted, and still feel an overpowering impulse to deploy the philosopher's enchanted verb 'cause'. So I want to spell out the other major dilemma which I think undermines, or at least diminishes the significance of agent causality doctrines.

## IX. WHY DO PEOPLE IMMANENTLY CAUSE THEIR BODIES TO MOVE?

This line of questioning deals with the beliefs, the knowledge, the emotions, ambitions, decisions and so forth, upon which we sometimes act. I am uninterested in reasons *for* acting, except when we go ahead and attempt to carry out a concrete individual action of the sort for which we have those reasons — and because of them. My dilemma is whether or not the reasons we act on are in any way connected with our agent-causing and the bodily movement we immanently produce. I choose the vague term "connected" because I want to allow for other than transeunt causal relationships between the event of our having reasons, and either our agent-causing or the immanently engendered bodily goings-on. But still one question I am asking is whether our reasons ever amount to, or form a vital part of, causally sufficient conditions for bodily happenings. Now there appears to be no plausible method of individuating a person's exercise of immanent causality, and separating it from the 'resulting' movement. So I shall assume that any transeunt sufficient causal condition of a bodily process will be just as much the transeunt sufficient condition of our agent-causing of the process. However, my dilemma about reasons does not hinge upon this assumption.

I used to be unsure what role Chisholm wishes to assign to the reasons on which we act. We recall his *dicta* that immanently produced events are caused "not by other events . . . but by the man himself". Chisholm goes on: "nothing — or no one — [transeuntly] causes us to [immanently] cause those events . . .". Specifically, "if our actions, or those for which we are responsible, are not causally determined, then they are not causally determined by our *desires*" (1966, pp. 23f). From these statements, one would gather that agent-caused bodily or cerebral happenings, particularly those which take place when we act freely, cannot be influenced by reasons which people are said to act on. But another passage undercuts this interpretation. Chisholm begins by noting that:

the agent's undertaking of [his] act . . . is not preceded or accompanied by any set of events consituting a sufficient causal condition for it . . . it is caused by the man . . . and his causing . . . need not have been capricious. For there is a state of affairs such that he caused these things to happen in the endeavor to make that [additional] state of affairs happen. Making that [additional] state of affairs happen, therefore, was one of his reasons for acting as he did. And he may have had other reasons; perhaps he *desired* that that state of affairs happen, or perhaps he thought he ought to make it happen (1969, p. 214; emphasis added).

I was hard put to harmonize the assertions that what we do is "not causally determined by our *desires*", and that we might do it because we "*desired* that" some "state of affairs happen". I looked to Chisholm's brief discussion of Leibniz's rather opaque doctrine that one's "motive for making *A* happen . . . *inclines but does not necessitate*" (1966, pp. 23–28). Chisholm appears to take it for granted that transeuntly sufficient conditions do "*necessitate*". In his Winnipeg typescript we read that if "*c* is a sufficient causal condition of *e*, then it is physically *necessary* that if *c* occurs then *e* occurs" (this volume, p. 201, emphasis added). Chisholm assumes that "lawlike generalizations ... express laws of nature — the physical necessity of certain states of affairs" (this volume, pp. 200–201; see 1971c, pp. 44f). What relationship of desire and belief to behavior would fall short of such necessitation? I found no examples in Chisholm's earlier writings. But he gives a hint now when he suggests:

One way of affecting another person's behavior is to restrict his options. We prevent him from making choices he otherwise would have made. We may indeed thus cause him to act in a certain general way and leave the further particulars up to him (this volume, p. 203).

I think the contrast between "a certain general" tendency and "the further particulars" is central to 'inclination without necessitation'. I shall paraphrase an example, which again has to do with one person influencing another, from an unpublished manuscript which Chisholm kindly sent me. The agent is on top of a pedestal. It is safe for him to jump off toward the west, the east, the north or the south. He believes that the landing on the west would be less agreeable than on the other sides. Now you heat up the pedestal. The heat becomes unbearable to him. As a result of your machinations, he must leap. So you have deprived him of one option: staying put. His belief that a westward leap would be painful, and his desire to avoid discomfort, take away another option. Now there is a causally sufficient condition for plunging generally — and for his plunging in a non-westerly direction. Perhaps it is one of the "laws of nature" — a "physical necessity" — that anyone like the pedestal-squatter, in a similar situation, with similar motives, will act thus. But with regard to "the further particulars", there is no such necessitation. For suppose our protagonist agent-causes his brain or legs to behave in such a way that he jumps eastward. Although you, together with his belief and desire, transeuntly caused him to jump, and not to jump westward, neither your thermal skullduggery nor his motives amount to a transeuntly sufficient condition of his eastward jump. In fact there may be no such condition.

One reproach against this case of 'inclining without necessitating' would be that, in Chisholm's own terms, it seems "capricious" for the jumper to go east. There was nothing arbitrary about his leaping in a non-westerly direction. His behavior was rational to this extent. But "the further particulars" do seem arbitrary: he might just as well have plunged northward or southward.

Another reproach would take the opposite line. Can Chisholm be sure that the jumper had no supplementary reason at all to plunge eastward, or to avoid north and south? If the motives you gave him, and the attitudes he had toward the west side, inclined him to leap in a non-westerly direction, why should we halt our inquiry there? Isn't it at least a good methodological bet that other factors — perhaps further beliefs and desires of the jumper — inclined him all the way, and that it is a law of nature that anyone with such motives would, in similar circumstances, plunge eastward? Reasons would thus *"necessitate"*, or be part of what necessitates.

Because of both these challenges, I would feel uneasy about the 'inclining without necessitating' analysis of the way our reasons are connected with our deeds. But Chisholm's present essay furnishes us a new account. He still denies that anything transeuntly necessitates our action, at least when we act freely (this volume, pp. 201–204). Yet "even if a man's undertaking has no sufficient causal conditions", Chisholm would allow it to have "indefinitely many necessary causal conditions . . . each of which is a *sine a qua non* [*sic*] of his undertaking what he does" (this volume, p. 204). Among such transeuntly necessary causal conditions, according to Chisholm, figure "our reasons and motives".

Once again I foresee two counter-arguments — also from opposite directions. First we could object to Chisholm's reliance upon the problematical dichotomy between sufficient and necessary conditions. Something like this has been under attack since John Stuart Mill denied that there was "any scientific ground for the distinction between the cause of a phenomenon and its conditions" (1843/1961, p. 214). Of all the attacks upon this dichotomy, I personally have been most impressed by H. L. A. Hart's and A. M. Honore's (1959). They illustrate the many "ways of distinguishing the cause from other equally necessary conditions", and how "relative to the context of any given inquiry" these methods will be (1959, pp. 30, 33). Evidently I shall not attempt to vindicate these authors, or any of the others who reject a rigid 'necessary'-'sufficient' distinction. But I would warn agent causationists that they are skating on thin ice. To deny that the reasons we act on may constitute a transeuntly sufficient condition, or even "parts" of one (Chisholm, this volume, p. 201; 1971c, p. 45), while admitting that they may form a necessary condition of our agent-causing, seems to me dialectically quite risky.

In any case this position is exposed to challenge from philosophers who accept the 'necessary'-'sufficient' dichotomy, but would surely demand a rationale for Chisholm's edict that beliefs and desires can only be necessary conditions of what we do. I find no supporting argument.

Perhaps, then, agent causationists should say that although we have reasons when we immanently bring about happenings in our brains or limbs, the hookup is not transeuntly causal. A weak version of this would be to say that reasons might have been transeunt causes of our immanent activities, but in fact are not. I prefer Taylor's stronger contention, that our motives cannot possibly be transeunt causes of our deeds. If Taylor's arguments persuade us, we can go on to ask what sort of non-causal relationship motives bear to motived behavior.

## X. TAYLOR'S DENIAL THAT REASONS TRANSEUNTLY CAUSE ACTION

Taylor realizes that our free acts, which by his definition (in Section V) cannot have transeunt causes, should nevertheless be "rational". He suggests:

an action that is free . . . must be such that it is caused by the agent who performs it, but such that no antecedent conditions were sufficient for his performing just that action . . . [A]n action that is both free and rational . . . must be such that the agent who performed it did so for some reason, but this reason cannot have been the cause of it (1974, p. 55).

But how can we act for a reason without the reason playing a causal role? All Taylor manages to prove, I think, is that our statements ascribing reasons to someone do not entail that the reason was a causal factor. Hence we do not contradict ourselves if we deny that it was. For instance, when we explain people's behavior "by reference to the aims, purposes, or goals of the agents", Taylor points out that our explanation *need not* contain "any references, hidden or other, to any causes" (1966, p. 141; see pp. 216, 222). He adds that "[t]he question, 'why did you do that?' . . . is almost never a request for a recital of causes". I agree: our linguistic practice of demanding and constructing a purposive, or 'why', explanation differs from our practice of requesting and listing transeunt causes. But does this demonstrate that a single event — the event of our having a purpose of some kind — may not be cited, perhaps under different descriptions, in both forms of explanation? But suppose anyway that teleological and causal accounts are so dissimilar that a single occurrence might not be mentioned in both. How could it follow that the occurrence itself — the event of my having a reason from $t_1$ until $t_n$ — may not engender concurrent motion of my limbs? I am unpersuaded that our linguistic practices could impose such limits on what transeuntly causes what.

Similarly when Taylor declares: "Purposes do not *cause* one to do anything; they only render intelligible whatever it is that he does" (1966, p. 142). Why not both? I have the same reaction when Taylor analyses preventive behavior:

A purpose, end or goal is not part of the *cause* of a preventive action. It is part of the very *concept* of such an action, just as being a sibling is part of the concept, but no part of the cause, of being a twin (1966, p. 199; see pp. 223, 252, 255; also 1960/62, p. 88).

We need a proof that whenever two concepts are logically connected, the corresponding objects or events may not have causal ties. Why, for example, shouldn't "deliberation . . . itself be one of the causes of . . . actions . . . that result from deliberation"? (1966, p. 182). I find it question-begging to be told that these concepts are logically interrelated, and that they carry no causal implications:

To say that some agent does something as a result of deliberation is very far from saying that he is caused to do what he does by his deliberation . . . It is part of the very concept of deliberation that it applies to situations in which there are, or are at least believed to be, alternative courses of action, and that as a result of one's deliberation he might do either one (1966, p. 192f; see pp. 147f, 176f).

In this last argument from concepts, Taylor seems to have suppressed a premise: If any antecedent of your behaviour — such as deliberation — were a transeunt causal factor, you would be robbed of freedom, unable to act otherwise than it causes you to act. So the claim that reasons cannot cause deeds is questionable in itself, and partly depends upon other assumptions like this, which we already found dubious (Section IV).

## XI. BUT SUPPOSE REASONS CANNOT BE TRANSEUNT CAUSES

Possibly I have not appreciated the force of Taylor's assault upon the 'reasons as causes' doctrine. So I shall imagine that it succeeds. An agent causationist could then say that the act-motive relationship is "logical and semantical" instead (Taylor, 1966, p. 223). For that matter, we could just as well grant to agent causationists either of the causal reclassifications we considered in Section IX: that a person's motivational state *"inclines but does not necessitate"*; or that it is a transeuntly necessary condition of what he does. My question now is what impact any of these concessions would have upon our second major dilemma, which we devised for agent causationists at the beginning of Section IX. Would it help agent causationists if the reason-action hookup were transeunt, but fell short of causal sufficiency; or if it turned out to be not transeuntly causal at all, but conceptual?

Paradoxically enough, it seems to me that any of these answers will deflate immanency doctrines almost as effectively as the old 'sufficient condition' view of motives. To illustrate, imagine that the body of a sane, waking adult has moved. Agent causationists will straightaway inquire: Did this result from immanent goings-on? We may assume so. But is that all we wish to learn about the episode? Do we not want to ask why the person immanently made his body move?

Here is the dilemma for agent causationists. If they say the person had no reasons, his immanent exertions will seem "capricious". The immanent origin of his bodily movements will make them no less freakish. But once an agent causationist grants, with Taylor, that the agent-causing was "rational" (Section X), or allows Chisholm to introduce "our reasons and motives", immanency hardly matters. Nor does the less-than-sufficient causal status of reasons, or their non-causal status, have any deep significance. For suppose our agent-causer brought about motion of his limbs in an unusual, non-transeunt manner. And suppose the reasons he acted on do play a peculiar causal or non-causal role. With all that, our 'Why?' question is more vital to our understanding and assessment of human behavior than the agent causationist's 'How?' question. So although I have not wished to anathemize the concept of agent causality, or to reduce it (Chisholm, this volume, p. 199) to its philosophically overrated transeunt congener, I think I have reduced its importance for action theory. This may be a benefit, since my two main dilemmas, as well as my preparatory endeavors to pin down Taylor's and Chisholm's notions of immanency, all bring out fundamental obscurities.

## XII. A STUNNING BUT DUBIOUS METAPHYSICAL CREATION

The idea that we immanently produce movement or repose of our limbs, or perhaps neural states of affairs, thus appears to defy consistent elucidation. Evidently, propositions like "Smith raised his arm" are true and epistemically "innocent" (see Chisholm, this volume, pp. 199–200). And there is no gainsaying that various initiatory and feedback processes went on in Smith's nervous system. But it evades the central issues we have discussed if you baldly assert: "'Smith raised his arm' implies that the raising [sic] of Smith's arm was something that was caused or brought about by Smith" (Chisholm, this volume, p. 199). It is equally question-begging if you infer that Smith agent-caused the firing of his neurons. Only when Smith performs a distinguishable "act A", which transeuntly "causes event E" (the levitation of his arm), may we deduce that Smith causes E (*pace* Chisholm, this volume, p. 199). Furthermore, the causation of E by Smith would be transeunt (see Goldman, 1970, p. 84). Generally, from the premise that someone moved his body, or that his neurons fired, you cannot conclude "that there is such a thing as 'agent causation'" of either happening (again *pace* Chisholm, this volume, p. 199). At least we can recognize instances of action, and a few of the cerebral events that accompany them. But we have not yet learned what agent-causing is, nor how to spot episodes of it. So we should not infer agent causality from action.

This brings me to a proposal, which I distill from our unsuccessful, though instructive, attempt to equate acting with agent-causing, and to understand the latter. Why not admit, provisionally, that we cannot analyse action — nor the relationship of agent, reasons, cerebral goings-on, limb motion and deed to each other. Unlike agent causation, these are things we can observe and depict in more detail. We would only enjoy the illusion of metaphysical progress if we adopt the immanent analysis of them. As I have documented, that analysis quickly plunges us into deeper obscurities and dilemmas than we face if we take moving one's body as our primitive notion.

I cannot elaborate my 'no analysis' alternative here. But I should remark that it is compatible with the position I improvised for determinists at the end of Section IV. We need not pretend to be analysing, or laying bare the essential nature of action, when we list motives, neural processes, muscular tensings, and other salient occurrences that coincide with action. None of these component events have to be identical with the action they coincide with, and none have to be further deeds that the agent 'performs' (see Weil and Thalberg, 1974; Thalberg, 1976).

The anti-analysis I propose will allow me to share the misgivings of agent causationists like Taylor toward volition theories (Section I). I can join all agent causationists in refusing to assimilate action to the corporeal movement that remains when we laugh away acts of will (Section II). I can endorse their rejection of standard deterministic and indeterministic analyses of what it is to act generally, and of free action in particular (Sections III, IV). I say, in Section XI, that the agent's reasons are more crucial than his immanency — if we want to decide what he was doing, and to what extent he may be held accountable. But I would not let his reasons take over. That would make him an automaton within which a motley crew of cognitive, affective and conative attitudes function as more or less independent agents. And recall that if we then emphasize that he is the one who develops and holds all these attitudes, we will begin to sound uncomfortably Prichardian. In such a cramped dialectical position, I can even share the urge to just assert that people simply cause their bodies to move. But as we discovered repeatedly, we have no inkling what 'cause' could mean here. We fail to understand how immanency might work.

In spite of this fundamental difficulty, I am firmly convinced that

Chisholm's and Taylor's theories of agent causation are imaginative and systematic attempts to deal with the most profound riddles about human behavior. These are brilliant metaphysical inventions, to be appreciated as such. I believe their intellectual merits will only be enhanced by the sort of critical scrutiny which I have devoted to them.

*University of Illinois at Chicago Circle*

## NOTES

[1] Formerly I believed that Aristotle and Thomas Reid were incipient agent causationists. Although I wish to avoid historical disputes here, I would now say that for Aristotle, the event which is our engaging in practical reasoning serves as the main cause of our intentional acts. With Reid, the volition-like event of exercising one's active power seems to have a similar function.

Johnson's notion of "immanent causality" applies to processes in inanimate nature as well as human behavior (1924/1964, vol. III, pp. xx–xxx, **69**, 93–98, 127–42, 171–7); and in any case Johnson is clearly a volition theorist (pp. xxv, 141).

[2] Refers to Chisholm's 'The Agent as Cause', pp. 199–211, this volume.

## BIBLIOGRAPHY

Aune, B., 1974, 'Prichard, Action and Volition', *Philosophical Studies* **25**, 97–116; see esp. p. 101.

Broad, C. D., 1952/1962, 'Determinism, Indeterminism, and Libertarianism', reprinted from Broad, *Ethics and the History of Philosophy*, in S. Morgenbesser and J. J. Walsh (eds.), *Free Will* (henceforth 'FW'). Prentice Hall, Englewood Cliffs, pp. 115–137.

Campbell, C. A., 1951/1968, 'Is "Freewill" a Pseudo-Problem?', reprinted from *Mind* in J. Margolis (ed.), *Introduction to Philosophical Inquiry*, Random House, New York, pp. 154–172.

Chisholm, R. M., 1964a, 'The Descriptive Element in the Concept of Action', *Journal of Philosophy* (henceforth '*JP*') **61**, 613–625.

Chisholm, R. M., 1964b, Review of J. L. Austin's *Philosophical Papers*, *Mind* **83**, 1–25.

Chisholm, R. M., 1966, 'Freedom and Action', in K. Lehrer (ed.), *Freedom and Determinism*, Random House, New York, pp. 11–44.

Chisholm, R. M., 1967a, 'He Could Have Done Otherwise', *JP* **64**, 409–418.

Chisholm, R. M., 1967b/1970, 'Brentano on Descriptive Psychology and the Intentional', reprinted from Lee and Mandelbaum (eds.), *Phenomenology and Existentialism*, in H. Morick (ed.), *Introduction to the Philosophy of Mind*, Scott, Foresman, Glenview, pp. 130–149.

Chisholm, R. M., 1969, 'Some Puzzles About Agency', in K. Lambert (ed.), *The Logical Way of Doing Things*, Yale Univ. Press, New Haven, pp. 199–217.

Chisholm, R. M., 1970, 'Events and Propositions', *Noûs* **4**, 15–24.

Chisholm, R. M., 1971a, 'States of Affairs Again', *Noûs* **4**, 179–183.

Chisholm, R. M., 1971b, 'On the Logic of Intentional Action', in R. Binkley *et al.* (eds.), *Agent, Action, and Reason* (henceforth '*AAR*'). Univ. of Toronto Press, Toronto, pp. 38–69.

Chisholm, R. M., 1971c, 'Reflections on Human Agency', *Idealistic Studies* **1**, 36–46.

Chisholm, R. M., 1971d, 'Problems of Identity', in M. Munitz (ed.), *Identity and Individuation*, N.Y.U. Press, New York, pp. 3–30.

Danto, A., 1970, 'Causation and Basic Action', *Inquiry* **13,** 108–125.
Danto, A., 1973, *Analytical Philosophy of Action*, Cambridge Univ. Press, Cambridge.
Davidson, D., 1971, 'Agency', in AAR, pp. 3–25.
Goldman, A., 1971, *A Theory of Human Action*, Prentice Hall, Englewood Cliffs.
Hart, H. L. A. and Honore, A. M., 1959, *Causation in the Law*, Oxford Univ. Press, Oxford.
Honderich, T., 1972, 'One Determinism', in Honderich (ed.), *Essays on Freedom of Action*, Routledge, London, pp. 187–215.
Johnson, W. E., 1924/1964, *Logic*, vol. III, Dover reprint, N.Y.
Mill, J. S., 1843/1961, *A System of Logic*, Longmans, London.
Prichard, H. A., 1945, *Duty and Obligation*, Clarendon Press, Oxford.
Ranken, N. L., 1967, 'The Unmoved Agent and The Ground of Responsibility', *JP* **64,** 403–8.
Taylor, R., 1958, 'Determinism and the Theory of Agency', in S. Hook (ed.), *Determinism and Freedom in the Age of Modern Science*, Collier, New York, pp. 224–236.
Taylor, R., 1960/1962, 'I Can', reprinted from *Philosophical Review* in FW, pp. 81–90.
Taylor, R., 1966, *Action and Purpose*, Prentice Hall, Englewood Cliffs.
Taylor, R., 1974, *Metaphysics*, 2nd edition, Prentice Hall, Englewood Cliffs.
Thalberg, I., 1967/1972, 'Do We Cause Our Own Actions?', revised from *Analysis*, in Thalberg, *Enigmas of Agency*, Allen and Unwin, London, pp. 35–47.
Thalberg, L., 1976, *A Component Approach to Perception, Emotion and Action*. Blackwell's, Oxford.
Weil, V., and Thalberg, I., 1974, 'The Elements of Basic Action', *Philosophia* **4,** 111–138.

PART 7

ABILITIES AND OTHER 'CANS'

KEITH LEHRER

# 'CAN' IN THEORY AND PRACTICE:
# A POSSIBLE WORLDS ANALYSIS*

The word 'can' stands at the intersection of our theoretical and practical interests. In science and rational inquiry, we seek to explain human behavior and assume there to be natural laws to be discovered in this domain as in others. Given such laws and suitable antecedent conditions every human action may be explained in such a way that it appears that the agent could have performed no other action than the one he did. Our legal and moral concerns, on the other hand, lead us to assume that people sometimes could have fulfilled their obligations when, in fact, they did not do so. To resolve the conflict, philosophers have argued that statements about what a person could have done should be analyzed in terms of conditionals. Others have demurred. The present moment is a propitious one for reconsideration because of recent research on conditionals using possible world semantics. Using such methods, I shall argue that 'can' and 'could have' statements should *not* be analyzed in terms of conditionals. I shall, moreover, provide an analysis of 'can' and 'could have' statements within the framework of possible world semantics. Finally, I shall argue that under the analysis provided, conflict between theory and practice, between freedom and determinism, may be resolved. The resolution shows that truth of the statement that a person could have done otherwise is independent of the truth of determinism.

## I. OBLIGATIONS, EXCUSES, AND 'COULD HAVE'

In some circumstances a man may excuse his failure to perform an action on the grounds that he was not capable of doing so. But if a person is obligated to perform some action he *could* have performed, then he may not excuse his failure to do so on the grounds of incapability. I do not assume that if a man is obligated to perform an action, then this logically implies

*I am indebted to many people for criticism of earlier versions of this paper, most especially, to D. Walton, P. Klein, J. Pollock, P. S. Greenspan, D. Sanford, and F. Raab.

*M. Brand and D. Walton (eds.), Action Theory, 241–270. All Rights Reserved*
*Copyright © 1976 by D. Reidel Publishing Company, Dordrecht-Holland*

that he can or could have performed the action. A person may promise to do what he cannot do and thereby obligate himself to do what he cannot. That he cannot perform the action may be an adequate excuse for failing to do what he was obligated to do. To have such an excuse is, however, quite different from not being obligated to perform the action in the first place.

Of course, the meaning of 'can' and 'could have' are multiply ambiguous. I wish to fix on a sense of these terms that will always suffice to defeat an excuse for failing to perform an action on the grounds of incapability. To insure that a person does not get off the hook on the grounds of incapability, we must be able to claim that he could have performed the action in a very strong sense of 'could have'. It is a sense implying that all those conditions required for the man to succeed in performing the action were fulfilled. If the action requires a special skill, the person has it; if instruments are needed, he has access to them; if information is essential; he is informed, and so forth. Austin referred to this as the 'all-in' sense of 'can' and 'could have'.[1] It has also been called the categorical sense.[2] But the term 'categorical' prejudges the question of how the use of sense of 'can' and 'could have' is to be analyzed.

It has been suggested that to say that a person could have done something in this sense is equivalent to saying that he had the opportunity and the ability to do it.[3] But other attributes may be required as well.[4] A man may have the ability to jump seven feet, but, if he is terrified of heights, he may be unable to jump a six foot chasm that lies before him. This example reveals that it may be difficult to tell whether a person is able to do something because it is difficult to determine his state of mind and the impact of the latter on his behavior. Fully appreciating such epistemic hazards, we sometimes are convinced that requisite conditions are in and that, consequently, a person could have performed the very action he in fact did not perform.

Some clarification is needed concerning the relation of 'could have' and the nonpast tense verb 'can'. If a man borrows money from another with the promise to pay back the sum on a given day, and deliberately places himself in position where he cannot repay the debt at the time in question, this is no excuse. He could have repaid the debt by handling his affairs differently. At the time he incurs the debt, he can repay it. At the time the debt is due, he cannot repay it. That he can repay the debt at the time he incurs it shows that he could then have repaid the debt. Similarly, consider some specific action such as my appearing in a lecture hall in Winnipeg at noon on May 10. On May 9, I can be in the lecture hall at that time, even though I am in Tucson on May 9. On the other hand, at ten o'clock in the morning on May 10 when I am still in Tucson, I cannot be in Winnipeg at noon on May 10. Yet on May 9 I could have been in that lecture hall in Winnipeg at noon on May 10.

As these remarks illustrate, and as I have argued elsewhere, statements affirming that a person can do something have a double time index, one time reference being to the time at which the person has the capability, and the second being to the time of action.[5] Similar remarks apply to the use of 'could have'. Again consider the matter of the unpaid debt from some time after the date at which the debt was due. At the time the man incurred the debt he could have repaid it on the date due, but a week before the debt was due, having mishandled his finances, the man could not have repaid the debt on the date due. The use of 'could have' parallels exactly the use of 'can', the only difference being an adjustment for tense of the verb.* Nevertheless, it is assumed that there are fully deterministic explanations of all human actions whether or not we can formulate them.

It has been argued that the antecedent conditions and laws that determine an action may fail to explain the action, that is, determination is not sufficient for explanation.[6] It has also been argued that an action may be explained, in terms of statistical relevance for example, even if the antecedent conditions and laws fail to determine the action, that is, determination is not necessary for explanation.[7] I am inclined to think that both theses are true, but that does not vitiate our problem. For, it is not unreasonable to suppose that there are fully deterministic explanations of all human actions. If there are fully deterministic explanations of all human actions, then every human action is determined by antecedent conditions and universal laws, and those conditions are also thus determined, and so forth. An action determined in this manner is determined *ancestrally*.

The assumption that actions are ancestrally determined appears to conflict with our earlier assumption that the debtor could have repaid his debt on the date due. If his failure to repay his debt is ancestrally determined, then it seems that there was no time at which he could have brought about any alternative course of events which would have culminated in the promised repayment of his debt. Though we may imagine scenarios leading to that action, it was determined by laws and antecedent conditions that such a course of action would not occur. Thus, the man could not have repaid his debt, and, indeed, no one could have performed any action he did not perform. This is an old conundrum, of course, but I make no apologies for calling it to your attention. In my opinion, past attempts to solve the problem have been based on analyses of 'could' that are either erroneous or inadequate. The conflict between theory and practice remains unresolved. I shall now offer a resolution using possible world semantics.

* See page 270 for Author's insertion in proof.

## II. POSSIBLE WORLDS

To obtain a semantic analysis of sentences containing 'could' and 'determined' as well as conditional sentences germane to our problem, we shall take the notion of a possible world as primitive and proceed to explicate these key terms.[8] There are various ways of conceiving of possible worlds, varying from completely linguistic conceptions to highly metaphysical ones. I shall speak metaphysically, for naturalness of formulation, but what I say could be recast linguistically. For example, instead of speaking of possible worlds, one might speak of sets of sentences that completely describe a world within a given language. Such a description would be a maximally consistent set of sentences, that is, a set to which no further sentence of the language may be added without contradiction.[9]

We may define various kinds of necessity and corresponding forms of possibility in terms of possible worlds. Thus, a statement is logically necessary if and only if it is true in all possible worlds. It is logically possible if and only if it is true in some possible world. Nomic necessity, or necessity in terms of universal laws, may be defined by placing a restriction on the possible worlds to be considered. A statement is nomically necessary if and only if it is true in all possible worlds having the same laws as the actual world. It is nomically possible if and only if it is true in some world having the same laws as the actual world.

Using the conception of possible worlds, we can reformulate conceptions of determinism and ancestral determinism as follows. Consider an action $A$ at $t_n$ in the actual world $W$. Condition $C$ occurring at $t_i$ ($i < n$) in the actual world $W$ determines $A$ at $t_n$ in $W$ if and only if (i) there is a possible world in which $C$ occurs at $t_i$ and $A$ does not occur at $t_n$ but (ii) for any possible world $w$ having the same laws as the actual world $W$, if $C$ occurs at $t_i$ in $w$, then $A$ occurs at $t_n$ in $w$. Clause (i) tells us that it is logically possible that $C$ occurs at $t_i$ without $A$ occurring at $t_n$ thus precluding that the occurrence of the former logically implies the occurrence of the latter. Clause (ii) insures that it is nomically necessary that, if $C$ occurs at $t_i$ then $A$ occurs at $t_n$. Action $A$ at $t_n$ in $W$ is determined if and only if there is some condition in $W$ that determines that $A$ occurs at $t_n$ in $W$. Action $A$ in $W$ is ancestrally determined if and only if there is a condition $C$ occurring at $t_i$ ($i < n$) in $W$ that determines $A$ at $t_n$ in $W$ and for any condition $C$ occurring at any time $t_h$ ($h < n$) in $W$ such that $C$ at $t_n$ in $W$ determines $A$ at $t_n$ in $W$, there is a condition $C'$ occurring at $t_g$ ($g < h$) in $W$ that determines $C$ at $t_n$ in $W$. An ancestrally determined action is, therefore, one that is determined by an antecedent condition, that antecedent condition is determined by an antecedent condition, and so forth.

## III. 'CAN' AND CONDITIONALS

The preceding formulation enables us to sharpen the focus on the problem. Anyone attempting to offer a unified theory according to which a person could have done something he did not do even though his omission was ancestrally determined must offer some truth conditions for saying that a person could (at $t_i$) have done $A$ at $t_n$ even though the fact that the person does not do $A$ at $t_n$ was ancestrally determined. To achieve this objective philosophers have argued that 'could have' statements may be analyzed in terms of conditionals. The most popular among such analyses are ones affirming that to say that a man could have done something is to say that he would have if he had chosen, or that he would have if he had tried.[10]

The subject of conditional analyses has been rather thoroughly debated, but I believe the debate is worth some further discussion. I argued against such analyses in an earlier article that has been discussed critically.[11] The distinction of some of my critics suggests that I should capitulate, but interest in truth suggests another course. Let me note that one who argues that there is *some sense* of 'could have' and *some sense* of 'if' in which these analyses are tenable, is someone with whom I may have no quarrel. What concerns me is whether the sense of 'could have' informally characterized above may be analyzed in terms of a conditional in such a way as to demonstrate the logical consistency of saying that a person could have done something when his not doing it was ancestrally determined.

This end may be achieved by arguing that such analyses succeed when the truth conditions for the conditional are provided within possible worlds semantics. The original treatment of conditionals with possible world semantics is due to Stalnaker.[12] Applying his results to the sort of conditionals with which we are concerned, Stalnaker's account would tell us that a statement of the form 'if $C$ were to occur at $t_i$, the $S$ would have done $A$ at $t_n$' is true in the actual world $W$ if and only if '$S$ does $A$ at $t_n$' is true in the possible world $w$ which is most similar to the actual world of all possible worlds in which '$C$ occurs at $t_i$' is true. Thus to evaluate the conditional, according to Stalnaker, you examine all those possible worlds in which, unlike the actual world, '$C$ occurs at $t_i$', is true, find the one that is most like the actual world in spite of this difference, and see whether in that world '$S$ does $A$ at $t_n$' is true. If it is, the conditional is also true, otherwise, it is not.

Stalnaker's analysis rests on the assumption that there is exactly one possible world that is the most like the actual world of all those possible worlds in which '$C$ occurs at $t_i$' is true. Lewis argued, to the contrary, that there might be an entire set of possible worlds in which '$C$ occurs at $t_i$' is true which are all as much like the actual world as any world in which that is true. Moreover, Lewis argues, there may not be any world, or any set of worlds, that are maximally similar to the actual world. Perhaps for every possible world $w$ in which '$C$ occurs at $t_i$' is true, there is another possible world $w^*$ which is more similar to the actual world that $w$. Possible worlds in which that statement is true get more and more similar to the actual world without limit. This leads Lewis to propose that 'if $C$ were to occur at $t_i$, then $S$ would have done $A$ at $t_n$' is true in $W$ if and only if there is some world in which '$C$ occurs at $t_i$ and $S$ does $A$ at $t_n$' is true which is more like $W$ than any world in which '$C$ occurs at $t_i$ and $S$ does not do $A$ at $t_n$' is true. Thus, according to Lewis, to evaluate the conditional we should consider all those possible worlds in which '$C$ occurs at $t_i$ and $S$ does $A$ at $t_n$' is true and all those in which '$C$ occurs at $t_i$ and $S$ does not do $A$ at $t_n$' is true. If one possible world in which the former is true is more like the actual world than any in which the latter is true, then the conditional is true in the actual world, otherwise it is not.[13]

A third analysis of conditionals was proposed by Pollock. It is Pollock's contention that minimal difference rather than comparative similarity should be used to evaluate the truth of subjunctive conditionals. Thus, to evaluate the truth of the sort of conditional we have been discussing, one should consider all those worlds minimally different from the actual world so that '$C$ occurs at $t_i$' is true and consider whether '$S$ does $A$ at $t_n$' is true in such worlds. If all such worlds are ones in which the latter is true, then the conditional 'if $C$ were to occur at $t_i$, then $S$ would have done $A$ at $t_n$' is true in the actual world, otherwise the conditional is not true.[14] As Pollock formulates the analysis, he adds the qualification that the minimally different worlds must also be ones having the same natural laws as the actual world. Throughout the remainder of our discussion, we shall assume that worlds minimally different from the actual world have the same laws as the actual world rather than explicitly adding this qualification. On this analysis, 'if $C$ were to occur at $t_i$, then $S$ would have done $A$ at $t_n$' is true in $W$ if and only if every possible world $w$ minimally different from the actual world so that '$C$ occurs at $t_i$' is true in $w$ is such that '$S$ does $A$ at $t_n$' is also true in $w$.

The difference between Pollock's account and those of Stalnaker and Lewis rests on the difference between the notion of minimal change and that of similarity. For Stalnaker and Lewis, the truth of the conditional depends on the comparative similarity of certain possible worlds, in which the antecedent of the conditional is true, to the actual world. For Pollock the truth of the conditional depends on certain possible worlds minimally changed from the actual world so that the antecedent is true. We may compare any two worlds with respect to their similarity to the actual world. One will be more, less, or equally similar to actual world in comparison to the other. On the other hand, two worlds might not be comparable with respect to magnitude of change from the actual world. We may have two possible worlds, each minimally different from the actual world so that some statement is true which is not true in the actual world, and it may not make sense to ask whether the change that yields the one possible world is a greater change from the actual world than the one that yields the other.[15] All worlds minimally different from the actual world so that the antecedent of a conditional is true are, therefore, equally germane to the evaluation of the conditional.

We shall adopt the analysis Pollock proposes. For our purposes either of the other two analyses would suffice and would yield similar results. My reason for choosing his analysis is that I think that the concept of minimal difference is a natural and fruitful one to employ in the analysis of 'could'. The question of what a man could have done depends, I shall argue, on what sort of minimal difference would be required to accommodate his performing the action in some possible world. We shall, therefore, take the notion of minimal difference, rather than the notion of comparative similarity, as the basis for our semantics.

On Pollock's analysis, a conditional statement of the form 'if $C$ were to occur at $t_i$, then $S$ would have done $A$ at $t_n$' is consistent with the statement that $S$ does not do $A$ at $t_n$ in $W$ and that this is ancestrally determined. In the first place, we are only concerned with possible worlds having the same laws as the actual world. Consider then all possible worlds minimally different from the actual world so that $C$ occurs at $t_i$. In all those worlds, $S$ does $A$ at $t_n$. Then consider all those possible worlds in which $S$ does not do $A$ at $t_n$. The two sets of possible worlds have no common members. All those worlds that contain conditions that determine that $S$ does not do $A$ at $t_n$ in the actual world and the same laws as the actual world are worlds in which $S$ does not do $A$ at $t_n$. That is perfectly compatible with there being another set of possible worlds containing the same laws as the actual world in which $S$ does $A$ at $t_n$ but which are different from the actual world in that they contain $C$ at $t_i$ and are otherwise minimally different from the actual world. To make this obvious, one need only reflect that the difference between the latter set of possible worlds and the former must be in part a difference in just those conditions that determine that $S$ does not do $A$ at $t_n$ in the actual world. Otherwise, the two sets of possible worlds would not have the same laws.

The foregoing may seem to be an excessively technical way of expressing the point that if a person had tried to perform an action which he, in fact, did not try to perform, then the conditions would have been different, and so would the subsequent outcome. There are benefits to the somewhat more technical way of formulating the matter. Primary among these is that we may sidestep a sticky issue. It has been disputed whether or not when we say that a person would have done something if he had chosen, or if he had tried, we are affirming a genuine conditional.[16] Such discussions, whatever intrinsic interest they may have, are beside the issue as we have formulated it. When the if-statements are treated in the suggested manner, then, whatever other properties they may have, they will, provided they explicate the meaning of 'could have', resolve the conflict that concerns us.

## IV. THE CONDITIONAL ANALYSIS: SOME COUNTEREXAMPLES

Analyses of the proposed variety have the advantage of resolving the conflict between theory and practise, and they have the further advantage of being very plausible. Yet they suffer the defect of being incorrect. Moreover, it is simple enough to explain why by appeal to the account of conditionals offered above. The minimal difference that would be required to accommodate a person trying or choosing to act in some possible world, when he does not try or choose to perform the action in the actual world, may be a difference that would render him capable of doing in the possible world what he could not have done in the actual world.

Take a very familiar example, imagine that a man is pathologically afraid of snakes. He is taken before a large basket containing a placid python, but he cannot see the snake because a lid conceals the reptile from his view. The lid is then removed and he is asked to reach inside the box to touch the snake. We may imagine various degrees of pathological fear. The fear might prevent him from touching the snake but not prevent him from making some attempt in that direction. In such a case it is false that he could have touched the snake and also false that he would have touched the snake if he had tried. He did try, but to no avail. Even in this case of what is almost ordinary pathology, it seems true that he would have touched the snake if he had chosen to. But the man does not choose to touch the snake nor can he bring himself to choose to do so. It is not true that he could have touched the snake but it is true that he would if he had chosen to. The latter is true because the minimal change we need to imagine to accommodate his choosing to touch the snake in a possible world with the same laws as the actual world is one in which his psychology is such as to allow him to choose to touch the snake. But it is precisely his psychological state, his pathological fear, that incapacitates him in the actual world.

Before turning to deeper pathology, it is useful to note that some people would say that the man in question could have touched the snake though they might admit that he could not actually bring himself to do so. In my opinion, this manner of speaking reflects a misunderstanding of human capacities. The assumption behind it is that only physical constraints genuinely incapacitate a person. Psychological conditions only incapacitate one in some degenerate sense. Therefore, when there are no physical constraints, the person really could have done the thing in question. This theory is erroneous. Paralysis that results from hysteria may incapacitate a person, even to the extent of causing his demise, as certainly as paralysis resulting from organic conditions. This brings us to the deeper pathology.

Suppose that the man in our example is frozen with paralysis when the snake appears. In this example, it is clearer that the man could not have touched the snake. The paralysis may, as I have suggested, completely incapacitate the man. He may, let us imagine, be stiff and rigid, his muscles exhibiting contracture, rendering him unable to make any effort to move. It may be true, nevertheless, that he would have touched the snake if he had chosen to, or if he had tried to. The difference we must imagine, however, to accommodate such a choice or attempt is one that would alter the very state that prevents him from touching the snake, his pathological fear.

Let us imagine yet a third form of pathological reaction. In this instance we imagine that the man is one who is usually able to conquer his fear, and, indeed, when he tries to touch a snake confined within easy reach, he usually succeeds in doing so. Sometimes, however, at the sight of a snake, the man immediately faints. Now imagine our man confronted with the python in the circumstances indicated. He immediately faints. He cannot touch the snake because he is unconscious. Yet he would have touched the snake if he had tried to. His problem is not that he would fail if he tried, it is that, having fainted, he cannot try. It is not true that he can touch the snake, but it is true that he would have touched the snake if he had tried. The former is not true and the latter is true because the minimal change required to accommodate his trying to touch the snake is his being conscious, instead of having fainted, but his having fainted, instead of having tried, prevents him from touching the snake.

There are other more interesting examples of when a person cannot try. People who believe in witchcraft and who are convinced that someone is a witch can sometimes be incapacitated by the witch. For example, if the person believed to be a witch openly attacks another with the intention of paralyzing the throat of someone she seeks to afflict, the victim may become convinced beyond all hope and doubt that his throat is paralyzed and, consequently, that he cannot swallow. He may die as a consequence. In this circumstance, the afflicted person exhibits a form of pathological hysteria in response to the activities of the witch. Because the afflicted person is convinced beyond all hope and doubt that he cannot swallow, he cannot make any genuine attempt to do so. Of course, with urging, the person may place food in his mouth and pretend to try to swallow. But he is not genuinely trying. He is in much the position that I would be in if you asked me to swallow my shoe. I could, of course, remove my shoe, shove it into my mouth and choke myself with it a bit to convince you that I was attempting to comply with your request. But I would not be trying to swallow my shoe, I would be feigning the attempt. I am convinced beyond all hope and doubt that I cannot swallow my shoe, and, therefore, I cannot even try to do it. People can try to do things they believe they cannot do provided they have some hope they will succeed, however slim, or some doubt that they will fail, however slight. But when a person is convinced beyond all hope and doubt that he cannot succeed, undertaking actions necessary to success is not the same as trying, it is ritualistic pretense.

In the case of the person afflicted by the witch, it may be difficult to determine whether the person would have succeeded in swallowing if he tried. It is, in fact, partially an empirical question. The minimal change that would be required for the afflicted person to try to swallow would be an alteration in the convictions of the person so that he would not be convinced beyond all hope and doubt that he cannot swallow. Such an alteration of conviction might produce a lessening of the hysterical contraction of the throat muscles so that the person would succeed in swallowing. At any rate, we may imagine that this is so. Thus, the person, as we conceive him, cannot and could not have swallowed anything, even though, had the situation been minimally different so that the afflicted person tried to swallow, he would have succeeded.

## V. OTHER CONDITIONAL ANALYSES

Other proposed analyses of 'can' and 'could have' statements in terms of trying should be mentioned. It has been proposed that to say that a person can do something or could have done something is to say that he usually succeeds or, subjunctively, that he would usually succeed if he were to try.[17] The plausibility of this proposal rests, in the first place, on confounding saying that a man could have done something with saying that he has the requisite abilities, and, secondly, on confusing verification conditions with meaning.

In an earlier paper, I argued that we can have adequate evidence that a man could have done what, in fact, he did not do, if we have observed him performing the action in relevantly similar conditions.[18] If we have observed that a person frequently succeeds in performing an action when he tries, and if the circumstances in those cases are similar to the present ones in all relevant respects as far as we can determine, and if in the present circumstances he neither performs the action nor makes any attempt to do so, then we have adequate evidence that he could have performed the action he does not perform. But this evidence does not entail the statement that he could have performed the action or provide truth conditions for it.

First, the proposal that to say a person can do something means he usually succeeds if he tries is defective because there are actions that a person could have performed though he never tries. When I began this lecture each of us could have placed the thumb of each of his hands in his mouth, winked first with the left eye and then with the right, closed his eyes and removed first the left thumb and then the right thumb from his mouth. But it would be incorrect, I presume, to describe anyone in this room as having usually succeeded when he tried to perform the action.

This objection is met by putting the proposal counterfactually, by saying that the person would usually succeed if he were to attempt to perform the action. Such a counterfactual may explicate the notion of having the ability to perform an action, but it fails to give us truth conditions for saying that a person could have performed an action at a specific time. There are actions that a person can do but once, for example, I could, at noon today have shaved the beard I began growing in Edinburgh. It is unclear what it means to say that I would usually succeed in shaving the beard I acquired in Edinburgh in 1967 at noon today if I attempted to do so. Since we are here concerned with the question of what it means to say that a person could have performed a specific action at a specific time, this objection is critical. Moreover, and more significant, it may be that, though in general a person succeeds in performing an action when he attempts to do so, he cannot do it at the time in question. An archer who shoots with consummate skill may usually succeed in hitting the bullseye from twenty paces when he attempts to do so, but sometimes, rather inexplicably, he loses the knack and is unable to do so. We all have a bad day, or at least a bad few minutes, when we cannot do what we ordinarily can.[19] Thus, it is perfectly consistent to say both that a person usually succeeds in performing a certain action, and yet deny that he could have done it on some specific occasion.

Having rejected such attempts to analyze 'could have' statements as conditionals I shall attempt to explain why such analyses have seemed so plausible to philosophers that some aver that no argument would undermine them.[20] Finally, we must offer some improved analysis of our own. The two tasks are interrelated in that the analysis we shall propose will explain the plausibility of the conditional analyses. I shall, however, first attempt to explain the plausibility of such analyses on intuitive grounds.

Many of the cases we have considered are ones in which the alteration of conditions that would be required to accommodate some person choosing or trying to perform the action would also give the person some advantage, a psychological one, that he lacks in the actual world. Ordinarily, we believe that men need no such alteration to merely try to perform an action, that is, it is a background assumption of customary discourse that there is nothing to prevent a person from trying. When someone says that a person would perform an action if he chose, or that he would succeed if he tried, the speaker would be taken to imply that nothing prevents the person from so trying or choosing. It would, consequently, be misleading to say that a person would have done something if he chose to or that he would have succeeded if he tried, when his psychological state precludes such a choice or effort. For the listener would surely take the speaker to be implying that the person could have performed the action. The implication is not, however, a logical consequence of the truth conditions of the conditional statements. It is, instead, a consequence of the conditional statement in conjunction with the usual background assumption that there is nothing to keep a person from trying or choosing to perform an action. Ordinarily that assumption is noncontroversial (which is not to say that it is correct!) and so a person affirming one of the conditionals would be taken to be implying that the person could have performed the action. That leads philosophers to erroneously confuse what the speaker could reasonably be taken to be implying with truth conditions of what the speaker asserted.[21]

## VI. THE ANALYSIS OF 'COULD HAVE'

To make this informal explanation stick, we shall offer an analysis of 'could have' statements that will enable us to explicate the relation between such statements and conditionals. As a preliminary step, let us consider a tempting but inadequate proposal suggested by our earlier remarks. We have said that sometimes some condition required for a person to be able to perform an action is lacking and therefore that the person cannot perform the action. This suggests that those cases in which the conditional statements are true and yet the person could not have performed the action are ones in which some necessary condition for the performance of the action is missing. From this, one might infer that a correct analysis of 'could have' would require that no necessary condition for the performance of the action was absent.[22] Schematically,

> $S$ could have done $A$ at $t_n$ only if no necessary condition for doing $A$ at $t_n$ was lacking.

This proposal is, however, too restrictive.

To understand why, imagine that I leave the fingers of my left hand relaxed at $t_n$. From the simple fact that I do this, it would be peculiar to suppose that I could not have clenched my fingers into a fist instead. Yet, there is a certain muscle in my arm, *flexor digitorum profundus* to be precise, that must be flexed for my hand to be so clenched, and that muscle is, in fact, unflexed. The flexing of that muscle is a necessary condition of my clenching my fingers into a fist, and that condition is unfulfilled. Hence, according to the proposal it would follow that I could not have clenched my fist because a necessary condition was lacking.

Some necessary condition is lacking for any action, or even any attempt to act, when that action does not in fact occur. Moreover if we suppose that there is always some antecedent condition that determines what occurs and what does not occur, then we also obtain the conclusion that whenever a person does not perform an action, then some antecedent necessary condition for performing the action is lacking. The antecedent condition determining that the action does not occur is sufficient for the non-occurrence of the action. Therefore, the nonoccurrence of the antecedent condition is a necessary condition for the occurrence of the action. From this it follows that whenever there is an antecedent condition $C$ that explains why an action does not occur, there will be some antecedent condition, the nonoccurrence of $C$, that is necessary for the action to occur, and that necessary condition will be lacking.[23]

The crux of the foregoing is that when we say that a person could have done something he did not do, we should not, and I believe do not, thereby affirm that every antecedent necessary condition for his performing the action is fulfilled. It is enough that there be some possible world minimally different from the actual world restricted in an appropriate way so that the person performs the action and those conditions are fulfilled. We may speak of worlds restricted in the appropriate way as possible worlds that are *accessible* to the agent from the actual world. In some possible world accessible to me, though not in the actual world, *flexor digitorum profundus* is flexed rather than unflexed, and my fist is clenched.

## VII. ANALYSIS ONE

In what way, then, must a possible world in which a person performs an action he does not perform in the actual world be restricted in order to be accessible to the agent from the actual world? First of all, the possible world must have the same laws as the actual world. That there are possible worlds with laws different from the actual world in which I perform an action that I do not perform in the actual world hardly shows that I could have performed that action. That there are possible worlds in which whispers move mountains hardly shows that I could have moved the Rincon mountains to Phoenix with a whisper in the actual world. Second, the possible world must differ minimally from the actual world. Possible worlds with wildly different conditions from the actual world, even if they have the same laws as the actual world, are irrelevant to the question of what a person could have done in the actual world.

Moreover, even if there is a possible world having the same laws and only differing minimally from the actual world so that I perform an action I did not perform in the actual world, it by no means follows that the possible world was accessible to me or that I could have performed that action in the actual world. If, for example, I am chained to a wall from which I am anxious to move, but do not because I am chained, we can find a possible world with the same laws, minimally changed to accommodate my moving from the room, namely, a possible world in which I am not chained. But it hardly follows that I could have moved from the room in the actual world. In the possible world I have an advantage I lack in the actual world, to wit, of being unchained. That possible world is not accessible to me.

This observation suggests a further modification that is needed to yield the analysis we shall defend. We must find a possible world that has the same laws, is minimally changed to accommodate my action, *and* these changes must not bestow on me any advantage for performing the action that I lack in the actual world. To illustrate, suppose I am standing in a room with nothing to deter me from leaving. It is natural to assume that I could have left the room rather than remaining. We can imagine my doing so without bestowing any advantage upon me I lack in actuality. This contrasts sharply with the case in which I am chained to the wall. For, in this instance, if we imagine that I leave, we must imagine a change in the circumstance that conveys upon me an advantage I manifestly lack. This suggests the following analysis.

A1.     'S could (at $t_i$) have done A at $t_n$' is true in W if and only if there is a possible world w having the same laws as the actual world W and only minimally different from W so that 'S does A at $t_n$' is true in w in such a way that S has no advantage at $t_i$ for doing A at $t_n$ in w that he lacks in W, and $t_n$ is past in W.

This analysis meets the objection that whenever a man does not perform an action there is some advantage that he lacks in the actual world which he will have in any possible world in which he performs the action. For there may be some time prior to the time of the action when the advantages the person has for performing the action in a possible world in which he does perform the action are all ones he has at that time in the actual world as well. For example, if I am sitting in an airport with a ticket purchased for a flight to Washington two hours before the flight, I can at that time take the flight two hours hence. There is nothing I need do at that time to insure that I will get on the flight. I can sip a milkshake at the ice cream bar without foregoing any advantage. If I subsequently decide not to take the flight, there will be a possible world in which, two hours before flight time, I am sipping a milkshake at the ice cream bar and have no advantages for getting on the flight which I lack in the actual world at that time. Yet, in the possible world I subsequently take the flight to Washington.

The current analysis remains defective, however. There may be some time $t_i$ at which I have the advantages I need at that time to do A at $t_n$ but by some time subsequent to $t_i$ and prior to $t_n$ something happens to prevent me from doing A at $t_n$. I might, for example, have promised to repay a debt in a loan house at a specific time, say between one and two o'clock on Friday. On Thursday, I have the money and am not far distant from the appointed place. But Friday morning a tornado strikes the loan house, sucking it up like a vacuum, and, as a result, I am unable to repay the debt at that place at the appointed time. Now one might be tempted to say that I could, on Thursday, have repaid the debt as promised. But this is false. I could have repaid the debt on Thursday, but not as promised. For I promised to repay the debt at the loan house on Friday between one and two o'clock, and that I could not have done because of the tornado. In such a case, there is a possible world having the same laws as the actual world, minimally different from the actual world so that I repay the debt in the

promised manner on Friday. Moreover, in the possible world I have no
advantages on Thursday for repaying the debt I lack at that time in the
actual world. I do, of course, have some advantages on Friday in the
possible world which I lack on that day in the actual world, because in the
possible world in which I repay the debt on Friday the tornado follows a
slightly different path and misses the loan house.

We face the following problem. In our analysis of '$S$ could (at $t_i$) have
done $A$ at $t_n$' we required that $S$ have no advantages at $t_i$ for doing $A$ at $t_n$
in a possible world accessible to him which he lacks at $t_i$ in the actual
world. That restriction is too weak because the possible worlds in which $S$
does $A$ at $t_n$ may all be ones which bestow some advantage upon $S$ at some
time subsequent to $t_i$ which he lacks at that time in the actual world. On the
other hand, if we required instead that $S$ have no advantages at any time up
to $t_n$ for doing $A$ at $t_n$ in a possible world accessible to him which he lacks
at those times in the actual world, the restriction would be too strong. For
some advantages a person acquires subsequent to $t_i$ may be a consequence
of what he does from $t_i$ to $t_n$. Arriving at a boarding area to get on a flight
to Washington fifteen minutes before the plane departs gives me an
advantage for getting on the flight I would lack if I had remained at home
instead. But when I fail to act so as to secure that advantage, it hardly
follows that I could not have gotten on the flight.

## VIII. ANALYSIS TWO

There is an obvious solution, to wit, to require any advantage the person
has in possible worlds accessible to him which he lacks in the actual world
result from what he does. We must insure, however, that what he does to
obtain those advantages either requires no additional advantages, or
requires no additional advantages except ones that result from what he does
earlier. We thus propose the following recursive analysis.

A2.     '$S$ could (at $t_i$) have done $A$ at $t_n$' is true in the actual world $W$
        if and only if there is a possible world $w$ having the same laws as
        $W$ and minimally different from $W$ so that '$S$ does $A$ at $t_n$' is
        true in $w$ in such a way that any advantage $S$ has in $w$ for doing
        $A$ at $t_n$ which he lacks in $W$ is admissible for $S$ from $W$ and $t_n$
        is past. An advantage $S$ lacks in $W$ is admissible for $S$ from $W$
        if and only if either (a) the advantage results from $S$ doing
        something $B$ at $t_j$ $(t_i \leqslant t_j \leqslant t_n)$ when he has no additional
        advantage for doing $B$ at $t_j$ in $w$ which he lacks in $W$ or (b) the
        advantage results from $S$ doing something $C$ at $t_k$ $(t_i < t_k \leqslant t_n)$

when $S$ has no additional advantages for doing $C$ at $t_k$ in $w$ which he lacks in $W$ except those advantages admissible to $S$ from $W$ resulting from what $S$ does prior to $t_k$.

Conditions (a) and (b) are restrictions concerning advantages which must be satisfied for a possible world to be accessible to $S$ from the actual world.

We need to provide truth conditions for saying that an advantage results from what a person does. Intuitively, this is equivalent to the subjunctive conditional that the person would not have had the advantage if he had not done what he did. Thus, using our analysis of subjunctive conditionals, 'the advantage $C$ $S$ has at $t_j$ for doing $A$ at $t_n$ *results* from $S$ doing $B$ at $t_i$ $(i \leqslant j \leqslant n)$' is true in $w$ if and only if any possible world $w^*$ having the same laws as $w$ and minimally different from $w$ so that '$S$ does not do $B$ at $t_i$' is true in $w^*$ is such that $S$ does not have the advantage $C$ at $t_j$ for doing $A$ at $t_n$ in $w^*$.

When we speak of what $S$ *does* in the analysis, we intend this expression to be construed in a naturally broad manner. Deciding, choosing, and trying are to be included in what a person does, though wanting, believing, and intending are not. It is difficult to draw the line in precise manner, but a question about what a person is doing at a given moment may be naturally answered by replying that a person is trying to climb a pole, choosing a sugar ball, or deciding which road to take. It is peculiar to answer the question by replying that a person is believing there is a pole before him, wanting a sugar ball, or intending to take the road to his left. Such answers do not tell us what the person is doing. Those states may influence what a person does, but they are not things he does.

The intuitive idea captured by our analysis is that a person could (at $t_i$) have done $A$ at $t_n$ just in case there is a possible world or scenario beginning at $t_i$ in which what the person does culminates in his doing $A$ at $t_n$.[24] It is crucial that at $t_i$ and subsequently to $t_n$ he not have any advantages in the scenario for doing $A$ at $t_n$ which he, in fact, lacks, except those that result from what he does earlier, though not prior to $t_i$. This restriction insures that what he does in the scenario is something he might actually have done. To see that the analysis has this effect, consider the situation at $t_i$. If the person takes some step forward doing $A$ at $t_n$ in the scenario which he did not actually take, such as doing $B$ at $t_i$, then he must do so without having any additional advantages at $t_i$ for doing so which he lacks in the actual world at $t_i$.

Suppose there is something in the actual world that prevents the person from doing $B$ at $t_i$ in the actual world. Then there is no scenario that meets our restriction in which the person does $B$ at $t_i$. For what prevents the person from doing $B$ at $t_i$ in the actual world is an obstacle to his doing $B$ at $t_i$. Hence, for the person to do $B$ at $t_i$ in the scenario, the obstacle to his doing so, whether physical or psychological in origin, would have to be removed. The removal of such an obstacle at $t_i$ constitutes an additional advantage for doing $B$ at $t_i$ in the scenario that the person lacks in the actual world. The advantage is not admissible nor is the scenario accessible to the person from the actual world.

When we consider the scenario subsequent to $t_i$, the person may have some advantages for doing $A$ at $t_n$ which he lacks in the actual world resulting from what he does, satisfying the restriction concerning advantages, at earlier times in the scenario. Moreover, such advantages may be ones he lacks in the actual world for doing something $C$ at $t_k$ ($t_i < t_k \leq t_n$) resulting in further advantages for doing $A$ at $t_n$ that the person lacks in the actual world. When, however, there is some obstacle in the actual world to the person doing $C$ at $t_k$ which has not been removed in the scenario by what the person does at earlier times without violating the restrictions concerning advantages, then the removal of that obstacle is an additional advantage in the scenario which the person lacks in the actual world. Again, the advantage is not admissible and the scenario is not accessible to the person from the actual world.

Thus, our analysis is recursive over times. A scenario satisfies the restriction concerning advantages only if what the person does at $t_i$ to obtain advantages for doing $A$ at $t_n$ does not require any additional advantages at $t_i$ which he lacks in the actual world, and what he does at the next moment, $t_i + 1$ to obtain advantages for doing $A$ at $t_n$ does not require any additional advantages at $t_i + 1$ except those resulting from what he does at $t_i$, and so forth.

To illustrate concretely, consider a scenario resulting in my taking a flight to Washington which I did not actually take. The flight leaves at noon on Friday. There is a familiar scenario that I might have enacted beginning at noon on Thursday that would have resulted in my getting on the flight. I might have decided at noon on Thursday to telephone for a reservation to take the flight. Now if we imagine that I do not have any psychological peculiarities, such as a pathological fear of flying, or for that matter of telephones, I might have made that decision without having any additional advantages in the scenario for doing so which I actually lacked. Having made this decision, I then head to a telephone to make a reservation. When, five minutes later, I arrive at the telephone, I have some advantages for getting on the flight that I did not have at that time in actual world. In the actual world, I was not, at that time, at a telephone. This advantage,

however, resulted from the earlier decision that was made without my
having any additional advantages in the scenario for doing so. Now, if the
telephone to which I proceeded is one that was operational in the actual
world, and other circumstances were also appropriate, then I might proceed
to make the telephone call for the reservation without having any additional
advantages for doing so which I lacked in the actual world except those
advantages that resulted from the earlier decision. Notice here that if the
telephone to which I proceeded in the scenario was not operational in the
actual world, then the scenario in which I use the telephone to make the
reservation is not accessible to me because the use of the telephone is an
additional advantage that is not admissible for me from the actual world.
The telephone being operational would give me an additional advantage in
the scenario that I did not have in the actual world which did not result
from earlier actions of mine in the scenario. Each of the steps I take in the
scenario resulting in my getting on the flight must be such as to require only
those advantages I had in the actual world or advantages admissible for me
from the actual world that result from steps in the scenario. The restriction
concerning advantages thus limits those scenarios that are accessible to me.
If there is a scenario resulting in my taking the flight accessible to me from
the actual world, then each step in that scenario must be one that I might
actually have taken given the situation I was in at noon on Thursday.

## IX. 'CAN' AND 'COULD HAVE'

The analysis of 'could have' that we have given treats 'could have' as the
simple past tense of 'can'. The analysis of 'can' may be obtained from the
analysis of 'could have' by deleting the qualification that $t_n$ is past and
inserting instead that $t_n$ is nonpast. The analyses yield the consequence that
if a person will do $A$ at $t_n$ then there is a time, $t_i$ ($i \leq n$) such that $S$ can (at
$t_i$) do $A$ at $t_n$. Similarly, if $S$ did do $A$ at $t_n$, then there was a time $t_i$ ($i \leq n$)
such that $S$ could (at $t_i$) have done $A$ at $t_n$.

Sometimes, 'could have' is used in a more general sense which may be
represented by changing the first time index to a variable and adding an
existential quantifier. Thus, $S$ could have done $A$ at $t_n$ if and only if there is
a time $t_i$ such that $S$ could (at $t_i$) have done $A$ at $t_n$. Where obligation is at
issue, however, there is usually some restricted if rather indefinite time index
that is implicit in the use of the expression. If I incur an obligation by some
action I undertake as an adult, and if, for reasons beyond my understanding, I am, at that time, incapable of fulfilling the obligation, it will
be conceded that I could not have done so. Here the implicit index is to the

time at which the obligation was incurred. There is, finally, an even more general use of 'could have' that results from quantifying over both time indices. Thus, $S$ could have done $A$ if and only if there is a time $t_i$ and a time $t_n$ such that $S$ could (at $t_i$) have done $A$ at $t_n$. Since time indices are often left implicit, this perfectly general use of 'could have' may appear to be the most commonly used in discourse. That is, I believe, an illusion created by the way in which time references, though ubiquitous in discourse, are usually covert and contextually indicated.

## X. 'COULD' AND CONDITIONALS RECONSIDERED

Our analysis enables us to clarify the relationship between conditionals and 'could'. According to our analysis, there must be some scenario accessible to the agent culminating in the performance of the action. This scenario may involve decisions, choices, and attempts leading to the action. Let us consider some obvious differences between this analysis and the conditional analyses. First, no single state like choosing, trying, or wanting enters into the analysis. As Taylor argued, one difficulty with conditional analyses is that there are too many equally qualified candidates, with no clear ground for selecting one rather than another.[25] For example, '$S$ could (at $t_i$) have done $A$ at $t_n$' might be analyzed as '$S$ would have done $A$ at $t_n$ if $S$ had *chosen* to do $A$ at $t_i$' or as '$S$ would have done $A$ at $t_n$ if $S$ had *tried* to do $A$ at $t_i$' or as '$S$ would have done $A$ at $t_n$ if $S$ had *wanted* to do $A$ at $t_i$'. Since choosing, trying, and wanting are different states, these analyses are not semantically equivalent. There do not seem to be any reasonable grounds for preferring one to another. Moreover, they are all incorrect. As we noted earlier, even if all three of the conditionals are true, it does not follow that $S$ could (at $t_i$) have done $A$ at $t_n$. For a change in the person might be required for the person to choose, try, or want to perform the action which would bestow upon the person an advantage, perhaps a psychological one, which he lacks in the actual world. The examples of pathological fear illustrate this sort of problem. Whatever sort of psychological state is used in the antecedent of the conditional, the question will arise as to whether the person might actually have been in that state. If the answer is negative, then the fact that the person would have performed the action if he had been in that psychological state does not logically prove that he could have performed the action.

The preceding sort of argument is familiar, and it shows that the 'could have' statements are not logically implied by the conditionals that are proposed as analyses of them. The proposed analyses are too weak. It has been less commonly observed that the proposed analyses are too strong as well. The 'could have' statements do not logically imply the conditionals either. The reason is that there may be some possible worlds with the same laws as the actual world minimally different from the actual world so that the person chooses, tries, or wants at $t_i$ to do $A$ at $t_n$ and does $A$ at $t_n$ but other such possible worlds minimally different from the actual world so that the person chooses, tries or wants at $t_i$ to do $A$ at $t_n$ but does not do $A$ at $t_n$. Thus, on Pollock's analysis, the conditional is false.[26] The analyses offered by Stalnaker and Lewis yield the same result.[27] The latter set of possible worlds in which the person does not do $A$ at $t_n$ may be as much like the actual world as the former set in which the person does perform the action. On all three analyses the conditional statements will be false, but it may well be true that the person could (at $t_i$) have done $A$ at $t_n$. If those possible worlds in which the person does do $A$ at $t_n$ satisfy our restriction on advantages, and thus are accessible to the person from the actual world, then it will be true that he could (at $t_i$) have done $A$ at $t_n$ in spite of the possible worlds in which he does not do $A$ at $t_n$ subsequent to choosing, trying or wanting at $t_i$ to do so.

An example will illustrate the point. Suppose, once again, that I contemplate the flight to Washington, but I decide that I belong at home with my family and students who are, for one reason or another, especially dependent on me at the moment. I decide on Thursday not to take the noon flight on Friday. Let us imagine that, though I am a conscientious man, my decision is by no means compulsive, or, for that matter, even free from ambivalence. Now suppose someone says that if, at noon on Thursday, I had chosen to get on the flight to Washington on Friday, then I would have done so. Is that true? Suppose I had so chosen. There are, it seems to me, two scenarios, each minimally different from the actual world so that I choose to take the flight, each equally similar to the actual world, but in one of these I take the flight and in one I do not. In the one in which I do, I simply proceed to take those steps that result in my getting on the flight. But there is another scenario. Might I not, having chosen on Thursday to go to Washington, perhaps even having gone so far as to make a reservation, change my mind on Friday morning and remain in Tucson? One scenario is no more or less similar to the actual world than the other. The very considerations that weighted in my actual decision to remain might lead me to change my mind if I had chosen on Thursday to go.

However, the question of whether I could have taken the flight does not depend on what I would have done on Friday if I had chosen on Thursday to take the flight. There is a possible world accessible to me in which I do take the flight and that suffices. If I need no additional advantages to decide to take the flight or to take any subsequent step to that end except those that result from the decision, then there is such a world accessible to me. The other worlds in which I choose to take the flight but subsequently change my mind do not matter. That there is one accessible world in which I take the flight reveals a scenario I might have followed and shows that I could have taken the flight.

The preceding argument shows that the conditional analyses are both too strong and too weak, too narrow and too broad. It is interesting historically to note that Hume, to whom the conditional analysis is often attributed, actually made a proposal that avoided the objection we have just considered. For he contended that to say that a person could have performed an action is equivalent to saying that he may have performed the action if he had so chosen.[28] And that is closer to the mark. Such an analysis would, however, still fall victim to the counterexamples mentioned earlier. Once again some psychological pathology might prevent the person from choosing to perform the action. It will be false that the person could have performed the action even though it is true that he might have performed the action if he had chosen to.

Moreover, our analysis reveals why such analyses have seemed natural. Usually, a person needs no special advantages to choose, or try to perform an action. If, moreover, choosing or trying to perform the action would result in the performance of the action, then, in such a situation, the person could have performed the action. Consider the set of possible worlds in which the conditionals are true. Consider then the subset of that set in which a further restriction is met to the effect that the person needs no additional advantages to choose or try which he lacked in the actual world. If that subset is nonempty it contains a possible world in which the person performs the action and which is accessible to him from the actual world.

If a person needs no advantages, psychological or otherwise, to try or to choose at $t_i$ to do $A$ at $t_n$, which is usually assumed to be the case, and if he would have done $A$ at $t_n$ if he had so tried or chosen at $t_i$, then he could (at $t_i$) have done $A$ at $t_n$. That would suffice. It is not, however, necessary. The closest approximation to our analysis formulated without the use of possible world semantics would be as follows. $S$ could (at $t_i$) have done $A$ at $t_n$ if and only if there is a course of action $C$ that $S$ really might have initiated at $t_i$ without having any additional advantages he actually lacked, and if $S$ had initiated $C$ at $t_i$, then $S$ really might have done $A$ at $t_n$. The expression 'really might' seems to come the closest to capturing the flavor the technical notion of there being a possible world accessible to the person.

That expression is not, however, quite adequate. For we would say of a man in a gambling hall that he really might have placed a wager on a certain number when the roulette wheel was in motion, and if he had placed the wager on that number, then he really might have won a thousand dollars. But it does not follow he could have obtained a thousand dollars in that situation. For, the odds were against him, and he would require the additional advantage of extraordinary luck to have won that sum. In our terminology, the possible world in which he places the bet on the winning number is one in which he has an advantage he does not have in the actual world, to wit, the good luck to win against extraordinary odds.

Finally, our analysis of 'could have' enables us to explain why the observation that person has frequently succeeded in performing some action in circumstances similar to those in which he now does not perform the action gives us evidence that he could have performed it. If we ascertain that the circumstances are similar in all the respects that we have any reason to believe to be relevant to the performance of the action, we acquire adequate evidence that the person required only advantages admissible for him to perform the action. The circumstances are discovered to be favorable enough by observing performance in other relevantly similar situations. Such performance renders it reasonable for us to believe that there are possible worlds, having the same laws as the actual world, in which the person performs the action, and which are only minimally different from the actual world in such a way that any advantages for performing the action he lacks in the actual world are admissible for him.

Moreover, the analysis enables us to understand how we can know that a person can perform an action that we have never seen him perform or an action that he can perform but once. We obtain such evidence by watching that person, or similar persons, perform similar actions. The closer the relevant similarity, the better our evidence.

## XI. THE BASIC CONFLICT. A SOLUTION

Let us now return to the crucial question with which we began. On our analysis what becomes of the apparent conflict between theory and practise? Suppose that a person does not perform an action at a specific time and that his not doing so is determined, indeed, ancestrally determined. Does it follow on our analysis that the person could not have performed the action at the time in question? The answer to the question depends on whether the presence of an antecedent condition determining the person's inaction entails the lack of some advantage he needed to perform the action.

If the presence of such a condition entails the lack of some advantage, then any possible world having the same laws as the actual world in which the person performs the action will be one in which the determining condition is absent and, therefore, one in which the person has some advantage for performing the action he lacks in the actual world, to wit, the absence of the condition in question.

Our earlier reflections indicate, however, that not every condition that determines the nonoccurrence of an action need entail the lack of some advantage to the person performing the action. Again suppose I do not clench my fingers into a fist at a specific moment. That *flexor digitorum profundus* was unflexed just prior to that moment determines the fingers not being clenched. Yet it hardly follows from the antecedent condition of that muscle being unflexed that I could not have clenched the fingers. On the contrary, I could have clenched the fingers, and had I chosen to do so, *flexor digitorum profundus* would have been in a flexed state at the required time. The nonoccurrence of an action at a time being determined and ancestrally determined by antecedent conditions does not entail that the person in question would require some advantage he lacks in the actual world for him to perform the action. Therefore, he could have performed the action even though the nonoccurrence of the action was determined and ancestrally determined.

## XII. OBJECTIONS AND REPLIES

There is an objection to the foregoing line of thought which is perplexing. It may be noted that the unflexed state of *flexor digitorum profundus* is a condition that the person could have altered, and therefore, that he could have clenched his fist because he could have flexed the muscle. But, the objection continues, if the nonoccurrence of the action is ancestrally determined, then there will be some condition that determines the non-occurrence of the action existing at some much earlier time, say when the person was an infant, or, for that matter, even before the person was born. It would, consequently, be incorrect to say that the person could have altered that condition, and since the condition has the nonoccurrence of the action as a consequence, it follows that the person could not have performed the action because he could not have altered the condition.[29]

My reply to the objection is as follows. On our analysis, whether a person can (at $t_i$) perform an action at $t_n$, depends on what advantages $S$ has at $t_i$ in the actual world and what advantages are admissible for him from the actual world from $t_i$ to $t_n$. This means that what happened prior to $t_i$, how the situation at $t_i$ arose, is irrelevant to the question of whether the man can perform the action at $t_n$. All that matters is what advantages he has at $t_i$ and thereafter. How he came to that state is beside the point. What the past has wrought in the present is, of course, crucial, but *how* the present was wrought is otiose.

A bit of fanciful speculation will, I believe, convince you of the correctness of this consequence of our analysis. Suppose that our universe has a duplicate which, at this moment, has suddenly popped into existence, and the present state of the new universe is indistinguishable from the present state of our universe to any observer. That universe has no past history, and so could not have the same laws as ours, but we imagine that the laws of both universes yield the same results for times subsequent to the present. Each of us has a duplicate in the new universe. There will be some actions that a person in the other universe could not be correctly described as performing because our descriptions of actions refer to the past. For example, if I embrace my wife, and my duplicate embraces my wife's duplicate, he is not embracing his wife, because, having just popped into existence, he has never married. Any action that may be described without reference to the past, however, such as embracing a person five minutes hence, and so forth, will be such that a person in our universe can do it if and only if the duplicate of that person in the new universe can also do it. We have the same advantages as our duplicates for performing all such actions.

This shows that it does not matter at all that we have a history our duplicates lack. Whatever has been wrought by the past on us, they suffer as well, but without any past. Therefore, the fact that our present state is determined by conditions existing before we were born and over which we have no control is irrelevant to the question of what we can do now. Whether we have a history or not, our present situation is the same. If our universe is, in fact, what I have called the new universe, we have exactly the same advantages and disadvantages, the same powers and weaknesses, the same beliefs and disbeliefs, and these are what matter for us. Whether a man can perform an action depends entirely on his present circumstances and the laws that determine what will occur henceforth. If the past has wrought a present state of affairs in which I cannot perform some action because I require some advantage I lack, then, of course, that settles the matter. But my duplicate in the new universe will be in the same situation because of his present state. Whatever the past, we find ourselves in some state or other. That state may be one in which, though we choose not to act, we lack no requisite advantage for performing the action, and the same will be true of our duplicates. That my present inaction is determined by conditions that existed before I was born is shown to be irrelevant to whether I can perform the action by considering that my duplicate's not performing the action is not determined by such conditions.

The argument just articulated may suggest that I believe that the knowledge of the past is irrelevant to discovering what a person can do. That is not my thesis. Our knowledge of the past may give us knowledge of the present, and thereby enable us to discover what a person can or cannot do. But our knowledge of the past is only relevant in so far as it gives us knowledge of the present. For it is what exists at the present that determines what a person can and cannot do then.

In summary, I can find no reason whatever for supposing that a condition that determines my not performing some action, even a condition that existed before I was born, should have the result that at every subsequent time I lack some advantage I needed to perform the action. To be sure, if I have the required advantages, I shall not use them because, by hypothesis, I do not perform the action. But the determination might explain why I do not make use of the advantages I have to explain my inaction and, therefore, not entail that I lacked some advantage needed to perform the action. It is my contention that many human actions are to be explained in just this way. For example, suppose an action is explained by assuming that a person is reasonable at a given time and that, being reasonable, he chooses to perform that action which has the greatest expected utility for him. His not performing some other alternative action would be explained in terms of that action having a lower expected utility for him than the action he chose. He could have chosen the action with lower expected utility, though perhaps that would have been unreasonable. It may well be the case that when he was very young, or even before he was born, conditions existed that determine why he would find himself acting the way he does, that is, reasonably. But why should we conclude from that he could not have acted otherwise? He lacked no advantage needed to act otherwise, it is simply that his so acting would have been less beneficial to him and, in this sense, unreasonable.

## XIII. CONVERGENT EXPLANATORY SEQUENCES

As a final foray against my detractors, I should like to point out that I have guarded myself against the preceding objection in a way that may not be readily apparent. I have defined ancestral determination so that to affirm that some action or inaction is ancestrally determined is to say that it is determined by some antecedent condition, that this condition is itself determined by some antecedent conditions, and so forth. From this definition, even in the technical formulation, it does not follow that when inaction is ancestrally determined, then the sequence of ancestral determination will extend indefinitely into the past. To see why not, suppose that I do not perform action $A$ at $t_n$, and this is ancestrally determined. There may be a condition $C$ at $t_i$ $(i < n)$ that determines this, but the condition that determines $C$ at $t_i$ occurs a length of time earlier than $t_i$ which is only half the length of time between $t_i$ and $t_n$. It may then be that the condition that determines this condition precedes it by only half the length of time that the condition preceded the condition it determined and so forth.[30] Shades of Zeno, but, I believe, without paradox. In fact, then, the sequence of events, rather than extending backward indefinitely into the past, will converge toward some point in time, a point in time that may be only ten minutes earlier than time $t_n$.

Thus it is logically consistent to suppose that action and inaction are ancestrally determined without supposing that the sequence of determination extends backwards indefinitely in time. The question is whether this is any more than a logical possibility. I confess I do, though I admit that anything said on this score is mere conjecture and speculation. In defense of taking the model seriously, notice that it has some common sense plausibility. Our natural view of human behavior is that people *initiate* actions. After the action is initiated, the sequence of events is perfectly explicable. Before the sequence is initiated, explanations appear dubious and *ad hoc*. If a man is reasonable, we may be able to understand what decision he will make, what course of events he will initiate. But before the fact, who can say who will be reasonable and who will not? If one could assume that men would behave reasonably, there would be less anxiety in human affairs, and, indeed, if one could assume that one would behave reasonable oneself, there would be less anxiety in one's personal affairs. These awfully mundane reflections suggest to me that it is worth considering whether certain sequences of events initiated by human agents may be explicable only internally, that is, each event in the sequence has some explanation in terms of an earlier event in the sequence, but the sequence extends backward in time only to the initiation of the sequence.

Let me consider some objections. First, it might be said that an action explained in this way is not genuinely explained because the sequence of events is not itself explained. Notice, however, that such argument is precisely the sort of argument that hard-headed philosophers have repudiated when offered by theists. If we suppose that an infinite sequence of events extends indefinitely into the past and that each event is explained in terms of some earlier event in the sequence, then, it has been averred, there is nothing more to explain. Theists have been wont to suggest that there must be some explanation for the whole sequence. If a hard-headed philosopher rejects the theist's claim, he must, by parity of reasoning, reject the argument that a convergent infinite sequence of events, in which each event in the sequence is explained by some earlier event in time in the sequence, must have some explanation. If we assume that we have adequate scientific explanation of events in a sequence when each event is explained in terms of earlier events, then a sequence of events that converge toward a point in time must be counted as providing adequate explanations too.

Secondly, laws that now occur in science employ variables that take as values all rational numbers. Hence a law concerning the sequence mentioned above would not incorporate any formal complexity that is not assumed in presently formulated laws. There is, therefore, no paradox to the assumption that an event explaining an action precedes it by a given length of time, that the event that explains that precedes it by half that length and so forth.

Thirdly, it may be objected that the events in such convergent sequences would not be predictable, nor would a universe containing such events be truly deterministic. Our reply is that such events may be statistically predictable, and, moreover, that appears to be the only form of prediction of human actions that is at all reliable. The world would not be deterministic in the usual sense that every possible world having the same laws as the actual world and sharing a complete temporal slice with the action actual world would have exactly the same slices as the actual world at all other times.[31] I am not sure that is an important objection. If all events can be explained by earlier events in terms of laws, the universe exhibits a high degree of order. To suppose that human actions are the culmination of self-contained sequences of events initiated at some point in time may fail to satisfy all of one's rationalistic passions, but we assume such a picture of human behavior in our practical reflections, and such a conception is consistent with the ideal that every event have an explanation. I concede, in conclusion, that I have not been able to discover a scrap of scientific theory or observation in defense of this idea. But then, nobody seems to have tried.

*University of Arizona*

## NOTES

[1] Austin [3].
[2] Campbell [7].

³ Austin [3], Brand [6], Walton [32].
⁴ Kaufman [14].
⁵ Lehrer and Taylor [18], Hilpinen [12], Walton [33].
⁶ Salmon. [25].
⁷ *Ibid.*
⁸ van Inwagen [30].
⁹ Pollock [24].
¹⁰ Moore [20], Nowell-Smith [21], Baier [4], Aune [1].
¹¹ Lehrer [16], Aune [1, 2], Goldman [10], Pears [22], Dore [8].
¹² Stalnaker [28].
¹³ Lewis [19].
¹⁴ Pollock [23].
¹⁵ *Ibid.*
¹⁶ Austin [3], Pears [22].
¹⁷ Nowell-Smith [21].
¹⁸ Lehrer [16].
¹⁹ Austin [3].
²⁰ Aune [2].
²¹ Grice [11].
²² Baier [4].
²³ Lehrer [17].
²⁴ Cf. Baier [4], Sellars [27].
²⁵ Taylor [29].
²⁶ Pollock [23].
²⁷ Stalnaker [28], Lewis [19].
²⁸ Hume [13].
²⁹ van Inwagen [31].
³⁰ Sanford [26].
³¹ van Inwagen [30].

## BIBLIOGRAPHY

Aune, B., 'Hypotheticals and "can": Another Look', *Analysis* **27** (1967), 191–195.
Aune, B., 'Free Will, "can", and Ethics: A Reply to Lehrer', *Analysis* **30** (1970), 77–83.
Austin, J. L., 'Ifs and Cans', *Proc. of The British Academy* **42**, *Oxford University Press*, 1956, reprinted in Brand (5).
Baier, K., 'Could and Would', *Analysis* suppl. vol. 1 (1963), pp. 20–29, and reprinted with modification in Feigl, Sellars, and Lehrer (9).
Brand, M., *The Nature of Human Action*, Scott, Foresman and Co., 1970.
Brand, M., 'On Having The Opportunity', *Theory and Decision* **2** (1972), 307–313.
Campbell, C. S., 'Is "Free Will" a Pseudo-Problem?', *Mind* **60** (1951), 441–465.
Dore, C., 'On a Recent Discussion of If's and Cans', *Philosophical Studies* **21** (1970), 33–37.
Feigl, H., Sellars, W., and Lehrer, K., *New Readings in Philosophical Analysis*, Appleton-Century-Crofts, 1972.
Goldman, H., *A Theory of Human Action*, Prentice Hall, 1970, pp. 199–200.
Grice, P. H., 'The Causal Theory of Perception', *Proc. Ar. Soc.* supp. vol. 20 (1946).
Hilpinen, R., 'Can and Modal Logic', *Ajatus* **32** (1970), 7–17.
Hume, D., *An Enquiry Concerning Human Understanding*, Open Court, 1956, p. 103.
Kaufman, A. S., 'Ability', *Journal of Philosophy* **60** (1963), 537–551, reprinted in Brand (5).
Lehrer, K., *Freedom and Determinism*, Random House, 1966.
Lehrer, K., 'An Empirical Disproof of Determinism?' in Lehrer (15).
Lehrer, K., '"Could" and Determinism', *Analysis* **24** (1964), 159–160.

Lehrer, K. and Taylor, R., 'Time, Truth, and Modalities', *Mind* **74** (1965), 390–398.
Lewis, D., *Counterfactuals,* Harvard University Press, 1973.
Moore, G. E., *Ethics,* Chapter VI, Clarendon Press, 1912, reprinted in Brand (5).
Nowell-Smith, P. H., 'Ifs and Cans', *Theoria* **26** (1960), 85–101.
Pears, D. F., 'Ifs and Cans', *Canadian Journal of Philosophy* **1** (1972), 369–391.
Pollock, J. L., *Subjective Reasonings,* Reidel, forthcoming.
Pollock, J. L., 'Four Kinds of Conditionals', *American Philosophical Quarterly* **12** (1975), 51–60.
Salmon, W. C., *Statistical Explanation and Statistical Relevance,* University of Pittsburgh, 1971.
Sanford, D. H., 'Causal Necessity and Logical Necessity', *Philosophical Studies,* forthcoming.
Sellars, W., 'Fatalism and Determinism', in Lehrer (15).
Stalnaker, R., 'A Theory of Conditionals', *American Philosophical Quarterly,* monograph series, Vol. 2 (1968), 98–112.
Taylor, R., 'I Can', *Philosophical Review* **69** (1960), 78–89, reprinted in Feigl, Sellars, and Lehrer (9).
van Inwagen, P., 'A Formal Approach to The Problem of Free Will and Determinism', *Theoria* **60** (1974), 9–22.
van Inwagen, P., 'The Incompatibility of Free Will and Determinism', *Philosophical Studies* **27** (1975), 185–199.
Walton, D., 'The Logic of Ability', *Philosophy Research Archives,* forthcoming.
Walton, D., '"Can", Determinism, and Modal Logic', *The Modern Schoolman* **52** (1975), 381–390.

Author's insertion in proof (see page 243)

To make the double time index explicit, I shall place a time index in parentheses after the verbs 'can' and 'could'. Thus, I shall be concerned with locutions of the form: $S$ can (at $t_i$) do $A$ at $t_n$ and $S$ could (at $t_i$) have done $A$ at $t_n$. The only difference in truth conditions for statements of these two forms is that the nonpast tense verb 'can' implies that $t_n$ is nonpast, while the past tense verb implies that $t_n$ is past. In statements of both forms $t_n$ cannot precede $t_i$. A person could (at $t_i$) have done $A$ at $t_n$ only if he required no additional advantages to bring about an alternative course of action culminating in his doing $A$ at $t_n$. Thus, in the case of debtor, who could, at the time he incurred the debt, have repaid the debt when it was due, there is a scenario of action beginning at $t_i$ or thereafter resulting in his repaying the debt on the date due. Moreover, the man required no additional advantages at $t_i$ beyond those he actually possessed to bring about that course of action.

*Explanation.* To resolve the conflict between theory and practice we shall require both an analysis of 'could have' and some explication of our theoretical commitments. We ordinarily assume that every human action is explainable in terms of natural laws and antecedent conditions, that those conditions are similarly explainable, and so forth. Moreover, it is also sometimes assumed that every human action has an explanation that is fully deterministic in the sense that it is based on completely universal laws rather than statistical generalizations. We need not, of course, assume that any one can actually formulate either the laws or conditions. First of all, there are more possible conditions than sentences, the latter being denumerably infinite, the former not. Secondly, it may be a consequence of laws that human beings cannot, because of intellectual or perceptual limitations, formulate laws or conditions of certain varieties.

DOUGLAS WALTON

# TIME AND MODALITY IN THE 'CAN'
# OF OPPORTUNITY*

This paper investigates some questions relating to the explication of the concept of opportunity as expressed by statements like 'I can pick up this pencil on my desk now.' This concept of 'opportunity', or something like it, has also been expressed by some writers through the term 'control' (see Walton [26] and Rescher [19]), and has been discussed by others under the heading of the modal auxiliary verb *can* (see the bibliography in Brand [3]). Myles Brand [4], p. 309, has achieved a helpful initial formulation of the notion we seek to clarify. Let $N$ be a conjunctive statement of the nomic universals that obtain and let $C$ be a conjunctive statement of the relevant initial conditions that obtain.

For every person, a, every individual action A, every time $t_1$, and some time $t_2$, a has the opportunity at $t_1$ to perform $A$ at $t_2$ if, and only if, statements expressing that a performs $A$ at $t_2$ are consistent with $N$ and $C$ (i.e., the conditions at $t_1$).

We will explore the hypothesis that Brand's conception of opportunity corresponds to a concept of possibility that, minimally, shares the formal properties of the $M$-operator in Feys' System $T$ of alethic modal logic. We investigate a contradiction outlined by Lehrer and Taylor [12] that, they argue, shows that the structure of opportunity is not $T$-like, and a two-part solution of Hilpinen [9] that purports to restore the feasibility of the hypothesis of the $T$-structure of opportunity. According to Hilpinen there are two distinct possibilities of formalization according to whether the initial conditions are regarded as (a) obtaining only previous to the time of the action, or whether (b) concurrent initial conditions are allowed as well. In Brand's terms, we can have it that (a) $t_1 < t_2$ or (b) $t_1 \leqslant t_2$: only in the former case are the relevant conditions truly *antecedent*. We will explore the question of which of these two conceptions better exemplifies the 'can' of opportunity sought in the literature on ifs and cans.

* I would like to thank Risto Hilpinen, Keith Lehrer, Kathleen Johnson Wu, and Myles Brand for comments and discussion. My thanks are also due to Arthur Burks for making available to me a manuscript copy of *Cause, Chance, and Reason.*

*M. Brand and D. Walton (eds.), Action Theory, 271–287. All Rights Reserved*

We restrict the scope of the inquiry in several ways. First, the basic notion of opportunity we have in mind is that according to which there is said to be no physical obstruction to an action. At least the paradigm case is that of a physical obstruction, although we may also want to include psychological conditions as possible obstructions as well (such as those disorders called "functional" by psychiatrists) if a more broadly applicable notion of opportunity is to be captured.[1] Although we do not reject the analysis of 'can' via intentions, choosing, willing, trying, and so forth, this is not the sense of 'can' we attempt to clarify here. Quite possibly 'can' is ambiguous, as suggested in Walton [28]. Second, while it is possible to speak of the time of an opportunity for an action at a period previous to and not temporally adjacent to the action (holding in abeyance the question of whether the opportunity is withdrawn or restored during the later interval), we shall idealize to the extent of mainly being concerned with the fuller kind of allegation of opportunity that is said to obtain right up to the time of the action. In this sense, if I truly have the opportunity to do $A$, it must not be possible for some intervening later development to prevent me from doing $A$. A third restriction: the agent is thought of as alone in nature. Interpersonal cases will not be considered here (but see [26]).

## I. THE LEHRER/TAYLOR PROBLEM

A contradiction due to Keith Lehrer and Richard Taylor [12] seems to show that the logic of *can* is inescapably un-$T$-like by requiring the rejection of one of the following axioms (see Hughes and Cresswell [10], p. 31).

(A5)    $Lp \supset p$    The axiom of Necessity

(A6)    $L(p \supset q) \supset (Lp \supset Lq)$

Consider the problem of Smith and the airplane. It is now shortly before 3:30 and Smith is at a country airport. The 3:30 plane is the only possible means whereby Smith can arrive at the city at 4:00. Assume that although there is nothing to prevent Smith from leaving on the 3:30 plane, he does not in fact do so. In this scenario, the following four statements are thought to be true.

(1)    If Smith does not leave at 3:30, then he cannot arrive at 4:00.

(2)    If Smith does leave at 3:30, then he will arrive at 4:00.

(3)    Smith can leave at 3:30.

(4)    Smith does not leave at 3:30.

These four statements are apparently consistent, but the problem is that they also seem to entail a contradiction. For (2) and (3), by (A6)$^2$, entail

(5)     Smith can arrive at 4:00.

Yet (1) and (4), by *modus ponens*, entail

(6)     Smith cannot arrive at 4:00.

And clearly (5) and (6) are contradictories.

Lehrer and Taylor consider and reject a number of solutions, finally arguing for the rejection of the inference from (2) and (3) to (5), and consequently the rejection of '$p$ is possible and $p$ entails $q$, therefore $q$ is possible'. They argue that we can perceive the fallaciousness of this inference by replacing 'a can (at $t$) do $p$ (at $t'$)' by a statement entailed by it: 'Nothing has happened (by $t$) sufficient to prevent a doing $p$ (at $t'$).' So reconstrued, the inference in question reads as follows.

(2)     If Smith leaves at 3:30, then he arrives at 4:00.

(3d)    Nothing has happened by 3:30 sufficient to prevent Smith from leaving at 3:30.

*to infer*

(5d)    Nothing has happened by 3:30 sufficient to prevent Smith from arriving at 4:00.

Cleaving to (A5) and the exclusion of its converse, Lehrer and Taylor argue that (3d) must be accepted as true: "... Smith's not leaving at 3:30 does not count as a condition that prevents Smith from leaving at 3:30, because if it did it would follow that no one can ever do anything he does not do, which is surely false." The impossibility of doing something should not follow from its mere falsity; this would be a clear violation of the ancient *ab esse ad posse* principle expressed in the standard rejection of the converse of (A5) in modal logics (see Hughes and Cresswell [10], p. 28). On the other hand, (5d) is seen as false by Lehrer and Taylor since Smith's not leaving at 3:30 can and does count as a condition that prevents Smith's arriving at 4:00.

## II. HILPINEN'S SOLUTION

Hilpinen in [9] points out the ambiguity of (1), observing that two formalizations are possible. Let $p$ stand for 'Smith leaves the airport', $q$ for

'Smith arrives in the city', s for 3:30, and u for 4:00 o'clock. Now (1) can be rendered as

(7)        $L(\sim p_s \supset \sim q_u)$

or

(8)        $\sim p_s \supset \sim M q_u$

Lehrer and Taylor specifically reject formalization via (7) as a solution and insist on (8) as the correct characterization of the scenario as they conceive it. Hilpinen then mounts a detailed and very interesting dilemmatic argument against (8), to the effect that (8) can be legitimately interpreted two ways — the first way it comes out false, and therefore contradiction does not arise, and the second way, (8) is true, but requires a different interpretation of the physical modalities that excludes the contradiction. Thus either way, there is no contradiction. Let us consider Hilpinen's dilemma in more detail.

*First Horn:* Hilpinen concedes with Lehrer and Taylor that, according to the scenario, it is true at 3:35 that Smith cannot make it to the city at 4:00. This concession depends on the principle that an individual cannot change the course of *past* events. But can Smith make it at 3:30 even granting that he does not leave at 3:30? This question seems to depend on whether an action is sometimes reversible right at the very time of its occurrence (or non-occurrence). And scope for disagreement seems possible on this question. First, continues Hilpinen, let us regard actions as sometimes reversible during their very times of commission. According to this view, (1) is false, for even if Smith does not leave at 3:30, it is still true at the exact time 3:30 that he can leave. And thus it is still true, at that very time, that he can arrive at 4:00. And therefore it is false that if he does not leave at 3:30, then he cannot arrive at 4:00, in this sense of *can*, according to which actions can be reversed at their time of commission. As Hilpinen puts it, the Lehrer-Taylor view is strongly counterintuitive because it implies that there is a time (3:30) at which Smith can board the plane at 3:30 but cannot arrive in the city at 4:00, despite the assumption that boarding the plane at 3:30 is a sufficient condition of arriving in the city at 4:00.

*Second Horn:* According to a second interpretation, actions are not held to be reversible during the actual time of commission — only the future is thought of as open to the possibility of change and the past and present are alike fixed. By the previous interpretation, we had accepted the principle,

(9)        If $t_i < t_j$,   $p_i \supset L_j p_i$

Now the principle is strengthened to read:

(10)    If $t_i \leqslant t_j$,   $p_i \supset L_j p_i$

Both (9) and (10) possess some intuitive plausibility. (10) seems more plausible if the $t_i$ are instants or very short intervals, (9) comes to seem more plausible if the $t_i$ are allowed to comprise longer intervals. Both principles have a history. (10) corresponds to the medieval dictum: *unumquodque, quando est, oportet esse* (anything, when it is, is necessary). (9) expressed the weaker interpretation of the dictum: anything, *once* it is, is *henceforth* necessary (see Rescher and Urquhart [20], p. 191f). Hilpinen also points out that (10) may be attributed to Aristotle in *De Interpretatione*, ix, 18a 27–30.

A problem inherent in the assumption of (10) is that if we interpret $M$ and $L$ as previously, we have as a consequence

(11)    $\sim p_s \supset \sim M_s p_s$

thus contravening the *desideratum* that physical possibility not be truth-entailing. (10) itself obviously exemplifies a non-T-like concept of necessity. Interestingly, however, $M$ and $L$ can be re-interpreted so as to be brought back in line with $T$. Here we reinterpret $\ulcorner M_t p_t \urcorner$ as '$p$ is possible relative to conditions *before t*.' A statement can be contingent only in respect to its future, its past and present being fixed, so to speak, and semantically, a statement could be said to be possible, in this sense, if it is true in at least one possible future. Under this interpretation (11) and (10) now fail to qualify as logical truths. Consider (11): even if $\ulcorner p_s \urcorner$ is false, it does not follow that $\ulcorner M_s p_s \urcorner$ is false. An instance: Smith fails to do p at s, but it is possible at s that, relative to conditions *before s*, Smith could have done either $p$ or not-$p$.

*The Second Horn Elaborated:* It has been shown independently in Walton [25], that according to this interpretation of the physical modalities, the Lehrer-Taylor contradiction is eliminated without rejection of (A5), and that rejection of (A6) is no longer warranted by the scenario. Restructured according to the most recent interpretation of $M$, the inference in Lehrer and Taylor becomes:

(2)      If Smith leaves at 3:30, then he arrives at 4:00.

(3e)     Nothing has happened before 3:30 sufficient to prevent Smith from leaving at 3:30.

(5e)     Nothing has happened before 3:30 sufficient to prevent Smith from arriving at 4:00.

Smith's neglecting to leave must have taken place at or before 3:30. If before, it cannot count as a sufficient condition for his not arriving at 4:00, since, by (2), if he leaves *at* 3:30, he arrives at 4:00. If Smith failed to leave at 3:30, then if (2) and (3e) obtain, then (5e) also obtains. At least we cannot say, as previously, that (5e) is false because something happened before 3:30 sufficient to prevent his arrival at 4:00, namely his neglecting to leave at 3:30. Thus in either case, the inference is preserved, the Lehrer-Taylor solution is vitiated, and the *T*-structure of *can* remains.

A solution is provided for the contradiction nevertheless, because (1) comes out false. Rendered according to the second interpretation, (1) reads:

(1d)     If Smith does not leave at 3:30, then something has happened
         before 3:30 sufficient to prevent Smith from arriving at 4:00.

But this is simply false, as Lehrer and Taylor envision the situation, since, by hypothesis, there is nothing to prevent Smith from leaving at 3:30. At 3:30 (relative to previous conditions) Smith can still arrive at 4:00. It is true, as Lehrer and Taylor have outlined the situation, that if Smith does not leave at 3:30, he cannot (at 3:31) arrive at 4:00. But he can at 3:30 still arrive at 4:00 unless something has happened *before* 3:30 sufficient to prevent his arrival at 4:00. Hence the contradiction is resolved.

Thus there are two ways of resolving the problem—relativizing to past conditions, or relativizing to past-and-concurrent conditions. Let us now attempt to further clarify the form of each of these alternatives.


III. THE SYNTAX OF OPPORTUNITY

The general proposal we suggest here to make the minimal syntax of opportunity more explicit is to add a statement constant, $K$, to the system $T$ of Feys. This strategy is reminiscent of the systems of Anderson [2] and Smiley [22] for deontic logic, antedated by some general suggestions of Lewis and Langford [13], 160f., concerning the notions of relative possibility and necessity. $K$ should be thought of as specified extra-systematically so that the modalities defined in terms of $K$ are *relative modalities*. This proposal stems also from four other sources. First, Reichenbach [18] analyzes the physical modalities as modal operators relativized to a set of laws and antecedent conditions. Second, Von Wright [23] has worked out systems of relativized modalities that exemplify the concept of dyadic versions of possibility and necessity. Third, McCall [14] has advanced two systems of relativized physical modalities and in [15] has suggested the application of the concept of physical possibility to 'can'.

Fourth, Wilfrid Sellars has explored relativized modalities in [21] in connection with 'can' and determinism. We will not concern ourselves here with the formalities of these systems but only with their general shape, some minimal syntactical features shared by them, and the connection of this syntax with the problems of time that arose in the previous section.

Intuitively, $K$ is meant to represent the class of nomic universals and initial conditions that pertain to a given statement. The set $K$ is composed exclusively of the set $N$ of nomic universals and the set $C = \{C_1, C_2, \ldots, C_i\}$, the set of initial conditions. In particular, we are interested in temporally definite statements and the defined relative modalities are to be thought of as temporally definite also. Accordingly, a sentence $p_s$, where $s$ represents the time at which $p$ is true, will be said to be necessary relative to the set $K^0$ where the $C_i \in K$ are true at times *before* $s$. The set $K^*$ is thought of as including $C_i$ true both *at* and *before* $s$, *but (i) excluding* $C_i$ that logically imply $p_s$ without any intermediary premises from the set $N$ of nomic universals within $K^*$.

Whether we think of necessity as relativized to $K^0$ or $K^*$ the basic $T$-structure of the resultant concept would still seem to be applicable. In other words, the notion of relative possibility, defined in the usual way,

$$Mp =_{df} \sim L \sim p$$

will obey Von Wright's axioms for $M$.

(M1)    $p \supset Mp$
(M2)    $M(p \lor q) \equiv (Mp \lor Mq)$

This is not to say that axioms added to the axioms for $T$ or the equivalent $M$ might apply to modalities relativized to $K^*$ but not to $K^0$, or conversely. That (M1) and (M2) apply to cases of 'can' wider than the purely logical sense has been suggested by Von Wright [24] and Kenny [11], and looking at the theorems of $T$ displayed by Hughes and Cresswell [10] there seems to be no good reason to dispute this claim at least for the *can* of opportunity. Thus at present, the only difference between necessity relative to $K^*$ (let us call this *concurrent necessity* in the sequel) and necessity relative to $K^0$ (call this *antecedent necessity*),[3] lies in extrasystematic restrictions laid on $K^*$ and $K^0$: Antecedent necessity is relativized to previous initial conditions exclusively whereas concurrent necessity is relativized to contemporaneous *and* previous initial conditions.

One question I should comment on, but would like to largely avoid, is that of the relation between these relativized modalities and the standard absolute (logical) modalities. Here I have excluded $C_i$ in $K^*$ that logically implies $p_s$ without requiring a law. The reason for this proviso (i) is outlined in Walton [25]. Perhaps this may suggest thinking of the logical and physical modalities as being independent. An all-in sense of 'can' would seem to require both logical and physical possibility, as in Von Wright [24], p. 50. But if we restrict ourselves to a narrower view of the 'can' of opportunity, we might want to think of opportunity as being disjoint from logical truth. That is, it might not be a theorem that every necessary truth is such that every agent has the opportunity to bring it about. We might, for example, restrict the scope of states of affairs that can be brought about to logically contingent states of affairs. I will not try to rule either way here on this difficult technical problem.[4]

Hilpinen [8] has suggested a notion of 'can' relativized to individuals. Here, going a different route, following in outline a scheme suggested by Rescher [19], I would like to propose that (what I call) antecedent and concurrent necessity can be usefully adapted to express a notion of opportunity in the context of human action by iterating the operators $L^0$ and $L^*$ over an operator relativized to an individual intended to express the notion of agency, 'a (an agent) brings it about that $p$'. The proposal is put forward by Fitch [7] that we have the following minimal axioms for $\ulcorner\delta_a p\urcorner$ read as 'a brings it about that $p$'.

(A$\delta$1)    $\delta_a p \supset p$
(A$\delta$2)    $\delta_a(p \& q) \supset (\delta_a p \& \delta_a q)$

A stronger axiomatization is suggested by Pörn [16] that we add to (A$\delta$1) instead of (A$\delta$2),

(A$\delta$3)    $\delta_a(p \supset q) \supset (\delta_a p \supset \delta_a q)$

This latter would make $\delta$ isomorphic with $L$ in Feys' $T$. Some problems in applying this proposal to the concept of agency are discussed in Walton [27] and [29]. Whatever the appropriate axioms for $\delta$ or other operators intended to express notions of human agency might be, we will follow the proposal of Brand [4] that opportunity must be expressed in terms of agency, however the latter might be analyzed, and accordingly consider two definitions pertaining to opportunity that utilize an agency operator: antecedent-necessity-to-do and concurrent-necessity-to-do. Read $\ulcorner\delta_{a,s} p_t\urcorner$ as 'a brings it about at s that $p$ obtains at t.

*Antecedent-Necessity-To-Do:* $L^0 \delta_{a,s} p_t$: that is, $\ulcorner\delta_{a,s} p_t\urcorner$ is necessary relative to $K^0$.

*Concurrent-Necessity-To-Do:* $L^* \delta_{a,s} p_t$: that is, $\ulcorner\delta_{a,s} p_t\urcorner$ is necessary relative to K*.

Here K* is thought of, as before, including restriction (i) and a further restriction on $C$ is also required, as made apparent by Hilpinen [6], p. 8:

(ii)        It is not the case that a controls any of the $C_i$.

We can see the need for restriction (ii) by observing that *Concurrent-Possibility-To-Do*, defined as $\ulcorner {\sim}L^* {\sim}\delta_{a,s} p_t \urcorner$ only expressed the ordinary notion of opportunity if the initial conditions of the action are *not* themselves controlled by the agent. This restriction automatically applies in the case of *Antecedent-Necessity-To-Do* since the initial conditions are in the past, relative to the action, and are thereby automatically out of the agent's control, according to the plausible and ancient principle that the past cannot be changed: *facta infecta fieri non possunt*. Note however that (ii) makes the definition recursive, or at any rate introduces a structural revision of the form of the definition. Ultimately, a definition of roughly this form seems to be needed: a has the opportunity to bring about $p$ if and only if a's bringing about $p$ is concurrently possible and it is not possible (in the same sense) for a to bring it about that any $C_i$ do not obtain.

Introducing the $\delta$-operator brings with it the nasty problem of interpreting iterations of the operators, $\delta$, $L^0$ or $L^*$. The formalities of the system that would be required to support *antecedent-possibility-to-do* and *concurrent-possibility-to-do* would appear formidable. Yet it is hard to see how any remotely adequate notion of opportunity could be expressed except in terms of an integrated notion of agency. Next, let us examine the question of concurrent initial conditions of actions more closely to see whether antecedent possibility or concurrent possibility is more akin to the notion of opportunity that is sought after in the literature on *ifs* and *cans*.

## IV. REVERSIBILITY DURING ACTION

We commonly think that on some occasion we could have done otherwise during certain periods of times preceding the occasion. Yet most of us would likely agree that once an action is done and in the past, from that time onward we cannot do otherwise with respect to that specific action. The future is thought of as sometimes open, the past always deemed closed to our efforts at reversal of a posited action. Agreement might be expected to be quite general on both these highly plausible statements, in contrast to the third question of the reversibility of an action during the actual time of its commission. Here is greater scope for philosophical puzzlement, *aporia*. I could have avoided signing the contract therebefore, not thereafter. But could I have avoided signing it while I was signing it? Obviously I could have stopped writing in the middle of my signature. At any stroke before the final flourish I could have avoided the act of signing. Of course I would have done something, irreversibly, before that final flourish, but not the deed in question, that of signing my name. Thus it would appear possible to reverse an act during the actual time of its commission. In regard to other acts, the point of reversibility comes sooner. At what point during Rocky's recent punching of the bag could he have pulled the punch? Not presumably after it was well on its way and had reached a certain critical point. In the case of other acts, this point is pushed back to the extent that no possibility of reversal at all during any time of commission seems open.

Consider an instance of my moving my finger. Having moved it at all, I cannot not have moved it, even during the very initial phases of actual movement. That the apparent total irreversibility in this case is deceptive can be shown by the specification of an exact duration of the finger-moving, however, and the case is thereby seen to be more similar to the previous two. For consider the time-specific action, my having moved my finger during the period beginning at $t$ and ending at $t'$. (1) It is true here that once I have moved my finger during the period $t + \Delta(< t')$, I cannot not have moved it at some time or other. That this assertion is correct simply follows from the statement that there is some time $t^0$ later than $t$ but previous to $t + \Delta$ — presuming the interval $\Delta$ is sufficiently long — at which I was moving my finger. Thus at $t + \Delta$ my moving my finger at $t^0$ is a past action and hence irreversible. The ordinary time-vague expression — "... if I moved my finger at all I cannot not have moved it, even during the initial phases of actual movement" — expresses a truth. But it is a truth that follows from the irreversibility of past actions and says nothing about the irreversibility of actions during the time of commission. (2) But it is also true, more germanely, that during the period $t - t'$, say at $t^0$ ($t < t^0 < t'$), where the interval between $t^0$ and $t'$ is sufficiently long for me to stop moving my finger before $t'$, I can bring it about that the action 'finger-moving at $t - t'$' is not committed by me. Of course it is trivially true, as shown in (1), that once I have moved my finger even slightly, I have done *something*. But the question remains whether *during* the time of doing that something, I could have not done it. Thus the apparent irreversibility of this case is a fallacy if we regard an action as relative to a specific duration of time. During my doing $p$ at $t - t'$ some act is irreversible, but not necessarily the specific action 'doing-$p$-at-$t - t'$'.

The general picture emerges that for a given action that takes place during $t - t'$, there is a critical point, $t_k$ where the action becomes irreversible. Where $t_k$ is located between $t$ and $t'$ appears to vary with the kind of

action that is involved. Some kinds of actions have what we would call a high inertial factor — once initiated they rapidly tend to irreversibility. Other kinds of actions are reversible nearly up to the point of termination.

Now let us consider the interval $\phi$ between $t_k$ and $t'$. Need there always

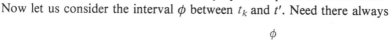

be some such finite interval $\phi$ between the point of irreversibility and the point of termination of an action? Or are there some actions that have the property of being reversible on the very instant of their termination? Just at $t'$, the action is not past, and therefore not irreversible on that count. Thus it might seem that just at $t'$ the action could still be reversible — that is, $\phi$ could be null. This expectation is a fallacy, however, if we cleave to the assumption that any action must take a finite length of time. For reversing an action is itself an action, and must also, on this assumption, take time. $\ulcorner \sim\delta_a p \urcorner$ and $\ulcorner \delta_a \sim p \urcorner$, on our account, constitute "actions" equally as well as $\ulcorner \delta_a p \urcorner$. On the contrary assumption that such "negative actions" are not genuine actions, it may be possible to characterize action-reversal as not requiring a finite interval of time of execution. But given our assumption that all actions take time, it follows that if an action at $t-t'$ is reversible during $t-t'$, there will always be a $\phi$-interval before $t'$ during which the action is irreversible.

It also follows as a corollary of this consequence that there are some actions that are not reversible at all during the time of their commission. For there will be some actions where the time required for reversal will exceed the stretch of time occupied by the action. Here $\phi$, the time of

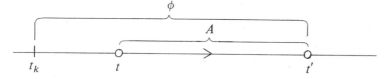

reversal, includes $A$, the time of action. One case fitting this paradigm is that where some external factor prohibits reversal. An especially interesting case is that where $A$ is simply too short an interval to physically allow execution of any act of reversal. Take the action of my moving my finger for a microsecond. Presumably there is a class of such actions that are too quick to be reversed at all, once initiated. In general, for any reversal-interval $\phi$, we can always pick out an action-segment that takes place within that interval and is therefore irreversible, so long as $\phi$ is finite.

## V. THE PRINCIPLE OF PRESENT-IRREVERSIBILITY

We are now in a better position to reflect on our third question that was laden with *aporia*: whether actions are reversible during the time of commission. Let us pose the three questions formally. Let $t_s < t_t < t_u$ obtain.

$$(P_{fut}) \qquad \delta_{a,u}\, p \supset \sim M \sim \delta_{a,t}\, p$$
$$(P_{pres}) \qquad \delta_{a,t}\, p \supset \sim M \sim \delta_{a,t}\, p$$
$$(P_{past}) \qquad \delta_{a,s}\, p \supset \sim M \sim \delta_{a,t}\, p$$

We could call these respectively the principles of future, present, and past-irreversibility. The last, for example, reads: If a brings it about at $t_s$ that $p$, then it is not possible for a to reverse[5] $p$ at a later time, $t$. As we suggested earlier, this principle, that of past-irreversibility, is generally accepted. The principle of future irreversibility (for all $p$) is generally rejected. And the principle of present-irreversibility, represented by the middle schema, appears open to contention.

Let us take a closer look at the middle schema. What it says is this: if a brings about $p$ at $t$ then it is physically impossible for a to not bring about $p$ at $t$. As before, we will assume that $t$ stands for an interval or stretch of time, although perhaps very small intervals may be allowed, rather than a point of time, or some such infinitesimal quantum. Thus we assume in interpreting $(P_{pres})$ that $t$ will be comprised of subtimes, $t_i$. Further, we assume that $(P_{pres})$ is meant to be true of all the $t_i$. In other words, the expression $\ulcorner \delta_{a,t}\, p \urcorner$ as it occurs in $(P_{pres})$ and other schemata of this type is meant to be read in such a way as to contain an implicit universal quantification of $t_i$: a brings it about that $p$ during the *entire* interval $t$. More explicitly, $(P_{pres})$ could be schematized:

$$(\forall_{t_i})\ (\delta_{a,t_i}\, p \supset \sim M \sim \delta_{a,t_i}\, p)$$

We are questioning whether this principle is logically necessary. Thus to overturn the allegation of logical necessity, we need to establish the logical possibility of the schema,

$$(\exists_{t_i})\ (\delta_{a,t_i}\, p \ \& \ M \sim \delta_{a,t_i}\, p)$$

Now our informal examples of the previous section have furnished instantiations of this expression. That is, there are actions that are reversible during certain time within the time of commission of the action (namely during the initial phases). Accordingly, the above schema is realizable and the previous generalization, $(P_{pres})$ cannot be asserted as a logical truth.

It does not follow that the principle of present-reversibility,

$$\delta_{a,t} p \supset M \sim \delta_{a,t} p$$

is logically false. For, as we have seen, for certain very small $t$, this principle is true. A correct appraisal of the situation is that both principles, that of present-irreversibility and that of present-reversibility, are logically contingent, sometimes true and sometimes false. If our earlier conjecture that there is always a $\phi$-interval is correct, however, a restricted version of the principle of present-irreversibility,

$$(\forall_{t_i}) \ (\delta_{a,t_i}) \supset (\exists_{t_j})(\sim M \sim \delta_{a,t_j} p)$$

would be concurrently necessary, if not logically necessary. In other words, if I bring about something during an interval $t$, there will generally be some sub-time of $t$ during which the action is irreversible. In this restricted sense, it seems generally true that actions are present-irreversible. But in a fuller sense more intuitively adequate to $(P_{pres})$, we have seen that it is not logically true that actions are present-irreversible.

Again, another principle similar to $(P_{pres})$ would come out as generally logically (or physically) true on our assumptions, namely,

$$(\forall_{t_i}) \ (\delta_{a,t_i} p) \supset (\sim M)(\forall_{t_i})(\sim \delta_{a,t_i} p)$$

Paraphrased: if a brings it about that $p$ during the entire duration of $t$, then it is physically impossible that a not bring about $p$ during the entire duration of $p$. For again, that there is always a $\phi$-interval implies that there are some sub-times during which the action is irreversible. Thus the consequent, which states that it is physically impossible that the agent reverse the action at all times of commission, will be true provided only the antecedent is true. The similarity between the above logical truth and the logical contingency previously discussed makes $(P_{pres})$ a source of considerable confusion. Perhaps this partly explains the aura of puzzlement that surrounds informal statements of $(P_{pres})$.

## VI. CONCLUSIONS

We conclude that actions are sometimes thought to be reversible during some times of their commission and therefore that the concept of concurrent possibility is more akin, *ceteris paribus*, to the sought-after sense of opportunity than the concept of antecedent possibility. Thus, of the pair of solutions suggested by Hilpinen, the one to be pursued more actively in the further analysis of the *can* of opportunity is the first solution, the one that utilizes the concept of concurrent possibility. Accordingly, a method I suggest we pursue is the addition of a constant, $K^*$, to $T$, while at the same time working on a set of axioms for agency such as those suggested by Fitch [7] or Pörn [16].

As with any project of this type, however, there are other ways to do it. One way, instead of making the modality of 'can' a purely relative matter, is to relativize to a fixed set, say, a statement constant representing the state of the "world" at $t$. Meredith, Prior, Suszko and others[6] have investigated the use of formal devices such as a "contingent constant" to represent a comprehensive statement comprising the set of the conjunction of all true statements at a time $t$. We could adopt this notion to our needs by ruling: a can do $A$ at $t =_{df}$ 'a does $A$ at $t$' is logically consistent with the world-statement at $t$. Or to yield a variant of antecedent possibility instead of the foregoing analogue of concurrent possibility, we could change the last occurrence of '$t$' to '$t - \Delta$'. While I believe that this proposal may initially seem more attractive and more substantive than the one I have put forward (so it seemed to me for a time), I have argued in [30] that it is so plagued with difficulties that there seems not much hope for it. Nor is the notion of a world-statement well understood enough to give us much assurance that it is free from paradox.

A second way, would be to treat 'can' as a variably strict modality, instead of as a strict, but relativized, modality. We could use a selection function $*$ after the fashion of Åqvist [1] where $\ulcorner *p \urcorner$ is read '$p$ in the circumstances' or '$p$, other things being equal'. Thus I can bring about $p$ if, and only if, my bringing about $p$ is possible in the circumstances. The syntactical form of a can-sentence, where $p$ is an action-sentence, is exhibited by the schema $\ulcorner M*p \urcorner$. Semantically speaking, I can bring about $p$ if, and only if, I do bring about $p$ in all the closest possible worlds to the actual world. In this line of analysis, much depends on which theory of counterfactuals one subscribes to, but perhaps enough has been said to indicate that there is much promise in the general approach. It is a live option for further research, in my opinion potentially the most competitive rival to the method of relativized modalities.

A third possible line of inquiry may be opened up through consideration of the causal modalities investigated by Burks in [5] and [6]. The language of action and opportunity is known to be closely linked to the causal relation, and thus work of Burks has important applications to Action Theory. Perhaps however the causal modalities may function more as an adjunct to, than as an alternative to, the devices of relativized modalities or selection functions in the analysis of the 'can' of opportunity. Certainly studies of varieties of indirect agency (see [29]) could be greatly advanced using Burks' concept of elliptical causal implication[7] through definitions like the following: a causally indirectly brings it about that $p$ if, and only if, a brings it about that $q$ and $q$ elliptically causally implies $p$. So here is a third avenue to the understanding of the 'can' of opportunity. Despite the existence of these three alternatives, the method of relativized modalities is a natural approach to the syntax of the 'can' of opportunity that, I hope to have shown, has much to recommend it.

Our investigations have shown that the basic $T$-structure of the 'can' of opportunity is preserved despite the problems posed by the anomaly discovered by Lehrer and Taylor. As a postscript, I would like to add that it seems likely that an adequate concept of opportunity requires a modal system even stronger than $T$. For the following inference would seem to be valid:

> a does not have the opportunity to bring about both $p$ and $q$
>
> a brings it about that $p$
>
> Therefore, a does not have the opportunity to bring it about that $q$.

I do not have the opportunity both to take the bus home today and walk home today. Suppose I take the bus home. Then it follows that I do not have the opportunity to walk home today. As McCall [14] points out, if the modalities are thought of as relativized then the following inference goes through, even though its counterpart in the absolute modalities is fallacious.

$$\frac{\sim M^*(p \ \& \ q)}{\sim M^*q} \quad p$$

This suggests that, for relativized modalities, (A6) should be strengthened:

$$(\text{A6L}^*) \quad L^*(p \supset q) \supset (p \supset L^*q)$$

This axiom would not suit the logical (absolute) modalities since, interpreted that way, it proceeds fallaciously from a *necessitas consequentiae* to a *necessitas consequentis*. But when the modalities are physical and relative the inference represented by (A6*) seems much more likely to be valid, as

McCall suggests. Thus not only does the concept of opportunity display a minimal $T$-structure in respect to (A5) and (A6), but also seems to require an even stronger version of (A6) such as (A6L*).

*University of Winnipeg*

## NOTES

[1] Even though, strictly speaking, our efforts of analysis are directed toward characterizing the class of statements that are "narrowly physically possible", it is easy to see how it could be extended to take other wider kinds of possibility into account, using physical possibility as a base notion. I view this flexibility of the account as an advantage.

[2] The theorem $\ulcorner (Mp \,\&\, (p \supset q)) \supset Mq \urcorner$ is a fairly direct consequence of (A6). See the proof in Hughes and Cresswell [10], p. 37.

[3] In [25] antecedent necessity is called "Laplacean necessity" but the context of the discussion there relates to determinism, a topic outside the scope of the present article (regrettably).

[4] But see the discussions in Burks [6], for an illustrative treatment of closely analogous problems.

[5] The expression 'a reverses $p$' is ambiguous, and may be rendered schematically as either $\ulcorner \delta_a \sim p \urcorner$ or $\ulcorner \sim \delta_a p \urcorner$. The former implies the latter, but not conversely. The same problems that we consider arise for both cases. Thus we might equally well have considered the analogues $\ulcorner \delta_{a,t} p \supset \sim M \delta_{a,t} \sim p \urcorner$ plus the corresponding pair for $(P_{fut})$ and $(P_{past})$.

[6] For a description of this literature, see Prior [17].

[7] See Burks [6], 7.3.3.

## BIBLIOGRAPHY

[1] Åqvist, Lennart, 'Modal Logic with Subjunctive Conditionals and Dispositional Predicates', *Journal of Philosophical Logic* **2** (1973), 1–76.

[2] Anderson, A. R., 'The Formal Analysis of Normative Systems', *The Logic of Decision and Action*, University of Pittsburgh Press, Pittsburgh, 1967, pp. 147–213.

[3] Brand, Myles (ed.), *The Nature of Human Action*, Scott Foresman, Glenview, Illinois, 1970.

[4] Brand, Myles, 'On Having the Opportunity', *Theory and Decision* **2**, (1972), 307–313.

[5] Burks, Arthur, 'The Logic of Causal Propositions', *Mind* **60** (1951), 363–382.

[6] Burks, Arthur, *Cause, Chance, and Reason*, forthcoming.

[7] Fitch, Frederic B., 'A Logical Analysis of Some Value Concepts', *Journal of Symbolic Logic* **28** (1963), 135–142.

[8] Hilpinen, Risto, 'An Analysis of Relativized Modalities', in J. W. Davies *et al.* (ed.), *Philosophical Logic*, Reidel, Dordrecht, 1969, pp. 181–193.

[9] Hilpinen, Risto, '*Can* and Modal Logic', *Ajatus* **32** (1970), 7–17.

[10] Hughes, G. E. and Cresswell, M. J., *An Introduction to Modal Logic*, Methuen, London, 1968.

[11] Kenny, Anthony, 'Freedom, Spontaneity and Indifference', in Ted Honderich (ed.), *Essays on Freedom of Action*, Routledge and Kegan Paul, London and Boston, 1973, pp. 89–104.

[12] Lehrer, Keith and Taylor, Richard, 'Time, Truth, and Modalities', *Mind* **74** (1965), 390–398.

[13] Lewis, C. I. and Langford, C. H., *Symbolic Logic*, Dover, New York, 1932.
[14] McCall, Storrs, 'Time and the Physical Modalities', *The Monist* **53** (1969), 426–446.
[15] McCall, Storrs, 'Ability as a Species of Possibility', in [2], 139–147.
[16] Pörn, Ingmar, *The Logic of Power*, Blackwell, Oxford, 1970.
[17] Prior, Arthur, *Past, Present, and Future*, Oxford University Press, Oxford, 1967, Ch. V.
[18] Reichenbach, Hans, *Elements of Symbolic Logic*, The Free Press, New York, 1947.
[19] Rescher, Nicholas, 'The Concept of Control', *Essays in Philosophical Analysis* (ed. by Nicholas Rescher), University of Pittsburgh Press, Pittsburgh, 1969, pp. 327–353.
[20] Rescher, Nicholas and Urquhart, Alasdair, *Temporal Logic,* Springer-Verlag, New York, 1971.
[21] Sellars, Wilfrid, 'Fatalism and Determinism', in Keith Lehrer (ed.), *Freedom and Determinism*, Random House, New York, 1966, pp. 141–174.
[22] Smiley, Timothy, 'Relative Necessity', *Journal of Symbolic Logic* **28** (1963), 113–134.
[23] von Wright, G. H., 'A New System of Modal Logic', in *Logical Studies* by von Wright, Routledge and Kegan Paul, London, 1957, pp. 89–126.
[24] von Wright, G. H., *An Essay in Deontic Logic and the General Theory of Action*, North-Holland, Amsterdam, 1968.
[25] Walton, Douglas, '*Can*, Determinism, and Modal Logic', *The Modern Schoolman* **52** (1975), 381–390.
[26] Walton, Douglas, 'Control', *Behaviorism* **2** (1974), 162–171.
[27] Walton, Douglas, 'Agency and Modal Logic', *Logique et Analyse*, forthcoming.
[28] Walton, Douglas, 'Ifs and Cans: Pros and Cons', *The Personalist* **56** (1975), 242–249.
[29] Walton, Douglas, 'Logical Form and Agency', *Philosophical Studies*, forthcoming.
[30] Walton, Douglas, 'Obstacles and Opportunities', forthcoming.

KEITH LEHRER

## COMMENT ON WALTON'S PAPER

What Professor Walton has written about the paradox Taylor and I propounded is quite correct. Indeed, the solution he and Hilpinen defend is a consequence of the analysis of 'can' I propose in my paper in this volume. In the paradox as originally formulated we have the following four statement forms:

(1)    If $S$ does not do $A$ at $t_j$, then $S$ cannot (at $t_i$) do $B$ at $t_n$.
(2)    If $S$ does $A$ at $t_j$, then $S$ does $B$ at $t_n$.
(3)    $S$ can (at $t_i$) do $A$ at $t_j$.
(4)    $S$ does not do $A$ at $t_j$.

From these four statement forms and the following principle one may derive a contradiction.

(5)    (If $S$ does $A$ at $t_j$, then $S$ does $B$ at $t_n$) $\supset$ (If $S$ can (at $t_i$) do $A$ at $t_j$, then $S$ can (at $t_i$) do $B$ at $t_n$)

In the original paper we concluded that when $t_i = t_j$ there are examples in which statements (1) to (4) all appeared to be satisfied. We proposed, therefore, that principle (5) should be abandoned. We admitted that if $t_i$ precedes $t_j$, then the statement instantiating (1) will turn out to be false. Even if $S$ is not going to do $A$ at $t_j$, he can (at $t_i$) do $A$ at $t_j$, and, by so doing, do $B$ at $t_n$ as well. If $t_i$ is subsequent to $t_j$, the statement instantiating (3) will not be true, because if $S$ does not do $A$ at $t_j$, then, at any time subsequent to $t_j$, $S$ cannot do $A$ at $t_j$.

Both of these results are consequences of the analysis I have articulated. If $t_i$ precedes $t_j$, and $S$ can (at $t_i$) do $A$ at $t_j$, then there is a possible world $w$ accessible to $S$ from the actual world $W$ in which '$S$ does $A$ at $t_j$' is true. Assuming that (2) is true in $w$ as well, '$S$ does $B$ at $t_n$' is also true in $w$. Hence, $S$ can (at $t_i$) do $B$ at $t_n$. If at $t_i$ there is a scenario accessible to $S$ in which $S$ does $A$ at $t_j$, then, given (2), that scenario remains accessible when it includes $S$ doing $B$ at $t_n$.

If, on the other hand, $t_i$ is subsequent to $t_j$, and '$S$ does not do $A$ at $t_j$' is true in the actual world $W$, then there is no scenario accessible to $S$ from $W$

*M. Brand and D. Walton (eds.), Action Theory, 289–290. All Rights Reserved*
*Copyright © 1976 by D. Reidel Publishing Company, Dordrecht-Holland*

beginning at $t_i$ in which '$S$ does $A$ at $t_j$' is true. Any possible world $w$ in which '$S$ does $A$ at $t_j$' is true will be one in which he has some advantage for doing $A$ at $t_j$ which he lacks in $W$. Admissible advantages are ones that result from what $S$ does at $t_i$ and subsequently. Since $t_i$ is subsequent to $t_j$, $S$ doing A at $t_j$ would involve some additional advantage for so doing that does not result from what $S$ does at $t_i$ or subsequently. Hence, the advantage would not be admissible.

The paradox, therefore, only appears to arise when $t_i = t_j$. What does the analysis tell us about that? What is in question is whether there is ever any action that a person does not perform at a specified time $t$ in the actual world such that there is a possible world having the same laws as the actual world and only minimally different from the actual world at $t$ so that the person performs the action at $t$ in the possible world without having any advantages for doing so that he lacks in the actual world. By speaking of *additional* advantages in the analysis, I meant advantages additional to the simple degenerate advantage of performing the action. Need $S$ have any advantage at $t_j$ for doing $A$ at $t_j$ in a possible world $w$ which he lacks in $W$ in addition to his simply doing $A$ at $t_j$? In the case of some actions which are simple and do not require antecedent preparation, for example, applying a very slight pressure on a button on which one's finger is resting, the answer seems to be negative. So statements (3) and (4) may both be so instantiated as to both be true when $t_i = t_j$. Statement (1) would, however, then become false for the same reason that it is false when $t_i$ precedes $t_j$. Given (2), there will be a scenario accessible to $S$ from $W$ in which '$S$ does $A$ at $t_j$' is true, and, given the truth of (2) in the scenario, '$S$ does $B$ at $t_n$' is also true. Hence. $S$ can (at $t_i$) do $B$ at $t_n$.

*Center for Advanced Study in the*
*Behavioral Sciences and*
*University of Arizona*

PART 8

# RESPONSIBILITY AND HUMAN ACTION

# ACTION AND RESPONSIBILITY

> "Since God is dead, nothing is forbidden."
> — DOSTOYEVSKI

The title of my remarks confronts me with two imponderables. The first, the concept of agency, has for the past decade or so been at the center of attention in philosophy. The analytical literature of action theory has accordingly grown very large, and I shall not add to it here except indirectly. I shall only say that the strangeness of this concept has not, as a result of all this attention, been reduced in the least, so far as I can see. It still contains two mysterious ingredients, namely, the idea of a *self* as a unique kind of being, and of *causation* by that self which amounts to absolute creation.

I shall, then, devote my attention to the second idea, that of responsibility. It is this idea, I believe, which is largely responsible for the philosophical concept of agency to begin with. Had people never conceived of themselves as responsible beings then it is doubtful whether they would ever have thought of themselves as agents either, in the philosophical sense of that term. The reason for this is that responsibility presupposes freedom. If anyone is responsible for what he has done, then he must have been free to do otherwise. But in that case he could not have been caused to do what he did, in the usual sense of causation. Nor must his behavior have been simply uncaused. The only description left, then, would seem to be that he, if he was responsible for what he did, must have been the originating cause of his behavior, and must, moreover, have been such that he could have behaved entirely differently. Or in other words, he must have been an *agent*, in the philosophical, or indeed the metaphysical, sense of that term.

That illation, briefly and crudely sketched here, is of course very familiar. From it one can at once see two things, one being the strangeness of the concept of agency, of which we need little reminder, and the other being how much the acceptance of that concept seems to rest upon the belief that people are sometimes responsible for what they do. If this latter were false,

*M. Brand and D. Walton (eds.), Action Theory, 293–310. All Rights Reserved*
*Copyright © 1976 by D. Reidel Publishing Company, Dordrecht-Holland*

then there would seem to be little reason for saying that people are ever agents, in the sense described.

I shall, then, concentrate on the idea of responsibility, with the aim of nourishing scepticism concerning its usefulness.

## I. RESPONSIBILITY AND LAW

What we are ultimately concerned with here is, of course, *moral* responsibility, and not responsibility in its purely empirical sense. Thus both the terms *action* and *responsibility* have an ordinary and unproblematical meaning having nothing to do with either metaphysics or ethics. This meaning of each appears in the remark, "Salt acted corrosively with respect to this iron and is responsible for its deterioration." All this means is that salt corroded the iron, which is not a metaphysical statement, and has nothing to do with ethics. The verbally similar remark, that "This man acted maliciously with respect to his rival and is responsible for his blindness", on the other hand, seems to express a totally different idea of acting and a totally different idea of responsibility. It is the concept of *responsibility* that is embodied in that second statement that I shall discuss, and not the equally strange and interesting concept of *agency* that is found there.

Generally, the idea of *moral responsibility* does not seem terribly mysterious to philosophers. They usually use the term confidently, even glibly. The apparent fact that this kind of responsibility, like the associated concept of agency, applies only to persons and is evidently, like agency, non-empirical, has not deterred philosophers from offering judgments of responsibility with utter confidence. What I want to show, however, is that this idea is not only very strange, like the idea of agency, but is really not a useful one to begin with. It has become a fond thing of philosophy, shedding darkness on our thinking rather than illuminating it, and even causing mischief in the relationships of people to each other.

## A. *The Presuppositions of Moral Responsibility*

A typical procedure for a philosopher addressing himself to this concept of responsibility would be to set forth, in an *a priori* way, its presuppositions and then, perhaps, delineate the implications of those presuppositions — implications with respect to the concept of personality, for example, or with respect to agency. And I think it is fair to say that such a procedure would receive the approval of almost any group of professional philosophers. Thus one could declare, on the basis of no empirical facts whatsoever, that for someone to be morally responsible for an act, then (i) that act must be caused by him, and not by another person or thing, (ii) that it must be free, that is to say, avoidable by him, and (iii) it must have the quality of moral wrongness, and be such that the agent knows this.[1] All of which implies a uniqueness of persons among all the other things in the world, a unique kind of free causation not found elsewhere in nature, and a unique kind of knowledge, the knowledge of right and wrong. These extraordinary implications should be sufficient to induce scepticism with respect to the whole idea of responsibility, in this sense. They also seem to nourish scepticism with respect to the idea of agency, but I shall not pursue that.

In the past philosophers who have cast doubt upon the idea of moral responsibility have usually done so by attacking the first two of the three presuppositions set out above, that is, by undermining the idea of a free cause. For me to do the same would involve an excursus into the concept of agency, and I have said I am not going to do that. Instead I propose to question the third of those presuppositions, which has hitherto seemed least questionable; namely, the distinction between moral right and wrong itself, and the correlative possibility of knowing what that distinction is. And I am going to do this by first showing how the basic distinction between right and wrong arises at various levels, that is, at levels having no necessary connection with moral right and wrong, and then show that a fundamental condition for drawing such a distinction is lacking in the special case of moral right and wrong. Since, moreover, moral responsibility is supposed to be the responsibility that an agent has for his morally wrong acts, then it follows that a necessary condition for applying that concept to anyone is similarly lacking.

## B. *The Nature of Right and Wrong at the Level of Games*

The first thing to note, then, is that the distinction between right and wrong is created by rules or laws of some sort, whether these be man-made or whether they be considered a part of the order of nature. The similar distinction between *good* and *bad*, on the other hand, is not thus relative to rule.

Thus, to begin at a very elementary level, a *right* move in chess is simply one that is permitted or (sometimes) required by rule, and a *wrong* move one that is forbidden. No sense whatever can be made of describing some chess move as wrong, even though no rule forbids it. There is nothing in the least wrong with moving a bishop from one color to another, for example, except that the rule defining the *permissible* moves of a bishop disallows this kind of movement. Right and wrong are at this level so clearly relative to rule that no one would be tempted to dispute it. The rules do not merely describe that distinction; they *create* it.

## C. *The Distinction between Good and Bad*

Good and bad, however, are at this level not relative to rules, not even to implicit ones. Chess moves are good or bad according to the purposes of the players, the ultimate purpose or end here being, normally, to deliver a checkmate. Sometimes the best move is one that is contrary to what virtually every player would do under the circumstances, and in that sense contrary to rule — for example, a brilliant sacrifice of the queen. And sometimes a good move can be one that promotes defeat rather than victory. Thus a player might, for example, skilfully render himself vulnerable to checkmate, and receive a checkmate, in order to advance his opponent's instruction in chess, (as in the case of a mother teaching chess to her daughter), which illustrates that good and bad are, at this level, relative to purposes or ends, and not to rules.

Here one other peculiarity of right and wrong, which seems to have no analogue in good and bad, should be noted, and that is that while there is only one sense in which an action can be wrong, namely, that of being forbidden by rule, there are two ways in which it can be right, namely, either by being *required* by rule, in which case it is obligatory, or by being merely *permitted* by rule, in which case it is innocent. Thus a chess player acts rightly, upon opening a game, whether he moves his king's pawn one square or two. Either move is permitted, neither is required. It is, however, required, and not merely permitted, that such a move be made with a white piece, not a black one. This distinction between right acts that are merely permitted and those that are required holds, I believe, with respect to every level of right and wrong.

## D. *Conventional Right and Wrong*

If we now move to another area of right and wrong, which some might consider more significant than game rules, namely, to the area of the unwritten conventional rules of etiquette and social intercourse, we find exactly the same thing. Most of these have little or nothing to do with right and wrong in any distinctly moral sense, and philosophers have therefore bestowed little attention on them. They do nevertheless define quite clearly a distinction between right and wrong, and indeed, they create that distinction at this level, which Thomas Hobbes aptly called the level of "small morals".[2] What is conventionally right is what is permitted or required by some conventional rule, and what is wrong at this level is what is thus forbidden. Thus it is right, or permitted, to co-habitate with one's spouse, but not with the spouse of another person, even when this is not contrary to law. And it is right, or conventionally required, to take an oath of high office with one's hand on a bible, even though not required by law. And it is in this sense wrong to giggle at a funeral or during public prayers, to use the flag as a mop, to utter vulgarisms in parlor conversation, particularly those associated with sexual behavior, to enter a holy place without a hat if one is a Jew, or with a hat if one is not, and so on. And so it is with respect to that whole body of conventional behavior: right and wrong are at this level quite clearly the creation of rules.

Such rules do not, however, any more than the rules of game, create any distinction between good and bad. More often than not they arise from such a distinction, that is to say, from practical considerations, but they certainly do not create these. It is better, for example, for children to have parents, that is, to belong to families, than not. No rule, conventional or other, is needed to see that. And it is because it is true that many of the conventional rules governing the relations of the sexes have arisen and are so assiduously upheld.

### E. *Legal Right and Wrong*

Consider next still another level of right and wrong, which some would want to call a still "higher" level, namely, that of the positive laws of a governed society. Again we find exactly the same thing. What is legally right is that which is permitted or required by the criminal law, and wrong is whatever is thus forbidden. The distinction between legal right and wrong is thus the creation of rules, that is, of enacted laws, and of nothing else. No sense can be made of describing some action as legally wrong, even though no law forbids it. There is, for example, nothing in the least wrong with filing one's income tax return on May 15, rather than on April 15, except that this is forbidden by law. So it is with respect to the movement of vehicular traffic, the possession and use of firearms, and indeed, the entire scope of the criminal law. That body of law does not merely *describe* the distinction between what is and what is not legally wrong, it creates it.

### F. *A Common Confusion*

Here it is not unusual for someone, imagining himself to be very perceptive, to say something to the effect that, for example, such things as assault, homicide, theft and fraud, all of which are forbidden by law, would still be wrong even if they were *not* unlawful. But this is only to confuse two senses of right and wrong, namely, the legal sense and the so-called moral sense, which we have yet to consider. True enough, most persons would detest and condemn assault, for example, even if it were not forbidden by law, but this is not to the point. Our detestation of the act does not render it wrong in any legal sense. Only a law can do that. When someone is assaulted under the legal institution of slavery, then his assailant acts with total innocence, at the level of the law, whatever others may think or feel, and in no way can he be charged with a crime or tried in any court of law. For that to be possible an actual or positive law must be created.

It is worth noting that this same confusion can arise at the levels of right and wrong with which we began, namely, at the level of what is right or wrong in a game as well as at the level of conventional morality. Thus, one might assert that it would be *wrong*, while playing chess with the valuable pieces belonging to your opponent, to move your rook in such a manner that it ends up in your pocket, even though such a move is not, in fact, prohibited by the rules of chess; or that bigamous marriage is wrong even among those whose conventional rules permit or even enjoin it. But all that is meant by such remarks as these is that such acts violate the criminal law even when they do not violate any rules of games or convention. What is involved here, as in the preceding case, is simply a confusion of different levels of right and wrong.

## G. *The Irrelevancy of Law to What Is Good and Bad*

Again we find, however, that while legal right and wrong are the creation of rules, good and bad are at this level not thus created, but are, like chess moves, relative to people's ends and purposes. Thus, one might manage his affairs — his business, for example — in a perfectly innocent way, and yet very badly. This would be the case if, for example, you squandered your capital on frivolous ventures and thus led yourself into ruin. Bad as this is, no law forbids it. The badness of such an outcome would thus be relative to no rule or law, but only to the presumed purpose of the agent. If, on the other hand, one's purpose in a given enterprise was not his own betterment but that of another person, or perhaps the strengthening of some cause, then behavior that would otherwise appear stupid and foolish might in fact be very good, by virtue of the fact that its purpose was achieved even at the expense of the agent's ruin. Examples of this come very easily to mind — the father who neglects his own affairs in saving his son from perdition, and that sort of thing.

## H. *Moral Distinctions*

Exactly the same things can now be said of *moral right and wrong*, and of *moral good and evil*, namely, that the former distinction is, and the latter one is not, the creation of rule or law. The difference here is only that, in this case, we are speaking not of the rules of games, rules of custom, nor the positive laws enacted by human legislators, but of the moral law, as it is called. Thus, an action is morally *right* in case it is either permitted by moral law (morally innocent) or *enjoined* by that law (obligatory), and a morally *wrong* (or wicked) act is one that is forbidden by that law. No sense can be made of describing some action as wrong, even though it violates no moral law. It cannot, for example, be morally wrong to remove a living fetus from its mother's womb, or to dispose of excess female infants, or of the aged, unless such actions should turn out to be inconsistent with some moral law — the prohibition of homicide, for example. Such a moral rule or law does not merely describe or give expression to some antecedent wrongness that is discovered to reside in a wide variety of actions; it creates it. People do, to be sure, have an abhorrence of certain actions, and there is no doubt that this abhorrence serves as a powerful inducement to honor the moral law. But feelings such as these can hardly *create* moral right and wrong.[3] This is the work of the moral law, and of nothing else.

Again, however, we find that *good and evil* are, at this moral level, not the creation of any rule or law, but exist antecedently to law and are discoverable in experience. It is a distinction of nature, as philosophers belonging to the age of Socrates would have expressed it. Thus no rule or law is needed to know that hunger and thirst are bad. Similarly, a wound is bad, whether inflicted or accidental; and while a law may render its infliction wrong, no law is needed to render the suffering of it bad. And just as one can innocently make a bad move in chess, or with both conventional and legal innocence bring ruin upon himself or others, so also someone holding great power might, in violation neither of any human law nor of any moral law, and in fact in response to the clearest perception of his duty, bring sorrow and misery to a whole nation through the sheer miscarriage of his efforts. Similarly, one might, in response to no moral incentive whatever, but simply pursuit of personal glory, bring great and lasting blessings to a nation, and at the expense of no one.[4] As at the other levels considered, then, we can see that good and bad, unlike right and wrong, are relative, not to rules or laws, but to ends or purposes. Indeed it is not easy to distinguish *moral* good and bad from other varieties except by considering these to be the fulfillment or defeat of peoples' *highest* aims and purposes; happiness, for example, or peace and security.

## II. LAWS AS IMPERATIVES

We need next to note that laws, from the relatively unimportant sort that govern the conduct of games up to the highest laws of morality and religion, are appropriately expressed as commands or imperatives, not as statements, predictions, queries, or any other grammatical form. "Thou shalt not kill" and "Honor thy father and mother" are perfect modes for the expression of law. Often, to be sure, positive laws, as well as game rules, have the apparent form of mere assertions and sometimes predictions, but they are not assertions or predictions. Thus, the formulation "Whoever shall take the life of another shall be punished by death" is not a prediction about what is going to happen to anyone, though it has that form. It is instead a prohibition of homicide, conjoined with a criminal sanction. Similarly, the formulation "Each player makes one move in alternation with the other, white moving first" is not a statement, though it has that form. It is instead a directive or simple command, and could be so expressed without the least change of sense.

And so it is with all laws and rules. Indeed it could hardly be otherwise, because all rules and laws are directives having to do with what actions are and what ones are not forbidden, permitted and required. Their clearest and most straightforward expression, therefore, is as commands, and they remain commands even when expressed obliquely.

### A. *The Sources of Laws*

Any command, however, presupposes a source, that is, a commander, and in order to have the force of a command, as distinguished from mere request or exhortation, it must rest also upon some sanction, some externally supplied incentive to heed and obey it. Without such a sanction or threat of penalty a law degenerates to a mere "rule of imperfect obligation", as it is aptly described in the literature of jurisprudence. And in fact the kinds of rules and laws we have been considering do all have these two characteristics, or at least once did.

Thus, the rules of a game, which are commands addressed to players, originate with certain human beings, namely, those who have created those games, and who from time to time introduce modifications into them. No one has ever pretended, for example, that the rules of chess were discovered as some part of the metaphysical fabric of the universe, by some process of reason or inquiry. They are the fabrications of human beings, enforced by human beings,[5] and subject to human revision. So likewise with respect to the criminal law of any political society. This is nothing but the commands of whoever holds sovereign power within such a society. No one ever supposes that the laws governing the movement of vehicular traffic are traceable to any higher source. Some commands of civil authority are, to be sure, thought to have some source higher than human, namely, Scripture, the Ten Commandments of God, or some similar revelation; but this only means that the positive laws of human society are sometimes formulated in accordance with what are thought to be the commands of God. So long as human authority with the power to command prohibits certain practices, and threatens with pains and penalties any who do not heed those prohibitions, then those prohibitions stand as laws of that society, whether or not they are thought to be also laws of God; and they would still be laws even if they were in fact *contradicted* by a divine law — not good laws, perhaps, but laws, all the same.

## B. *The Sources of Conventional Morality*

Who, then, fabricates the rules of conventional morality? Where is the commander who has declared them, and who are their enforcers? These rules define no game — or at least, no *mere* game — nor do they have the force of criminal law, for no one can be prosecuted for their violation.

The answer to this question was perfectly given by Protagoras, who said, in effect: Everyone commands them, and everyone enforces them. He was clearly right, and his celebrated dispute with Socrates on this question was nothing but the product of a confusion between different levels of law like those already noted.

Thus, Socrates was deeply perplexed by the question: Who are the teachers of virtue? What he had in mind, of course, was a kind of virtue that is not merely man-made, something that is higher than the laws and conventions of human beings. So construed, his question was indeed a good one, and one which, as we shall shortly see, still appears to be unanswered independently of certain theological assumptions. But Protagoras had long since decided, not only that there is no natural or true law of morality, but that, in fact, nothing whatever is true "by nature", in this or any other realm. Virtue, therefore, could for Protagoras be nothing more than the conventional practices of human beings, which admittedly differ from one time and place to another. So construed, it is quite obviously true that "everyone" is the teacher of virtue or, in the terms in which I have been expressing it, "everyone" (persons generally) is the source and the enforcer of the commands in which conventional virtue is expressed. No particular person commands us not to giggle at funerals or during public prayers, yet we do learn this, from those around us. And violations of all such rules bring a swift and certain imposition of sanctions, in the form of disapprobation from every side, a kind of sanction having dreadful effect in keeping all persons, herd-like, from straying from the path. That Socrates was left speechless by Protagoras' lengthy disquistion to this effect was not the result of his not knowing all those things, for they are quite obvious to anyone possessed of any sense. Socrates' puzzlement resulted from the fact that, while he and Protagoras expressed themselves in much the same terminology, they simply were not talking about the same thing.

### C. *Four Varieties of Conventional Morality*

Before applying the considerations thus far elicited to the special case of moral law, it is worth remarking that Protagoras was far from unique in identifying morality with mere rules of custom. Indeed, it is characteristic of small minds everywhere to do exactly that, and Protagoras' greatness lay in the fact that he created a brilliant philosophy of ethics and politics around this narrow identification.

Thus we can find four quite distinct types of person who base their conduct and their lives largely upon this strange identification. Let us call them, respectively, the *prude*, the *pedant*, the *formalist*, and the *zealot*.

The first of these, the prude, takes for granted that the moral law is expressed in the conventional rules of his culture, particularly through his church, and then, consistently with this, measures his own moral goodness by the sheer *number* of such rules that he is able to uphold. The extreme expression of such prudery is: Everything to which one inclines as a natural good, particularly by the solicitations of pleasure, is forbidden. Such rules, then, need not be of great significance, need not advance any good or reduce any evil, and can indeed defeat felt goods without being abandoned for that reason. All that is required, for the style of life called prudery, is that such rules be numerous, hence largely trivial, and that they be entirely identified with the moral law. The latter ensures that they will be heeded, and the former that the path of such a life will be exceedingly narrow.

The *moral pedant*, on the other hand, euphemistically called the person of fixed principles, is characterized, not by the numerousness of the purely conventional rules he honors, but by his uncompromising adherence to them. Unlike the prude, whose rules are beyond counting, the pedant's are usually reduced to just two or three, usually those prohibiting lying, stealing and sometimes infidelity. Mendacity, for example, is a conventional wrong, the prohibition of which has quite clearly arisen from the evils that it normally spawns. The moral pedant treats this human fabrication as a moral law, and does not lie even on those occasions when veracity is nasty and petty. So likewise with the conventional rule of marital fidelity. The moral pedant, instead of identifying this with faith in the sense of trust and constancy of feeling, construes it narrowly as inflexible adherence to a rule of sexual conduct, and from exclusive devotion to this loses sight of its larger meaning. So likewise with the prohibition of theft, which the pedant congratulates himself for honoring even when it is plainly stupid to do so.

The third type to identify moral law with convention is the *formalist* who, without the moral fervor exhibited by the other two, is absorbed in the visible conventions of social life, or what are aptly called "externals", such as mode of dress, speech, and manners. These are precisely what are conventional, that is customary. The formalist is neither innovative, spontaneous nor creative, but instead totally imitates what he finds around him. It is a characteristic of politicians, and indeed of all whose fortunes depend upon the opinion of many. Such a person dresses much as others do, restricts himself to a vocabulary that offends no one, conducts himself unobtrusively everywhere, and is genuinely shocked by deviations from such norms. It is this latter that makes the formalist of some ethical significance, for, inasmuch as his capacity for shock is reserved for morally insignificant deviations, he is, like both the pedant and the prude, quite likely to be insensitive to larger concerns. This is sometimes forcibly brought home to us when it is discovered that some politician, conventional right down to the polish on his shoes, has without apparent feeling of guilt engaged in extortion, the exploitation of the weak, the obstruction of justice, or some one or more of the other arts at which persons in public life are often so skilled, and which the external conventionalism of their lives serves so effectively to mask, even sometimes, from themselves.

And finally, the moral *zealot* is one who identifies the moral law with some *one* purely conventional rule and then, exceeding the pedant, is not content with the inflexible observance of that rule on his own part, but strives to impose it on everyone else too. The rule forbidding the use of spiritous beverages, for example, born of evangelical enthusiasms of the previous century, lacks even a scriptural basis. The zeal of those whose mission is to impose it on the world blinds them even to the fact that Jesus' first miracle was the conversion of water to wine. Other examples of moral zealotry come easily to mind, such as the fanatical opposition to abortion, patriotic chauvinism, and so on.

## D. *The Source of Moral Law*

If, then, the three levels of law — the laws of games, of custom, and of political societies — are so easily traceable to their sources, where shall we look to find the source of the highest law, that is, the moral law? If the moral law is a command or imperative, as it surely is if it is a law, who has commanded it? Or is this law just a command that is laid upon human beings by no one at all, or that has issued from no commander, from sheer nothingness, or from thin air?

Actually, wherever human beings have upheld moral law, they have, at least originally, assumed a source of it, and that source has been some god. The commandments of God, the moral law, and the law of nature, as it has sometimes been quaintly called, were once all assumed to be one and the same.[6] And this, of course, made perfectly good sense, for it preserved the presuppositions of law, and thus the presuppositions of moral law. That law is a command, and its commander is no human or other created being, but God. And that is what distinguishes it as the *moral* law, namely, that it is commanded by the highest authority, higher than any king, priest, or other merely human authority. The clearest way to think of that moral law is to identify it with explicit commands, explicitly enunciated by God — for example, the Ten Commandments. Here it is not at all to be supposed that these were fabricated by Moses and delivered by *him* to the Israelites, even if we should assume him to have been the wisest man in the history of the race, or assume his purposes to have been noble beyond comparison. Or if anyone *does* make such a supposition, then he is reducing those commandments to the level of mere legality, at best, on a par with other human enactments, such as those governing vehicular traffic, and not expressions of any moral law at all.

No, these commands were enunciated by God, and laid upon all persons, and the distinction between moral right and wrong was the result of that fact alone. Furthermore, those commands were implicitly conjoined with a sanction, that is, an externally supplied incentive to obedience, for it was believed that their author could reward with the sweetest blessings, and punish with dreadful pains, those who did and those who did not heed and obey. They were not, then, mere exhortations to virtue or wise prescriptions for life, but laws in the full and complete sense.

## E. *The Historical Deterioration of the Moral Law*

It is very much worth noting what has happened to this moral law, its historical metamorphosis from a genuine moral law to a mere philosophical abstraction that is still called "moral law" even after the preconditions for such a law have been forgotten and even assumed non-existent. Briefly, what happened is that philosophers abandoned the belief in a divine source of this law, and imagined that they were still making sense in discoursing about it! That there should be a god, having the power to punish and reward, who has laid down commands for his creatures, makes perfectly good sense, whether one believes it or not. And that those commands should be considered higher and more compelling than the commands or laws of any human being also makes perfectly good sense, given their supposed source. And that it should be considered the height of folly to disregard them, for whatever reason, and the clearest wisdom to heed them, considering salvation to depend on this, also makes perfectly good sense. What happens, however, when the very presuppositions on which all this rests are swept aside or disregarded? What happens is that what was hitherto reasonably regarded as the moral law becomes instead an abstraction, a toy of philosophy having not the slightest claim to reverence or respect from anyone, a command that lacks any commander, a law that lacks any source, an injunction or prohibition without any hint of a sanction and one that therefore supplies not the slightest incentive to obedience. What happens, in short, is that the moral law becomes a non-entity, a verbal formulation in the mouths of philosophers which signifies nothing.

### F. *The Attempt to Replace God with Things Human*

Philosophers have, of course, not been entirely oblivious to this strange development, and some have accordingly tried to replace the original source of this law with something having at least some semblance to a commander, and something which, without too much violence to intelligence, might be viewed as exalted, or even divine. The most heroic attempt was made by Kant, who replaced God's will with human reason, then deified this as something of transcendent worth or as an "end in itself". Thus Kant clearly recognized that the moral law is a command or, which means the same thing, an imperative. Who, then, issues that command, if not God? If its source is some human being, such as Moses or the king or some wise philosopher, then how can it claim to be anything more than the positive law of a political society? How indeed can it pretend to be more than wise counsel, which one may disregard as he pleases? How can the sagacity of even the wisest of men, or even, as Plato fondly dreamed, of a host of these, having the power of kings, convert a command from a mere human edict, however laudable, to something having the grandeur of the moral law?

Kant's answer was that this law emanates, not from some person, but from *every* person, or better, from that in every person which is of more than mundane worth, namely, from *reason*. And Kant even went a considerable direction in supplying this moral law with a more than human sanction, replacing the blessings of heaven and the pains of hell with what he imagined was the practical impossibility of disobedience. One must not with impunity disregard the moral law because, to the extent that he is rational, he cannot.

It is a pleasant fable, and one that human beings will probably always cherish. It appears to restore to ethics some semblance of what philosophers, by their rejection of revelation, took from it. We still have before us something having the appearance of a command, which the moral law must be, and something which can, with a bit of artifice, be made to look like a commander, that is, a source for this law. It has also the great strength of feeding human conceit, in two ways; first, by giving to mankind at least one ingredient of religion that was precious, namely, a foundation of morality that is not merely a conventional or more or less arbitrary human fabrication; and second, by professing to find some purely human faculty having the authority, hitherto possessed only by God, to command every human being, and worthy of a respect that supersedes even the commands of a king. Kant himself, in one of his more fervid exultations, compared the supposed awesomeness of this moral law, and implicitly its source, with the very heavens above.

### III. THE GROUNDLESSNESS OF MORAL RIGHT AND WRONG

Now I come to my final point, and the real point of these remarks, which is, that there evidently is no moral law, and hence, no moral right and wrong at all. The distinction between right and wrong at any level, we saw, requires rules or laws, and moral right and wrong is no exception. One can, of course, as most people do, have strong feelings about certain kinds of action, such as the use of spiritous beverages, the practice of polygamy, the abortion of the unborn or the destruction of infants, and so on, and we have become accustomed to expressing these feelings in utterances having the form of moral judgment. I am of course not denying this. But I do wish to make the important point that there really is no moral law, that there can therefore be no real distinction between right and wrong at this level, and that most of the literature belonging to the genre of philosophical ethics is therefore devoid of intellectual content — something that has, in fact, often been suspected by philosophers themselves. Such books, which have been produced in great profusion throughout the period of modern philosophy, and are still being written and placed before students to read, should all be removed from the libraries, as books in the areas of witchcraft and phrenology long since were, for like these they are devoid of a real subject matter. Exceptions are, of course, such books as rest explicitly upon divine revelation, as well as books that deal only with the history of ethical practices and opinions, and also ethical treatises, if there are any such, that do not presuppose any distinction between moral right and wrong, plus those relatively few classics in this area that charm by their quaint prose and sometimes poetic quality. Apart from these, such books are without content and serve more to muddle and confuse than to edify.

My argument for this conclusion consists of two parts. The first is, that God has evidently issued no commands, and there is no other source adequate to the creation of a genuinely moral law, or a law higher or more authorititative than the expression of a human will. My own reason for believing that God has issued no such command is that no god, as thus conceived, exists. (This is not intended as a declaration of atheism, but rather, as a divorcement of religion from the totally human ethics with which it has become entangled.) Of course, this consideration is conclusive for anyone who happens to share that theological scepticism. A supposed moral law that is not a command is no law to begin with; and a command that issues from no commander, but is instead plucked from thin air by a philosopher, is no "command" even deserving that name, much less deserving the slightest respect of anyone.

But — and this is the second part of my argument — the case is actually much stronger than this, for we can now see that even those who profess to believe that God has commanded his creatures, and who therefore at least appear to possess the preconditions of belief in a moral law, do not in fact believe in any such law, for they do in fact without hesitation substitute their own feelings for this supposed law, without realizing that they have thereby abrogated it. These who profess to believe in the moral law and its divine source, and who accordingly believe they can draw the distinction between moral right and wrong, thus have no more than the rest of us have, namely, strong feelings about certain kinds of behavior which they imagine to be the expression of that moral law in their hearts, even though their own procedure amounts to a disclaimer of that conviction.

## A. *The Defeasibility of Moral Rules*

This follows from the fact there is no rule of conduct, or no moral law, which is not in fact abandoned in favor of their own feelings by those who unreservedly honor that law. At least I have never met any person, of whatever moral conviction, about whom this did not turn out to be so.

Consider, for example, a perfectly clearcut case of what purports to be a moral law, the injunction against killing. It is exactly expressed in the command: Thou shalt not kill. This is probably the most widely honored of any moral precept, even by those who disbelieve its divine origin. Even those, however, who most sincerely profess to believe that it is a commandment of God, and that it can never be violated without guilt, do not in fact believe this, for even they treat that law as "deafeasible", or in other words, they feel free to make exceptions to it that were never enunciated by any god and are in no way implied in the command.

Thus there is no one who does not immediately qualify that terse law by adding the words, "any person", such that it is taken as a prohibition of homicide only, not of killing as such. We can, perhaps, treat this as the intended meaning and not quibble. But having done that, note now how extensively subject to exception that law is, not just by this or that morally obdurate person, but by those who deem the law an absolute, who even imagine that it expresses the very will of God. Even these readily substitute their own will for God's whenever their feelings sufficiently prompt them to.

To illustrate this, let us begin with the straightforward imperative, "Thou shalt not kill any person." Do we have here what expresses a moral law? Hardly, for even those who suppose we have such a law before us are willing to say that you may innocently kill sometimes. Thus, it is said to be morally wrong to kill any person *except*, of course, in the case of:

(a) self defense.
(b) infant females.
(c) a just war.
(d) an unquickened fetus.
(e) a Jew who has had carnal contact with a gentile women.
(f) the terminally ill.
(g) the avenging of the murder of a kinsman.
(h) the aged and infirm.
(i) a criminal deserving of a death penalty.
(j) idiots, imbeciles, morons and nitwits.
(k) sparing the lives of others.
(l) obviating great and irreparable suffering.

And so on. It is not hard to see that the list could be easily extended to a considerable length.

The usual response of anyone presented with such a list is to examine it, to see which exceptions are, and which are not really allowable. But that is wholly to miss the point! The command itself is inconsistent with *any* exception, and the moment one begins to make these exceptions, he substitutes for the moral law, upon which the original distinction between moral right and wrong was supposed to rest, something entirely different — namely, his own feelings on the matter. But if *that* is how things are in the last analysis decided, why was there this ceremonious bowing in the direction of a so-called moral law to begin with? And if that moral law was supposed to emanate from God — as I should think one must suppose, if it is a moral law or command to begin with — then where has God made these amendments?

## B. *The Law of God and Human Feeling*

Actually, that last question raises a curious point which seems to strengthen the very point I am trying to make. For one can, in fact, find scriptural sources for some of these exceptions — for innocently taking the life to avenge the death of a kinsman, for example, or to punish a Jew's carnal contact with a gentile woman.[6] But here what we actually find is that those who profess to uphold this law consult their feelings once again, in order to decide whether exceptions which appear to have been explicitly granted by God are really to be allowed as exceptions! Where, then, is the moral law to which we are supposed to yield? And why was it not formulated, at the outset, as: Thou shalt not kill, except on those occasions when you find you can do so with the feeling of innocence!

Of course, there remains one other possibility, and that is to treat this supposed moral law (or any other such command that one might come up with) as being in truth a moral law, and decline to permit of *any* exceptions whatever. Many have in fact tried this. But no one, I think, has ever succeeded, which amounts to saying that no one appears to consider this or any other command to express a genuine moral law. Even those, for example, who have most vigorously upheld the right of the unborn fetus to its life have found it necessary, out of deference to their own feelings in the matter, to allow an exception for ectopic pregnancy, and cases of the murder of the terminally ill can be described which meet with no objection whatever from any quarter.

And this does, I think, sufficiently show that, whether or not there is any moral law, and hence any real distinction between moral right and wrong, at least there is no one who actually believes this, in spite of what they profess. Or if such a person does exist anywhere, I at least have not seen him.

## NOTES

[1] Of course one may be morally responsible for his exemplary acts, too, but I have limited myself to wrong acts for simplicity.

[2] *Leviathan*, Chapter XI.

[3] This is one of the enduring points of Kantian ethics.

[4] I believe Winston Churchill once conceded this to have been the chief incentive of his great career.

[5] One should have in mind here tournament chess, not parlor chess.

[6] See, for example, Deuteronomy 19.

P. H. NOWELL-SMITH

# ACTION AND RESPONSIBILITY

Taylor's conclusion is breath-takingly simple. The concept of moral responsibility should, like the concept of witchcraft, be given up because it has implications which are either senseless or false or not believed in even by those who profess to believe in them — or all three. And his argument is equally simple: moral responsibility entails moral wrongdoing; moral wrongdoing entails a law which forbids the conduct in question; a law requires a law-giver; there is no moral law-giver, (the so-called Moral Law being nothing but the ghost of God's commands sitting crowned upon the grave thereof). From these premises it does indeed follow that there is no such thing as moral responsibility. So the concept of moral responsibility must go, and with it — since we would have no occasion to speak of moral agents if there were no moral responsibility — goes the concept of a moral agent. But I do not think it can really be as simple as that — nor, I suspect does Taylor. So I shall take his paper to be not so much a proof of the vacuity of the concept of moral responsibility as an invitation to us to make coherent sense of it.

First, let us suppose that all Taylor's premises are true. The concept of *moral* responsibility must go; but we still need the concept of responsibility in connection with breaches of the laws of the state and of positive morality (convention). So, if he is to relieve us of the obligation to try to make sense of agency and responsibility, he would have to attack the first two conditions of responsibility (causation and avoidability) since, according to him, an act *could* have the qualities of legal and/or conventional wrongness. So even if it were true (which it isn't) that judges applied legal rules which are pure and unadulterated by moral considerations, they would still have to decide whether a killer knew that his act had the quality of *legal* wrongness before they could convict him, and all of us would still have to decide whether he knew that it had the quality of conventional wrongness before we undertook to hold him guilty under a rule of conventional morality.

Secondly, Taylor's premises are, to be blunt, not true; they have as minimal a relation to the actual operation of any legal system as a tailor's

*M. Brand and D. Walton (eds.), Action Theory,* 311–322. *All Rights Reserved*
Copyright © 1976 *by D. Reidel Publishing Company, Dordrecht-Holland*

dummy has to the noble contours of Michelangelo's Moses. I shall argue that Taylor is entitled to neither of the sharp distinctions on which his entire case for the vacuity of morality rests. The first of these distinctions is that between the deontological concepts of right and wrong, which are relative to rules, and the teleological concepts of good and bad, which are relative to purposes. The second is that between law and conventional morality on the one hand and the non-conventional morality that Taylor thinks vacuous on the other. I shall try to undermine these distinctions — or at least the sharpness of them that Taylor's argument requires — first in connection with the concept of law and then in connection with that of responsibility.

I

Taylor tells us that the distinction between right and wrong is relative to a system of rules, while that between good and bad is not. In a loose and general way this is true, and nowhere can this distinction be more clearly seen than in the context of a game, particularly the game of chess. To say that a move is illegal and to say that it is a bad move are distinct forms of criticism — which is not to say that they are unconnected, since a bad move must at least be a legal one. (Putting your opponent's piece in your pocket is not a chess move at all.) But it is a mistake to suppose that the operation of a system of legal rules can be understood in terms of the rules of a game. Aside from other objections[1] two are relevant here. First, while there is clearly some connection in law between 'he did something wrong (a forbidden act)' and 'he is legally responsible', a connection I shall examine in the next section, it is difficult to introduce the latter locution into the game of chess at all. In a legal context we can say that he did something wrong but cannot, for some reason, be held responsible; but what could be meant, at chess, by saying 'He moved his bishop horizontally, which is against the rules, but cannot be held responsible'? Rhetorical questions are not arguments, and this first point is only intended to insinuate a doubt as to the propriety of drawing an analogy between law and chess. In the case of chess the concept of responsibility for a wrong seems to have no application.

Secondly, the question whether someone's act was legally wrong is seldom if ever, as it is in chess, a matter of applying a crystal clear rule to a crystal clear fact situation. A killed B; no doubt about that; but a doubt can arise as whether what A did 'amounts to' murder at law. Legal rules are, and have to be interpreted in the light of many factors, not least the purpose (moral or other) which the rule is supposed to serve. A justification (self-defence) or an excuse (mistake) can be offered and, if successful, will result in an acquittal. (What could be the justification for moving a bishop horizontally at chess?) The point of mentioning these obvious facts is that they blur, in the context of law, the distinction between the deontological group of concepts and the teleological; and they blur it at two different stages, that of the charge against the accused and that of the judicial decision.

At the first stage, the question whether what someone did was legally wrong may turn on its goodness or badness since the rule itself is interpreted in the light of its stated or presumed purpose. A man who drives a Ford car onto the park is clearly in breach of the rule 'No vehicles are permitted in the park', but he would not be found guilty of an offence if he drove his car onto the park to succour an injured child. Taylor's distinction might be saved from such counter-examples by saying that, in the special circumstances which constitute his justification, the driver does not commit a forbidden act. If the rule against 'vehicles in the park is correctly and carefully spelt out it will include all excuses and justifications within its terms, so that a correctly formulated rule admits of no exceptions. On this view the chess rule that a pawn moves diagonally when it captures is not an exception to the rule that a pawn may only move forwards. The alleged rule 'a pawn may only move forwards' is an inaccurate statement of the rule governing pawns, a rule which, when accurately stated, allows of no exceptions whatever.

This manoeuvre, however, will not help Taylor's case in the end since, outside the context of a strictly rule-governed game, it cannot be carried through. As Hart has shown,[2] legal rules are *inherently* open-textured. They are *interpreted in the light* of many disparate considerations: the interests of the parties, the public interest, positive morality, economic policy, ease of administration, the need to arrive at a decision within a reasonable time, and so on. No legislator can determine in advance what unforeseen circumstances might make it reasonable for a judge to acquit someone who has clearly committed an act forbidden by the 'rule', so that it is a fundamental mistake to treat interpretation as simply a matter of allowing exceptions to rules. The policies and principles to which judges appeal when interpreting legal rules are just as much a part of 'the law' as are the statutory rules themselves, so that what may appear to a casual eye as a purely deontological system in which acts are required, permitted or forbidden is seen, on closer inspection, to be infected from the start by the teleological ideas of principle, policy and purpose.

The second way in which the right/wrong and good/bad distinction is blurred in law follows from the first. No sharp line can be drawn between the question whether a judge's decision was 'wrong' and the question whether it was 'a bad decision'. This follows from the first since an appellate court (or an academic lawyer writing after the highest court has spoken) may say that the judge did not interpret the relevant rule correctly, and the reason might be that the judge gave too much or too little weight to this or that principle or policy. Moreover, even in a case about which we could say flatly that the judge's decision was clearly wrong, 'wrong' does not mean, as Taylor thinks it does, forbidden by a law-giver subject to a sanction. For nobody commanded the judge to give the opposite decision and he will not, in the absence of special circumstances, be subjected to any sanction. The Hobbes/Austin theory that "the criminal law is nothing but the commands of whoever holds sovereign power within a society" is essential to Taylor's thesis, since his rejection of non-conventional morality depends on his view that wherever we can properly speak of laws there must be a law-giver and a sanction. But this theory, though incorporating the valuable insight that legal systems are indeed coercive, that they do threaten those who disobey the rules with sanctions, and that in the absence of a cohesive source of power they are inefficacious, will not stand up to examination even as a summary account of what a legal system is.[3] The crucial points for our purpose are that a rule of law is not a command, that there is often no locatable sovereign, and that legal obligation cannot be understood in terms either of the fear or of the likelihood of a sanction.

## II. RESPONSIBILITY, ACTS AND HARM

The upshot of my argument so far is that Taylor is entitled to neither of the sharp distinctions that are essential if he is to make out his case for the vacuity of moral responsibility. In this section I shall examine the concept of responsibility and try to show that Taylor's account of legal responsibility is radically mistaken. If I am right, the "presuppositions of moral responsibility" which Taylor attributes to those philosophers who believe that there is such a thing incorporates the same radical error, so that his attack on moral responsibility must miss its target. I shall argue that no one is ever, either legally or morally, *responsible for his acts*, so that Taylor's three presuppositions, which are given as presuppositions for someone to be morally responsible for an act, are presuppositions of nothing at all. This is, of course, Taylor's own conclusion, but whereas he treats it as a refutation of the idea of moral responsibility I treat it as an erroneous account of what moral responsibility is.

The thesis that no one is ever responsible for his acts is a strong one and appears to be open to numerous counter-examples. Is not the night porter responsible for locking the doors and also, in another sense, responsible for having on some occasion left them unlocked? I shall not argue against the frequency or propriety of such locutions, but rather that they have to be unpacked in terms of a basic sense of 'responsible' in which no one is ever responsible for his own acts or omissions.

Responsibility, as is now well understood, is a polymorphous concept, and the right way to handle such concepts is not to set out a single definition held to apply to all cases of responsibility which is then tested by counter-examples, but to explicate a central sense and then show how other senses can be understood as extensions or modifications of that sense. That there are at least two senses of 'responsible for' is already shown by the example of the night porter, since it could hardly be maintained that he is responsible for locking the doors and for omitting to lock them in the same sense. To say that he is responsible for locking the doors is to say that locking the doors is one of his responsibilities, which doesn't get us very far; and to say that he is responsible for having left them unlocked last night is to say that he is to blame for having left them unlocked and that he is to blame because he did not discharge one of his responsibilities.

All the relevant senses of 'responsible' stem, historically, from the idea of someone's being 'answerable' or 'accountable', and when it first appears in English in that sense it has a strongly legal flavour. In 1643, Prynne (a lawyer) wrote of "the erronious opinion that [kings] are in no case responsible to their whole Kingdomes or Parliaments for their grossest exorbitances", and at about the same time 'responsible to' became a common legal phrase in the United States in the sense of 'answerable to a charge'.[4] A man who is responsible is a man who may be required to answer. Sanctions appear at two points in this basic use. First, his being *required* to answer implies a sanction in case he does not, and secondly he is open to a sanction if the account he gives of himself is unsatisfactory. He is responsible *to* (a) a charge or accusation and (b) the person to whom he is required to answer. Our problem is 'What is he responsible *for*?'

Taylor's reply to this question is that he is responsible for his legally or morally wrong *acts*. Well, philosophers do sometimes speak in this way and I suppose we have all grown so accustomed to it that it elicits no surprise; but it should do so, since it is a very odd way to speak. If *A* murders *B*, he is responsible (in a now archaic sense) to a charge of murder, and murder is an act; but it would be a mistake to argue from those premises that he must be responsible for his act of murder. What he is responsible for is *the death of B*. In general, it is for good or bad states of affairs that we are, by our acts or omissions, responsible, and we are responsible for those states of affairs when they have been caused — in some sense and to some degree — by our acts and omissions. The connection between responsibility and causation has now become so close that we can even speak, without even a hint of a 'fiction', of unusually dry weather being responsible for a forest fire; but that does not alter the fact that the root meaning of 'responsible' — a meaning still heavily present in legal and moral contexts — is 'accountable'; and the fact that 'responsible' is, in some cases, simply equivalent to 'cause' cannot easily be accounted for except on the supposition that what we are accountable for is (by and large) those states of affairs that we cause.

(To say of a murderer that he is responsible for his act of murder rather than for the death of his victim is a solecism, and I should like to suggest in passing that this solecism may be at the root of the concept of agent-causation that has puzzled philosophers recently. People are responsible for what they have done; but 'what they have done' could refer either to the harm they have done or to their doing of it; and since being responsible for the harm one has done is in part a matter of having caused the harm, we are apt to slip into thinking that it makes sense to talk of someone's being the cause of his doing the harm (the act). Hence the queer idea of agent-causation.)

The relations between causation and liability are, as Hart and Honoré have shown,[5] enormously complex. First, a standard analysis in terms of necessary and sufficient conditions, though it may be true, is of little help when our interest in the question whether a person's act or omission caused a certain state of affairs lies in the need to decide whether or not he is responsible for that state of affairs. This is so because the standard analysis has mainly been concerned with the concept of cause in scientific contexts, and in those contexts all necessary conditions are equally necessary. A scientific explanation of the cause of a fire would have to include the presence of oxygen and of combustible material as well as the arsonist's match without any distinction between these necessary conditions in *status*. It is when our interest in the question of causation arises from a need to attribute responsibility that we need to understand how and why we pick on someone's act or omission as the *cause* as opposed to a 'mere condition'.

Secondly, as Feinberg has noted, in attributive contexts we sometimes treat causation as a matter of empirical fact and sometimes treat it as infected from the start by evaluative notions. An outstanding example of the first treatment is the New York rule under which a person who negligently starts a fire is liable to pay only for the first of several houses which it destroys.[6] Here it would be absurd to say that, while his act did indeed cause the destruction by fire of the first house, it did not cause the destruction of the others. Liability can be cut off by a legal rule; but causality, being a matter of fact, cannot. On the other hand a dispute as to whether the Second World War was caused by Hitler's invasion of Poland or by Chamberlain's guarantee to Poland would seem to be from the start a dispute about who was to blame, whose act was wrong. Though the language of causation is used, it is hardly even a disguise.[7]

'Let the doer suffer.' This ancient maxim lies, whether on a retributive or on a utilitarian view, at the heart of all criminal liability and of all civil liability wherever some kind of fault is a necessary condition. The principle is that a person should be held responsible (answerable to a charge and liable to suffer if his answer is unsatisfactory) for all and only those harms for which he is, by his acts or omissions, causally responsible, and he is responsible in the first sense *because* he is responsible in the second.

Most legal systems, however, depart from this basic principle in two main ways. First, at several points the law holds someone liable even though his act or omission would not, by ordinary criteria, be picked out as the cause or even *a* cause of the harm for which he is held liable. Conspiracy is an obvious example; someone who plays a very minor role in an assassination plot could not be said to have caused the death of the tyrant, but the law might hold him liable. Strict liability, collective liability, and vicarious liability are other examples. The law makes these exceptions to the basic principle for reasons of policy, and it is no part of my project to say what these are or whether they are justifiable.

Another and more important, because more pervasive, way in which the law departs from the basic maxim is that it makes harm neither a necessary nor a sufficient condition of liability. Harm is not a necessary condition, because the law imposes liability on anyone who commits an *injuria* whether or not this 'forbidden act' caused harm. Careless driving is an offence even if no one is hurt; and if you forcibly restrain someone from embarking on an aeroplane which subsequently crashes, you are guilty of an offence even though you have conferred on your victim the greatest benefit by saving his life. On the other hand, harm is not a sufficient condition since the law will not hold someone liable for causing harm if he has not committed an *injuria*. It is not an offence to hurt someone's feelings even though the wound may be more painful to the victim than would be a slight bodily wound which would constitute an offence. What counts as an injury in law is any harm the causing of which the legislator declares to be an *injuria*; hence the connection between 'wrong' and 'forbidden by legal rules'. Here again it is not difficult to see why the law departs from the basic maxim and it is no part of my project to assess the merits of the reasons for which it does so. The interest here lies in the fact that the substitution of *injuria* (offence) for injury (harm) lends colour to the view which I am attacking, namely that in law we are responsible for our acts rather than for the harm we cause by our acts. The illusion, however, disappears when we see that the careless driver is responsible in the sense of being called to account for his offence and liable to suffer if his account is unsatisfactory; he is not causally responsible for the act of careless driving or for any harm which his careless driving caused, since it caused none.

Infants and lunatics and normal sane adults in certain abnormal conditions are said to be 'not responsible for their acts' and the fact that this phrase applies only to special classes of individuals shows (according to the rules of common sense logic) that normal sane adults in a normal condition *can* properly be said to be responsible for their acts. But this objection, though natural, obscures the complexity of the thought involved. A normal sane adult is responsible for the harm that he does by his acts; a lunatic or infant cannot, in the required rather Aristotelian sense, 'act' at all; hence he cannot cause harm by his acts; hence he cannot be held responsible for the harm caused by his acts. That all this is telescoped into the phrase 'not responsible for their acts' is neither here nor there; the phrase is an idiom and cannot be construed in terms of the valid inference '*A*, being a sane adult, is responsible for his acts; so he is responsible for each of his acts; so he is responsible, not only for the death of *B*, but also for the act of killing *B*.' (The real philosophical problem here is, of course, to identify and explicate the relevant sense of 'act'; for the things that infants and lunatics, in some broad sense, *do* can certainly cause harm.)

Another apparent counter-example to my thesis is provided by the case of attempts. *A*'s attempt to kill *B* is certainly an act and, in most legal systems, a forbidden act. But this, like the example of the careless driver, is due to the fact that, for obvious reasons, the law often forbids conduct which, though in a particular case it causes no harm, is very likely to do so. If *A* himself attempted to kill *B*, to say that he was responsible for the attempt could, I think, only mean that, since the attempt is an offence, he is liable to be called to account for it. On the other hand '*A* was responsible for the attempt on the life of *B*' is much more likely to mean, not that *A* made the attempt himself, but that he master-minded a plot carried out by others, and here 'responsible for' is used in a causal sense. *A* might have ordered, or bribed, or threatened, or induced *C* to carry out the attempt on

$B$'s life, and these are causal notions even though they are not 'causal' in the sense in which most philosophers now use that word. We need not go into the difficult problems raised by these inter-personal transactions, since in any case this example is not a counter-example to my thesis which is only that a man is not causally responsible for his own acts.

The upshot of this section is, therefore, the same as that of the last. Taylor is not entitled to his sharp distinction between deontological and teleological concepts, the reason this time being that the concept of 'responsibility' is a conflation of the deontological concept of liability for an offence and the teleological concept of causing harm. Other concepts in this area, for example 'injury' and 'charge' exhibit the same duality, and the duality itself can be best explained in terms of the basic principle 'Let the doer suffer.' This is not to say that either law or morality always follows this principle; for good reasons or bad, exceptions are often made; but they are best understood *as* exceptions, as departures from a principle that remains basic to, and gives point to systems of legal and moral rules. Deontic logicians may construct systems using the familiar trio 'required', 'forbidden', and 'permitted' since, as logicians, they are not concerned with the field to which their constructs might be usefully applied. But systems of moral and legal rules are not merely formal systems, and it would be impossible to understand, except in a purely formal way, any such system in which the concept of an *injuria* bore no relation, direct or indirect, to that of an injury.

## III. RESPONSIBILITY AND MORAL WRONG

So far I have considered responsibility in a context in which the idea of 'forbidden act' is at least a prominent part of 'wrong', even though it is not, as Taylor seems to think, the whole of it. So, in approaching morality, let us examine it in a setting that most closely approximates to a system of rules under which acts are either forbidden, required or permitted — the idea of morality as God's commands. Even here, I shall argue, purely deontological concepts are insufficient for a complete picture. On this view it is a necessary and sufficient condition of its being wrong to kill that God has commanded us not to, and it is (or at least might be) just a coincidence that, when we look at any *actual* list of commands alleged to have been given by a God, we find a close correspondence between forbidden acts and acts that cause, or are believed to cause harm. But any believer is apt to find that some of God's laws are, to his way of thinking, pointless or even perverse and at this point there are two ways in which he can proceed. He can say, first, that it is not for him to question God's commands or to try to fathom God's purposes. But there are limits to how much he can do with this line of thought and still be accounted sane. Could any sane person 'believe in' a God *none* of whose commands bore any relation that he can see to human benefit and harm or believe that he had a moral duty to obey the commands of such a God? And if he did, could we (whether we are theistic in our approach to morality or not) say that his 'religion' had anything whatever to do with morality?

What is wrong with Taylor's prude, pedant, formalist, and zealot is not, as he thinks, that they employ a notion of 'moral rule' which is illegitimate because, in the sphere of morality, there is no law-giver and no sanction. That cannot be what is wrong with them since these unpleasing characters are to be found also in the legal sphere where law-givers and sanctions abound. What is wrong with them in both spheres is that they treat legal and moral rules, as Taylor himself does, as resembling the rules of chess, first in being hard-and-fast affairs (either you may move your bishop to that square or you may not) and secondly as having little or nothing to do with any point that rules serve, with good and evil.

The second route that might be taken by someone who finds some of God's commands repugnant is that of the casuist; and Taylor is unnecessarily hard on casuists. Exceptions to the law against killing are made, he tells us, "by those who deem the law an absolute, who even imagine that it expresses the very will of God. Even these readily substitute their own will for God's whenever their feelings sufficiently prompt them to do so." But why should not a Christian or Jew who takes the sixth commandment to be an absolute command of God — to be obeyed without exception — *still* not be in doubt as to precisely what God forbade us to do when he said something to Moses in words which we translate 'thou shalt not kill'? Was it the taking of any human life? Or only of innocent human life? The same God who issued the sixth commandment sometimes ordered his subjects to kill. So what are his subjects to do? No doubt God's will is consistent — but it can sometimes only be made so by interpretation. To accuse generations of scholars who have tried to interpret God's will of substituting their own is altogether too sweeping, especially as they often found themselves driven to most unpalatable conclusions. Nor were their conclusions always prompted by their *feelings*, though no doubt this is often the case. Current debates over the morality of capital punishment or abortion often give colour to the suspicion that the arguments used by each side are little more than a smoke-screen of rationalization; but this does not have to be so.

The same reflections apply to the interpretation of the law. A judge who finds for defendant because he does not like plaintiff's long hair is guilty of being swayed by his feelings, his duty being to decide the case on the basis of acceptable reasoned arguments. Legal cases, especially those which find their way up to an appellate court or higher, are such that it is possible to give an acceptable reasoned argument on either side. This may be unfortunate, but it is a permanent feature of all reasoning that cannot be cast into the form of a calculus. Rational men who are honestly trying to find the correct solution to a problem will often, in the end, disagree; but it by no means follows that their conclusions merely give vent to their feelings. The same is true of moral disagreements.

Once we see that deontological concepts can never be cast loose from their teleological moorings — an attempt that even Kant did not make — a foothold is gained for the kind of critical morality that Taylor wants us to consign to the flames. His argument cannot go through unless he can show that the concept of harm itself is illusory or subjective or so culture-bound that rational treatment is impossible. No doubt what counts as harm in one culture will not always count as harm in others; no doubt people will differ as to the relative gravity of different types of harm. But Taylor himself seems not to want to say that what counts as harm is just a matter of individual feeling or convention, of what some individual or some community happens to dislike.

For he tells us that "good and evil are, at this moral level, not the creation of any rule or law, but exist antecedently to law and are discoverable in experience ... no rule or law is needed to know that hunger and thirst are bad. Similarly a wound is bad, whether inflicted or accidental; and, while law may render its infliction wrong, no law is needed to render the suffering of it bad." So, according to Taylor, suffering is bad, and its badness is not created by any rule or convention. Why, then, does he insist on the view that when people make exceptions to what they claim to be a genuine moral rule, they must do so in response to their feelings? Might they not do so on the grounds that refusing to make the exception increases the amount of suffering in the world — a matter, according to Taylor, of objective fact?

That suffering is, in general though not always, bad is a truism; but it is a truism that raises problems. Is one kind of suffering worse than another? If the same act causes both suffering and joy, should it be done or not done? Does it matter whose suffering is involved? It is with such questions that moral *thinking* begins. Conventional or positive morality is a set of traditional 'rules' — in a very loose sense — for the avoidance of natural evils. As Taylor suggests, *we* collectively and often unconsciously, are both the authors and the enforcers of these rules. These systems are sometimes called 'conventional', but it is not wholly clear what this means. Is it that they have been agreed on at a moral constitutional convention? Or that no reason can be given why we should adopt this rule rather than that? The rule of the road is conventional in both senses. There is, as far as I can see, no reason why we should drive on the right rather than on the left, and the rule has (if only by a constitutional fiction) been laid down by agreement. Rules of what Hobbes called "the small morals" are conventional in the second sense, if not in the first. But since Taylor takes the line that some states of affairs are naturally good and others naturally bad, it is not open to him to take the line that all moral rules are conventional in the second sense. For once it is conceded that there are natural evils, a foothold is gained for moral *philosophy*. On a contract theory, genuine moral rules are those rules which would be adopted by rational men seeking agreement at a constitutional convention; on a utilitarian theory they are, more directly, rules for the prevention of natural evils. Many such critical moralities have been constructed — ostensibly by rational argument rather than by appeals to feelings — and one of their functions has always been the criticism of positive law and positive morality. These are the works that Taylor bids us consign to the flames. It is not for me to say which of them deserves to be saved from the holocaust; but so long as Taylor holds to the view that there are natural evils and that natural evils are to be avoided, he needs a stronger argument than any he has given to show that they all deserve that fate.

*York University*

## NOTES

[1] Graham Hughes has drawn attention to a number of ways in which it is misleading to draw an analogy between legal rules and the rules of a game in 'Rules, Policy and Decision Making', *The Yale Law Journal* **77**, (1968), No. 3.
[2] Hart, H. L. A., *The Concept of Law*, p. 125.
[3] The inadequacies of this theory of law are exposed in detail by Hart, *Op. cit.* Chapters 2–4.
[4] *Oxford English Dictionary* s.v. 'Responsible'.
[5] Hart, H. L. A. and Honoré, A. M., *Causation in the Law*.
[6] Hart and Honoré, p. 63.
[7] *Doing and Deserving*, pp. 200–1.

# PART 9

# DECISION THEORY AND HUMAN ACTION

ALEX C. MICHALOS

# THE MORALITY OF COGNITIVE DECISION-MAKING

## I. INTRODUCTION

In this paper an attempt is made to clarify the fairly old idea of an ethics of belief and to show that at least one plausible version of such an ethics is inescapable.

Briefly, the positive thesis defended here is that insofar as one engages in an activity designed to discover truth or to avoid falsehood one is engaged in an activity which is essentially moral in the narrow sense of the word, i.e. it is not morally neutral. After specifying the question in the next section, the cases for and against a negative ethics of belief are presented in sections three and four. In the fifth and sixth sections the cases for and against a positive ethics of belief are developed. Following this, in section seven I offer a critique of *prima facie* plausible but faulty objections to any version of an ethics of belief.

## II. THE QUESTION

The shortest and, I suppose, the historically most familiar way to put the question I want to consider in this essay is this: Is there an ethics of belief? A longer and philosophically more lucid way to put it runs thus: Is cognitive decision-making subject to moral appraisal? The extra length of the latter question will be granted immediately. Its additional lucidity will take some time to explain.

By 'cognitive decision' I mean a decision *that* something is or is not the case. For example, one might decide that two plus three is five, that the tracks in the snow were left by a beaver or that sugar is water-soluble. Such decisions are traditionally contrasted with so-called practical decisions which are decisions *to do* something or to bring something about, e.g. to swim, to write a poem or to twiddle one's thumbs.

From a psychological point of view, when one makes either kind of decision some kind of disposition or mental set is voluntarily acquired. If the decision is cognitive, one believes that something is the case. If the decision is practical, one is disposed to behave overtly in some particular way in some circumstances.

*M. Brand and D. Walton (eds.), Action Theory*, 325–340. *All Rights Reserved*
*Copyright © 1976 by D. Reidel Publishing Company, Dordrecht-Holland*

From a logical point of view, we may say that the object of a cognitive decision is a proposition and the object of a practical decision is an action.

As our basic question is put above, it might be understood as a question about the moral propriety of (a) a decision process (the input or means side of decision-making), (b) an act of deciding (the output, product or end which terminates the process), (c) holding the belief (decision that) resulting from the act, (d) the propositional content of the belief held, or (e) all of these. As we shall see shortly, our predecessors have often slipped unwittingly from (a) or (b) to (c) and back.

The question of the relation of belief to physically overt action is, I suppose, still largely open. I have argued at length elsewhere that there is a logical gap between the two which is impossible to bridge, but no one need believe that for what is to follow. Briefly there are four possibilities. One might hold that a belief can be

(1)     logically independent and irrelevant to every overt action
(2)     logically independent but not irrelevant to every overt action
(3)     not logically independent and irrelevant to every overt action
(4)     not logically independent and not irrelevant to every overt action.

The first position (1) is defended by Levi and called 'critical cognitivism'.[1] The second makes the relation of beliefs to action contingent, and this is my view (as well as Martin and Leach). The third is silly if not logically absurd, and no one I know of holds it. The fourth is a natural resting place for pragmatists and behaviouralists of one sort or another, e.g., Clifford, James, Dewey and Lewis.[2] Very often it is difficult to determine whether a given author holds a second or fourth class view and, since I think the former is more plausible than the latter, I tend to assume people want to be counted there unless they reveal some fairly explicit preference for the fourth class. At one time or another the people whose names follow 'Clifford' above all seem to have opted for the fourth view. I shall return to these options shortly.

'Moral' and 'ethical', as most philosophers know, may be contrasted with their complements 'nonmoral' and 'nonethical' or with their contraries 'immoral' or 'unethical'. In the case of contraries, goodness and badness are attached to the connotations, but not in the case of complements. In the latter 'moral' is contrasted with things like political, psychological, technical and so on. C. I. Lewis divided the moral or ethical into a wider class of principles dealing with action generally and a narrower class dealing with what we usually regard as morality proper. The wider class of moral concerns seems to be coextensive with what some people call 'praxiology' nowadays.[3] At any rate, the only thing that hangs on this distinction is one's understanding of Lewis's ethics of belief. In his view "... cognitive correctness is itself a moral concern, *in the broad sense of 'moral'*."[4] (Emphasis added.) Hence, little more will be said about his view here.

It is the narrower sense of 'moral' that is of primary interest in this paper. I take it that something is morally good if and only if it is good from a (narrow) moral point of view, good on moral grounds or good for moral reasons. Such a view, such grounds or reasons would include maxims like "One ought to be fair minded and treat people fairly or justly" (Principle of Justice), "One ought to be honest and speak the truth as one sees it, deceive no one" (Principle of Honesty or Integrity), and "One ought to be or do good rather than evil" (Principle of Benevolence). We need not be concerned with the justification or the operationalization of these principles, so long as we all find them acceptable, i.e. we believe that violations are *prima facie*, at least, morally wrong. However, it should be noticed that each one is formulated as a prescription for being a certain sort of person as well as for acting in a certain way. This was done following Frankena's observation that morality concerns both character and action.

One other distinction is necessary before we can lay out our central set of options. The following quotation from James will serve as an introduction.

There are two ways of looking at our duty in the matter of opinion ... *We must know the truth*; and *we must avoid error* ... they are two separable laws. ... We may regard the chase for truth as paramount ... or we may, on the other hand, treat the avoidance of error as more imperative, and let truth take its chance.[6]

Roughly speaking, the distinction James is suggesting is the sort that obtains between so-called affirmative action and equal opportunity employers, or between a mother who urges her son to try to find honest work and one who tells him to at least stay out of trouble. In other words, one might subscribe to a *positive* ethical maxim of cognitive decision-making such as "One ought to pursue the truth and believe it" or a *negative* maxim such as "One ought to avoid falsehood and disbelieve (or at least withhold belief from) it." Accordingly, we have four new options. One *might* hold that there *can* be logically coherent and plausible

(1)    positive and negative moral maxims of cognitive decision-making
(2)    positive but not negative maxims
(3)    not positive but negative maxims
(4)    neither positive nor negative maxims.

Moreover, since the maxims would provide the backbone of a moral code, anyone accepting the fourth (4) position would be opposed to an ethics of belief on logical grounds and anyone favoring such an ethical system would accept one of the other three positions.

Given the five alternatives of process, terminating act, product (belief), content, all these; the three plausible views of the relation of belief to action; and the four views about maxims; we have at least 60 possible ways to answer our question. (Actually, there are more than 60, since the negative maxim cited above is divided into two distinct types later and the agnostic position mentioned parenthetically is not strictly equivalent to a negative one.) Obviously I am not going to consider all of them. Instead, I will present the cases for and against those positions which have been more or less strenuously argued by our predecessors. This way we will be able to avoid red herrings, to keep our analyses tidy and, hopefully, to satisfactorily answer the question with which we began, i.e. Is cognitive decision-making subject to moral appraisal? In short: Is there an ethics of belief?

## III. THE CASE FOR A NEGATIVE ETHICS OF BELIEF

By the phrase 'negative ethics of belief' I mean an ethical code based on a negative maxim like "One ought to avoid falsehood and disbelieve (or at least without belief from) it" or "One ought to avoid believing anything on insufficient or inadequate evidence." Strictly speaking, these two maxims are not equivalent unless it is assumed that *the only* way to avoid falsehood is to withhold belief in propositions for which one has inadequate evidence. In fact, in W. K. Clifford's classic defense of such an ethics, this assumption is frequently, if not always, made. I will say more about these maxims later.

Clifford offers several different but closely related arguments which are as intriguing as they are vague.[7] For those to be considered below, it may be assumed that the relation of belief to action is at most contingent. That is almost certainly a weaker assumption than Clifford would have preferred, but it is strong enough to do the job.[8] I also assume, though Clifford does not make the distinction, that it is *prima facie* duties or obligations that are our concern rather than duties or obligations *simpliciter*. Finally, since he pretty clearly shifts from talking about *holding* a belief to acquiring it in the first place (i.e. the act of deciding that), I will try to straighten out his views with paraphrasing. The first argument we will consider (3.1) is not sound, but it is used so often in one form or another by Clifford that it is worthwhile to get it out in the open and dispose of it. The other three arguments in this section (3.2–3.4) seem to provide good reasons for the maxim of avoiding falsehood.

Clifford's most frequently used argument runs as follows.[9]

3.1. Because we are social beings, beliefs tend to be held in common.

For any task men pursue in common with others, each man has a moral obligation to hold up his own end.

If one holds a belief on insufficient evidence, one neglects that duty.

To neglect a duty is to violate the Principle of Justice. Hence, it is morally wrong to hold a belief on insufficient evidence.

Clifford spells out the first premise of 3.1 thus:

And no one man's belief is in any case a private matter which concerns himself alone. Our lives are guided by that general conception of the course of things which has been created by society for social purposes. Our words, our phrases, our forms and processes and modes of thought, are common property, fashioned and perfected from age to age; an heirloom which every succeeding generation inherits as a precious deposit and a sacred trust to be handed on to the next one, not unchanged but enlarged and purified, with some clear marks of its proper handiwork.[10]

Ignoring the flowery parts of this passage, it seems unobjectionable as do the first, second and fourth premises. It is really only the third premise that might create problems. Why should holding a belief on insufficient evidence count as neglecting one's duty to contribute a fair share of the labour necessary to sustain a collective good? Presumably what is required here is the assumption that the structure of beliefs held by a community is bonded together by sufficient evidence also held jointly. Then, anyone holding a belief without sufficient evidence would, as it were, be guilty of trying to hold only the structure without holding the foundation too. Altering our metaphor slightly, imagine a tent held up by several people with one hand on ropes holding the roof on and the other hand on ropes holding the floor taut. Then one who dropped his floor rope would be guilty of jeopardizing the shape of the tent. Similarly, one who holds beliefs on insufficient evidence only does part of what one is required to do to keep the total shape of our beliefs intact.

Plausible as this argument may sound, I think it is question-begging insofar as it requires the assumption that the structure of beliefs held by a community must be bonded together by sufficient evidence — held jointly or not. To see that this is so, one need only ask: Why is sufficient evidence required to bond the structure of beliefs together? Why not merely some significant evidence or, indeed, some nonevidential reason like faith or hope? That, of course, is roughly the sort of question James put to Clifford in 'The Will to Believe'. Clifford would be assuming here precisely what has to be demonstrated, namely, that if one has a good reason for believing any proposition to be true then one must have sufficient evidence for it, i.e. sufficient evidence is *the only* warrant for believing a proposition is true.

Another argument suggested by Clifford arises from the following.

Habitual want of care about what I believe leads to habitual want of care in others about the truth of what is told me.[11]

That is,

3.2. When one is careless about the reasons one has for the beliefs one holds, others tend to become careless about the reasons for the views they express toward one.

As others become careless, they tend to supply one with falsehoods so one becomes surrounded by "a thick atmosphere of falsehood and fraud".

To surround a person with "falsehood and fraud" is to violate the Principle of Honesty.

Hence, it is morally wrong to be careless about the reasons one has for the beliefs one holds.

Beginning with the first two premises of 3.2, Clifford also suggests the following finish.

3.3. To encourage others to surround a person with "falsehood and fraud" is to violate the Principle of Benevolence.

Hence, it is morally wrong to be careless about the reasons one has for the beliefs one holds.

The difference between 3.2. and 3.3. is that the former focuses on the evil of drowning a person in "falsehood and fraud" while the latter focuses on the evil of encouraging people to perform such an act. It's wrong to do it and to help people to do it.

Although I have not run any controlled experiments to determine whether the effects posited in the first premise of 3.2 and 3.3 occur always, usually or hardly ever, casual observation seems to suggest that the effects occur often enough not to be swiftly discounted. There is, of course, a lot of evidence on the pressures for and likelihood of individual conformity to group norms which is at least indirect support for this premise.[12] The second premise is also basically empirical, though it presupposes that in fact careless thinkers have more false beliefs than careful thinkers. If this is not true, then one of the main prudential reasons one might have for being a careful thinker is lost. I presume it is true. Similarly, I presume the final premises of 3.2 and 3.3 are unobjectionable.

Again, Clifford argues[13]

3.4. Insofar as one holds beliefs dogmatically one is less inclined to give issues a fair hearing.

Insofar as one is less inclined to give issues a fair hearing one is inclined to violate the Principle of Justice.

Hence, it is morally wrong to hold beliefs dogmatically.

As the first premise is formulated, it is virtually analytic. To hold beliefs dogmatically is just to automatically reject contrary views and arguments, and that is certainly not compatible with fairness. Unless one insists that 'fair-mindedness' can only apply to the adjudication of conflicting interests among people, the second premise is also unobjectionable. I should think, however, that the burden of proof would be on the insister in this case. Accordingly, the conclusion of 3.4 strikes me as true.

A couple of pages later Clifford asserts that "Every time we *let ourselves believe* for unworthy reasons, we weaken our powers of self-control, of doubting, of judicially and fairly weighing evidence."[14] (Emphasis added.) This suggests a variant of 3.4 in which the error is not in holding the belief but in deciding that it is true, i.e. in voluntarily acquiring it.

## IV. THE CASE AGAINST A NEGATIVE ETHICS OF BELIEF

As indicated earlier, William James sought to discredit what he took to be Clifford's position. In fact, as I also insisted, Clifford unwittingly presented arguments in defense of at least two different basic maxims for a negative ethics of belief. Furthermore, as will be explained shortly, it is only the maxim linking belief to sufficient evidence that James opposes, not the maxim against belief in falsehoods. In the following passage James suggests three reasons for finding

... it impossible to go with Clifford. We must remember that these feelings of our duty about either truth or error are in any case only expressions of our passional life ... he who says 'Better go without belief forever than believe a lie!' merely shows his own preponderant private horror of becoming a dupe ... but I can believe that worse things than being duped may happen to a man in this world: so Clifford's exhortation has to my ears a thoroughly fantastic sound. ... In a world where we are so certain to incur errors in spite of all our caution, a certain lightness of heart seems healthier than this excessive nervousness on their behalf.[15]

The first suggestion, that "these feelings of our duty" are "only expressions of our passional life" seems to be tantamount to the admission that we have reached a level of analysis at which the giving of reasons necessarily gives way to the expression of attitudes. That hardly seems plausible even to James, since he does try to present reasons for his view. His second suggestion is that considering the evils which may fall upon a person in this world, believing a falsehood is among the least of our worries. I suppose this should only be taken relativistically (even assuming a contingent relation between belief and action), since the consequences of some beliefs turning out false might be the overturning of one's whole orientation toward life, one's whole *Weltanschauung*, and that could be serious indeed. Finally, he suggests that we are so prone to error that one ought to maintain "a certain lightness of heart" toward it — rather than become what Lyndon Johnson used to call "a nervous Nellie". I imagine neither James nor anyone else knows how prone to error most people are, but again, I would think that the claim must be taken relativistically at best.

Taking these arguments together, I do not think we get to the heart of James's position. The latter comes out most clearly in the following passages.

There are ... cases where a fact cannot come at all unless a preliminary faith exists in its coming. *And where faith in a fact can help create the fact,* that would be an insane logic which should say that faith running ahead of scientific evidence is the 'lowest kind of immorality' into which a thinking being can fall. ... *A rule of thinking which would absolutely prevent me from acknowledging certain kinds of truth if those kinds of truth were really there, would be an irrational rule.*[16]

Thus, for example, one cannot have trusted friends unless one believes that they are trustworthy without sufficient evidence, i.e. without evidence that would guarantee their fidelity. Since a maxim proscribing belief on insufficient evidence would "absolutely prevent" one from deciding that a friend was trustworthy without serious testing, such a maxim should be rejected.

What James has hit upon in this passage is a species of prudential or pragmatic reasoning leading to *belief.* Schematically it might be represented thus:

### Pragmatic Schema

1.
$$p \left\{ \begin{array}{l} \text{only if} \\ \text{usually only if} \\ \text{probably only if} \end{array} \right\} X \text{ believes that } p.$$

2.      $X$ would like it to be the case that $p$.

3.      So, $X$ believes that $p$.

This pragmatic schema is roughly similar to traditional maxims of practical reasoning, e.g.

> If $\phi$ing is (usually, probably) a necessary condition of it being the case that $p$ and $X$ wants the latter, then $X$ ought (rationally, prudentially) to $\phi$.

For example,

> If believing that I can outrun Newberry is (usually, probably) a necessary condition of my being able to outrun him, and I want to be able to outrun him, then I ought (rationally, prudentially) to believe that I can.

However, the conclusion of our schema is not that one *ought to do* something, but that one believes something. Although the premises do, I think, provide good grounds for the practical conclusion, it is the cognitive conclusion that is most interesting. For here we have not evidential (e.g. straight deductive or (narrowly) inductive) grounds for believing that something is the case, but purely pragmatic, prudential or teleological grounds. We have good reasons for belief, but not good evidence! And that I find at once exciting and frightening. It is exciting because such grounds have been almost entirely neglected by epistemologists so far as I know,[17] and it is frightening because God knows *what* one might have good pragmatic reasons for believing. I wish I could pursue all the niceties of pragmatic schemata with you now, but that is both beyond me and the plan of this paper. So I will return directly to James.

What surprises me about James's approach here is that he does not try to rest his case on moral grounds, following Clifford, for instance. Instead, he complains that it would be "an insane logic" and an "irrational rule" which would proscribe belief without sufficient evidence. But why, after all, isn't it just plain morally wrong to prevent people from deciding that their friends or indeed, their fellow citizens are trustworthy prior to tests? "Don't trust anyone until he has proven worthy," is the sort of maxim which, if followed, would virtually destroy the social fabric of any community. One must trust the butcher not to color the meat, the doctor to conscientiously prescribe therapy, the mechanic to fix exactly what is broken, the teacher to try to put decent ideas into our kids heads, and so on. Without such trust there can be no community, no social or moral life, no friendship and no love. A maxim with these consequences must be pronounced morally offensive, and that seems to be as strong an objection as one could raise against it.

In James's final shot against the negative maxim, he says

... if we believe that no bell in us tolls to let us know for certain when truth is in our grasp, then it seems a piece of idle fantasticality to preach so solemnly our duty of waiting for the bell.[18]

In other words, there is no *logical* point in proscribing the acceptance of beliefs on insufficient evidence because no one knows when evidence really is sufficient. One might as well tell people not to believe anything at all or, on the contrary, to believe whatever they damn well please.

Although I think it must be admitted that there is no single, all purpose, sure-fire criterion of sufficiency for evidence, it is hardly the case that we are entirely at sea in this area. For all sorts of everyday occurrences as well as scientific research and judicial proceedings we are able to reach widespread agreement about what counts as sufficient evidence. Case by case, the problems are by no means insurmountable, although in general and in the abstract they may be.

## V. THE CASE FOR A POSITIVE ETHICS OF BELIEF

Briefly and roughly the conclusion reached in the preceding two sections is that there is a negative ethics of belief, i.e. cognitive decision-making can be morally right or good, wrong or bad. Furthermore, it was shown that James clearly saw that there is a difference between such a view and what I have called a positive ethics of belief, and he evidently opted for the latter. From what was said in the preceding section and the following remarks we may formulate the sort of argument he would want to use.

The importance to human life of having true beliefs about matters of fact is a thing too notorious. We live in a world of realities that can be infinitely useful or infinitely harmful. Ideas that tell us which of them to expect count as the true ideas in all this primary sphere of verification, and *the pursuit of such ideas is a primary human duty*. The possession of truth, so far from being here an end in itself, is only a preliminary means towards other vital satisfactions. ... *Our obligation to seek truth* is part of our general obligation to do what pays. (Emphasis added.)[19]

That is,

We have a moral obligation to try to preserve human life.
"The possession of truth ... is only a preliminary means ..." toward that end.
The pursuit of truth is often if not always necessary for its possession.
Hence, "the pursuit of such ideas is a primary human duty".

In short we are obliged to pursue that course of action which, often enough, is necessary to obtain a morally prescribed end.

The first premise of this argument follows immediately from the universally recognised Right to Life. The second premise strikes me just about as it struck James, namely as "a thing too notorious". The third premise is phrased as it is to avoid the objection that one might after all just stumble upon the truth. Of course one might, but I do not believe that is the usual or most promising way to find it. Given these premises then, there does not seem to be any escape from the conclusion. That is, James has given us one good reason to accept a positive ethics of belief.

As James laments elsewhere, he and other pragmatists paid dearly for all their references to payments, cash value, practical consequences, working and utility. The cost, he suggests, was in the form of the "solemn attribution of ... rubbish to us ...".[20] I will not review the literature on the nature of the pay-offs actually or usually envisioned by pragmatists generally or

James in particular. However, I should point out that if the reference to payment in the last sentence of the quoted paragraph above is understood in terms of the preservation of human life, then that sentence is roughly only a truncated version of the argument set out for him.

Another argument in favor of a positive ethics of belief runs as follows.

If there is a moral obligation to speak the truth as one sees it then there is a similar obligation to try to see it as it is.

There is a moral obligation to speak the truth as one sees it (Principle of Honesty).

Hence, there is a moral obligation to pursue the truth, i.e. to try to see the world as it is.

This argument clearly stands or falls with the first premise. Suppose it is false. If one has no obligation to try to find the truth, then the obligation to speak the truth is pointless. "Believe whatever you like for whatever reasons you like but always say what you believe" is a silly commandment because there is no virtue, intellectual or moral, in speaking falsehoods or in some kinds of reasons. That is, not all reasons are good reasons and not everything one likes is worth sharing. Thus, an unconditioned command to say whatever you believe cannot be a moral maxim, though it may be great for psychotherapy. Consequently, the first premise of this argument must be accepted and with it, the argument itself.

## VI. THE CASE AGAINST A POSITIVE ETHICS OF BELIEF

It might be argued that because, for example, a little philosophy makes one an atheist or at least an agnostic, one has no obligation to pursue the truth. Better to be a dogmatic believer than a doubter or a disbeliever! I do not doubt at all that one could imagine cases in which blatant dogmatism has better short run results (maybe even long run results) that are preferable to the results of disbelief or agnosticism. But to admit that is to admit nothing more than that the obligations and duties we are discussing are necessarily *prima facie* in character. There is a big step from this to the conclusion that we have a *prima facie* obligation to be dogmatic *because* sometimes dogmatism has more benefits than costs. If that line of argumentation were accepted then we would have similar obligations to lie and steal as well. In fact, the moral realm would be turned virtually up-side down. Accordingly, I reject this line without reservation.

## VII. THE CASE AGAINST ANY ETHICS OR BELIEF

At this point everything that I have to say in favor of an ethics of belief based on a negative and a positive maxim has been said. In the remaining paragraphs of this section then, I will present *prima facie* plausible objections to the position defended above and try to show that they are unacceptable.

7.1. The idea of an ethics of belief or of cognitive decision-making being moral or immoral is just so much self-serving sop. Only an academic mind or worse, a philosophic mind, would seriously entertain the notion that deciding that something is the case or holding on to a belief once acquired could be a moral act. No one else would be inclined to try to get moral credit for thinking straight.

*Reply*. This objection is obviously just an *argumentum ad hominem*. Of course an ethics of belief would have special relevance for academics of all kinds, philosophers, scientists or whatever. But that does not make the idea true or false, sound or silly. Our critics will have to aim higher.

7.2. Suppose it is granted for the sake of argument that there is, as some ancient philosophers might say, moral virtue in intellectual virtue. It still would not follow that cognitive decisions are moral or immoral. Recall, for example, Lewis's view that the sense of 'moral' involved is wide rather than narrow. Alternatively, consider the following remarks by Thomas Aquinas.

Other intellectual virtues [wisdom, science and art] can, but prudence cannot, be without moral virtue. The reason for this is that prudence is right reason about things to be done, and this not merely in general, but also in the particular, where action takes place. ... Consequently ... in order that he be rightly disposed with regard to the particular principles of action, viz., the ends, he needs to be perfected by certain habits, whereby it becomes connatural to man, as it were, to judge rightly about the end. This is done by moral virtue, for the virtuous man judges rightly of the end of virtue, because *such as a man is, such does the end seem to him.* Consequently the right reason about things to be done, viz., *prudence*, requires man to have moral virtue.[21]

In other words, Aquinas holds that morality can play a role in decision-making only insofar as beliefs are related to overt actions, i.e. only in the realm of what he calls 'prudence'. In that realm there *is* moral virtue in intellectual virtue, but that is only possible because the decisions made are not merely cognitive.[22]

*Reply*. Aquinas's view may be true, but it is question-begging to merely assert it in this manner. After all, what has to be shown is *not* that one can classify so-called intellectual virtues so that cognitive decisions never have any moral import, but that such a classification does justice to all the relevant facts or arguments. This sort of a justification has not been provided.

7.3. If cognitive decision-making has moral import then all good scientists, philosophers and mathematicians must be morally good. Ho, Ho, Ho! If that doesn't destroy the thesis once and for all, what else can?

*Reply.* This argument is a *non-sequitur.* One might just as well argue that anyone who performs lots of morally good actions is morally good. What if he is also performing lots of morally bad actions on the side? For example, he might be murdering people for money and giving all the money to his favorite charity. Or, what if he performs lots of morally good but trivial actions and one or two morally horrendous and highly significant actions? For example, he might regularly pay his grocery bills until one day he murders his grocer and every one else in the store. Clearly, the first premise of 7.3 will have to be tightened up in order to have any plausibility. Thus,

7.4. If cognitive decision-making has moral import then a mathematician doing his sums correctly (with no inclination or opportunity to share his results with others) is doing something that is morally right or good. That is, granted that he is not neglecting some duty or doing anything else on the side which is morally reprehensible, we must say that there is moral virtue in what he is doing. That is just an outrageous departure from common sense and ordinary usage. Imagine trying to persuade a man on the street that an accountant correctly multiplying 3728 by 261 is doing something that is as morally significant as telling his neighbour the true product!

*Reply.* In fact, of course, the last sentence is misleading. Insofar as both acts have moral significance they are in the same class, but it does not follow that each act has the same amount of moral virtue. The fact that all moral acts are praiseworthy does not imply that they are all equally praiseworthy. Whether or not finding the correct product would be as morally praiseworthy as truthfully giving the information to one's neighbor is a debatable question. Would giving the information to a total stranger merit more praise than giving it to a friend? I don't think one can answer such questions without considerable development of the cases.

For its relevance, if not for the sheer beauty of the prose, the following passage for Ferdinand Lundberg's classic *The Rich and the Super-Rich* is worth repeating.

... in the process of being educated there is always the danger that the individual will acquire scruples, a fact dimly sensed by some of the neo-conservatives who rail against the school system as "Communistic". These scruples, unless they are casuistically beveled around the edges with great care, are a distinct handicap to the full-fledged money-maker, who must in every situation be plastically opportunistic. But a person who has had it deeply impressed upon him that he must make *exact* reports of *careful* laboratory experiments, must conduct *exact* computations in mathematics and logic, must produce *exact* translations and echoes of foreign languages, must write *faithful* reports or *correct* readings and must be at least imaginatively aware of the world in its diversity, and who has learned these lessons well, must invariably discover that some element of scrupulosity — even if he hasn't been subject to moral indoctrination — has been impressed on his psyche. If he enters upon money-making in a world bazaar where approximate truths, vague deceptions, sneak maneuvers, half promises and even bald falsehoods are the widely admired and heavily rewarded order of the day he must make casuistic adjustments of his standards. The very process of laboriously making the adjustment, even if he succeeds, puts him at a disadvantage *vis-à-vis* the unschooled, who need waste no energy on such adjustments, who pick up anything lying around loose as easily as they breath. Some educated people can't make even a partial adjustment to the market bazaar, and their disgraceful bank accounts show it. They are, as even their wives sometimes kindly inform them, failures, though they are doing something conceded to be useful such as instructing children or enforcing the law. They can inscribe after their names a big "F" and go stand in a corner under a dunce cap as the propaganda dervishes scream about success.[23]

The rest of 7.4 is straightforward, but answerable. If one believes, as I and many others do, that it is logically possible to, say, dedicate one's life to learning and leave the comfort of human communities (with all that such a severance implies) and be or become a good person by doing just that, then there is nothing outrageous or extraordinary about the thesis being defended here. In short, if hermits can be morally good and can continue to perform morally praiseworthy acts in their hermitage, then the thesis of the moral significance of cognitive decision-making must be not only logically coherent but true as well.

7.5. As Campbell pointed out a while ago, no amount of nonmoral value can be added to produce moral value.[24] That means one cannot be morally praiseworthy or blameworthy for cognitive decision-making.

*Reply.* On some views of the nature of moral and nonmoral value, the former is constructed out of the latter. "Teleological theories" Frankena tells us ". . . make the right, the obligatory, and the morally good dependent on the nonmorally good."[25] Thus, considerably more than is said in 7.5 would have to be said in order to sustain the objection.

### VIII. CONCLUSION

If the preceding analysis has been accurate then the answer to the question "Is cognitive decision-making subject to moral appraisal?" or "Is there an ethics of belief?" in the sense specified above is: Yes.[26]

*University of Guelph, Ontario*

### NOTES

[1] Levi, I., *Gambling with Truth*, Alfred A. Knopf, New York, 1967.
[2] Clifford, W. K., *Lectures and Essays*, Macmillan and Co., London, 1886. James, W., *Pragmatism*, Meridian Books, Inc., New York, 1955. Dewey, J., *Essays in Experimental Logic*, University of Chicago Press, Chicago, 1916. Lewis, C. I., *Values and Imperatives*, J. Lange (ed.), Stanford University Press, Stanford, California, 1969.

³ See, for example, Kotarbinsk, T., *Praxiology: An Introduction to the Science of Efficient Action*, Pergamon Press, Oxford, 1965, and my critique 'Efficiency and Morality', *The Journal of Value Inquiry* (1972), 137–143.

⁴ Lewis, *op. cit.*, p. 163. My impression is that Price understands Locke's "ethics of belief" in this wider sense too, although I think part of the time at least Locke was concerned with the narrower sense. See, Price, H. H., *Belief*, George Allen and Unwin, Ltd., London, 1969, pp. 130–156, and Locke, J., *An Essay Concerning Human Understanding*, Vol. II, Dover Pub., Inc., New York, 1959, pp. 413–427. The following remarks by Locke p. 413 for instance, do not seem to be offered merely in the interests of efficiency or ethical action in a broad sense.

> "He that believes without having any reason for believing, may be in love with his own fancies; but neither seeks truth as he ought, *nor pays the obedience due to his Maker*, who would have him use those discerning faculties he has given him, to keep him out of mistake and error." (Emphasis added.)

⁵ Frankena, W. K., *Ethics*, Prentice Hall, Inc., Englewood Cliffs, 1963.

⁶ James, W. *The Will to Believe and Other Essays in Popular Philosophy*, Dover Publications, New York, 1956, p. 17.

⁷ Clifford, W. K., 'The Ethics of Belief', *op. cit.*, pp. 339–363.

⁸ "Nor is that truly a belief at all" he writes "which has not some influence upon the actions of him who holds it." *Ibid.*, p. 342.

⁹ A form of it appears on pages 342 and 344 in 'The Ethics of Belief', and also in James, *op. cit.*, p. 140 and in V. Tomas (ed.), *Charles S. Peirce Essays in the Philosophy of Science*, The Liberal Arts Press, New York, 1957, p. 16.

¹⁰ Clifford, *loc. cit.*, pp. 342–343.

¹¹ *Ibid.*, p. 345.

¹² See, for example, Hare, A. P., Borgatta, E. F., and Bales, R. F. (eds.), *Small Groups*, Alfred A. Knopf, New York, 1966.

¹³ Clifford, *loc. cit.*, p. 342.

¹⁴ *Ibid.*, pp. 344–345.

¹⁵ James, *The Will to Believe*, pp. 17–19.

¹⁶ *Ibid.*, pp. 25–28. The single quoted phrase is a reference to a quotation from T. Huxley which James cites on page 7 without telling us where it comes from. ". . . Huxley exclaims:" according to James "My only consolation lies in the reflection that, however bad our posterity may become, so far as they hold by the plain rule of not pretending to believe what they have no reason to believe, because it may be to their advantage so to pretend [the word 'pretend' is surely here redundant], they will not have reached the lowest depth of immorality."

¹⁷ The so-called pragmatic justification or vindication of induction supported by men like Feigl, Kneale and Reichenbach could be regarded as a special case of the general pragmatic line of argumentation schematized above or of ordinary practical reason. For an analysis of pragmatic justification see Salmon, W. C., 'Should We Attempt to Justify Induction?', *Philosophical Studies*, 1957, pp. 33–48, and for a review of ordinary practical reasoning schemata see Rescher, N., *Introduction to Value Theory*, Prentice-Hall, Inc., Englewood Cliffs, 1969.

¹⁸ *Ibid.*, p. 30.

¹⁹ James, *Pragmatism*, pp. 134 and 150.

²⁰ James, W. *The Meaning of Truth: A Sequel to 'Pragmatism'*, Longmans, Green and Co., New York, 1909, p. 212.

²¹ *Basic Writings of Saint Thomas Aquinas*, Vol. II, A. C. Pegis (ed.), Random House, New York, 1945, p. 447.

²² This is how E. Gilson interprets Aquinas too in *The Christian Philosophy of St. Thomas Aquinas*, Victor Gollancz Ltd., London, 1957, pp. 260–261.

[23] Lundberg, Ferdinand, *The Rich and the Super-Rich*, Bantam Books, New York, 1968, pp. 107–108.
[24] Campbell, C. A., 'Moral and Non-Moral Values: A Study in the First Principles of Axiology', *Mind* (1935).
[25] Frankena, *op. cit.*, p. 13.
[26] Several people have given me advice about this paper and I would like to thank them: Myles Brand, Charles Goodbrand, David Hall, William Hughes, Margaret Kumagai, John Leslie, Michael Martin, Jay Newman and Douglas Odegard, Ray Panavas.

# INDEX OF NAMES

# INDEX OF SUBJECTS

# SYNTHESE LIBRARY

Monographs on Epistemology, Logic, Methodology,
Philosophy of Science, Sociology of Science and of Knowledge, and on the
Mathematical Methods of Social and Behavioral Sciences

*Managing Editor:*
JAAKKO HINTIKKA (Academy of Finland and Stanford University)

*Editors:*
ROBERT S. COHEN (Boston University)
DONALD DAVIDSON (The Rockefeller University and Princeton University)
GABRIËL NUCHELMANS (University of Leyden)
WESLEY C. SALMON (University of Arizona)

15. C. D. BROAD, *Induction, Probability, and Causation. Selected Papers.* 1968, XI + 296 pp.
16. GÜNTHER PATZIG, *Aristotle's Theory of the Syllogism. A Logical-Philosophical Study of Book A of the Prior Analytics.* 1968, XVII + 215 pp.
17. NICHOLAS RESCHER, *Topics in Philosophical Logic.* 1968, XIV + 347 pp.
18. ROBERT S. COHEN and MARX W. WARTOFSKY (eds.), *Proceedings of the Boston Colloquium for the Philosophy of Science 1966–1968,* Boston Studies in the Philosophy of Science (ed. by Robert S. Cohen and Marx W. Wartofsky), Volume IV. 1969, VIII + 537 pp.
19. ROBERT S. COHEN and MARX W. WARTOFSKY (eds.), *Proceedings of the Boston Colloquium for the Philosophy of Science 1966–1968,* Boston Studies in the Philosophy of Science (ed. by Robert S. Cohen and Marx W. Wartofsky), Volume V. 1969, VIII + 482 pp.
20. J. W. DAVIS, D. J. HOCKNEY, and W. K. WILSON (eds.), *Philosophical Logic.* 1969, VIII + 277 pp.
21. D. DAVIDSON and J. HINTIKKA (eds.), *Words and Objections: Essays on the Work of W. V. Quine.* 1969, VIII + 366 pp.
22. PATRICK SUPPES, *Studies in the Methodology and Foundations of Science. Selected Papers from 1911 to 1969,* 1969, XII + 473 pp.
23. JAAKKO HINTIKKA, *Models for Modalities. Selected Essays.* 1969, IX + 220 pp.
24. NICHOLAS RESCHER et al. (eds.), *Essays in Honor of Carl G. Hempel. A Tribute on the Occasion of his Sixty-Fifth Birthday.* 1969, VII + 272 pp.
25. P. V. TAVANEC (ed.), *Problems of the Logic of Scientific Knowledge.* 1969, XII + 429 pp.
26. MARSHALL SWAIN (ed.), *Induction, Acceptance, and Rational Belief.* 1970, VII + 232 pp.
27. ROBERT S. COHEN and RAYMOND J. SEEGER (eds.), *Ernst Mach; Physicist and Philosopher,* Boston Studies in the Philosophy of Science (ed. by Robert S. Cohen and Marx W. Wartofsky), Volume VI. 1970, VIII + 295 pp.
28. JAAKKO HINTIKKA and PATRICK SUPPES, *Information and Inference.* 1970, X + 336 pp.
29. KAREL LAMBERT, *Philosophical Problems in Logic. Some Recent Developments.* 1970, VII + 176 pp.
30. ROLF A. EBERLE, *Nominalistic Systems.* 1970, IX + 217 pp.
31. PAUL WEINGARTNER and GERHARD ZECHA (eds.), *Induction, Physics, and Ethics, Proceedings and Discussions of the 1968 Salzburg Colloquium in the Philosophy of Science.* 1970, X + 382 pp.
32. EVERT W. BETH, *Aspects of Modern Logic.* 1970, XI + 176 pp.
33. RISTO HILPINEN (ed.), *Deontic Logic: Introductory and Systematic Readings.* 1971, VII + 182 pp.
34. JEAN-LOUIS KRIVINE, *Introduction to Axiomatic Set Theory.* 1971, VII + 98 pp.
35. JOSEPH D. SNEED, *The Logical Structure of Mathematical Physics.* 1971, XV + 311 pp.
36. CARL R. KORDIG, *The Justification of Scientific Change.* 1971, XIV + 119 pp.
37. MILIČ ČAPEK, *Bergson and Modern Physics,* Boston Studies in the Philosophy of Science (ed. by Robert S. Cohen and Marx W. Wartofsky), Volume VII. 1971, XV + 414 pp.
38. NORWOOD RUSSELL HANSON, *What I do not Believe, and other Essays* (ed. by Stephen Toulmin and Harry Woolf), 1971, XII + 390 pp.
39. ROGER C. BUCK and ROBERT S. COHEN (eds.), *PSA 1970. In Memory of Rudolf Carnap,* Boston Studies in the Philosophy of Science (ed. by Robert S. Cohen and Marx W. Wartofsky), Volume VIII. 1971, LXVI + 615 pp. Also available as a paperback.

40. DONALD DAVIDSON and GILBERT HARMAN (eds.), *Semantics of Natural Language.* 1972, X + 769 pp. Also available as a paperback.

41. YEHOSHUA BAR-HILLEL (ed.), *Pragmatics of Natural Languages.* 1971, VII + 231 pp.

42. SÖREN STENLUND, *Combinators, λ-Terms and Proof Theory.* 1972, 184 pp.

43. MARTIN STRAUSS, *Modern Physics and Its Philosophy. Selected Papers in the Logic, History and Philosophy of Science.* 1972, X + 297 pp.

44. MARIO BUNGE, *Method, Model and Matter.* 1973, VII + 196 pp.

45. MARIO BUNGE, *Philosophy of Physics.* 1973, IX + 248 pp.

46. A. A. ZINOV'EV, *Foundations of the Logical Theory of Scientific Knowledge (Complex Logic),* Boston Studies in the Philosophy of Science (ed. by Robert S. Cohen and Marx W. Wartofsky), Volume IX. Revised and enlarged English edition with an appendix, by G. A. Smirnov, E. A. Sidorenka, A. M. Fedina, and L. A. Bobrova. 1973, XXII + 301 pp. Also available as a paperback.

47. LADISLAV TONDL, *Scientific Procedures,* Boston Studies in the Philosophy of Science (ed. by Robert S. Cohen and Marx W. Wartofsky), Volume X. 1973, XII + 268 pp. Also available as a paperback.

48. NORWOOD RUSSELL HANSON, *Constellations and Conjectures* (ed. by Willard C. Humphreys, Jr.), 1973, X + 282 pp.

49. K. J. J. HINTIKKA, J. M. E. MORAVCSIK, and P. SUPPES (eds.), *Approaches to Natural Language. Proceedings of the 1970 Stanford Workshop on Grammar and Semantics.* 1973, VIII + 526 pp. Also available as a paperback.

50. MARIO BUNGE (ed.), *Exact Philosophy — Problems, Tools, and Goals.* 1973, X + 214 pp.

51. RADU J. BOGDAN and ILKKA NIINILUOTO (eds.), *Logic, Language, and Probability.* A selection of papers contributed to Sections IV, VI, and XI of the Fourth International Congress for Logic, Methodology, and Philosophy of Science, Bucharest, September 1971. 1973, X + 323 pp.

52. GLENN PEARCE and PATRICK MAYNARD (eds.), *Conceptual Chance.* 1973, XII + 282 pp.

53. ILKKA NIINILUOTO and RAIMO TUOMELA, *Theoretical Concepts and Hypothetico-Inductive Inference.* 1973, VII + 264 pp.

54. ROLAND FRAÏSSÉ, *Course of Mathematical Logic — Volume 1: Relation and Logical Formula.* 1973, XVI + 186 pp. Also available as a paperback.

55. ADOLF GRÜNBAUM, *Philosophical Problems of Space and Time.* Second, enlarged edition, Boston Studies in the Philosophy of Science (ed. by Robert S. Cohen and Marx W. Wartofsky), Volume XII. 1973, XXIII + 884 pp. Also available as a paperback.

56. PATRICK SUPPES (ed.), *Space, Time, and Geometry.* 1973, XI + 424 pp.

57. HANS KELSEN, *Essays in Legal and Moral Philosophy,* selected and introduced by Ota Weinberger. 1973, XXVIII + 300 pp.

58. R. J. SEEGER and ROBERT S. COHEN (eds.), *Philosophical Foundations of Science. Proceedings of an AAAS Program, 1969.* Boston Studies in the Philosophy of Science (ed. by Robert S. Cohen and Marx W. Wartofsky), Volume XI. 1974, X + 545 pp. Also available as paperback.

59. ROBERT S. COHEN and MARX W. WARTOFSKY (eds.), *Logical and Epistemological Studies in Contemporary Physics,* Boston Studies in the Philosophy of Science (ed. by Robert S. Cohen and Marx W. Wartofsky), Volume XIII. 1973, VIII + 462 pp. Also available as a paperback.

60. ROBERT S. COHEN and MARX W. WARTOFSKY (eds.), *Methodological and Historical Essays in the Natural and Social Sciences. Proceedings of the Boston Colloquium for the Philosophy of Science, 1969–1972,* Boston Studies in the Philosophy of Science (ed. by Robert S. Cohen and Marx W. Wartofsky), Volume XIV. 1974, VIII + 405 pp. Also available as a paperback.

61. ROBERT S. COHEN, J. J. STACHEL and MARX W. WARTOFSKY (eds.), *For Dirk Struik. Scientific, Historical and Political Essays in Honor of Dirk J. Struik*, Boston Studies in the Philosophy of Science (ed. by Robert S. Cohen and Marx W. Wartofsky), Volume XV. 1974, XXVII + 652 pp. Also available as paperback.
62. KAZIMIERZ AJDUKIEWICZ, *Pragmatic Logic*, transl. from the Polish by Olgierd Wojtasiewicz. 1974, XV + 460 pp.
63. SÖREN STENLUND (ed.), *Logical Theory and Semantic Analysis. Essays Dedicated to Stig Kanger on His Fiftieth Birthday*. 1974, V + 217 pp.
64. KENNETH F. SCHAFFNER and ROBERT S. COHEN (eds.), *Proceedings of the 1972 Biennial Meeting, Philosophy of Science Association*, Boston Studies in the Philosophy of Science (ed. by Robert S. Cohen and Marx W. Wartofsky), Volume XX. 1974, IX + 444 pp. Also available as paperback.
65. HENRY E. KYBURG, JR., *The Logical Foundations of Statistical Inference*. 1974, IX + 421 pp.
66. MARJORIE GRENE, *The Understanding of Nature: Essays in the Philosophy of Biology*, Boston Studies in the Philosophy of Science (ed. by Robert S. Cohen and Marx W. Wartofsky), Volume XXIII. 1974, XII + 360 pp. Also available as paperback.
67. JAN M. BROEKMAN, *Structuralism: Moscow, Prague, Paris*. 1974, IX + 117 pp.
68. NORMAN GESCHWIND, *Selected Papers on Language and the Brain*, Boston Studies in the Philosophy of Science (ed. by Robert S. Cohen and Marx W. Wartofsky), Volume XVI. 1974, XII + 549 pp. Also available as paperback.
69. ROLAND FRAÏSSÉ, *Course of Mathematical Logic — Volume II: Model Theory*. 1974, XIX + 192 pp.
70. ANDRZEJ GRZEGORCZYK, *An Outline of Mathematical Logic. Fundamental Results and Notions Explained with All Details*. 1974, X + 596 pp.
71. FRANZ VON KUTSCHERA, *Philosophy of Language*. 1975, VII + 305 pp.
72. JUHA MANNINEN and RAIMO TUOMELA, *Essays on Explanation and Understanding. Studies in the Foundations of Humanities and Social Sciences*. VII + 435 pp.
73. JAAKKO HINTIKKA (ed.), *Rudolf Carnap, Logical Empiricist. Materials and Perspectives*. 1975, LXVIII + 400 pp.
74. MILIČ ČAPEK (ed.), *The Concepts of Space and Time. Their Structure and Their Development*. Boston Studies in the Philosophy of Science (ed. by R. S. Cohen and M. W. Wartofsky) Volume XXII. 1976, LVII + 570 pp. Also available as a paperback.
75. JAAKKO HINTIKKA and UNTO REMES, *The Method of Analysis. Its Geometrical Origin and Its General Significance*. Boston Studies in the Philosophy of Science (ed. by Robert S. Cohen and Marx W. Wartofsky), Volume XXV. 1974, XVIII + 144 pp. Also available as paperback.
76. JOHN EMERY MURDOCH and EDITH DUDLEY SYLLA, *The Cultural Context of Medieval Learning. Proceedings of the First International Colloquium on Philosophy, Science, and Theology in the Middle Ages — September 1973*. Boston Studies in the Philosophy of Science (ed. by Robert S. Cohen and Marx W. Wartofsky), Volume XXVI. 1975, X + 566 pp. Also available as paperback.
77. STEFAN AMSTERDAMSKI, *Between Experience and Metaphysics. Philosophical Problems of the Evolution of Science*. Boston Studies in the Philosophy of Science (ed. by Robert S. Cohen and Marx W. Wartofsky), Volume XXXV. 1975, XVIII + 193 pp. Also available as paperback.
78. PATRICK SUPPES (ed.), *Logic and Probability in Quantum Mechanics*. 1976, XV + 541 pp.
80. JOSEPH AGASSI, *Science in Flux*. Boston Studies in the Philosophy of Science (ed. by Robert S. Cohen and Marx W. Wartofsky), Volume XXVIII. 1975, XXVI + 553 pp. Also available as paperback.

81. SANDRA G. HARDING (ed.), *Can Theories Be Refuted? Essays on the Duhem-Quine Thesis.* 1976, XXI + 318 pp. Also available as a paperback.
84. MARJORIE GRENE and EVERETT MENDELSOHN (eds.), *Topics in the Philosophy of Biology.* Boston Studies in the Philosophy of Science (ed. by R. S. Cohen and M. W. Wartofsky) Volume XXVII. 1976, XIII + 454 pp. Also available as a paperback.
85. E. FISCHBEIN, *The Intuitive Sources of Probabilistic Thinking in Children.* 1975, XIII + 204 pp.
86. ERNEST W. ADAMS, *The Logic of Conditionals. An Application of Probability to Deductive Logic.* 1975, XIII + 155 pp.
89. ASA KASHER (ed.), *Language in Focus: Foundations, Methods and Systems. Essays in Memory of Yehoshua Bar-Hillel.* Boston Studies in the Philosophy of Science (ed. by R. S. Cohen and M. W. Wartofsky) Volume XLIII. 1976, XXVIII + 679 pp. Also available as a paperback.
90. JAAKKO HINTIKKA, *The Intentions of Intentionality and Other New Models for Modalities.* 1975, XVIII + 262 pp.
93. RADU J. BOGDAN (ed.), *Local Induction.* 1976, XIV + 340 pp.
95. PETER MITTELSTAEDT, *Philosophical Problems of Modern Physics.* Boston Studies in the Philosophy of Science (ed. by R. S. Cohen and M. W. Wartofsky) Volume XVIII. 1976, X + 211 pp. Also available as a paperback.
96. GERALD HOLTON and WILLIAM BLANPIED (eds.), *Science and Its Public: The Changing Relationship.* Boston Studies in the Philosophy of Science (ed. by R. S. Cohen and M. W. Wartofsky) Volume XXXIII. 1976, XXV + 289 pp. Also available as a paperback.

# SYNTHESE HISTORICAL LIBRARY

Texts and Studies
in the History of Logic and Philosophy

*Editors:*

N. KRETZMANN (Cornell University)
G. NUCHELMANS (University of Leyden)
L. M. DE RIJK (University of Leyden)